The Philosopher-Lobbyist

The Philosopher-Lobbyist

John Dewey and the People's Lobby, 1928–1940

Mordecai Lee

Published by State University of New York Press, Albany

Printed in the United States of America

For information, contact State University of New York Press, Albany, NY
www.sunypress.edu

Production, Eileen Nizer
Marketing, Michael Campochiaro

Library of Congress Cataloging-in-Publication Data

Lee, Mordecai, 1948–
The Philosopher-Lobbyist : John Dewey and the People's Lobby, 1928–1940.
pages cm
Includes bibliographical references and index.
ISBN 978-1-4384-5529-7 (hc : alk. paper)—978-1-4384-5528-0 (pb : alk. paper)
ISBN 978-1-4384-5530-3 (ebook)

10 9 8 7 6 5 4 3 2 1

In memory of my dad, Jack H. Lee, born Jacob Levy (1915–2007), who had the patience to wait; and to Bill Houghton, who knows why.

Contents

Part III
Dewey as Honorary President of the People's Lobby and After

Preface and Acknowledgments

Part of the fun of researching history is the occasional "huh?" or "huh!" moment when the story you're pursuing takes you to places you didn't expect to go or didn't even know about. That was the genesis of this inquiry. I was researching the emergence of government PR during the twentieth century and especially its development during FDR's presidency. I became especially interested in his National Emergency Council and its later incarnation as the Office of Government Reports as part of the New Deal (Lee 2005). A few years later, I pursued another strand and wrote about the Division of Information in the Office for Emergency Management during World War II (Lee 2012).

In both books, I quoted from Bruce Catton's 1948 memoir of his service as a federal public relations officer before and during World War II. He called it *The War Lords of Washington*. It was a politically liberal retelling of the controversial arms production mobilization before and during the war. (In the 1950s and 1960s, Catton became a best-selling and award-winning author of popular histories of the Civil War.) Inevitably, I got curious about the reviews Catton's book received when it was published. Partly by luck, I stumbled across a favorable review in a publication called *The People's Lobby Bulletin*, which was published by something called The People's Lobby, Inc.[1] Never having heard of that periodical or organization, I idly wondered what it was. It was an intriguing name, hard to forget. I eventually wrote a short piece on Catton's book (Lee 2009). Now, years after that accidental discovery of the People's Lobby, this book answers my curiosity about it.

It took me several years before I could take a deeper look into the People's Lobby. By then, America was in the depths of the Great Recession. Democrat Barack Obama had been elected to his first term as president in the context of voters' apparent repudiation of the policies of his Republican predecessor or, at least, of the Republican party's ideology of tax cuts, spending cuts, and deregulation. Obama's first term was dedicated to repairing the economy, in part through stimulus spending, which increased the deficit. Things got better very slowly. In the meantime, the president was attacked vociferously from the right, which said he was too liberal, too much of a big spender, and didn't care about the impact of his policies on the national debt. To top it off, he had persuaded Congress to enact a major new policy: health care reform. Republicans depicted it as a government takeover of health care and a major threat to personal liberty. Yet, at the same time, Obama was also being attacked from the left for not being liberal *enough*, for his stimulus being too small to kick-start the economy, for his deficit-cutting policies as undermining economic recovery, and for a version of health care reform that was too timid because it was *not* a government takeover.

Over my morning coffee, I would be reading news coverage of the Great Recession and the criticisms of the president. Then I would head to work and read about the Great Depression and the criticisms of *that* president. The more I learned about the People's Lobby (which was founded in in 1928, before the 1929 stock market crash), the more I saw rough parallels in American history. First came the prosperity of the 1920s and 2000s, then the Great Depression and the Great Recession, with their political debates over FDR's and Obama's Democratic policy prescriptions. Finally, FDR and Obama were both reelected to a second term after fierce ideological arguments and partisan claims that in their first terms they had not done enough to reverse the economic crash to justify a second term.

I gradually became intrigued by the policy agenda of the Lobby and the statements of its president, professor John Dewey, who criticized FDR and the New Deal for not being leftish enough. This was new to me, especially coming from such a major and respected American figure as Dewey. These rough historical similarities drew me in. What was it that FDR had rejected as too liberal? What were the policy alternatives to the New Deal from the non-Communist left? I was seeing the now-familiar movie of American history through new lenses. As often happens with repeated viewings of the same film, looking at the same piece of art, or rereading the same book, new and interesting details jump out that one missed earlier. I was hooked.

When I started graduate school in public administration at Syracuse University in 1970, one of the professors kept talking about how, once we graduated, he wanted us to view public service. We should be "philosopher kings," he said. I had no idea what he was talking about, and it went right over my head. Years later (I'm embarrassed to say how many), I finally figured out he was using Plato's phrase, of the ideal for leaders of Plato's Utopian republic. "Aha," I thought, "now I understand." The professor felt that our *values* as public servants were at least as important as—perhaps more important than—our technical skills in management and leadership.

Everything came full circle when I stumbled on Dewey's People's Lobby. It initially seemed like an odd combination: a philosopher wanting to lobby government on the granular problems of public policy. Not only was Dewey a philosopher interested in improving the quality of life, but he also wrote a book about what a democratic society should look like. Then, impressively, he took tangible steps to help move his utopia toward reality. The People's Lobby was Dewey's effort to implement his philosophical values. So if Plato's ideal was the philosopher king, then Dewey was something of a variation on that: he was a philosopher-lobbyist.

I was fortunate to benefit from the libraries of the University of Wisconsin. My home campus had an excellent Inter-Library Loan Department, whose indefatigable staff was able to obtain (by hook or by crook, it seemed) just about every item I asked for. Second, I benefited from a cooperative relationship among all the libraries of the university's twenty-five other campuses. Using an online form, I was able to request any volume owned by any of them. Presto, via a regular van shuttle service, a day or two later the item was delivered to my library. Third, during this period I was appointed as a libraries research fellow by the Madison campus. That permitted me to access all online databases and journals in Madison's collection. As would be expected, the larger flagship campus (my alma mater, class of 1970) had a more extensive online collection than my home library. Not only was such access enormously helpful and convenient, but it also sharply reduced the carbon emissions I otherwise would have caused by dozens of 150-mile round trips between Milwaukee and Madison to use those databases in person. Go Badgers. The downtown central branch of the Milwaukee Public Library also had an excellent collection from that era.

In addition to the archival sources cited in the text and identified in the Bibliography, I was greatly helped by the advice and guidance of information professionals and archivists at the Center for Dewey Studies of Southern Illinois University (Carbondale), Martin Dies Papers at the Sam Houston Regional Library (Liberty, Texas), Minnesota Historical Society, New-York Historical Society, the Peace Collection at Swarthmore College (Pennsylvania), Special Collections at the University of Virginia (Charlottesville), Walter P. Reuther Library of Labor and Urban Affairs at Wayne State University (Detroit, Michigan), *Washington Star* morgue in the Washingtoniana Collection of the Martin Luther King Jr. branch of the District of Columbia Public Library, and the Manuscripts and Archives Department of Yale University's Library (New Haven, Connecticut). My thanks to all of them, sadly too numerous to name individually.

Also, my thanks to Athan Theoharis, emeritus professor of history at Marquette University, for helping me decipher some opaque terminology in the FBI's files on John Dewey and Benjamin Marsh, the People's Lobby executive secretary. My recurring appreciation to Andrea Zweifel, a program associate at my school, for proofing the entire manuscript with her eagle eyes. She has an amazing talent for spotting a typo a mile away.

Finally, my thanks to the staff of SUNY Press, who were uniformly helpful and patient. A special expression of my gratitude to senior acquisitions editor Michael Rinella, who bent over backward to reduce the anxiety that authors typically experience while their manuscript is undergoing external review. Above and beyond the call of duty, he made a point of being supportive of the project, of keeping me apprised of the status of the review and telling me when he'd likely have some news. I greatly appreciated his author-calming skills. His attitude seemed contagious. The reports from the two anonymous readers were detailed and rigorous, yet friendly. They conveyed a desire to help an author succeed, rather than merely looking for faults in a manuscript to criticize. My thanks to those two readers as well.

Naturally, any errors remaining in the book are mine alone.

Abbreviations

AAA	Agricultural Adjustment Administration
AC	*Atlanta Constitution*
AML	Anti-Monopoly League
AP	Associated Press (news wire service)
BG	*Boston Globe*
BS	*Baltimore Sun*
CR	*Congressional Record*
CSM	*Christian Science Monitor* (a daily newspaper headquartered in Boston)
CT	*Chicago Tribune*
FBI	Federal Bureau of Investigation, US Department of Justice
HC	*Hartford Courant*
HUAC	House Un-American Activities Committee, US Congress
LAT	*Los Angeles Times*
NRA	National Recovery Administration
NYT	*New York Times*
PL	People's Lobby
PLB	*People's Lobby Bulletin* (monthly publication, beginning in May, 1931)
PRL	People's Reconstruction League

RFC	Reconstruction Finance Corporation
SU	Soviet Union (also known as the *Union of Soviet Socialist Republics [USSR])*
UP	United Press (news wire service)
WP	*Washington Post*
WPA	Works Progress Administration
WWI	World War I
WWII	World War II

Introduction

Why Study the People's Lobby?

The story of the People's Lobby is a different retelling of the familiar trope of American history. After all, history is what the present chooses to remember about the past (Foner 2010, 71). This commonly accepted version of the story tends to tilt toward the conventional civics textbook narrative. Seeking to be nonpartisan, it focuses on the pre-crash prosperity, on Hoover's inability to right the economy, and then depicts FDR's New Deal as the unprecedented left-of-center success in getting the economy going again. Continuing further along in this given tale, while WWII was a necessary war to protect freedom and America's role in it was justified, it was also the final chapter in beating back the Great Depression. In all, it is a proud tale of success, collapse, fighting to come back economically, improvement, more success, and then maintaining the prosperity through war and postwar eras into the 1950s. There is also a second and revisionist narrative from right of center, which argues that FDR muffed the recovery and could have done so much better (Shlaes 2007).

There is a lesser-known third interpretation of the Great Depression, a perspective heretofore largely discounted—that of lost alternatives. This study seeks to add more texture to the retelling of American history and public policy in the 1930s and early 1940s with the policy agenda offered by the further left, the social democratic and socialist alternative to the policy choices that FDR and Congress actually made. This is a story of the non-communist left, a movement of progressives and radicals who opposed violent revolution and instead wanted to pull the political center of gravity of the country further to the left by activist and constitutional methods. For them, not only was Hoover unsatisfactory, but so was Franklin Roosevelt. In their eyes, FDR was too conservative, too timid, too protective of the basics of the political economy, too prone to compromise, and too accepting of incremental change. In a sense, they were right, in that FDR had protected the principles of the free-market economy and only tinkered around the edges to smooth things out for the have-nots and left-behinds. The conservative vitriol aimed at him was, in retrospect, mere propaganda. He had saved their economic standing. The further left understood exactly what was happening and was, in that sense, FDR's authentic opposition. By being the squeaky wheel, these activists wanted to pull FDR and Congress to the left, at the very least counterbalancing and neutralizing the well-funded and vocal pressures from the right. These leftists sought to keep federal politicians' feet to the fire, letting them know that if something were to be packaged as a compromise, then it needed to bring into consideration the left's alternatives, not just the right's.

If FDR was a mildly left-oriented but cautious politician, what was it that he was opting *not* to do? What policy alternatives were suggested that he did not care to pursue? The People's Lobby (PL),[1] a small but articulate voice on the left that existed from 1928 to 1950, has bequeathed to history a comprehensive platform from those who were disappointed in FDR and tried to push for more radical reforms to help American society. In that respect, the policy views of the People's Lobby present a counterfactual agenda of what was not adopted, but theoretically could have been. The PL was a historical path not taken. For example, history tends to view the pre–Pearl Harbor isolationists as coming from the right, a movement of conservatives. Yet, at the same time, the People's Lobby was equally vehement against US involvement in WWII—it was a voice on the left that saw no compelling reason for the United States to enter that war.

Still, why a book that focuses on this small group on the margins of Washington's political players? John Dewey. Dewey was a major figure in American intellectual history, philosophy, and education (Menand 2001; Ravitch 2000). The Center for Dewey Studies at Southern Illinois University has collected and published all of his writings and correspondence.[2] Some of the issues he raised about American democracy "seem equally, if not more, relevant in today's political climate" (Rogers 2012, 29). Yet most Dewey biographies mention the PL only in passing (Rockefeller 1991, 447; Bullert 1983, 28, 129, 148). Even a book-length study of Dewey and democracy limited discussion of the PL to a few pages of a 552-page text (Westbrook 1991, 445–446). And that brief discussion was later challenged for misinterpreting Dewey's thinking (Eldridge 1996, 14).

Even in its heyday, the People's Lobby was a small national organization. In 1936, it had about 3,700 members or subscribers to its monthly publication (US Senate 1936a, 388). Its peak membership was 4,280 in

1944.[3] It operated on a shoestring budget and had only one professional staffer, Benjamin Marsh. Dewey cofounded it with Marsh in 1928 and then served as the PL's president and public voice until stepping down in 1936. He continued his association with the organization afterward, serving as its honorary president until 1940. The organization lasted a decade after his link with it ended. In total, the Lobby existed for twenty-two years (1928–1950), disbanding when Marsh retired because of ill health. (Dewey and Marsh both died in 1952.)

Contemporary scholarship has occasionally mentioned the People's Lobby, Dewey's presidency of it, or Marsh's work as executive secretary. But these tend to be fleeting walk-on roles, such as John Atkinson Hobson's influence on Dewey's economic views (Deen 2013, 657), the political activism of F. J. Schlink (Donohue 2010, 440), rhetorical argumentation (Breuning 2003, 235), foreign aid (Kennedy and Ruttan 1986, 321n101), New Deal taxation (Leff 1984, 104–105), Dewey's theory of social reconstruction (Campbell 1984, 366–367), antitrust legislation (Lande 1982, 136n273), pre-WWII anti-imperialism (Papachristou 1974, 69, 76n30), and lobbyists (Westwood 1970, 616).

The People's Lobby received a somewhat more extensive treatment in Tobin (1986), but his inquiry extended only through 1933, while the PL existed another seventeen years after that. An excellent history of lobbying in the United States, even bearing the title *The People's Lobby*, actually concludes in 1925, three years before Dewey cofounded the People's Lobby (Clemens 1997). Seeking to add to this literature, this project entails a more in-depth examination of the People's Lobby, its political positions, and its legislative advocacy.

Disciplinary Foci and Audiences for the Book

This inquiry adds to the historical literature by bringing into view a comprehensive presentation of the policy agenda and political activities of John Dewey and his People's Lobby, especially during FDR's first and second terms. As such, it is likely to be of interest to several disciplinary areas, including Deweyian studies, political history (of FDR and the American left and of lost policy alternatives), history of the American nonprofit sector (especially advocacy activities), public relations, political science's subfield of interest group history, and public administration's interest in the history of the American good-government reform movement and, separately, in citizen participation in government.

From the perspective of Dewey studies, Dewey was a not-very-closeted socialist and sought to base his activism on creating a viable third party in US politics, one that was authentically left wing compared with the conservative, racist, and then mildly liberal Democratic Party. Dewey and Marsh were both radicals, but they were not revolutionaries. They were fully committed to working within the US constitutional system. In that regard, their legislative advocacy through the People's Lobby represented a fully developed and comprehensive manifesto of a political agenda. So the book presents a kind of counterfactual retelling of American history during the crucial years of the market crash and Great Depression, FDR's presidency, the New Deal, and WWII. If the effort to create a third party in the United States—most vivid and politically vigorous from the 1880s to the 1910s—had been successful, what might the history of the United States have looked like during these periods? What did the populists, progressives, and the left want to do and actually propose to do while their chances for political success were dimming, but not extinguished? How were their policy ideas different from the moderately liberal, but always politically pragmatic presidency of FDR?

Dewey continues to fascinate educators, philosophers, and historians for the originality of his thinking (Menand 2001; Ravitch 2000). For example, between 2000 and 2014, SUNY Press alone published fourteen books that named Dewey either in their titles or subtitles.[4] As another indication of his ongoing importance and influence, in 2012, Penn State University Press republished his *The Public and Its Problems* with a new introduction and commentary (Rogers 2012).

For historians, learning more about that which is largely unknown can be valuable because it adds to the texture, nuance, and understanding of the American historical narrative. In an arresting metaphor, Beschloss noted that, regarding some interesting and important people and events, "as we move further and further away from the period, have shrunk almost to a pinpoint in our rearview mirror."[5] This study seeks to un-shrink the People's Lobby so that it won't fade totally from history's sight and may be considered for its role in America's past.

In particular, the study of American political history is undergoing a revival (Zelizer 2012). While the PL was small potatoes in terms of size, it was a vocal and articulate "outsider" group, consistently criticizing the president in power, whether it was Hoover or FDR. It chose that role, trying to influence events further leftward than the status quo seemed to accept. It is nearly impossible to provide a quantitative tally of its wins and losses, though the latter are much more obvious and frequent than the former. But the role of agitator who opts to oppose the conventional wisdom and does not care about being politically realistic is not automatically a role of failure that should be ignored. For example, Tobin concluded about PL and two other like organizations that "they failed more often than they succeeded, yet they made a difference by forcing friends and adversaries to consider their views" (1986, 245). This perspective opens up the examination of history to a larger view, not limited to just to the winners and major players of elections and legislative enactments. The voice of the outsider may ultimately be that of the loser, but it is not necessarily irrelevant to political events and eventual outcomes. While Americans love winners, losers also play a role. In the longer perspective of history, ideas matter.

History is not inevitable and shouldn't present itself as such (Foner 2010, xx). There are always forks in the road and choices that are clearly or murkily made. Contingency is a major factor in the unfolding of history. An approach to policy history that has recently become more in vogue is what Zelizer calls the "Lost Alternatives" approach (2012, 55). If one of the purposes of historiography is to show what could have been, then a history of PL helps make more vivid the options and policy choices that were presented to decision makers at the federal level in those years. In that sense, the story of the People's Lobby presents the road not traveled.

Regarding the history of the United States nonprofit sector, the People's Lobby is an early example of a phenomenon that is common today, that of the public interest lobbying group, although that term has somewhat faded from contemporary usage (Berry and Wilcox 2009, 26). Berry defined it as one that focuses on a collective good that its members do not materially (or differentially) benefit from (1977, 7). The People's Lobby was not the earliest nonprofit lobbying for seemingly altruistic and nonmaterial benefits, in contradistinction to the more common special interest lobbies. McCarthy traces early manifestations of social advocacy for public policy making to before the Civil War (2003, 204). Tichenor and Harris categorized all interest groups and organizational appearances at congressional hearings between 1889 and 1917. They concluded that civic groups were anywhere from a fifth to a third of all testifiers (2002–03, 599).

However, many such civic groups were lobbying for single-issue social goal that, while nonmaterial, would directly or indirectly advance their members' interests, such as women's suffrage, Prohibition, and protections for African-Americans. Each of these more common kinds of social and civic goals was a powerful mobilizing incentive for members to join and then be active in the organization. In contrast, the People's Lobby was an early manifestation of a nonprofit group lobbying not for single or a handful of policy goals, but rather for a multiplicity of issues almost as broad as the range of the federal government itself. The PL was a multiple-issue public interest group. As a result, it did not have the built-in appeal to citizens to be members that some of the social movement groups had. Benefits to joining it were even more amorphous and non–self-benefiting compared with the more traditional and earlier civic groups. In fact, one distinct feature of the PL that separates it from other early public interest groups is that the Lobby was advocating for economic policies that were to the *detriment* of the interests of its members. The PL called for higher taxes and less deficit spending, which would have increased the tax burden on its middle-class members. This continues to be an oddity of American interest politics. This study, therefore, examines more closely an early American prototype of a broad-agenda nonprofit public interest lobby. What did it do, and how did it do it?

Nonprofit advocacy (whether for public or special interests) is a subfield of nonprofit studies, the latter a rapidly growing disciplinary focus in American institutions of higher education in recent years. Advocacy by nonprofits is also developing a distinct academic literature (Schmid and Almog-Bar 2014; Boris and Maronick 2012; Prakash and Gugerty 2010; Avner 2010; Reid 2006; Jenkins 2006) and an applied literature for practitioners and professional training (Hoefer 2012; Hessenius 2007; Richan 2006). Dewey and Marsh helped advance the scope and techniques of nonprofit lobbying. They had a "do everything" approach, practically making PL a kind of mega mall of such techniques. Their tactics included congressional testimony, public letters to leading officials (released to the press), newsletters, conferences, radio programs, speaking tours, brochures, press releases with provocative claims (and often on slow news days), and all other manner of communication. In retrospect, PL expanded the concept of nonprofit legislative advocacy to encompass both direct lobbying and indirect lobbying through efforts to influence public opinion and grassroots activities. This was lobbying to the max. So this biography of an early public interest lobby contributes to a more historically based understanding of nonprofit advocacy. It also contributes to a related subfield, the history of nonprofit public relations (Lee 2011a).

Nonprofit history is also a growing subfield of nonprofit and philanthropic studies. Yet none of the recent summaries of the literature has noted the People's Lobby role in that history (Hall 2010; 2006; Young 2006; Hammack 2002; 1998). While this may be because nonprofit historians have judged it as wholly unimportant, it is more likely because it has been largely unknown to that literature.

For the academic field of public relations (sometimes called mass communication or public affairs), the People's Lobby stands out as a prominent early example of the centrality of publicity. It engaged in extensive lobbying in media and politics. Unusual for many other interest groups at the time, the PL invested major efforts at media relations. Marsh was one of three men whom Tobin singled out as "*publicists* of postwar liberalism" while identifying Dewey as one of a trio of leaders who "never stopped exhorting, *propagandizing*, and organizing" for the left (1986, 133, 221, emphases added). PL's media strategy was two-pronged. First, by generating news covered in the Washington, DC, media market, PL was able to get its message directly to the policy makers it was lobbying, namely legislators and executive branch officials as news consumers. Second, national media coverage was pursued because it could help influence public opinion and reach grassroots activists, who, in turn, might lobby their hometown legislators. As an outsider group, lobbying through the media was an important strategy, if only for influencing public opinion in the long term.

One interesting public relations innovation by the PL was taking advantage of the growth of radio as a relatively new form of mass communication. At that time, broadcasters were eager for product to fill their schedules, especially those that could be categorized as educational and in the public interest (the latter often a requirement for keeping their licenses). PL helped fill that vacuum. At its height, almost every week it hosted a live public affairs discussion on Saturday that was broadcast on a national network. This gave an enormous reach to such a small organization. (The panels were not always balanced, often tilting disproportionately to the PL's political philosophy.) Further indicating a shrewd understanding of the media's ravenous appetite for news, by scheduling these events on Saturday, reporters often covered them as spot news to help fill the big, high-circulation Sunday newspapers.

Political scientists interested in the history of lobbying and pressure groups also may find the PL intriguing. While public interest lobbying is de rigueur today in Washington policy politics (Berry and Wilcox 2009), that was not the case when the PL was founded in 1928. This history of the PL helps to explore some early manifestations of nonprofit public interest lobbying, helping to overcome "a somewhat cavalier ahistoricism" of the literature (Tichenor and Harris 2005, 264). The PL emerged in the late 1920s, in the wake of the increasingly important and then-permanent roles that special interest groups (including business, labor, and farmer) played in the Progressive era (Clemens 1997). In the context of American Political Development (a subfield of political science), Hansen identified the

PL as "a left-leaning *prototype* of the public interest groups" (1987, 193, emphasis added).

Dewey cofounded the Lobby in 1928, a year after his seminal *The Public and Its Problems*. The PL was Dewey's effort to implement the ideas about lobbying he had developed in the book. Dewey's thinking about interest groups had a major impact on the emergence of the study of interest groups. David Truman's 1951 influential and path-breaking study of lobbying in the American governmental process cited Dewey's book as accurately laying out the philosophical basis and dynamics of lobbying (1993, 14, 16–17, 47, 157, 218, 335). Therefore, what Dewey actually *did* to implement his ideas about lobbying can add texture to the academic study of interest group history in American government, a scholarly field he influenced significantly.

Finally, public administration faculty focusing on the field's history might find the People's Lobby of interest. The roots of public administration are in the Progressive era reform efforts of good-government citizen groups that sought to reduce political corruption, increase governmental competence, and promote policies in the public interest. The People's Lobby can be seen as a successor to that historical period, presenting a case study of *post*–Progressive era advocacy for governmental reform. From 1928 to 1933, it focused in part on the enactment of clean government initiatives such as regulation of lobbying and increased transparency of governmental operations. The next historical stage after that was the FDR presidency. The conventional narrative of American public administration lauds his efforts to strengthen the presidency vis-à-vis Congress and his initiatives to improve the management of the executive branch. This is generally presented as an unalloyed good. The PL's fierce opposition to this trend and its ongoing support for a congressionally centered federal government presents a counter historical narrative to the traditional public administration perspective. Therefore, a history of the PL might add nuance and texture to the field's largely uncritical support for FDR. (The other part of the PL's work was its left-of-center initiatives for legislation. That orientation is beyond the traditional scope of public administration history, which tries to avoid political ideology.)

Another strand of public administration studies focuses on citizen participation in government. In the world of Washington's bureaucracy, the PL stands out as something of an odd duck. Federal departments were, and are, habituated to dealing with stakeholders who have intense interest in their agency's work. Whether supporters or opponents, these permanent interests (usually economic) are always in an agency's view. These interest groups are often formally represented on agency advisory committees and other citizen participation vehicles. But what of the amorphous public interest? What about those who do not have an economic stake in their lobbying? Public administration faculty interested in citizen participation are sometimes flummoxed by how to deal with such odd manifestations. How to incorporate non–self-interested views in citizen participation processes can bedevil public administrators who need a formal record of such views to justify not being responsive to *special* interests. The conception of the PL sought to do precisely that, by representing a public interest to countervail special interest lobbying of agency policy making. The PL had limited success. Can such an effort to concretize the non–self-interested views of the public-at-large be accomplished in the twenty-first century's iteration of citizen participation in public administration? Who lobbies for the citizenry as a whole? Can sentiment ever trump interest? The PL's history is a case study of how difficult this is to organize and institutionalize.

Historiographic Approach

Whether consciously or not, the historical researcher often gravitates toward a narrative arc to impose on past events or at least to make sense of them. This is a natural element of storytelling. However the impetus to give logic, momentum, and internal consistency to what occurred might contradict a reality that was not necessarily so. Sometimes the quest for order and coherence stifles the conveying of the actual unfolding of a story. Murphy cautioned that "the ways things turn out is often interpreted as the way things *had* to turn out" (2012, 115, emphasis in original). Not so. Contingency is an element of public and human affairs. Luck, coincidence, external events, unplanned developments, and the unexpected can deflect events from their apparent direction. Therefore, a historian "must avoid telescoping the actual course of events into a predetermined linear progress" (Foner 2002, 170).

In this case, there is some degree of artificiality in the overt completeness of a history of the People's Lobby. There truly was a birth (1928), young adulthood (1929–40), maturity (1940–49), and death (1950). Yet even when a story goes full circle on its own, there still can be a temptation to make it seem complete and inevitable. I have tried to avoid this. Rather, as suggested by Delbanco (2008, 215), I have sought to depict events as they looked at the time, with the players having no idea how things would actually turn out.

In particular, the People's Lobby existed in a time of major historical flux. The country was in great crisis and the economy virtually at a standstill in early 1933. FDR was quite nonideological, willing to experiment with just about anything that might help. He sometimes tacked right, sometimes left, sometimes both at the same time. The truculent rhetoric thrown at him (especially from the right) insinuated that he was governing in a way that destroyed the Constitution, the federal system of government, and personal liberty. He was accused of seeking to be a dictator, of being a threat to democracy, and even of trying to establish a dynasty for his sons. Somewhat similar to the economic and political instability of the early 1890s, "the issues were important, the outcomes unknown" (Williams 2010, 171). The policy proposals by the People's Lobby were as viable as anyone else's. No one knew what ideas might become law or what proposals might be pursued. So, in that respect, the path suggested by the People's Lobby needs to be read historically as an alternative voice in the cacophony of Washington at the time, when people were desperate and politicians even more so.

While history tells us what actually and eventually happened, it is important to reenvision those times as events that were unfolding. For example, in the retrospect of economic history, FDR (almost unknowingly) followed a mildly Keynesian economic policy. His decisions "helped to save the free [market] system at a time *when much more radical changes* in it were being seriously advocated" (citing Herbert Stein, Wapshott 2011, 294, emphasis added). In that respect, this is a story of those much more radical changes, which the PL generated as fair and reasonable alternatives to the status quo or the mild liberalism of the New Deal.

One methodological way to overcome this almost unconscious bias of history telling is to rely as much as possible on contemporaneous sources. Those primary sources tell us what people were thinking and saying *at that time*, wholly untainted by any post hoc insight or trimming of sails. In this case, I engaged in mixed-methods research using qualitative methodologies (Riccucci 2010, chap. 7). In particular, the most useful was the triangulation approach recommended by McNabb for political science and nonprofit studies (2010; 2013) and by Daymon and Holloway for public relations and communication research (2011). This approach calls for identifying multiple primary sources to weave together into as comprehensive a narrative as possible. Multiple sources help not only to fill gaps of other sources, but also to confirm or discredit a particular claim or assertion. As is often the case, archival documents were especially helpful (Piotrowski 2008).

Given the potential problems of post hoc accounts, especially telescoping, revisionism, and justifications, I have been quite parsimonious in relying on Marsh's autobiography, which he wrote after retiring in 1950 and which was published posthumously (Marsh 1953). While interesting, it benefits from the wisdom of hindsight and selectivity. I have preferred to quote from Marsh's contemporaneous observations, such as his congressional testimony, correspondence, press releases, and articles in the PL newsletter. In a few cases, when I could find no other archival or documentary sources, I was compelled to use his autobiographical version.

Part I

Inventing the People's Lobby

Chapter 1

John Dewey and Benjamin Marsh before the People's Lobby

Sketch of Dewey's Life and Philosophy, 1859–1927

Before he cofounded the People's Lobby in 1928, John Dewey (1859–1952) was already one of the most prominent, well-known, and respected professors in America. (The most famous was probably political scientist Woodrow Wilson as a result of being elected president. He died in 1924.) Long before the term "public intellectual" came into usage, Dewey played such a role. He did not shy away from controversial positions, whether related to his academic work or stances on a broad range of public policy issues. In Chicago and New York, where he had taught during that period (University of Chicago and Columbia), he was a news figure, mentioned 67 times between 1898 and 1927 in the *Chicago Tribune* and 117 times during the same time period in the *New York Times*. Indicating a lesser degree of a national stature, even in non-hometown papers he was occasionally mentioned, about half a dozen times each in the *Hartford Courant, Los Angeles Times*, and *Christian Science Monitor*.[1] Adding to his public profile, Dewey was also a frequent contributor to several highbrow, but still popular, national magazines, publishing scores of short pieces from the 1890s to 1928. He wrote about 110 columns in the *New Republic*[2] and also published in other broad-circulation magazines as *Atlantic Monthly*, *The Nation*, *Foreign Affairs*, *Science* (published by the American Association for the Advancement of Science), *Christian Century*, and *Dial* (Dewey 1970).

Dewey was a professor of philosophy, most well known for his theories about public education. He was reacting to the then-dominant model from Germany, which emphasized passive students memorizing abstract information lectured at them by authority-figure teachers. Order and teacher-centered hierarchical power were paramount. He suggested a revolutionary upending of that model by making it child centered. In his view, knowledge was inseparable from doing. Students learned by *doing*, by working out in real-world situations an understanding of such areas of knowledge as chemistry, biology, and math when engaging in such activities as growing and making food. Just covering all aspects of cereal took up three school years (Menand 2001, 323)! Then what they were learning would make sense, rather than repeating by rote seemingly irrelevant facts in a dry textbook. This also encouraged critical thinking, problem-solving skills, self-learning, curiosity, cooperation, and growth. According to Menand, "what Dewey accomplished helped to change the way children are taught, and it gave him a reputation as a great educator" (2001, 316). This came to be called Progressive education, although sometimes Dewey was obscure and opaque about precisely what it meant (and, especially, what specific practices were OK or not).

His approach to education had an underlying philosophy that related not only to the *process* of learning, but also to one of the primary goals for education. It was to help students' maturation into members of a democracy, where the citizenry would be involved in governance processes and decision making, rather than the passive and even sterile act of merely voting on election day and then withdrawing from any other involvement. Good education led to good citizens who were "socially responsive" (Blacker 2007, 42). In other words, Dewey wanted schools to be an instrument of social reform, to catalyze eventually a more progressive and fair society (Ravitch 2000; Westbrook 1991). Fixing the inequalities and deficiencies of the United States was to begin in the grade-school classroom. Progressive education could be seen as closely linked to the philosophy of pragmatism and the reform orientation of Progressive-era politics. However, it should be emphasized that there was no single definition of what Progressivism stood for as an ideology. Some reformers were relatively conservative, even antidemocratic, while others were left of center (Lee 2011b).

After a falling out with the president of the University of Chicago over Dewey's and his wife's roles in the university's experimental school and its teacher training, Dewey moved in 1905 to Columbia University. It was to be his academic home for the rest of his working career, and after retirement, he stayed in New York City engaging in social and political activism.

Inevitably, Dewey fused his thinking about education and philosophy to democracy and politics. It was but a short step for Dewey to begin opining about the issues of the day. The *New Republic* began publishing in 1914, and Dewey was one of its stars. Along with Walter Lippmann, Herbert Croly, and other leading progressives, he made regular contributions to the magazine. These were often short pieces reflecting his views on headline issues. The *New Republic* was Dewey's principle journalistic outlet for engaging in this form of adult-oriented civic education for nearly two decades. He was prolific and opinionated, and his columns largely were consistent with his underlying principles.

Generally, these *New Republic* progressives were pessimistic about the ability of the reigning regime and the establishment to enact fundamental reforms in the American political economy. Some were so far to the left that they were socialists (whether card-carrying or not), believing in a more active role for government to curtail the excesses of the private sector. Some were for public ownership of utilities, and generally all were for social welfare legislation to assure the rights of organized labor and improve the conditions of the poor. Like most of his confreres, Dewey had been disappointed by the election of Woodrow Wilson in 1912, having supported Socialist Eugene V. Debs (Westbrook 1991, 194). Wilson had presented himself as a moderate reformer and had actually been preferred early in his campaign for the Democratic Party's nomination by its more conservative elements because of his status quo and state's rights views on race and other related matters. But once Wilson was in office, Dewey gradually warmed up to his reform, even progressive, policies (except on race). Eventually, Dewey endorsed Wilson for reelection in 1916.

By then, what came to be called World War I was in its third year (with the United States, up until then, ostensibly neutral). After his reelection, Wilson maneuvered to make the United States more openly supportive of the Allies (France and Great Britain) and, conversely, against Germany. He practically provoked an incident of a German attack on American shipping to justify entering the war. It was at this point that Dewey broke with the general early consensus of European and American socialists against a war they had generally viewed as between various capitalist conservative regimes that were antithetical to labor. Rather, Dewey jumped in with both feet, approving of Wilson's framing of the US war aims as promoting democracy and human rights, fighting against the conquering of territory, fostering national self-determination, and supporting a postwar international structure to prevent future wars. Westbrook's view was that "Dewey's support for American intervention in World War I was rooted less in pragmatic reason than in blind hope" (1991, 202). Whatever his motivation, he was all in, including cooperating secretly with the Army's Intelligence Bureau about the internal politics of Polish-Americans.

Dewey's disillusionment with WWI was largely in the postwar stage, which included the traditionalist goals of France and the United Kingdom for the peace conference, the ignoring of some national groups' claims of self-determination, the continuing vitality of colonialism (for the winners), Wilson's inability to incorporate into the postwar settlements the noble goals he had articulated for the war, and the weaknesses evident in the League of Nations (which the United States did not join). Still eager for policy reforms, Dewey was active in postwar efforts to outlaw war, joined the socialist-leaning League for Industrial Democracy, opposed the repressive and anti–civil liberties Red Scares of the 1920s, and supported the creation of a truly left third party to enact progressive reforms that neither of the major parties seemed interested in. It would be fair to characterize him as a de facto socialist—a political and social radical—in comparison to the dominant conservatism and status quo orientation of the United States in the 1920s. Like his popular writings, these political positions were consonant with his educational philosophy, as they were oriented toward social reform.

But Dewey was a realist, too. Several developments in the mid-1920s likely were key in his decision to cofound the People's Lobby in 1928. In the run-up to the 1924 presidential election, he again supported a third-party candidate for president, and it again failed to attract enough support to threaten the viability of the two-party system. In the retrospect of history, that presidential election "would be the last significant national effort to put together a farmer-labor movement" (Sanders 1999, 416). Alternatives were needed. A trip to Mexico in 1926 forcefully showed him the economic imperialism of the United States, where diplomatic power was used to promote the interests of American corporations. Dewey abhorred the casual assumptions that American national interests were identical to those of US corporations, and he intensely disliked the way the United States meddled in the internal affairs of this Latin American country. This theme was to be an ongoing one for the People's Lobby.

In 1928, Dewey was part of a group of American lefties to visit the SU. Like most of his ilk, he wrote glowingly about what he saw that interested him (i.e., education), but mostly he saw what he wanted to see. Dewey interpreted what he liked and believed were the tenets of the new educational system as largely echoing his own doctrines of project-centered education and of schools as seedlings of social reform. Still, it was no brainwashing or exculpation of the extremes of the Communist regime that were just beginning to be noted. He said that "for selfish reasons I prefer seeing it tried in Russia rather than in my own country" (quoted in Ravitch 2000, 208).

Walter Lippmann's Public Opinion (1922) and The Phantom Public (1925)

Probably the most important development contributing to Dewey's decision to cofound the People's Lobby was his 1927 book *The Public and Its Problems* (2012). That book needs to be seen as a reaction to two important developments that preceded it earlier in the century, namely the fervent belief by Progressive-era reformers in publicity, which, in turn, influenced Walter Lippmann's thinking in his seminal 1922 book *Public Opinion* (1997).

It is hard a century later to conceive of the breakthrough brought about by the focus on publicity and its consequent evolution. From its beginning, publicity had two meanings. First, it was an end, that of shining a light on the corrupt activities of corporations and politicians. In modern argot, reformers wanted transparency of business and government. The mere threat of publicity would also be a prophylactic protecting the public interest from mal-doers. In this sense, publicity, in and of itself, was a goal. Second, publicity campaigns could be mounted by reformers (and the politicians they liked) to enact reforms they felt were in the public interest. Publicity would convince public opinion (then often called sentiment) of the benefits of a particular legislative proposal and, in turn, prompt lawmakers to enact such reforms if they wanted to bask in the approval of the voters. In this sense, publicity was a means (Sheingate 2007; Stoker and Rawlins 2005). However used, publicity contributed to the goal of a fairer and more just political economy.

Dewey agreed with both roles for publicity that progressive reformers had formulated. As an end, a 1908 textbook on ethics he coauthored applauded using publicity as a weapon against private sector corruption. Writing about unsavory practices of for-profit corporations, the text noted that "publicity is not a cure for bad practices, but it is a powerful deterrent agency so long as the offenders care for public opinion and not solely for the approval of their own class" (Dewey and Tufts 1929, 520).[3] By 1922 (i.e., after WWI), Dewey had not changed his views. In a short piece on industrial change he noted, "Publicity about the activities of industrial and financial captains and the consequences of their doings would bring an overwhelming check of public sentiment to bear upon what they do" (1983, 285).

On other occasions he endorsed publicity as a means to accomplishing a more fair society. For example, in an evaluation of Theodore Roosevelt's life, Dewey particularly endorsed that president's use of publicity to accomplish his reformist political successes (Greenberg 2011). He also praised America's international publicity during WWI as contributing to the support for US war aims by other countries (in this case, Japan). Given that Dewey had supported Wilson's goals for the war, he was glad to see publicity used to increase the support of public opinion (Dewey 1982, 150).

The idea that publicity was an unalloyed good for social reform nearly came to a screeching halt in the post-WWI disillusionment. The most prominent instance during the war of the professionalization of publicity had been President Wilson's Committee on Public Information (CPI). After Congress declared war, Wilson signed an executive order in April 1917 to create CPI as a propaganda agency to mobilize public opinion in support for the US role in WWI. National unity was the goal, and CPI engaged in emotion-laden (and sometimes factually inaccurate) claims to horrify the nation in order to obtain unqualified civic support for victory regardless of cost. It blanketed the country with all manner of publicity, including posters, parades, pamphlets, and press releases. It also invented the medium of four minutemen, local volunteers who gave canned talks on war aims and war news in nearly every movie theater in the country before the beginning of a show. CPI's staffing was something of a who's who of the good-government progressives who had enthusiastically helped to develop the concept of publicity (such as its head, George Creel) along with business-oriented professionals who saw the dawning of a new age of corporate communication (such as Edward L. Bernays). CPI successfully demonstrated how public opinion could be shaped by publicity (St. John 2010).

The intellectuals' reaction to what publicity had morphed into began with one of Dewey's similarly prolific *New Republic* colleagues, Walter Lippmann. In 1922, Lippmann released a book on *Public Opinion* (1997). It was a pathbreaking and seminal consideration of the changing roles of publicity and public opinion in a modernizing society and democratic government. The book was "his most original contribution to political thought, social psychology and the study of mass communications" (Curtis 1991, xv). In it, Lippmann tried to assess the evolution of journalism and its impact on democracy. He concluded that it was never possible to report the objective and whole truth about something, no matter how conscientious a reporter might be. The newspaper version was simply a partial truth of what a reporter concluded were the most important aspects of a news event. This created, in Lippmann's immortal phrase, "pictures in our heads" that inevitably were increasingly distant from reality. Public opinion was therefore shaped by stereotypes, not facts. It was artificial, not authentic. These were amazingly powerful insights, which later became the conventional wisdom of the modern media age. But it was Lippmann who so perceptively identified, described, and analyzed them. As would be expected of someone identifying a problem, Lippmann tried to follow up these observations with a proposed solution. That was the weaker (though still interesting) latter part of the book. He conceptualized a class of policy analysis and research specialists who would tease out the true facts of a situation for the benefit of political decision makers and as a corrective to (false) public opinion. In all, it was a powerful book. Lippmann had zeroed in on the weaknesses of the Progressives' faith in publicity and in the reliance of government policy makers on public opinion. Modern democracy had such weaknesses that it could be perverted by those who knew how to shape information and stereotypes.

Dewey's review of *Public Opinion* in the *New Republic* was extremely positive. Overall, the book's "brilliancy does not impress one as fine writing; rather the material dealt with shines through. To read the book is an experience in illumination." Without reservation, Dewey endorsed the accuracy of Lippmann's analysis of stereotypes, news, and public opinion. He acknowledged that Lippmann had identified a valid and important problem, saying, "Mr. Lippmann has thrown into clearer relief than any other writer the fundamental difficulty of democracy" (Dewey 1983, 337, 344).

Being consistent and reflecting his own philosophy of education, Dewey nonetheless demurred from Lippmann's solutions. He wanted to help make democracy work, rather than isolate decision makers from democracy and public opinion. These demurrals were early glimpses at what later was reflected in the work of the People's Lobby. First, instead of a cadre of information specialists advising only politicians and administrators, he wanted these corrective mechanisms to communicate with the public-at-large so that the resulting public opinion would be more valid and accurate. This led to the People's Lobby engaging in a great amount of publicity, viewing such efforts as a corrective to the incrementalism of daily news coverage (who criticized who today?) and journalism's tilt to the sensational over important (though eye-glazing) developments in public affairs Second, he suggested the need to help readers "see underlying forces moving in and through events seemingly casual and disjointed." In other words, an ongoing effort was needed to link a meta-narrative to daily news—the bigger story of ideology, privilege, economic disparity, and the self-servedness of those who already had economic power. This, too, morphed into a running theme of the People's Lobby publicity work—of constantly relinking the bigger picture to what was essentially hidden in the press of daily journalism.

Three years after *Public Opinion*, the irrepressible but pessimistic Lippmann published something of a sequel to it called *The Phantom Public*

(1993).[4] In it, he was even gloomier about the ability of mass democracy to make the right decisions. He saw it as inherently defective and essentially absent from any substantive public debate over an important issue. People were not only diverted by inaccurate, sensational, and manipulated reporting. Citizens also had many other aspects of their lives that called their time and attention away from dispassionate and well-informed thinking about complicated issues of public policy. Lippmann's desire to limit the power of elections and public opinion corresponded to the thinking of many of the public administration reformers during that period (Lee 2011b). Lippmann had "opened the way to a post-Progressive conception of politics as a 'realistic' process of brokering an openly interest-based pluralism" (McClay 1993, xxxiv).

Dewey also reviewed *The Phantom Public*, also in the *New Republic*. As with his review of *Public Opinion*, it showed how Dewey's thinking about publicity, public opinion, and democracy was being refined in reaction to Lippmann's work. Dewey again praised Lippmann's incisive analysis of contemporary public affairs. Also, he was pleased that Lippmann's "philosophical background gives his book a reach and force which distinguish it from almost all other contemporary writing in the field of [public] affairs" (Dewey 1984a, 220). Coming from Dewey, a philosopher, that was a major compliment.

But, again, Dewey resisted the direction Lippmann took to deal with the problems he had identified and ably analyzed. This book review, too, sketched some of the rationales and actions of the subsequent People's Lobby. First, Dewey did not like the cause and effect that Lippmann assigned to mass democracy (and the emerging phenomenon of diminished voting turnout) as having a deleterious impact on quality of governmental policies and decision making. Dewey's interpretation focused on "the inherent problems and dangers the Great Society has brought with it, with respect to which the weakness of democracy [was] *symptomatic rather than causal*" (219, emphasis added).[5] In other words, democracy per se was not the cause of whatever problems Lippmann said were occurring in public affairs. Second, Dewey felt that there were methods of reorganizing society to strengthen the workings of democracy as an alternative to insulating public policy from democracy. If one were to describe the results of elections and tilt of public opinion as "meddling" in decision making, Dewey pointed out, then one was automatically accepting the validity of the framing of reality by laissez-faire economics. Instead, for example, he suggested experimenting with what came to be called syndicalism, a method of organizing social groups by "something that approximates a 'guild' or 'soviet'—please note I do not say Bolshevist—organization" (217).

In addition, there was a need to keep working at "making the press a continuous, systematic and effective revelation of social movements" (219–220). The goal, in Dewey's view, was to improve democracy so that the public could "discriminate between the group whose policies genuinely further the public interest and those who are making use of the public to promote private ends" (216). If the electorate could receive through the news media more factual and contextual information, then voters would "see private activities in their public bearings and . . . deal with them on the basis of the public interest" (220).

Here was the germ of an idea that Dewey was gradually formulating and that became manifested in the People's Lobby. There was a need to (1) promote the dissemination of otherwise unknown, but important factual information; (2) magnify such efforts by working to maximize its press coverage; and (3) analyze policy options to see if they were covert private interests or were truly in the public interest. Dewey's review kept returning to the existence of an authentic public interest. Identifying it and pressing for it as the underlying rationale for all policy decisions was to be a major driving force in the work of the People's Lobby.

Dewey Responds to Lippmann: The Public and Its Problems, 1927

Dewey was not satisfied that his two book reviews provided a comprehensive alternate framework to Lippmann's pessimism about mass democracy. He wanted a more full-throated "rebuttal" of Lippmann (McClay 1993, xviii), with a detailed examination of the subject of modern mass democracy. The intellectual debate between the two became famous as a showdown between two progressives with different takes on modern mass democracy (Gary 1993). Dewey soon had a platform for elaborating on his side of the argument. In 1926, he delivered a series of lectures at Kenyon College on the subject that elaborated on the ideas he expressed in the two book reviews. Dewey then revised the lectures and expanded his comments further for publication. In the fall of 1927, he released *The Public and Its Problems* (2012). He attributed some of the ideas of the book to a reaction to Lippmann's two books, acknowledging the strengths of Lippmann's analysis, but stating that he had reached "conclusions diverging from" Lippmann's (104n).[6]

It was a powerful and densely argued book. Dewey, as a philosopher, was comfortable with discussion of abstract and remote concepts, though he largely brought those discussions back to earth for his readers. It was not as opaque and highly theoretical as some of his earlier books, but rather somewhat more accessible to the less specialized reader. Assessing the importance of the book in 2012, Rogers described it as "perhaps one of his richest meditations on the future of democracy in an age of mass communication, governmental bureaucracy, social complexity, and pluralism" (2012, 1).

In the retrospect of later developments, *The Public and Its Problems* can be read as the theoretical underpinning of the People's Lobby, the organization's political stances, and its modus operandi (without detracting from Marsh's contributions). Dewey defined the proper scope of governmental actions (a hotly argued topic to this day) as when the consequences—bad or good—of private interactions between individuals significantly impacted others. That was when something became a public matter. In those cases, government was needed to intervene "whether by inhibition or by promotion" (48). But he also cautioned that government was not the totality of the society, of all human interactions, rather only a portion of it (53, 79).

Dewey criticized the stale dogmatism of political conflict, warning that self-serving interests would propagate interpretations of events as causal, rather than simply symptomatic (50). To use a contemporary example, does government regulation always hurt business efficiency (causal)? Or do problems with the operations of business require government regulation (symptomatic)? Similarly, he warned of the need to interpret the activities of public officials: Were they covertly pursuing their own private interests, or were they truly making decisions based on the public interest (57)? The former needed to be removed from power.

In particular, Dewey was critical of the determinism and triumphalism attached to the democratic status quo. He argued that the existing form of American democracy was not planned, but rather the result of a series of ad hoc decisions, solutions, and reactions (58). In that case, the then-form of democracy was not necessarily perfect unless "history is ended" (57). Assuming it was not, then democracy would and should continue to evolve through the same "experimental process" that had shaped it to that point. For Dewey, any oratory about the status quo being sacred and holy was suspicious and probably used to rationalize the privileges enjoyed by some in the current setup (58). He was especially critical of the increasing disparity between the fast pace of economic and technological advances in contrast to the resistance by the haves to additional political reforms. This was an effort, in his view, to retain the increasingly anachronistic economic laissez-faire doctrine in control of a political economy that no longer could function constructively under such a principle (100). Echoing Voltaire's mocking in *Candide*, Dewey's was a powerful critique of the oft-made claim by conservatives (and others) that the present was the best of all possible worlds. (Presciently, Dewey also predicted that "the present era of 'prosperity' may not be enduring" [116].)

Using an unusual argument, Dewey suggested that one of the trends in the expansion in the scope of government was due to taking over once-innovative but now-common economic activities. Taking over such "habitual" activities would free people to continue innovating and experimenting (73). Therefore, he dismissed as nonmeritorious claims of the propertied classes that public ownership of certain enterprises was Socialism. To him, that was a vacuous, lazy, and fact-free argument. In general, he supported a broader state role when economic disparities were too large. Government needed "to form a level on which bargaining takes place" between the haves and have-nots (74).

As he had in his reviews of Lippmann's two books, Dewey agreed with Lippmann's analyses of the faulty thinking about public opinion and modern democracy. There was no Public (a term he capitalized) in the sense of a viable and working entity that sequentially considered issues, coalesced into public opinion, and then shaped governmental decisions (118). But he saw these developments in a hopeful way, countering Lippmann's pessimism and inherently antidemocratic views. For example, Dewey noted that the huge waves of immigration to the United States had not upset the basic functioning of American government and had not prompted disintegration or instability. On the contrary, the absorption of the new immigrants into the electorate was "an extraordinary feat" (104). Rather than adding new democratic vitality, which, in turn, would prompt political innovation, he saw these new Americans as quickly fitting into the status quo of political values and the two-party system. Dewey was indirectly admitting to pessimism about his own longtime efforts to create a third party (106).

Picking up from his earlier writings, Dewey was optimistic about the ability to have social reform (partly coming from his ideas on public education), which in turn would lead to the creation of an authentic Community. What would that look like?

> A good citizen finds his conduct as a member of a political group enriching and enriched by his participation in family life, industry, scientific and artistic associations. There is a free give-and-take: fullness of integrating personality is therefore possible of achievement, since the pulls and responses of different groups reenforce [sic] one another and their values accord. (122)

Moving from the theoretical to the more specific, Dewey essentially outlined what he felt was lacking in modern political discourse and what, specifically, could be done. Here he was prophetically describing the mission of an organization to promote such democracy, a de facto description of the People's Lobby. Dewey focused on the importance of communication (124) as a prerequisite for a working democracy. Communicate about what? A true public could not come into being "without full publicity in respect to all consequences which concern it" (132). There was a need to convey what daily journalism was not, in particular to give coherence to alternatives that the economic status quo was suppressing or that the news media did not find interesting. This often artificial manufacturing of what was being covered had the effect, in Dewey's view, of alienating the citizenry, further detaching the public from a sense of being involved in the democratic process or having the ability to affect it. Using modern terminology, Dewey had identified the impact of disjointed and sensationalist news coverage—it made the citizenry the spectators of public affairs rather than participants. News, for Dewey, was more than what was happening or what was unusual. Instead, news should include context, alternatives, and discussion of what was not being talked about (132–133, 138–139).

In particular, Dewey wanted to see a more robust effort by someone or some organization to be sure that relevant knowledge (such as research results from the academy) be injected into news coverage. Possessing information from systematic and comprehensive "inquiry" (i.e., research) would significantly enhance the knowledge base of the electorate, especially about approaches and alternatives that may have had validity, but were suppressed by the beneficiaries of the economic status quo. It was a call for "a politics of knowledge" (Westbrook 1991, 316).

Here, then, was the kernel of the People's Lobby, initially expressed in his book reviews and now more fully formulated:

- engage in maximal publicity to reach the citizenry;
- use such publicity efforts to give a larger coherence to the episodic nature of news;
- disseminate information and alternatives that the economic and political oligarchy may be suppressing; and
- provide relevant and credible new knowledge that may contribute to a public debate about policies.

Dewey concluded the book with a call to arms that, as it turned out, identified the need for the People's Lobby: "Until secrecy, prejudice, bias, misrepresentation, and propaganda as well as sheer ignorance are replaced by inquiry and publicity, we have no way of telling how apt for judgment of social policies the existing intelligence of the masses may be" (155). What came to be the People's Lobby would contribute to the functioning of a democratic public, restore to proper functioning the increasingly absent public interest, and contribute to the creation of an authentic community. No wonder that, a year later, Benjamin Marsh would consider Dewey as a good candidate for heading some kind of a non–special interest group lobbying effort. It also explains why Dewey would agree with alacrity, but only with specific reformulations of the idea before starting. He had thought long and deeply about it and was ready to act. In retrospect of later historical developments, *The Public and Its Problems* was the theoretical underpinning and manifesto for the People's Lobby.

Hence, the organization was an example of Dewey trying to do more than philosophize, but also to implement his philosophy of democracy and citizenship, parallel to his support for specific schools that implemented his thinking about pedagogy. Throughout his life, Dewey welcomed opportunities to actualize his many ideas. In this case, the PL became a vehicle for him to be a philosopher-lobbyist who was trying to implement the views he coalesced and refined in *The Public and Its Problems*.[7]

Sketch of Marsh's Life and Politics, 1877–1921

Benjamin Clarke[8] Marsh (1877–1952) was a preternatural rabble-rouser: inflamed, passionate, combative, argumentative, never satisfied—and never caring about being popular or nice. He was always sure he was right, regardless of what anybody else thought, and was never at a loss for words. Marsh was the antithesis of the cerebral, soft-spoken, and polite-to-a-fault Dewey. But they nearly always agreed on their left-leaning ideological interpretation of public affairs. Both had the brains, but Marsh also provided the brawn; he was a born debater and rhetorical brawler. Dewey leaned toward expressing himself in writing, Marsh toward talking. Dewey used high-toned vocabulary, Marsh hot adjectives. They were fire and ice—it was a political match made in heaven.

In particular, Marsh had an intuitive understanding of the news media. He was ever ready with a quotable sound bite, provocative accusation, or generalization; was eager to create conflict and public theater at legislative hearings; and had an ability to turn a phrase and an ever-ready news release on slow news days. And he was a workaholic with seemingly endless energy. These skills made him a fabulously successful publicity hound for whatever cause he was espousing.

Marsh was born to American Congregationalist missionaries in Bulgaria and grew up there. He viewed his parents' theology as "pretty dour," but believed that they had "innate compassion and humanism" (Marsh 1953, 11). The Ottoman Balkans at that time were in near constant political upheaval, as the empire was disintegrating and ethnocentric nationalism rising. He recalled nearly being snatched for conscription into the Ottoman army and a few years later fantasizing about running away to enlist with the Bulgarian army in its war with Serbia. He returned to the United States to attend college at his father's alma mater, Grinnell in Iowa. He then was awarded a fellowship at the University of Pennsylvania for graduate work in sociology (Personal Notes 1902, 104). Showing the beginnings of an academic career, he published an article in an academic journal of the results of some of his research (Marsh 1904) but never finished a degree program. Instead, his do-good Protestant-based background and education quickly lured him to the real world of social activism and reform.

In quick succession, he was involved in the YMCA, the American Board of Missionaries, the Philadelphia Society for Organizing Charity, and the Pennsylvania Society to Protect Children from Courts. Then, in 1907, he became the secretary of a new group, the Committee on Congestion of the Population. Based in New York City, it was a nonprofit advocacy organization created by some leading social reform and philanthropic activists. Their central idea was that decreasing congestion would improve the quality of life in urban areas. Pursuing that goal would ostensibly decrease overcrowding in tenements, spread out the population of the poor over a larger area, promote improved housing conditions, and create space for new parks and recreation areas. Marsh jumped in feet first and had a knack for promoting the cause. He obtained the endorsement of leading politicians, civic activists, and philanthropists for investigating the subject; organized meetings; wrote about it; and generated news. In its essence, the anti-congestion camp was trying to capture control of the nascent enterprise of city planning by giving it a focus on improving the living conditions of people. This was, through the back door, social reform with a left-of-center orientation below the water line.

By getting there first, Marsh was hoping to *define* city planning. He moved fast. In 1909, he organized in New York City the first-ever City Planning Exhibition. That year, he self-published what was probably the first American textbook on city planning (Marsh 1974) and organized the first National Conference on City Planning, which took place in Washington, DC. For the moment, he was the most influential voice and thinker in the city planning movement. But a reaction against embedding this left-leaning ideology into the profession quickly set in. Led by Frederick Law Olmsted, Jr., a more politically neutral and technocratic approach to zoning trumped Marsh's message. Within a year, he had lost control of the annual conference and his views had been marginalized (Kochtitzky 2011, 131; Frumkin et al. 2011, 19; LeGates and Stout 1998, xxi–xxii; Kantor 1974). In Peterson's vivid metaphor, Marsh would "suddenly streak like a comet through the American planning skies," but then disappear as quickly as he had come (2003, 236).

That did not slow Marsh down. He continued writing, publicizing, and lecturing for his causes. He presented a somewhat academic paper at a conference on public recreation (Marsh 1910), wrote a 272-page final report of the Congestion Committee (reviewed in *Political Science Quarterly* by Charles A. Beard [1911]), self-published a 112-page treatise endorsing Henry George's single-tax proposal (Marsh 1911), authored a pamphlet on giving women the right to vote (Marsh 1912), and published another article in an academic journal on population congestion (Marsh 1914). In between all that, he testified at public hearings for his causes, joined committees, lectured, spoke at rallies, wrote letters to the editor, and traveled Europe as a freelance reporter. He managed to garner publicity for trying to milk a cow at a Greenwich Village fair and got himself expelled from the City Club for "conduct unbecoming a member" for an accusatory comment in the press about another member.[9]

By then, Marsh was a well-known political activist in New York and deeply involved in politics and causes on the left. According to the FBI, "his principal duties were the making of 'soap-box' speeches on the east side of that city, in which he attacked Wall Street and its activities."[10] But he was neither overtly nor formally a socialist. Marsh did not support a revolution and didn't want to be associated with any of groups advocating it, nor, for that matter, with the Socialist Party (even if it, ambiguously, opposed a revolution). He was, in Tobin's phrase, "a radical Progressive," that is, a moderate in the sense of wanting to work for reform from within the system and aiming to win elections. While his political goals often overlapped with those of socialists, he was not a card-carrying member of any party (1986, 19, 21, 45).

During WWI (but before the United States became a combatant), he was active in the Committee for Real Preparedness, which called for resolving social justice issues in the United States as a way to strengthen the country (Marsh 1916). He strenuously opposed the US entering the war (as the left generally did) and was active in the National Emergency Peace Committee. (It will be recalled, from earlier in this chapter, that Dewey, breaking with the left, had supported Wilson and the war.[11])

Once the United States declared war, accusations of traitorous behavior by left activists were common and in some cases led to arrests and imprisonment. Marsh diplomatically opted to downplay his opposition to the war in principle and instead to voice criticisms of how the war effort was being pursued. Moving to Washington, he became involved in the Farmers National Headquarters, which declared itself the joint voice in Washington for all "progressive farm organizations," listing fourteen sponsoring organizations on its letterhead.[12] In some respects, this was the contemporary manifestation of the southern and western farmers who had been active in national politics since the 1890s as an independent populist movement (Sanders 1999; Clemens 1997). They saw the left as separate from the Democratic Party and took vociferous stances against the business sector, especially banks, Wall Street, and the Republican Party. As publicity director of the coalition, Marsh noisily raised concerns about how the draft was degrading farmers' ability to maximize production, that the wartime emergency had loosened US Department of Agriculture (USDA) regulation of meatpacking factories, and how the tax burden to fund the war was malstructured.[13] Marsh wanted to tax the rich and wartime corporate excess profits. He later claimed he said that to President Wilson at a twenty-minute meeting with him (Marsh 1938, 81).

After the war was over, he helped reorganize the coalition into a successor organization called the Farmers' National Council. Its motto was "Guarding the Farmer's Interests at the National Capital."[14] It listed twenty-four members of a board of directors, encompassing about a dozen organizations. But the letterhead was more impressive than the reality. Marsh described the Council as "a very loose organization" in terms of formal membership, local chapters, and dues contributions (Marsh 1953, 49). He was its managing director.

Largely working alone on a shoestring budget and with little oversight, Marsh continued voicing farmers' interests, such as urging continuation of federal wartime control of the railroads because farmers feared a substantial postwar (and post–federal-control) increases in shipping rates.[15] He complained about the low wartime tax rates on millionaires who, he said, supported the war "to make their foreign investments secure." The rich, not suffering farmers, should now be expected to pay off the federal war debt, given their ability to pay and how little they were currently paying.[16] At a 1921 congressional hearing, he called for the federal government to take over and manage the export of farm surpluses, rather than leaving it in private hands.[17] The year before, he had urged a veto of a bill privatizing the wartime Atlantic shipping fleet and expressing farmers' fears about its impact on their costs.[18] A constant critic of administration agricultural policies, he was well known at the USDA. According to the FBI, he sent "insulting letters, advocating extreme radical abuse regarding farm legislation and criticizing the Secretary of Agriculture."[19]

Marsh saw little differentiation between legislative advocacy aimed at current office holders and involvement in electoral and partisan politics. For example, he testified before the Platform Committee of the Republican presidential nominating convention in Chicago in 1920. He urged a platform plank supporting the program of the Farmers' National Council.[20] When it of course did not do that, he loudly denounced the Republicans for ignoring the interests of farmers.[21] After the convention, he then tried to provoke the nominee, Warren Harding, into a public fight over the subject.[22] Harding didn't bite.

By this point, Marsh's continuing and aggressive criticisms prompted some of the conservative congressional targets of his barbs to try to challenge his credibility as a voice of farmers. At a hearing, Marsh provocatively said he represented those farmer organizations "which are not controlled by Wall Street," the latter including the Farm Bureau. Fighting rhetorical fire with fire, a Republican legislator made an equally inflammatory charge that was more of an insinuation than a question. He asked Marsh if there was any alliance between his organization and "the Russian Soviets." No, said Marsh.[23] At another congressional hearing, Marsh was asked to "explain the status of their organization and the number and character of the farmers that they represent," implying that Marsh was not an authentic representative of any major farm organizations.[24] When a farm bill was opposed by all farm groups except the Council, even sympathetic committee members dismissed Marsh's legitimacy to speak for any producers, especially after compelling him to answer where his voting residence was. "I voted in New York the last time," he said (Hansen 1987, 202).

A reporter covering one of those hearings flagged readers that he agreed with Marsh's congressional critics, characterizing Marsh and the Council as "the radical wing of organized farmers."[25] Similarly, the *New Republic* also identified the Council as representing "the Left."[26] The historical literature has since agreed with the validity of those perceptions. Guth identified the Farmers' National Council and Marsh as "radical" (1982, 75).

Marsh and the People's Reconstruction League, 1921–28

The results of the November 1920 elections were a victory for a Republican return to normalcy and a deflating setback for those in Marsh's circle trying to create a viable progressive-populist and farm-labor third political force. One attempt to keep the movement alive was led by Senator Robert M. La Follette Sr. (R-WI) to create a "People's Legislative Service," which would provide ostensibly neutral and factual analyses of bills introduced in Congress.[27] The formulation "People's" was in part a shortening of "Working People's," a term used at the time by some in the movement, such as the Working People's Nonpartisan League (Olssen 1978, 380).[28] Largely funded by the increasingly politicized unions of railroad workers, it had some modest success in the early 1920s. By the mid-1920s, the unions, having lost most of their legislative goals, cut back their funding. While it struggled on until 1933, the People's Legislative Service never became a major player (383).

In any case, the People's Legislative Service was to be an *observer* of legislative politics, not a participant. Marsh quickly saw political daylight and ran toward it, perceiving a political vacuum that could be filled with a counterpart that would be a player, actively lobbying for the same progressive agenda. Besides, the Farmers' National Council had been losing credibility on Capitol Hill, and its agricultural orientation precluded Marsh from involvement in issues that were tangential or unrelated to farmers' interests. Therefore, in early 1921, without abolishing the Farmers National Council outright (which he kept in a kind of inactive reserve status), Marsh created the People's Reconstruction League (PRL). According to Tobin, PRL was "the most aggressive and innovative lobbying group then formulating a progressive program," and its policy positions "typified contemporary liberal thinking" (1986, 132). Williams identified the PRL as one of four "new institutions" that were central to the progressive movement in the 1920s (2013, 60).

Like the People's Legislative Service, PRL began largely as a labor union organization. The railroad unions in particular provided almost all of its (meager) initial funding and comprised most of the two dozen members of its executive committee (a de facto board of directors). The funding from unions was modest, with Marsh—as before with the Farmers National Council—a one-man band operating on a shoestring budget. However, different from the Council, PRL also solicited *individual* memberships.[29] This was not only an expedient decision in terms of raising adequate funds, but also meant that PRL's views could not automatically be dismissed as parroting its organizational funders. Also, with members around the county, Marsh could turn to them to engage in letter writing to their legislators. Here was grassroots advocacy long before the term came into use. Marsh's title was executive secretary.[30]

The term "reconstruction" was used to convey the goal of "progressive forces to carry out a reconstruction program of economic justice."[31] More specifically, PRL had six legislative goals: resumption of federal operation of the railroads (as had occurred during WWI), effective controls over the meatpacking industry, increasing taxes on the rich and reducing taxes on the poor, strict banking regulation to prevent use of depositors' funds for speculation, public ownership and control over natural resources, and opposition to any military draft. Indicating its orientation, PRL stated that its modus operandi would be "publicity, pamphlets, conventions and organization."[32] Here was a declaration that lobbying was more than testifying at public hearings; it entailed mobilizing the public through publicity to the point of influencing public opinion.

The public unveiling of the organization took place in late January 1921.[33] According to the *New York Times*, the new lobbying group would be nonpartisan and focus on "economic justice" for workers and farmers. PRL asserted that its legislative program "will save American workers with hand and brain $6,000,000,000 a year."[34] The league quickly announced that it was convening a two-day national founding conference in April to flesh out its program and mobilize an active membership.[35] At the conference, speakers called for nationalization of the railroads, breaking up monopolies, legislation to enact a bill of rights for unions, a more progressive income tax, and criticism of the Federal Reserve for higher-than-necessary interest rates and constricted lending.[36] At the end of the conference, Marsh issued a public statement describing the now-sanctioned policy agenda of the PRL. Then League leaders went to Capitol Hill to lobby for those legislative goals. They claimed they represented 2 million members.[37]

Even before the conference, the new organization plunged in and supported enactment of legislation to oversee, inspect, and regulate meatpackers.[38] Marsh quickly became a frequent and combative presence at congressional hearings. He testified on domestic and international issues, farm-labor policies, and other progressive causes. Challenging his claims of whom he spoke for, at a Senate hearing he was grilled about PRL's actual membership. "Anyone can come in here with a fancy name of some league and claim they represent the earth," said the committee chair. Marsh patiently listed the names and organizational affiliations of the League's executive committee, but the senators who were the butts of his criticisms would have none of it. Giving as good as he got, Marsh expanded the scope of the hearing to criticize munitions makers "as spreaders of propaganda." The senators tried to cut him off.[39]

In addition to speaking at congressional hearings, he was a fount of public statements, including frequent press statements,[40] an issue brief to Congress,[41] and obtaining the endorsement of twenty-two senators for a request that the Federal Trade Commission investigate corporate mergers.[42] He also engaged in civil disobedience at least once, getting arrested for picketing the White House to protest the president's meeting with a (conservative) delegation from Hungary.[43]

In particular, Marsh peppered the president and his cabinet members with hectoring letters about their mistakes. When he received a reply, he then had an opportunity to respond further and keep the matter alive. These never-ending tos-and-fros were like perpetual grist for the mill. All these he released to the press, which welcomed such confrontational and quotable exchanges on the controversial issues of the day. Marsh's harsh and very public criticisms of the Republican administration triggered some of those exchanges. Commerce Secretary Herbert Hoover replied to a PRL letter addressed to the president, calling it "offensive" and punching back by criticizing "the warm support you give to the Bolshevik Government."[44]

While PRL was a Washington-based and -oriented group, Marsh was hoping to have state chapters to promote grassroots support and lobbying for its legislative agenda. He even envisioned memberships organized by congressional districts. In April, the League boasted that "already branches of the league are forming in ten states."[45] For example, Senator La Follette tried to create a chapter in Wisconsin (Saloutos 1946, 248), and the Machinists' union promoted having one in Boston.[46] But these local efforts died aborning. In lieu of formal chapters, when Congress was out of session, Marsh went on speaking tours to reach activists. He called himself the "poor man's lobbyist"[47] and addressed civic groups about the PRL's goals and his views on current developments. By this method, he sought to influence public opinion gradually and possibly convince some listeners to become PRL members. Marsh traveled to all sections of the country, speaking, for example, in Des Moines, Iowa; Portland, Oregon; Los Angeles; Omaha, Nebraska; Denver; and Salt Lake City.[48] On another occasion, he was an invited speaker at a national conference in New York City of Henry George single-tax supporters. In that appearance, he focused on the PRL's concern that land speculators were driving up agricultural land values, greatly to the detriment of farmers.[49]

Another organizing tool was the convening of PRL conferences. Marsh saw many benefits flowing from such meetings, including keeping the League vital, demonstrating its legitimacy in the eyes of others (i.e., that it was more than a letterhead), drawing more groups and individuals into activism, and, quite importantly, gaining press coverage. An early example was a public meeting in 1925 to oppose high tariffs, which were the standard GOP pro-business position.[50] Over the next few years, there were similar events on single topics, including opposing US intervention in Mexico,[51] American economic imperialism,[52] and economic concessions that the United States forced on other countries.[53] These events usually did not have a balance of pro and con speakers; rather, most (sometimes all) were in agreement with the PRL's positions. In 1927, a two-day conference covered PRL's multiple issues, including federal radio control, China, civil rights, labor rights, Nicaragua, outlawing war, and freedom of the press.[54] Almost all took place in Washington, but at least once, Marsh convened a conference in New York City.[55]

From the beginning, PRL was in the crosshairs of the red hunters in the US Justice Department's Bureau of Investigation (later the FBI). The files of the FBI's Washington Field Office on Marsh stated that it wanted "to see whether Marsh was a radical."[56] In 1921, a bureau agent came to interview Marsh at the PRL office. He said to Marsh that his assignment was "to get a line" on the League, its finances, names of contributors, and purposes. Marsh, typically, turned the tables on him, first having a stenographer present to make a formal transcript of the interview, then asking persistently why PRL was being visited but not pro-business lobbying groups. He kept badgering the agent about whether other lobbying groups would also be asked for the same information. The hapless agent kept demurring.[57] In the FBI's version of the meeting, Marsh "expressed considerable resentment because of the inquiry. . . . He requested to be advised if the so-called Capitalistic Lobbies in the city were being investigated as well."[58]

After the dramatic start to the meeting, Marsh made a point not to appear defensive or secretive (or personally insulting to the agent). He opened the League's books to the investigator. (Nowadays, that would be called transparency.) After the meeting was over, Marsh followed up with a letter to the attorney general demanding "a letter which I can make public stating whether you find anything in connection with the League which justified such an investigation."[59] The attorney general declined.[60] Meanwhile, the leftist press loved it, the FBI noted.[61]

Conservatives kept up a drumbeat against PRL and Marsh, along with many other groups and individuals. Those who feared antidemocratic subversion from the left viewed PRL and Marsh as part of a covert conspiracy of leftist revolutionaries. A book purporting to be the contents of documents seized by authorities in a 1922 raid of the Communist Party in Michigan listed Marsh and PRL as part of the Communists' covert but well-organized "Political Field." The giveaway was that Marsh supported "nationalization of public utilities" (*Reds in America* 1924, 46). A front-page story in the *Los Angeles Times* summarized a report released by the railroads identifying PRL as part of a nest of "Domestic Reds" with radical aims. PRL was "ostensibly operated as a farm lobby but actually under the control of a group of labor leaders and political extremists who advocate government ownership of railroads."[62] A congressman inserted in the *Congressional Record* (*CR*) a report from a conservative activist who claimed that the PRL was part of "a system of interlocking committee memberships . . . that play into the hands of the communists."[63] A few years later, another member inserted a document stating that PRL (among other organizations) was not openly Communist, but was a prominent liberal and pacifist organization that deliberately concealed its affiliation with communism. He said that the PRL was one of the five most dangerous groups in this larger category because it "operate[d] particularly in the political field."[64]

In part, Marsh knew that progressives and union supporters were almost automatically being smeared as Communists and there was nothing he could do to prevent it. But on one occasion, when invited to speak at a conference sponsored by the League for Industrial Democracy (a socialist organization in which Dewey was active), Marsh made a point of saying that "it is pure nonsense to talk revolution" and that he was not in that camp. Instead, the left should focus on pursuing its goals "gradually and through a long educational campaign" (Laidler and Thomas 1927, 216–217). Later in the conference, when another speaker called him a "professional revolutionist," Marsh insisted that the published transcript of the proceedings insert an editorial note that he "emphatically disclaims" supporting a revolution in the United States (229).

By 1927, PRL was sputtering out. Financially, no more funding was coming from unions, and it was hard to survive on individual membership fees alone. More generally, Marsh was shouting into the wind—that of prosperity. In his memoir, he confessed that it was hard enough in American politics to fight for non-mainstream principles, but nearly impossible in "the roaring days of the Coolidge Administration." PRL simply could not "survive prosperity" (Marsh 1953, 87).

Marsh had had a decent run. He had vigorously promoted PRL's agenda, attaining a high (if controversial) public profile, at least high enough to be included in Herring's census of interest groups in Washington in the 1920s (1967, 282). Marsh felt it had had "some success" (1953, 87). However, as Tobin noted, "there is a danger in attributing excessive influence to an organization like the PRL simply because it had a published program, a

Washington address, and letterhead stationary" (1986, 132). As a result, it is difficult to determine PRL's effectiveness. Still, working on a shoestring budget, Marsh deserves some credit for trying to keep alive the farm-labor progressive policy agenda during much of the roaring twenties. But it was a relatively lonely task. Political and economic conditions led to a fading constituency for a third party or for any major policy changes in the status quo. There was little he could accomplish beyond showing the flag. It was true that PRL was committed to working *within* the system, but it was widely seen as "composed mainly of radical elements" and lacking a significant grassroots presence outside the capital.[65] Even Henry A. Wallace (later FDR's USDA secretary, still later vice president), no shrinking violet on the need for progressive farm policies, wrote of PRL in 1921 as limited to representing the "more radical farm organizations" (Sillars 1952, 133).[66] In the prosperity and conservatism of the 1920s, this was generally a political kiss of death.

With PRL clearly fading, especially in terms of financial support from unions, in 1927, Marsh tried to reconstitute it as the Anti-Monopoly League (AML), focusing on the unfair economic benefits that accrued to monopolies. (The title was not new. An Anti-Monopoly League had existed in New York in the 1880s.) While the theme for its organizing prism was different, the policy issues were "substantially the same" as PRL's (Marsh 1953, 87): federal control over natural resources on public lands, private utility companies, Standard Oil, and foreign concessions. When the AML was unveiled in late 1927,[67] it released a position paper of its legislative program,[68] convened a founding conference,[69] received favorable coverage from a syndicated columnist,[70] sent a mailing to small rural newspapers,[71] and criticized Congress in a press statement.[72] But, as might be expected, pouring old wine into a new bottle did not help much. It was still an era of prosperity, progressives were out of the political and governmental mainstream, and ideas to expand the role of government and regulate corporations were easily smeared as communistic. Much faster than Marsh expected, AML was quickly approaching a political dead end. PRL had lasted seven years. For AML, within a year of its founding, the organization's death rattle was becoming clear. Its president, having served less than a year, insisted on stepping down, and no successor was in sight.

Earlier Efforts at Forming a People's Lobby

The moniker "people's lobby" was not original to Dewey and Marsh. It had been used in various ways, often more informally than officially, at least as early as 1906. That year, allies of President Theodore Roosevelt announced that they were planning on organizing a people's lobby. Its goal would be to make Congress more transparent so that voters could identify behind-the-scenes efforts by special interests to pass legislation favorable to them. The organization would be a wholly passive one, not engaging in lobbying itself, but rather providing information. Early sponsors were Mark Twain and Lincoln Stephens.[73] But conservative voices quickly chimed in, questioning the idea as possibly using the seemingly noncontroversial goals of good government and clean politics as a subterfuge for progressive, left-leaning, and anti-business reformers. The *Chicago Tribune* editorialized against such an organization "if partisanship, or spleen, or too much of the 'muck raking' is indulged in."[74] The organizing committee convened a meeting in Washington to found the organization and name its leadership.[75]

A year later, the group held a rally in Indianapolis to recruit members. Senator Albert Beveridge (R-IN), a political progressive, chaired the meeting and endorsed the effort.[76] By then, the *Tribune* was even more indignant. If it claimed to represent all the people instead of narrow special interest groups, then this kind of organization could intimidate legislators who might fear that if they opposed its views, then they would be branded as against the people. And who were the funders of this new organization? What were *their* special interests? Who were they to claim they had a monopoly on what was good for the people? "If the plan was successful, [it] might easily bring about more evil in the way of hasty or ill considered legislation than [the] state or nation suffers from now," the paper editorialized.[77] For reasons that are unclear, nothing ever came of this effort to create a people's lobby in Washington.

After the first news of the idea of a people's lobby to monitor Congress, similar efforts were made in some state capitals. A relatively formal People's Lobby briefly was active in New Jersey politics in Trenton (Tobin 1974) and in New York politics in Albany.[78] The creation of what probably was the first legislative reference bureau in Wisconsin's capital was sometimes described informally as a people's lobby.[79] Lesser efforts to create peoples' lobbies oriented at state government were at least initiated in Massachusetts, Illinois, and (much later) Nebraska.[80] Clemens's book title *The People's Lobby* emanated from the *rumor* in California in 1909 that such an organization was coming into existence and would be lobbying the Legislature in Sacramento. It never happened (Clemens 1997, 1–2, 55). Just in case, the conservative *Los Angeles Times* editorialized against it.[81]

In his 1929 review of public interest–oriented lobbying on a national level, Logan considered the National Community Board in the early 1920s as something of a precursor to the Dewey and Marsh People's Lobby (Logan

1929, 76–77). This assertion was quite a stretch and is not credible when comparing the two organizations. The Board sought to facilitate creation of public interest–oriented organizations at the local level, which, in turn, would then lobby local governments to enact their ideas. The Board's vision was that "everybody is organized except the one class which represents the public interest," and that organization's mission was to be the "attorney for the public."[82]

Marsh stated in his posthumously published memoir that the People's Lobby he and Dewey cofounded in 1928 was the first national organization with this electrifying title and audacious purpose (1953, 88). His appears to be a creditable claim. The effort to create a people's lobby in Washington in 1906 had failed and, significantly, even if it had succeeded, it would have been a passive, information-sharing organization only. The handful of efforts to create people's lobbies on the state level, including engaging in active lobbying, had had some brief existences. Dewey and Marsh were thinking on a national level and not just monitoring Congress, but also actively advocating for specific public policies. They wanted to do nothing short of upending the influence of special interest groups in Washington or, at least, balancing the scales a bit by promoting their view of the public interest. Dewey and Marsh earn credit for going further than anyone else had gone before.

Chapter 2

Constructing the People's Lobby, 1928–1931

By the winter of 1927–28, both Dewey and Marsh had relatively well-developed progressive political philosophies and were at a point of welcoming a new venue to pursue such legislative and policy goals in Washington. For Dewey, the publication of *The Public and Its Problems* had helped to crystallize his views on public affairs and how to accomplish democratic change. For Marsh, the slow fadeout of the People's Reconstruction League and then the even quicker one of the Anti-Monopoly League (Chap. 1) made a change imperative.

That winter, the AML's president resigned after less than a year in office. What to do? The remaining members of the executive committee (akin to a board of directors) met in a gloomy mood. None was willing to be the new president, and all felt there was a need for a major jolt if the League were to survive. Running out of ideas and in something of a long-shot Hail Mary pass, one of the board members suggested that Marsh go to New York City and see if John Dewey was interested (Marsh 1953, 87).

At around the same time, a longtime ally of Theodore Roosevelt and Bull Moose Progressivism revived the idea, first floated in 1906 by TR's political allies, of creating a People's Lobby in Washington to monitor Congress (Chap. 1). Along with TR, Gifford Pinchot had been a founder of the conservation movement.[1] President Roosevelt appointed him to head the US Forest Service. After being fired noisily by President Taft, Pinchot was elected as a reform-oriented governor of Pennsylvania. When his term ended, Pinchot ran for US Senate and lost (in a close election, possibly affected by ballot stuffing by the urban political machines who opposed him). Casting about for a continuing role in public affairs, he decided to move (back) to Washington and get involved in promoting progressive policies.[2] In late 1927, musing out loud to a reporter, Pinchot said he was playing with the idea of naming his proposed new group the "People's Lobby" as a way to capture its purpose and mission. It was a good story and was picked up by newspapers nationally.[3] As it turned out, Pinchot never followed up on that specific idea for the name of an organization to promote his views. But Marsh, an acquaintance of Pinchot's, would have known about the trial balloon.[4] With Pinchot ultimately not using it, in early 1928 it was free for the taking.

Dewey and the Founding of the People's Lobby

Marsh arranged an appointment with Dewey in New York in the early spring of 1928. Dewey, then sixty-eight, was a faculty member at Columbia and, separately, vigorously engaged in public affairs. He remembered Marsh from Marsh's social work activist years in Pennsylvania and then New York and thought well of him. However, the two had parted company over World War I (then called the Great War). Dewey, in a somewhat surprising decision for people of his political ilk, had supported the United States entering the war. Marsh, taking a more traditional leftist stance, was a pacifist and not willing to make an exception for this particular war. Such major disagreements often ended friendships, in the way that the Vietnam war did for some liberals in the mid-1960s. But Dewey—never the hater—didn't hold it against Marsh. From the beginning of the meeting, Dewey received Marsh in a warm manner.

Marsh told Dewey the purpose of his visit and asked if he would accept the presidency of the AML. Dewey amiably and somewhat impishly replied that he was a philosopher, not a lobbyist—humorously ignoring the implicit lobbyishness of his scores of writings, many in the *New Republic*, when he did take positions on public policy issues and thereby tried to influence public opinion and decision making by public officials. But it was true that his policy advocacy had almost always been indirect, through his writings (and overt political activities, such as for a third party), and he was not involved in leading any ongoing direct lobbying efforts.

Dewey had only once testified before Congress, about a decade before their conversation. In early 1917 (before the United States entered WWI), he was part of an organized delegation of educators to testify against a military draft bill. In his testimony, Dewey stated that conscription went against American civic traditions, though he was careful to say he was not a pacifist who was automatically against any military-oriented policy. He also didn't like the impact it might have on the educational system, in a sense militarizing them by expecting them to prepare boys for service. He also lightly challenged the presumption that only men would be drafted, not women, too. (At this point in the transcript, it notes "[Applause]" from the audience, evidently endorsing the strong debating point, not likely in favor of drafting women.) Generally, Dewey based his comments on his large body of abstract theorizing about education, applying those theoretical principles he sometimes densely wrote about to this specific matter. Members of the committee, whether agreeing with him or not, treated him with courtesy, even deference, given his public standing and their presumption that he was without guile and not there to score political or partisan points (US Senate 1917, 560–571). That was Dewey's sole personal involvement in lobbying Congress in person. So when he genially told Marsh he did not view himself as a lobbyist, he was being accurate.

In the course of their conversation, it was clear that both were in full agreement about the need for legislation to make major reforms in the social and economic direction of the country. Marsh said to Dewey that he had sometimes viewed PRL as a kind of people's lobby,[5] but that the board of directors strongly felt that the term "lobby" was inexorably odious, a pejorative epithet. It was routinely used to describe the legislative efforts of major economic interests, such as Standard Oil, Wall Street, and other major corporations. In those days, there were no "good" lobbies (Clemens 1997), and these very powerful Interests[6] and their lobbies were always on the right side of the ideological spectrum. Dewey perked up at this potential contrarian usage of a term, an approach he had often applied in his intellectual and philosophical work, of arguing that much of the conventional wisdom got things backward and needed to be reseen in a wholly different, even opposite, light (Menand 2001, 304, 330). A lobby that fought for the public interest, not the Interests![7] Dewey later explained that he "did not hesitate to call it a 'lobby,' for that is what it is" (Dewey 1984b, 429). Heading such an organization with that specific title was also a logical continuation of the views he expounded on in his 1927 book *The Public and Its Problems*. Dewey gave his answer on the spot. He told Marsh he would accept the presidency, but only on one condition: that the name of the organization would be the People's Lobby (Marsh 1953, 87–88).

It was a perfect pairing, Dewey the famous philosopher and leftist political figure; Marsh the indefatigable polemicist, writer, speaker, lobbyist, and organizer. Dewey would be the front office man whose prominence practically guaranteed a perception of legitimacy and gravitas; Marsh would be the back-office worker bee, churning out publicity material in every possible packaging.

The new organization came into being in April 1928.[8] That the People's Lobby was a distinctly different organization than Marsh's PRL and AML was clear from its debut or, more precisely, lack thereof. When PRL and AML had started, each began with a kick-off announcement of their creation in a press statement, a kind of declaration of birth and high hopes of impact. Not so for the People's Lobby. Instead, it went for a soft launch. Reflecting Dewey's quieter style, PL gradually came into public view and then only as an existing organization at work, as a fait accompli. The absence of a grand opening helped tamp down high expectations and grandiose-sounding aims. Instead, the new organization would gradually earn its spurs, developing a record based on its activities rather than premature promises. It would garner a reputation based on the deed, not on claims before any action at all. This seemed consonant with Dewey's approach and philosophy. He preferred to focus on behavior and action as central and inseparable from knowledge (Menand 2001, 322, 361).

Marsh's first public testimony at a congressional hearing as representing the PL was in April 1928. Reflecting this new style, he was more tentative than usual. Marsh said he represented an organization the senators had known up to then as the PRL, but that it was now "sometimes known as the People's Lobby" (US Senate 1928, 220). Fittingly, he was opposing a bill requested by Treasury Secretary Andrew Mellon to cut taxes and, in Marsh's view, doing so disproportionately for the wealthy. Later in the month, he spoke at a civic forum in Washington and identified himself as "secretary of the People's Lobby."[9] Dewey's first public appearance on behalf of the new organization occurred the next month, May 1928, when he addressed a symposium-style meeting Marsh organized in Washington on the interventionist and pro-business American foreign policy in Latin America. Dewey criticized it.[10]

Dewey and Marsh were both careful about protecting their new creation as a nonpartisan and nonpolitical group. Using Berry's definition (as discussed in the Introduction), the PL was a public interest group because its members did not have an economic stake in the positions it was advocating, in contradistinction to special interest groups, which did. The PL focused on public policy issues and not on political organizing, partisan involvement, or any other direct appeals to voters. Yes, it understood the link between elections and policy making, but it tried to steer clear of the former. For Dewey, within a year, he had an outlet for the latter. In May 1929 (so slightly more than a year after cofounding the PL), Dewey accepted the presidency of the League for Independent Political Action (LIPA), a group of progressive and liberal activists. It was an organizational home for the remaining believers in creating an authentically left (but non-Communist) third party.[11] (One of the few occasions when LIPA and PL overlapped was a jointly sponsored conference in Washington in November 1929, shortly after the stock market crash.[12])

Similarly, Marsh was also careful that his personal activism and views could not easily be used by the right to smear the PL as a red organization. For example, only a few months after the PL was established, he was an invited speaker at a conference on socialism. He was at pains to clarify his politics. When it was his turn to address the audience, his first sentence was, "Let me at once state that I am not a socialist" (Laidler and Thomas 1929, 168). Later in the conference, he somewhat chastised the participants for seemingly being more interested in "self-expression" than in accomplishing better conditions for the masses (277). He positioned himself in the latter category, the pragmatic lobbyist with his sleeves rolled up, working in Washington to affect public policy, rather than luxuriating in political clubhouses or coffeehouses engaging in rhetorical and ideological purity.

Building an Initial Organizational Structure

In Dewey's view, a people's lobby should be precisely that: an organization of *people*. This was a dramatically different organizational template from the one that Marsh had been using since the late 1910s, when he formed the Farmers' National Council, then the PRL (predominantly an organizational membership, though individual memberships were offered), and finally the AML. All three were essentially organizations of organizations. In other words, the members of the organization were themselves organizations. They were really coalitions or umbrella groups that tried to amalgamate preexisting and independent entities into a united front. From Dewey's perspective, this would not do. Coalitions can be feeble, falling apart when their member organizations disagree on a policy position. Also, coalitions can be unstable, because they depend on the goodwill, continued cooperation, and funding of their member organizations. Instead, Dewey conceived of the People's Lobby as having a membership of individual citizens. This would give the organization a more anchored and concrete base of real people sending in real money to maintain their annual memberships. Such an organization would have greater credibility with veteran pols, who could see through seemingly impressive letterheads. And it would be an effort to operationalize the more idyllic democratic form of governance that he had advocated in *The Public and Its Problems.*

Furthermore, policy positions adopted by such an organizational structure would likely have a greater political impact, again because of the real people at the ground level. That was the distinct lobbying benefit to having individual members. These were likely to be grassroots activists and likely to be spread around the county. Every member would have his or her own member of Congress and pair of home-state senators. They were *constituents*, a magic word for elected officials. It is one thing to dismiss a lobbyist claiming to represent the public, but it is altogether different to know the organization has constituents as members and sometimes even hearing directly from them in support of the organization's recommended position.

Hence, an organization of people had several distinct advantages over an organization of organizations. (It also had some disadvantages, which are discussed in the next subchapter.) The change in *who* comprised the organization quickly became apparent. The People's Lobby started out with the (outgoing) board of AML, but then it gradually eliminated all organizational representatives and replaced them with individuals. There were twenty-seven members of the executive committee of AML (including officers). Of them, ten were unaffiliated (37 percent).[13] All the affiliated members were from labor and farm organizations. Going farther back, PRL's Executive Committee (and officers) consisted of twenty-two people, only five of whom had no organizational affiliation (23 percent). Again, the other seventeen were exclusively from organized labor and farm groups.[14] Within a year of its founding, PL had a thirty-six-member Advisory Committee, twenty-five of whom were private citizens not representing any organization (69 percent).[15] It was gradually moving toward a wholly different paradigm of what kind of organization it was and whom it spoke for. A *people's* organization.

Related to the change in the nature of the membership of the organization's steering group was a change in the title of that body. For PRL and AML, it was an executive committee, but for the new People's Lobby, it was downgraded to an advisory committee. Why the change? If this truly was to be a people's lobby, there couldn't be an intellectually honest justification for having a board of directors *from inception*. Rather, the board of directors should come into existence only *after* the new organization had existed long enough to have an open process of designating its first board of directors. Then, after that initial stage, as a true people's lobby should be, the Board of Directors would always be elected by the citizen members. Dewey was being consistent with his view of the workings of democratic citizenship.

Dewey was also personally active in recruiting some of these initial members of the PL's steering group. He wanted people who not only agreed with his basic leftist philosophy of fighting pro-business conservative special interest groups, but also were intellectually independent and would have worthwhile judgments and insights to contribute to the PL's initial decision making. Dewey asked Columbia Economics Professor Rexford Tugwell and Oswald G. Villard, editor of *The Nation*, to serve. Given Dewey's standing, being invited by him was something of an honor. Also, Dewey selected his recruits carefully, wanting to have people of a caliber who "gave some respectability" to PL immediately (Sauter 1991, 226). His selectees gave PL a kind of instant credibility in terms of how it represented itself.

Six years later, in 1934, Tugwell's "yes" to Dewey came back to haunt him politically in an incident that also helps to convey the suspicions that Dewey's conception of the PL had triggered. Tugwell had been part of FDR's brain trust and an assistant secretary of agriculture. This made him something of a lightning rod for the emerging opposition to the New Deal on Capitol Hill, mostly the noisy protestations of the conservative coalition of minority Republicans and conservative Democrats (usually southern). They warned of the Red menace that was behind the curtain of the New Deal and that the federal government was slipping into the control of communism, insinuating that FDR himself was at the very least a front or dupe of the hard left. In 1934, Roosevelt nominated Tugwell to be promoted from assistant secretary to under-secretary. The Senate confirmation hearing turned into an early version of an "Are-you-now-or-have-you-ever-been . . . ?" interrogation, including Tugwell's affiliation with the People's Lobby. It was a "stormy" four-hour "inquisition," with conservatives intent on showing that Tugwell's politics were un-American, a threat to constitutional government, and anti–free enterprise.[16]

Late in the hearing, probing for some accusation that would stick to Tugwell, Agriculture Committee Chair Ellison Smith (D-SC) dramatically displayed a piece of paper and then handed it to Tugwell (US Senate 1934a 172–173; all following quotes from this source). It was from the March 1933 issue of the *People's Lobby Bulletin.*

> SMITH: I have been asked to ask you if you are still a member of this concern? If so, I would like to put it in the record.
>
> TUGWELL: No, sir.
>
> SMITH: You are not?
>
> TUGWELL: No sir.

SMITH: Were you a member at one time?

TUGWELL: I don't think I ever was . . . or perhaps I made a 1-year contribution to them and then dropped out.

SMITH: I would like for it to appear in the record that I have handed Dr. Tugwell a statement here showing that he was at one time a director in what is known as "the People's Lobby." He says he was not.

In a highly irregular action, to strengthen his hand, the chair had invited two conservative Democratic senators who were not members of the committee to participate in the committee's questioning of Tugwell. They were Harry Byrd (VA) and Josiah Bailey (NC). Bailey jumped in at this point: "I want to read this. These are the officers of the People's Lobby" and proceeded to read out loud the entire masthead of the PL into the record, starting with Dewey as president and ending (literally) with Tugwell as a member of PL's Council (which was separate from and listed after PL's Board of Directors).

BAILEY: I suppose "Rexford G. Tugwell" means you?

TUGWELL: I suppose so.

BAILEY: But you don't know whether you were a member of the council or not?

TUGWELL: I am sorry, but I do not. I hope I am a very good friend of Dr. John Dewey, and if he asked me to be a member of some organization at some time I probably did it without any further request, and I should do it again—glad to. I am proud to be associated with him in any enterprise.

BAILEY: Would you authorize a statement to be issued such as this bulletin purports to carry?

TUGWELL: I don't know what it is.

SMITH: Read it and see.

At this point, Burton Wheeler (D-MT)[17] and George Norris (R-NE)[18] (who were committee members) could not refrain from jumping in to defend Tugwell and the People's Lobby.

> Wheeler: Here are some of them . . . [reading the names of some other PL Council members]
>
> Tugwell: Pretty good company.
>
> Wheeler: Yes; I would say they would be.
>
> Norris: A role of honor, isn't it?
>
> Tugwell: They are people whom I respect very much.
>
> Smith: Let him read the statement and see whether or not he subscribes to it.
>
> Norris: We ought to be able to find something that he does not subscribe to and get it on the record.[19]
>
> Tugwell: . . . I see I am listed as a member not of the board of directors but of something they call the "council." The board of directors is different.

As directed by the chair, Tugwell proceeded to read out loud some excerpts from the *Bulletin*. It made him and the Lobby sound like radical, subversive, and perhaps commie revolutionaries. After finishing, he said

> Tugwell: Well, I never saw this before. There are some things in it that I believe in and some that I don't.
>
> Committee member Peter Norbeck (R-SD): I have heard nothing in that paper that has anything to do with his qualifications or preparation for this.

That was the end of it. Tugwell's opponents had fired their last bullet and failed to score, even to the extent that a *Republican* senator dismissed the excerpt from the *Bulletin* as damning Tugwell in any way. Guilt by (tenuous) association with the People's Lobby was not persuasive.[20] The hearing promptly adjourned.

It turned out that the paper he was given was a mishmash of two separate articles in that issue. The first two paragraphs were the last two of the lead article authored by Dewey, which was titled "The Banking Crisis." The remainder came from a different article titled "Technocracy, Taxation and Tactics." It was largely a summary of the contents of the writings by three different authors (all unrelated to the PL) and likely drafted by Marsh.

Tugwell was recommended by the committee the next morning by a vote of sixteen to two and then confirmed by the Senate fifty to twenty-four. Nonetheless, the conservative onslaught against him and insinuations of his supposedly secret but true hard-left ideology continued fiercely until he left Washington in 1937. (In 1941, FDR named him governor of Puerto Rico.) In retrospect, the combative and accusatory confirmation hearing raising questions about his and the PL's fidelity to the United States was a foreshadowing of the direction that the conservative movement in American politics was about to undertake for the next few decades. Tugwell was lucky to have survived it, as was the People's Lobby and its reputation.

Getting to Financial Viability

Dewey (and Marsh) did not want the PL to have the same fate as Marsh's earlier organizations. They wanted to create a sustainable economic model for the Lobby. This went hand in hand with their decisions on the PL's organizational structure. Breaking from dependence on labor unions, they were hoping that the voluntary dues paid annually by the members would sustain the Lobby. This would not only guarantee authentic political independence, but also would be another way to demonstrate the Lobby truly being a people's organization by relying mostly on funding from the rank and file of the citizenry. Other contributions would be accepted and welcome, but only if no strings were attached. Dewey and Marsh understood that the appearance of independence was as important as the actual fact of it.

This was all easier said than done, especially when an annual membership cost $1. Just covering Marsh's subsistence-level salary and office expenses would require at least ten thousand members at that level of basic membership. Higher membership status called for higher annual contributions: $10 for sustaining member and $25 for active member. In an effort to jump-start a new member base, the PL announced its existence and solicited enrollment in the *New Republic*. This was a natural audience for potential members because readers were familiar with and sympathetic to Dewey's political views. About a year after PL was founded, the magazine published a letter to the editor from Marsh that briefly explained the purpose of the (relatively) new organization and inviting readers to enroll.[21]

At first, Dewey and Marsh were optimistic that they could keep PL afloat on membership dues only. A year after its founding, the Lobby stated that it had "hundreds" of members (Logan 1929, 77). By its third year of existence, things were looking somewhat better. In 1931, when pressed at congressional hearing about whom he *really* represented, Marsh testified that the Lobby had about 1,400 to 1,500 members in about thirty-four states (US Senate 1931, 209–210). That reflected a healthy growth curve, but it was not nearly enough to sustain the organization at minimal levels. Also, it was not clear if continued growth rates could be maintained or if the Lobby had already largely maxed out on its likely members.

Dewey was actively involved in trying to make the Lobby financially viable. For example, in addition to recruiting Oswald G. Villard, editor of *The Nation*, to serve on the PL's initial Advisory Committee, Dewey also asked him for a major contribution. In a January 1929 letter to Villard, Dewey described the new PL and its financial needs thus:

> Money is needed to enable us to capitalize the results of present information and to carry on further investigations and circulate their findings. Our releases have a wide distribution, and we have frequent proof of their efficacy in affecting action at [sic] Washington. Officials are, I need not say, highly sensitive to public opinion . . . and every cent given counts in creation of this public opinion. There is no other organization, it is safe to say, with such a small percentage of administrative and overhead expense.[22]

On another occasion, he wrote fellow professor and social activist Eduard Lindeman for help, financial or otherwise. Lindeman was affiliated with many local organizations and was in a position to facilitate contributions by those organizational boards of directors to PL. Dewey conveyed how affected he was by the social and economic suffering and frustrated by President Hoover's unwillingness to set aside his principled opposition to federal aid to those in hardship: "The stories I hear of suffering are getting worse, and the indications are that we may have a terrible winter."[23] Lindeman replied, "I am sorry that there has been so much delay in appropriating the money for the People's Lobby" from one of the organizations in which he was active and promised to finalize a contribution as quickly as possible.[24]

In addition to writing to request contributions, Dewey was also willing to give of his time. For example, in late 1929, he went to Philadelphia to address a meeting of local members of the PL and other liberal activists. He was hoping that the event would help to recruit more members and convince current ones to give more generously or, at least, keep renewing their annual membership. With 150 people there, he described the "plans for the protection and advantage of the general American public which will be carried out in the near future by the People's Lobby."[25]

Still, even with Dewey's personal efforts, the membership dues and other minor contributions were not adequate to keep PL going. By spring of 1931, after three years of struggling, Dewey wasn't sure the Lobby was going to make it. Then, in April, Dewey excitedly wrote Marsh: "Dear Ben, The Lord Livith—enclosed please find Mrs. Clyde's check for $1616. Pay yourself for God's sake: I'm not a Godsaker as a rule."[26]

Mrs. Ethel Clyde was the granddaughter of the founder of the successful Clyde steamship line and had inherited substantial wealth from it (Auerbach 1966, 46n53). She was determined to use that money very differently from so many members of New York's society who gave to mainstream cultural institutions and were quite passive in their relations with these philanthropic organizations. Clyde wanted to use her wealth to help promote social change, and she wanted to be actively involved in such efforts, not just write checks. Having been a student at Columbia when Dewey taught there, she liked what he stood for and how he pursued those goals.[27] Her contribution was prompted by a desire to help the Lobby pursue its agenda. In particular, she felt that the Lobby's influence on decision makers and public opinion could be enhanced if its publications had a more professional look. She was willing to pay for the costs of shifting from newsletters that were typed and stenciled to a more attractive and appealing format of typeset and printed ones.[28] The first issue of the new monthly *People's Lobby Bulletin* (*PLB*) was in May 1931. (The format, presentation, and template of that inaugural issue were retained for the duration of the Lobby's existence.) Mrs. Clyde also suggested expanding the reach of the Lobby by adding to its mailing lists such categories as college libraries and faculty in relevant academic disciplines like economics and sociology. Clyde was an early example of an engaged philanthropist. She continued covering PL's deficit into the future and accepted a role as an officer of the Lobby.

While this was not quite the financial scenario that Dewey had hoped for, it was certainly next best. As the patroness of PL, Clyde kept the organization financially viable, sincerely believed in its goals, and invested not only her money, but also her time in the organization. From his delighted letter to Marsh informing him of the good news, Dewey's relief is palpable. He could now count on PL being financially safe for the foreseeable future. Dewey continued to be attentive to Clyde, signaling that he knew of the importance of his personal involvement for this crucial source of funding of the lobby. For example, in 1931, he accepted her invitation to drive him to a meeting[29] and, a different time, noted that "Mrs. Clyde is certainly wonderful" in how much she cared about the PL.[30]

Determining a Legal Status

The last act in the creation of the People's Lobby was to decide on its legal status. Out of the blue, in late 1929, Marsh received a letter from (what later came to be called) the Internal Revenue Service (IRS). A citizen's tax return had listed a tax-deductible contribution to it. As the IRS was not familiar with this organization, it needed "to determine the status" of PL. The IRS requested "an affidavit sworn to by the principal officer" with basic information about the organization. In particular, the IRS wanted to know if the organization was incorporated, if there was any capital stock, and if any financial benefits inured to private shareholders.[31]

Marsh promptly complied. In an affidavit, he stated that the People's Lobby was not incorporated, did not have any capital stock, and, therefore, no financial benefits inured to shareholders. Indicating that the legal template of nonprofits and their tax-exempt status in the internal revenue code had not yet gelled, as it would later in the twentieth century, he did not describe PL as a nonprofit or any other similar term, nor did he assert that contributions were tax deductible. Rather, the PL was similar to many of its peers at the time—an informal, nonprofit organization that was not incorporated, registered with the IRS, or issued stock or shares.[32] A little more than a year later, Marsh was obliged to submit a similar affidavit covering the actions and status of PL in 1930. He added to the 1929 filing the statement that it had "no assets and liabilities—its only assets being furniture in the office which it occupies."[33]

The necessity for a second affidavit confirmed that as long as the PL remained unincorporated, such documents would be required. This prompted Dewey and Marsh to confer on what permanent legal status PL should have. It could continue as it was or it could incorporate, thereby regularizing its status in formal legal terms. With Mrs. Clyde's ongoing financial commitment to cover PL's necessary expenses when they were higher than member dues, Dewey and Marsh felt more certain about PL's future and relative permanence. Finally, in the fall of 1931 they decided the PL should incorporate.

A second reason for incorporating was that it would give them proprietary ownership of the term "people's lobby" and could ostensibly prevent others from using it, even with legitimate threats of legal action if necessary. In a kind of de facto way, they would be trademarking the term. As the formal and legal name of a corporation, they would own the term, an important phrase that went to the heart of what they were trying to create, on an exclusive basis. This was no minor detail. As late as 1948, Marsh would still be calling out the improper use of the term by another organization, in this case a conservative group in Los Angeles calling itself the People's Lobby of California.[34]

They decided to incorporate in Delaware. That was the preferred state for incorporation of all the major businesses in the United States, a kind of incorporation national capital. By incorporating in Delaware, Dewey and Marsh were opting for the most widely recognized venue for it. Placing PL in the mainstream of convention for this action, they earned a kind of blue ribbon status that other major national corporations had. This was helpful, given that they wanted to be the voice of the American people who were not represented by special interest groups. Hence, they would establish a nationally recognized corporate status for a (hoped for) national organization.

The decision to incorporate in Delaware was a choice, not a requirement. By the 1920s, nonprofits could routinely incorporate in any state, and they did not need to obtain a charter issued by a legislative body, as had been the case in early American history. In particular, PL could have incorporated in the District of Columbia without needing a congressionally issued charter. While Congress held on tightly to some prerogatives in controlling the governance of the District, it let go of the power to control incorporations. In 1901, Congress passed a law permitting nonprofits to incorporate in the District in the same way they could in other states (Lee 2007, 132). Nonetheless, one can discern in Dewey and Marsh's action a logic of wanting to incorporate like the major national corporations against which the PL would be fighting. While not equal in economic terms, at least they would be equal in legal standing.

Incorporating in Delaware may have been common, but it was not simple. On October 13, 1931, Marsh had to arrange for the filling out of eleven legal documents to be filed with the Delaware secretary of state. The Certificate of Incorporation stated that the new entity "shall have no capital stock and is not organized for profit."[35] The corporation's statement of the purpose provided a concise summary of which interests Dewey and Marsh believed were not represented in Washington's world of lobbyists. Some of the new corporation's goals were[36]

- to join in the discussion, and devising, of ways and means for the correction of conditions known to be causing a general unrest and dissatisfaction among the masses of the people;
- to look to sane, proper and considerate solution of vital public questions;
- to improve conditions of labor; and
- to investigate, better, and assist in bettering social conditions and to secure better living conditions for the people generally.

The initial bylaws specified that the organization would have an annual meeting for the election of officers. Any member of the organization (i.e., dues payer) was eligible to attend the annual meeting and cast a vote. While $1 was the minimal level of annual dues for membership, those members who contributed more for a higher category of membership (such as $10 for sustaining and $25 for active) still could cast only one vote per person. Annual meetings would take place in January. In an unusual determination, the quorum necessary for an annual meeting to conduct business was seven members. This hinted that Dewey and Marsh were not expecting mass meetings and, in any event, did not want a modest turnout to prevent the PL from legally engaging in formal business at the meeting.[37]

By prearrangement, the incorporators promptly elected Dewey and two others as the initial Board of Directors of The People's Lobby, Inc.[38] As it routinely did, the *New York Times* reported the next day that one of the new Delaware corporations was The People's Lobby, Inc., registered in Wilmington, and that it had "No capital," unlike most of the other new registrations that day.[39]

While Delaware may have had the reputation of the most corporate-friendly legal code, its regulations for maintaining corporate status were strict and exacting. As a result of choosing to incorporate in Delaware, the PL was required to submit annual reports, including a comprehensive audited financial statement, to renew its registration, and to pay an annual registration fee. While these were relatively cumbersome for such a small organization, Dewey and Marsh felt the legitimacy it imparted was worth it. For all of the years of its existence, Marsh was punctilious about preparing and submitting the annual paperwork and payment necessary to maintain the PL's legal standing and its continued validity as a Delaware-based corporation.

Dewey and Marsh's Partnership

While Dewey and Marsh had known (or known of) each other for years, the founding of the People's Lobby in 1928 was the first time they had ever worked closely and continuously together. The initial years of this relationship established a pattern for the entirety of Dewey's PL presidency through 1936. Some of the historical literature has implied that Dewey did little more than permit the Lobby to use his name and that he was a passive and inactive president, little more than a front or puppet for Marsh. For example, McGlashan stated, "Dewey was the titular head of the People's Lobby, lending his national reputation and voice to the organization" (1976, 11). According to Westbrook, from the founding of the PL in 1928 to 1931, "Dewey's role consisted principally of issuing press releases to the *New York Times* (many of them coauthored by Marsh)" (1991, 445–446).

These insinuations are wholly inaccurate. Dewey was an engaged and active president. No figurehead was he. Preceding sections have already documented some examples of his personal participation in the work of the Lobby: giving a speech at the PL's first public event in May 1928 in Washington that was critical of the administration's Latin American policy, initiating correspondence to recruit members for the PL's initial Advisory Committee and to request contributions, traveling to Philadelphia to speak at a meeting of PL members, and attracting Ethel Clyde to underwrite the organization's deficit. Additional documentary and archival evidence of those early years shows how much time and effort Dewey gave to get the People's Lobby off to the right start and to achieve sustainability for it. For example, in the spring of 1931, he gave a talk on the NBC national radio network about the economy.[40] A few weeks later, he traveled to Harvard to address a joint meeting of its liberal and socialist clubs, also on the economy.[41] Given how many organizations in which Dewey was active, in both cases he made it clear that he was speaking in his capacity as PL president. He was also protective of the standing and reputation of the People's Lobby. In 1931, the National Association for the Advancement of Colored People (NAACP) was seeking organizations to sign a petition to present to President Hoover criticizing his policy toward the largely African-American nation of Haiti. Dewey replied that he would sign it (on behalf of the PL) only if six other organizations would, too. He would not lend his name or the PL brand willy-nilly and would pick and choose carefully what the Lobby should get involved in and what it should not. In this case, he wanted to be sure that the petition demonstrated a broad base of support, rather than just a handful of organizations supporting that cause. This would help create an ongoing coalition of groups committed to working on the issue in the future.[42] There was strength in numbers, although on some other issues, Dewey did not mind the PL standing alone against the world.

Dewey and Marsh worked as partners, frequently in consultation with each other, sometimes disagreeing, always with a clear view of what the role of the volunteer president should be in comparison to that of a nonprofit's salaried and full-time executive director. Dewey and Marsh did most of their work by mail. They corresponded frequently, with Marsh carefully touching base with Dewey, especially about public statements. For example, the first surviving letter is from January 1929, about nine months after the PL was founded. Dewey enclosed a draft of a statement he had prepared for PL to issue but then added, "any changes in wording you think advisable, you can make of course."[43] This showed not only Dewey's role in preparing the draft, but also his trust in Marsh's judgment early on in their partnership. He did not require that Marsh get Dewey's approval for any changes. The pattern that emerged was that Marsh usually prepared a first draft of a position statement for Dewey to review and then Dewey would give his feedback to Marsh, at which point the draft was finalized. Another time, Marsh shared with Dewey the final version of a newsletter. Dewey caught a few specifics attributed to him that had to be corrected before going to print and in a few others asked Marsh to double check them for accuracy. He regretted holding up the newsletter, but it was better than "to let them go & get jumped on."[44] Printing incorrect information could undermine the Lobby's credibility with the press and decision makers.

Marsh once had drafted a letter to be sent to the assistant secretary of commerce. Dewey had made numerous and detailed edits to the draft, sometimes changing specific wording, sometimes raising questions that were unaddressed ("—but why?") and flagging what he felt "[wasn't] very clearly expressed." Finally, indicating Marsh's slash-and-burn style versus Dewey's etiquette and politeness, Dewey told Marsh to "be sure and make a courteous acknowledgement" to an earlier response by the assistant secretary "at both [the] opening and closing" of the final version of the letter.[45]

Dewey did not always play the role of toning down Marsh's hot rhetoric. The opposite also happened occasionally. Marsh submitted a draft of a letter from Dewey to President Hoover criticizing Hoover's economic policies. Dewey was more than glad to sign it, but first he made "considerable" changes to the draft. He lightedheartedly told Marsh that "for once perhaps I've made your statements stronger instead of toning them down."[46] The eventual release to the *Times* quoted Dewey as charging Hoover with "tragic failure" to understand the suffering occurring in the country.[47]

Many times Dewey approved a draft as is. For a letter Marsh drafted, Dewey told him he signed it "without change" and then sent it out (rather than returning it to Marsh to send out).[48] Another time, Dewey signed a letter prepared by Marsh and returned it to Marsh for dissemination. He also said that a draft for a letter from PL to the Interstate Commerce Commission (ICC) about railroad rates "is fine" as is.[49] Other times he said a draft "seems to me all right"[50] or that a draft "farm article is ok" for the next newsletter.[51]

This was not always the case. Sometimes Dewey flatly turned Marsh down. Marsh had an idea for the PL to write a public letter to John D. Rockefeller Sr. on the need to tax unearned income because of the needs of people who were starving. Dewey agreed that it was "undoubtedly a good publicity stunt" but declined to sign. He had a practice of only signing public letters (i.e., that would be released to the press) that were addressed to public officials. As Rockefeller was a private citizen, Dewey felt compelled to be consistent with his past practice because "there is too much personal exploitation in it." However, he explicitly permitted Marsh to sign the letter and send it "in behalf of the Lobby," if Marsh felt strongly about following through with his idea.[52]

While most of this working relationship occurred by mail, Marsh occasionally went to New York and was able to confer with Dewey in person.[53] When both were scheduled to speak at a Labor Party conference in London in the summer of 1929 against colonialism, they would have been able to spend leisurely amounts of time together while en route.[54] Also, whenever Dewey spoke to or presided at a Lobby event, he and Marsh had opportunities to discuss organizational business in person. For example, Dewey spoke at a PL meeting in Washington in May 1928[55] and presided at PL public meetings in New York in June (one of the issues was the tariff) and October 1930.[56]

In general, Dewey thought well of Marsh—his capacity for work, his energy, and his modest economic needs. Their early correspondence during those initial years of establishing the PL was replete with Dewey's compliments. In early 1929, Dewey generously wrote Marsh that "it makes me feel rather small when I think of what you've done & are doing. It's wonderful for me to be associated with some one who is doing something badly needed neither from selfish interest nor from 'altruism' & and uplift zeal, but simply because he sees the need & likes to do something about it."[57] Two years later, he continued feeling that way. After a particularly busy period, Dewey lamented that Marsh's behind-the-scenes work meant "you won't get the credit you deserve."[58] In another letter, he urged Marsh to take a break, because "you need a real vacation." Reversing the normal hierarchical relationship between a lay board president and an executive director, he told Marsh, "it has been a pleasure to be of use to you."[59] Coming from a person of such eminence as Dewey, this was a high compliment indeed. Further confirming the sincerity of these comments, Dewey shared his good opinion of Marsh with others. For example, less than a year after founding the Lobby, Dewey wrote to an acquaintance that Marsh was "the wheel horse" of the organization and that he had a "reputation for integrity and discretion, as well as for energy."[60]

In summary, in the first three years of the existence of the People's Lobby (1928–1931), Dewey and Marsh had accomplished much organizationally. With little to build on from the PRL and AML, they essentially started from scratch. They then established a new organization, set its philosophy and orientation, created an interim board of directors they called an Advisory Committee, began recruiting annual dues-paying members, obtained the underwriting of a wealthy patroness, convened several public meetings, initiated a newsletter with wide circulation, and obtained significant press coverage for such a new and young organization. Finally, they incorporated the PL in Delaware as a way to make its existence more formal, to give it a recognized legal template, and to try to protect their rights over the term "people's lobby."

All in all, it was a pretty good organizational start. As a capstone to all this unglamorous and behind-the-scenes work, Dewey and Marsh unveiled a motto to describe succinctly the Lobby's mission and vision: "To Fight for the People, We Get and Give the Facts."[61] (In the mid-1930s, they slightly revised it to "We Get the Facts and Give Them."[62]) This nicely captured their Progressive antecedents, the belief in facts and publicity as the levers of influence in mass democracy, and the desire to represent the public interest in the face of the power of the lobbies for special interest groups. (However, it masked their Progressive, even leftist, ideology.) Now for the hard part: influencing the national public policy agenda.

Part II

Dewey as President of the People's Lobby

Chapter 3

Policy Advocacy during the Coolidge and Hoover Presidencies, 1928–1932

The People's Lobby was cofounded by Dewey and Marsh in April 1928. From then until the stock market crash in late October 1929, the Lobby was trying to promote a policy agenda amid the cresting of the roaring twenties, a period of economic boom and prosperity. So the initial year and a half of the Lobby's work occurred when leftist policy proposals to help the underprivileged and left-behinds were quite in the wilderness and out of harmony with the national mood. Corporations were king, government deferred to the private sector, and the marketplace was the seemingly perfect mechanism for decisions about the political economy. With the exception of the PL, lobbies were the domain of the right—of the Interests—who used money and influence to control what Washington did and did not do. In that respect, this period is an interesting way to begin tracking the views of the non-Communist left and the suggestions it offered *not* in reaction to economic crisis and failure, but rather to economic success and enrichment.

Advocating for the Disadvantaged during Prosperity, April 1928–October 1929

The good times were rolling. Nobody seemed to care about those left behind. President Coolidge had announced that he would not run for another term, and his Secretary of Commerce Herbert Hoover was in hot pursuit of the Republican nomination for president. Ignoring the odds, Dewey and Marsh jumped into the arena, full of ideas of what should and should not be done, irrespective of being politically pragmatic or realistic. Theirs were alternatives to the laissez-faire and "what, me worry?" atmosphere of the times. That they were shouting into the wind mattered to them not at all.

In his first congressional testimony after the PL was founded (mentioned briefly in Chap. 2), Marsh aggressively criticized the Coolidge administration's proposal to cut taxes in a way that disproportionately benefited the rich. He said Treasury Secretary Mellon's plan would "reduce taxes on those best able to pay, the wealthy of this country," and consequently farmers and the unemployed would "pay more taxes in proportion to their ability." Ranging far from the bill at hand, he also criticized the long-standing high tariff policy of the Republican Party because "it protects the few against the many." When the chairman tried to pull him back to the specifics of the bill, he said he wanted to discuss "the organic principle" embedded in such legislation, especially anything dealing with the economy. He also talked about war debts, farm bankruptcies, estate taxes, and loose credit (US Senate 1928, 220–224). In this public debut for the People's Lobby, Marsh wanted to set the baseline of what it advocated for and its tone of aggressive political rhetoric.

When the Federal Reserve increased the rediscount rate to discourage highly leveraged Wall Street stock speculators, the PL criticized the action as not only ineffective for the stated goal, but also having unintended consequences for smaller investors as well as of making loans for farmers more expensive, thus driving some farmers into bankruptcy.[1] The Republican presidential platform presented another occasion to make similar points about economic policy. The PL criticized the Republican plank in Dewey's name (but likely Marsh's rhetoric), saying it was predictable that "the party devoted to big profits for large property [owners] should give the farmers policemen's black-jacks and political bunk."[2]

Yet in this initial debut as a public voice leading up to the 1928 presidential election, Dewey and Marsh mostly concentrated on foreign affairs. Both spoke fiercely against the-then presence of Marines in Nicaragua and, more generally, against US interventionism in Latin America. They viewed it as an extension of American corporate interests and not authentically in the interests of the nation as a whole. In this regard, they were indeed trying to articulate a policy perspective of the public interest rather than the organized lobbies of the moneyed interests. The PL challenged all presidential candidates to accept its proposal for peaceful and reciprocal relations between the United States and all Latin American countries and that international mediation and negotiations should replace unilateral military intervention.[3] A magazine ridiculed these ideas as naive and unrealistic, saying they came from "reforming wiseacres." It sarcastically referred to "the distinguished organization known to contemporary fame as the People's Lobby" and wondered "how this poor old earth of ours contrived to get along for so many thousand years before the advent of some of our contemporary sages."[4]

Making it more personal and therefore tangible to the citizenry, the PL garnered front-page coverage by provocatively asking President Coolidge, "[W]ould your wife and you want your son John to risk his life in marine rule in Nicaragua? If not, what right have you to send the marines there?"[5] Before and after the November election, Dewey and Marsh peppered other public officials about US policies in South America,[6] at one point claiming that American corporations were looting Bolivia.[7] Their sympathy toward Latin America prompted favorable front-page coverage in *La Prensa*, a Spanish-language newspaper based in New York.[8]

These kinds of potshots were usually successful in obtaining public attention (as indicated by media coverage) and therefore consistent with one of PL's goals of getting information to the citizenry and trying to influence public opinion. But they ran the risk of lacking coherence and rootedness in a more systematic policy agenda. Therefore, beginning what became an annual tradition, around the turn of the year, the PL released a program for 1929. This was a comprehensive summary of its policy goals and views on current affairs in the context of an integrated whole, reflecting consistent principles. For domestic policy, the PL had four goals:

1. Increasing taxes on the rich and decreasing taxes on the working and farming classes;
2. Opposing tariffs that had the effect of protecting inefficient or profiteering industries or of pushing down domestic farm prices;
3. Federal relief for poor children; and
4. Establishing publicly owned power systems.

For foreign policy, PL had two goals:

1. Getting US military out of Nicaragua; and
2. Ending any US military or political intervention in other countries, especially when motivated to protect the commercial interests of US corporations, banks that had loaned to foreign countries, and beneficiaries of exclusive concessions.[9]

Hoover replaced Coolidge in the White House in March 1929.[10] While the stock market was wobbly in midyear, the crash and following depression did not occur until late October. So the first half-year of Hoover's presidency overlapped with the ongoing prosperity. During that period, economics continued to be a major issue on the policy agenda of the federal government and, in reflection, for the People's Lobby. In particular, the conflict over tariff legislation gave Dewey and Marsh the perfect opportunity to demonstrate that the PL was the only lobby in the capital for the public-at-large. Tariffs were part of the orthodoxy of the Republican ideology. High tariffs could be depicted as protecting American jobs, but often were little more than rewards to very narrow, but highly motivated, industrial lobbies. The tariff issue epitomized the asymmetry of political power in Congress. While the public-at-large wanted lower prices of goods as a general principle, tariff legislation was not fought out in the halls of Congress on general principles. Rather, the decision making was motivated by the salience of particular industries and producers clamoring for protection and advantage. For members of Congress, there were significant upsides to rewarding these lobbies and virtually no downside backlash from the voters-at-large. Even with "widespread public sentiment for change, those narrow interests had far more effect than the public on the legislative decisions that constituted 'the tariff' " (Arnold 2009, 112). Here was a true David and Goliath battle. Dewey and Marsh had little illusion about a happy ending in terms of a legislative victory. They felt that merely being vocal advocates for consumer interests was a step forward in shaking up the incestuous and mutually benefiting relationship between pols and the lobbies of the Interests. The two of them knew the difficulties of organizing the unorganizable, but speaking out for them was better than nothing and—who knows—maybe in the long run would lead to some substantive victories.

Marsh testified against yet another congressional proposal to increase tariffs, saying the PL "represents the consumers" in contrast to the "millionaires' bread line" waiting to testify for tariffs. He vividly depicted Republicans as "a party whose doctrine is the survival of the fattest" and argued that the impact of a raised tariff was to "give oxygen to a dying patient and he will seem to be healthy, until the oxygen wears off . . . and they come back worse than they started" (US Senate 1929, 735, 738). Separately, a PL statement issued in Dewey's name raised questions about the lack of balance in congressional hearings on tariff proposals. Echoing the progressives' faith in experts, Dewey suggested that the subject-matter experts of the US Tariff Commission be invited to question those testifying at congressional hearings in favor of tariff increases. Surely, he suggested, this would help expose weak arguments, false data, and overly optimistic predictions. Congress needed facts, he said. Opposition to the PL's suggestion "would be prima facie evidence of the spuriousness" of a self-serving tariff request.[11] He criticized Hoover for supporting tariff legislation and for serving corporate interests with the effect of economic "world domination."[12]

The PL continued pressing for aggressive regulation and oversight of meatpackers, complaining that the administration was being too friendly to the industry's efforts to weaken the consumer protections then in place. Dewey complained that President Hoover's stated hope that the growing wealth of the country could reduce remaining poverty "if the consumers are to be ruthlessly exploited by highly protected manufacturers and equally ruthlessly plucked by a meat-packers' food monopoly."[13]

But it was the apparent shakiness of the stock market that year that prompted one of Marsh's most pointed criticisms of the banking industry and reflected the worldview he and Dewey imbued in the People's Lobby. Marsh said he could not understand why Washington policy makers were giving such deference to the advice of bankers, who were not really promoting the best interests of the national and international economy, but rather their own financial self-interest. He raised fears of a secret plan by major banks for "an international bank to be the real fiscal super-government of the world."[14] Here was a classic Midwestern and farm-based populist fear of Wall Street and its influence. Instead, Marsh hoped that "the stentorian mouths of bankers will be permanently closed on such matters, and they will be taught that this country is run for the benefit of the people and not of the few directors and other stockholders of banks." He also criticized the banks' playing favorites with their easy credit and not sharing the loose money policy with less privileged segments of the population, such as small investors. He presciently raised alarms that banks were relying on reserves that were only one-eighth of the sum they were lending, risking their solvency and depositors' money in case of changed economic conditions.[15]

As the stock market weakened in the summer and fall of 1929 (September 3 was the end of the bull market), the sensitive antennae of politicians quickly picked up on the potential of a public clamor for the blame game. (This was repeated after the 2008 crash.) Suddenly the question of lobbies was on the political agenda. The PL used it as a news peg for its more general fight against special interest lobbies. It also called for registration of all lobbyists trying to influence Congress as a first step to spotlighting influence peddlers in politics.[16] After the crash, the PL specifically suggested an investigation of "the superlobby—the banking and credit octopus."[17] Dewey also proposed that all members of Congress reveal their stockholdings so as to clarify any hidden conflicts of interest or instances of taking advantage of inside information. Such "publicity" (nowadays one would say transparency) of the equities they owned would inevitably lead to lawmakers holding only plain vanilla portfolios, hence helping to improve the disinterestedness of policy makers.[18] (Dewey was on to something. A 2004 study found that senators' investments beat market averages by 5 to 10 percent *a year* [Ziobrowski et al. 2004]. Finally, in 2012, Congress passed the Stop Trading on Congressional Knowledge [STOCK] Act to tighten regulation of use of insider information by members of Congress.) Several Senate committees began inquiries into the influence and power of lobbies, and those initiatives were welcomed by Dewey and Marsh.

A prominent Manhattan minister said in his Sunday sermon that all lobbies in Washington should be investigated, including so-called peace organizations. He specifically mentioned the People's Lobby as needing to be examined.[19] Dewey and Marsh were more than glad to be caught in the political net being cast against lobbies, knowing it would expose the misdeeds of organized economic interests and highlight the need for a people's lobby. In a letter to a Senate committee chair, "Dewey asked that his organization be investigated."[20]

With the heightened interest in the influence of lobbyists, two newspaper reports tried to convey what the PL was in contradistinction to the rest of the lobbyists. Shortly after the crash, an article in the *Times*' Sunday magazine summarized the concerns about, and investigations of, lobbying in Washington. Noting the existence of the PL, it viewed the creation of this new organization as "a rather desperate confession by some of our best thinkers that without a lobby the people cannot express themselves in government."[21] A syndicated columnist tried to describe the world of lobbying in Washington, but noted that the PL did not fit in his generalizations. It was, he wrote, a lobby for "the public interest but is none the less a lobby and is maintained by private funds."[22]

Dewey and Marsh also emphasized the PL's international perspective, especially against American imperialism. They felt it was true that the flag followed trade and the United States was continuing to intervene in Latin America to protect corporate interests. The PL issued a four-page "Questions and Answers on Imperialism" detailing its critique of American foreign policy.[23] While one of Dewey's pet projects was outlawing war, the PL broke with most peace groups by criticizing the Kellogg Pact against war as well as a counterpart plan to build more cruisers for the US Navy.[24] Once the treaty was approved, the PL then argued that its implementation should compel the repeal of the law permitting the US military to be assigned to duties in Latin America, referring to the marines stationed seemingly permanently and without any clear military mission in Nicaragua.[25]

The flurry of initial news coverage of the Lobby in 1928–29 reflected Dewey's views about the power of publicity as it had emerged during the Progressive era (Chap. 1)—the more, the better. For example, in a mailing to current and future members, the PL explained its modus operandi: "America is governed by headlines—The People's Lobby gets its share."[26] The frequency of public statements also led to the press developing a shorthand way of explaining who the PL was. Many stories used a relatively fixed phrase along the lines of "The People's Lobby, of which Professor John Dewey is President, released a statement today . . ." This indicated Dewey's prominence and helped—as he intended—give the new organization instant standing and authority when issuing press releases.

However, the bad came with the good. For example, an official of the relatively conservative American Federation of Labor criticized Dewey (without mentioning the PL) as "a propagandist, not for special interests, but for Communist interests."[27] Dewey handled it with equanimity; by then, he was used to such attacks, but that was just the beginning of the right's attacks increasingly naming the PL.

In the meantime, Marsh was trying to take advantage of the PL's sudden high profile in the news as a way to recruit new members. He prepared a four-page pamphlet with blurbs of "Leading *Progressives* Tell Why the Peoples' Lobby."[28] Here was the key signal of PL's intended constituency. It was neither a liberals' organization nor a socialists' one. Rather, this would be the organizational home for the non-Communist left, which still believed in the values generated during the Progressive era, and supporters of Senator La Follette's third-party progressive candidacy for president.[29] Marsh mailed the flier as widely as possible. His goal was to recruit 10,000 members,[30] but he never came close. PL's effort to appeal to the remnants of the progressive movement was a recurring theme. For example, later that year, in a fierce criticism of Congress for passing an income tax cut after the market crash, Marsh described the Democrats' support for the bill as "knavery [that] removes the last pretenses of that party to progressivism, however much diluted." As for the other side of the aisle, he criticized "the pseudo-Progressives in the Republican party" for supporting a bill giving disproportionate benefits to the wealthy, often their contributors.[31]

Lobbying After the Crash, November 1929–December 1930

The stock market crash began on Black Thursday, October 24, 1929, with equities losing about half their value by mid-November. In a flash, everything changed, economically and politically. Now optimism was replaced by pessimism, prosperity with depression, loose credit with tight credit, expansion with bankruptcies, and success with failure. The headwinds against PL's agenda over the preceding year and a half suddenly were filling its sails. Almost instantly, PL was on the side of the angels in the dramaturgy of the given narrative of American history. Trying to help the have-nots now meant helping the bulk of the country. This was an opening for PL to push for a more fair and balanced political economy.

For Dewey and Marsh, the crash was a mere confirmation of the concerns they had already raised beforehand about imbalance and unfairness in the economy. They did not change their policy prescriptions significantly. The big change was now having a more attentive audience. Just a week after Black Thursday, while the crash was still ongoing, PL was ready to provide its explanation for the events and the needed remedies. It issued a statement hoping that the citizenry now understood "who rules the country." There was now a need "to prevent excessive capitalization, speculative bankers' control and excess profits."[32]

Much of the focus of the PL's work from the crash to the November 1930 elections was on domestic policy, submitting suggestions for national action that, for conservative Republicans, were automatically off the table. The PL persisted in bringing them back to decision makers' and the public's attention. It wanted to show that there were alternatives to what the federal government was doing (or not doing) and that the cozy conventional wisdom of Washington, including that of liberal Democrats, was far too narrow a prism for action. These post-1924 progressives sought to prick the balloon of what was politically pragmatic or acceptable. Perhaps politicians were obsessed about what was doable or popular, but Dewey and Marsh were not. The People's Lobby was a vehicle to try to shake the complacency not only of laissez-faire Republicans (such as Treasury Secretary Andrew Mellon), but also of Democrats who were comfortable merely criticizing the president's administration without providing much substance as an alternative. (By a nice coincidence, Dewey turned seventy in late 1929 and retired from Columbia in 1930, giving him more time to dedicate to his many causes, including the Lobby.)

If there were ever a time that the policy agenda of the left might resonate with citizens who were suffering and demanding action, this was it. On the surface, PL's work was limited to public policy and lobbying for its views, but this was also a broader opportunity to buttress the left's political and electoral efforts throughout the country. The PL was gradually constructing the "what" of a progressive political platform for the Great

Depression. As the crisis of the crash and its permanence sank in, the PL sought several policy responses. It pushed for new or different domestic and economic policies in the areas of unemployment and relief, taxation, tariffs, farming, children, meatpacking, public power, and even Prohibition.

Economic Policy

Marsh stated the central premise for all of the PL's policy recommendations: "We have ended forever the fetish that government is not responsible for the economic condition of the country."[33] On another occasion, he said that this new realization was "the most significant event of the century."[34] At the time, this was a controversial position, but within decades it became part of America's bipartisan conventional wisdom, namely that the federal government had a central role in macroeconomic policy (Wapshott 2011).

But Dewey and Marsh went much further than merely a generic call to action; they identified the core ideology driving the PL's economic theory. Dewey viewed the income inequalities in the country as "a moral iniquity" as well as an economic problem. One of the causes of the depression, he felt, was the disproportionally small buying power of the masses, which led to destabilization of industrial production and consumption. In a talk to a PL conference, he said that the federal government needed "to reduce the inequality in the distribution of incomes. The first and foremost urgent step in this process consists in the levying of higher taxes on swollen fortunes" to pay for programs to ameliorate unemployment and poverty.[35]

Marsh elaborated. The federal government is failing "because it has no control over industry or the distribution of wealth. Lacking this control it cannot remedy the inefficiencies of free competition and distorted distribution. Contrary to popular assertion, over-production is not at the basis of the present depression, it is under-consumption. . . . The reason for under-consumption is the distribution of the national income. No matter how the rich live, they cannot possibly consume everything."[36] This viewpoint would be a recurring theme or unstated premise of the PL's proposals in reaction to the market crash and onset of the Great Depression. It was too radical even for most Democrats.

Nonetheless, Dewey and Marsh found multiple ways of articulating their agenda without automatically scaring away decision makers or citizens with PL's underlying ideology. For example, they focused on identifying economic data that the political establishment was less interested in highlighting and on articulating policy responses without necessarily stating the underlying ideology. Marsh released a dry and statistics-laden analysis of economic data from the IRS for the preceding year showing that only 20 percent of Americans had incomes greater than $2,000 a year. In particular, unearned income was disproportionately distributed, with the bulk going to people with incomes of greater than $100,000 a year. Yet the effective tax rate on these higher-income people was lower than the rates of low-income taxpayers.[37] The lack of a truly progressive tax, he hoped, would generate support for more fairness in its structure, even by those policy makers who would not agree with the underlying ideology that Dewey and Marsh held.

To deal with mass unemployment, the PL presented several ideas, virtually all anathema to Hoover and the GOP, most beyond the comfort zone of opposition Democrats. It suggested several times that the federal government engage in deficit spending of at least $250 million for unemployment insurance to match an equal amount from state and local governments.[38] Hoover was not interested and the PL excoriated him for it. Hoover's favorite term to criticize such ideas was "panacea," that is, that these were not permanent solutions to a problem. At the same time it was slamming Hoover, the PL was equally critical of an unemployment bill by a liberal senator, Robert Wagner (D-NY), which the PL felt was tepid, misdirected, and insufficiently targeted to the victims of the depredations of corporations.[39] In late 1930, the PL cobbled together a coalition of twenty-six labor and civic groups to endorse and lobby for a three-part economic program consisting of $500 million for relief, $100 million for unemployment insurance, and increased federal spending on public works.[40]

The idea that the federal government had a role in relief for individuals who were unemployed, as opposed to macroeconomic stimulative policies, was a nearly alien precept to Washington. At that time, almost all welfare agencies were small, local nonprofits supported by the charitable contributions and volunteerism of more affluent families. Social work, as a profession, had little to do with *government*. The PL and other like organizations were looking to the federal government for an unprecedented principle of involvement in relief and welfare programs that would touch individuals in need. This was a radical concept that naturally appealed to people like Dewey and Marsh, but, symmetrically, was anathema to Republicans and some Democrats. Shrewdly, Dewey and Marsh decided to promote the issue by focusing on the least responsible and most deserving of that population, namely the children of the unemployed. (This was repeated in the 2010s, when proponents of immigration reform focused on the proposed DREAM Act, which would educate minor children of illegal residents who were blameless for their status. Similarly, Democrats' defense of antipoverty programs from conservative attacks focused on the benefits to children of such programs as food stamps and Head Start.[41])

These children, Dewey and Marsh said, were "the nation's first responsibility." Children, through no fault of their own, did not have adequate food or shelter if their families were suddenly unemployed or living in chronic poverty or on small farms. The PL urged adoption of a program of direct federal relief to those children. They proposed the establishment of a Federal Child Relief Board, building on the recent precedent of the new Federal Farm Board. They said the program would be family based, not oriented to taking children from their homes to institutions. Given that aid could not really be given directly to children, this proposal embodied the principle of federal responsibility for relief costs, except that it was through the back door of helping children. The PL made a big push for federal child relief. It prepared and widely distributed a fact sheet justifying the legislation.[42] Dewey sent a message to a conference emphasizing that even robust reemployment programs would not be able to hire all those seeking jobs, and therefore there would still be economic difficulties for those "in the marginal class to earn enough to maintain a good standard of living for their families."[43] About a month later, Dewey tried to keep the focus on children and away from political ideologies about macroeconomics. He linked his early philosophizing about the role of public education with the current crisis. "Unless [children] have a chance for proper nutrition and an education, they become either public charges or drags on the community at a later time, because of inefficiency, bad health and lack of preparation for the duties of citizenship," he said.[44]

Other Domestic Issues

Besides dealing directly with unemployment and relief, the PL had suggestions for changes in other aspects of economic policy that were intertwined with unemployment, especially in the areas of taxation, tariffs, and agriculture. For practically opposite reasons, conservatives and liberals supported the principle of cutting income taxes to stimulate the economy. Marsh was more than willing to crash the party. At a congressional hearing in late 1929 on a tax-cutting bill, he was the only one to speak in opposition. He said that the benefits of income tax cuts would largely go to the wealthy. In the meantime, no reductions were proposed in consumption taxes (such as excise and, indirectly, tariffs), which by their nature were regressive. He said that "indirect taxation is the subtle method by which the Government picks the pockets of the poor" (US House 1929, 21). Furthermore, if Congress really wanted to ameliorate the economic situation, increases in expenditures would be more direct and targeted than an equal sum of tax cuts. He also called for increases in surtaxes because they amplified the progressive taxation principle of income taxes based on the ability to pay. He followed up his testimony with an irresistible press release that shifted from a dry discussion of abstract tax principles to attacking some of the wealthiest. He said that people with "swollen incomes," like publisher William Randolph Hearst and Treasury Secretary Andrew Mellon, would benefit greatly from the bill, while the poor would see no distinct benefit.[45]

Before the crash, the PL had consistently opposed tariffs. Now it retained that position, but with new arguments. For public consumption, the PL explained in plain terms why this was a bad idea: "It will lead to exporting jobs instead of goods. It will increase unemployment through heavy duties on raw materials."[46] Marsh also used more heated rhetoric against the promoters of yet another tariff-raising bill. He was bipartisan in his criticism, saying the tariff bill was the work of "a coalition of Republican and Democratic flunkeys of the plunderbund which owns both parties."[47] But in addition to his skills with mass media–friendly language of plain explanation and hot rhetoric, Marsh was equally a policy wonk comfortable with a wholly different style of communication. He released for an expert audience an analysis of the Smoot-Hawley bill examining in detail how it proposed to change tariffs on seventeen specific products ranging from lemons to smoking pipes to manganese ore to phonograph needles. Methodically using statistics, he rebutted the claims of the sponsors of the bill. Here was unjustified protectionism, he argued. The seeming arbitrary scope of the bill selectively benefited special pleaders who had lobbyists in Washington and would do little to lift the economy, given that the problem was unemployment.[48]

Along with tariffs, before the crash the PL had also sought to support farmers. The crash had greatly amplified their inability to break even because of declining demand and prices. The Lobby suggested several innovations in traditional federal agricultural policy. For example, the collapse of wheat prices in the first year of the Great Depression was a major problem that federal politicians tried to deal with. The PL suggested the focus be on increasing exports to prop up demand and doing so through federal financial assistance to foreign governments needing wheat but unable to pay for it in hard currency.[49] When a drought compounded the farm situation, the PL suggested that the federal government sponsor crop insurance. It was a novel, even odd, proposal, but eventually a common policy tool.[50] Both a farming and a consumer issue, the PL also continued its pre-crash concerns about weakening the regulation of meatpackers. It wrote President Hoover asking that he direct the attorney general not to agree to an industry request to loosen oversight as a result of a court suit and consent decree.[51] A month later it issued a vehement statement wondering why the president would acquiesce to the meatpackers desire to "throw off government control in order to start a profiteering combine?"[52]

One of the PL's policy interests was public power. It believed in the public ownership of utilities and natural monopolies generally, and the generation of electricity specifically. This was a common position for the left. The PL opposed what came to be branded as investor-owned utilities. One of the long-running post-WWI political battles was over what the federal government should do with its Muscle Shoals (AL) facility, built by the government to help in its need for power to manufacture nitrates for military explosives. A conservative farm group in Alabama, supporting the sale of the facility to the private sector, attacked the People's Lobby (along with the League of Women Voters) for its opposition to such a plan.[53] On another occasion, the PL submitted a petition to Congress urging it to create an independent utility regulatory commission for the District of Columbia so that it could regulate utilities in the same way that the states did instead of the direct control of Washington's government by Congress.[54]

Marsh was in a long-running battle with the relatively new Federal Power Commission over what he felt was its excessive friendliness to private utilities and disfavor of public ownership. He charged that a power trust of large, private utilities had co-opted the Commission and that the Commission was not fulfilling its duty to the public interest.[55] For example, the Commission's secretary, he said, was the industry's "inside man" there to protect it from vigorous regulation.[56] Specifically, Marsh waded in to a controversy over development of electric-generating dams in the Flathead Indian Reservation in Montana. He charged that Indian interests were not being protected, especially because the two senators from Montana did not want to oppose the largest corporate interests in the state. He was ultimately subpoenaed to testify on what he knew. It was largely circumstantial inferences. But that did not stop him from denouncing the "gutless inactivity" of government officials in face of "the unscrupulous power combine" (US Senate 1930, 3539). This got him into a running spat with one of Montana's senators, and he, typically, refused to back down from his charges or be cowed by a senator's fury.[57]

Foreign Policy

The short version of American history from the Crash to the 1932 election tends to tread lightly on foreign policy. Domestic problems were so dire and so riveting that the attention of the country on foreign affairs seemed to disappear. The People's Lobby worked hard to prevent such geocentrism. It continued a vigorous lobbying effort relating to international matters during this period. (Of course, many international economic issues bled into domestic economics, but the focus here is on noneconomic-related matters.) Dewey and Marsh continued their pre-crash position against US hegemony in the hemisphere. The Lobby criticized American interference in Haiti's domestic affairs, the use of American troops in Nicaragua to weaken the labor union movement there, and loans to support the sugar interests in Cuba; and it called for the repeal of a law permitting the use of US troops in Latin America.[58] The Lobby also spoke out against continued British colonialism in India and against American bans on importation of goods from the SU.[59]

Marsh and Dewey were quite acerbic about various disarmament and arms limitations conferences. For example, a treaty for reduction of naval fleets was, in their eyes, merely a self-serving American maneuver for foreign governments to have more funds to repay their WWI loans.[60] Marsh suggested that with the development of germ warfare during WWI, future wars needed only a few airplanes to drop chemical bombs and, all other military equipment was now obsolete.[61] Instead of the half-measures the PL criticized, Dewey and Marsh showed their idealistic pacifism for truly outlawing war, disbanding navies completely, and reordering priorities from military to domestic spending.[62]

Alternatives to Hoover's Policies, 1931–32

As the country settled into the seeming permanence of the Great Depression, the second half of President Hoover's term unfolded on two closely related tracks. The most obvious one was public policy: what to do to help the country? The other track, more of interest to politicians than the public-at-large, was the political sphere. Both parties were jockeying for electoral advantage come November 1932. That era was very comparable to the Great Recession politics in Washington during 2011–12, when, in anticipation of the next presidential election, the party holding the White

House said the economy was getting better and the opposition party said it was not. Each side was eager to act in a way that created a self-fulfilling prophecy.

Contrary to the historical (and Democratic-inspired) caricature of Hoover as an inflexible dogmatist who opposed any economic policies that went against pure laissez-faire economics, Hoover was actively and constantly seeking new initiatives that harmonized with his political philosophy (Jeansonne 2012). His Treasury Secretary, Andrew Mellon (until early 1932), who *was* a true laissez faire believer, was often exasperated with the new ideas Hoover was constantly generating and suggesting (Cannadine 2006, 392–394, 444–445).

Congress, while deeply politicized because of partisan politics, did not want to appear to the country to be inept or unconcerned. So this period continued to be a rich one for policy proposals emanating from differing values and political philosophies. Reflecting the desperation of the times, no idea was automatically DOA. The PL was very active as a generator of suggestions for what the federal government should and should not do. Some activities, of course, likely had a political view toward influencing the upcoming elections, but this perspective should not obscure the substance of what Dewey and Marsh thought the country could do about the economy. In a sense, what the PL brought into the mix was a policy agenda from the old-line progressives, who were now more liberal than mainstream Democrats, but not overt socialists or Communists.

Economic Policy

As a policy-oriented lobby, it is understandable that virtually all of the PL's criticisms of what Washington was doing (or not doing) from the crash in October 1929 to November 1932 election were aimed at President Hoover and the Republican 71st Congress (1929–31).[63] But its underlying motivation was *not* to assist the Democratic Party in the 1932 elections. (A reminder that, separate from his PL presidency, Dewey was also active in promoting third-party politics, giving him ample outlets and opportunity to express his views on the election season as it was unfolding.) For example, the PL did not hesitate to criticize publicly a group of old-line progressive senators who were not, in the PL's view, providing the leadership for legislation to deal with the Depression.[64] On another occasion, it described congressional Democrats' lack of policy initiatives as, "to put it mildly, disingenuous." It called one of the leaders of the House Democrats a "mental and moral nonentity."[65] A month later, the PL denounced congressional Democrats as "double-crossing."[66]

During 1932, the PL also expressed its dissatisfaction with the record of Governor Franklin Roosevelt in New York State and his campaign positions leading up to the election. About a month before the election, it complained that, as governor, FDR had made no effort to lobby for passage of economic stimulative policies in Washington. Furthermore, it asserted that he had a "record of subserviency to Tammany Hall."[67] In late October, it blasted him for refusing to support a state income tax that would impose a higher rate on the rich than the middle class. It also said that FDR as governor and candidate for president was protecting the "predatory wealth" that was concentrated in New York City.[68] These were not the actions of a covert Democratic political organization.

By criticizing FDR and fellow progressive senators, the PL not only demonstrated its political independence, but also was documenting that its policy platform would not be tailored to make Democrats look good. The issue was of substance, and the PL was applying the same yardstick to both parties. It was not engaging in the more typical political relativism of American politics, where one stood depending on where one sat. The consistency of the PL's economic program adds credibility to the argument that its work in 1931 and 1932 was not motivated primarily to provide political and rhetorical cannon fodder to Democrats. If Dewey and Marsh wanted to bash Hoover and the Republicans exclusively, then one might expect their policy proposals and public rhetoric to change during 1931 and 1932 to adapt to changes in the policy environment and to the needs of Democrats. That was not the case. The PL's economic proposals to deal with the Great Depression were consistent over time and showed little change as the presidential election got closer.

For example, in late 1931, Marsh prepared a comprehensive position paper on the PL's "National Employment Program."[69] It was a detailed, four-page explanation of what the Lobby proposed to do, listing about two dozen specific recommendations. These were largely a compilation of the individual suggestions the PL had made in 1929–30 relating to unemployment insurance, relief, and taxation. The Lobby released this integrated position paper in February 1932. Then, six months later, it distributed an updated version.[70] The changes and differences were minor. In most cases, the levels of appropriations it was recommending for relief and unemployment insurance were higher, but little else was different. The only significant substantive difference was the last item. In February, it was about taxing gifts and bequests to nonprofits. In October, it was replaced by taxing government bonds and corporate surpluses. The lack of significant change in the two versions of the policy paper reflects the ideological basis from which PL derived its policy positions. This was the ideology of the old-fashioned progressives who declined to merge back into the Republican Party or shift to an increasingly liberal Democratic Party. Dewey and Marsh were to the left of political liberals. Their views did not change much, nor did they trim their political sails based on political expediency. For them, the prescriptions for getting out of the Depression were not affected by how close or how far the next election was.

One could try to make the case that at least the timing of the October release of the revised version was somewhat suspicious and was aimed at affecting the election. If so, that would indicate deliberate collusion with Democrats. However, such a motivation is unlikely because of the PL's lack of enthusiasm for FDR and published criticisms of him. There is a strong policy-based rationale for an October position paper. The second session of the 72nd Congress was scheduled to begin on December 5 and to go until the day before the presidential inauguration in early March. For the PL to release a detailed action program in advance of Congress reconvening makes sense in terms of trying to influence the policy-making process.

While the economic program of the PL was quite stable in 1931–32, its lobbying methods show a greater variety than earlier ones had. The PL wanted to influence decision makers and public opinion with its remedies for the Depression. New formats and venues for persuasion were ways to reach audiences multiple times or reach new segments of the population. And reporters liked variety and drama. The PL also played well with other like groups and understood the potential benefits of coalition politics or, at least, coalition-based lobbying and persuasion efforts. Another feature of its 1931–32 economic efforts was a distinct increase in fervency and poignancy. Dewey and Marsh were clearly affected by the reality around the country. The suffering of the unemployed, the poor, and the dirt farmers were not abstract concepts to them. People were hurting. They wanted to do whatever they could so that the federal government would respond to the growing urgency of the deteriorating conditions.

One of the major efforts of the PL in 1931 was to get Congress to come back to work. The 3rd session of the 71st Congress (elected in the 1928 presidential election, that is, before the crash) adjourned on March 3, 1931. The new 72nd Congress (elected in November 1930) was not scheduled to be sworn in and have its first session until December 7, 1931. This leisurely (and delayed) pace of congressional sessions reflected a lingering style of the 1800s. Given the crisis of the Great Depression, the PL felt that going from March to December without any congressional action was out of touch with the country's suffering. People could not just *wait*. They needed help *now*. So one of the PL's major initiatives was to press for a special session of Congress. The problem was that Congress met based on a schedule it adopted for its regular sessions. Only a president could call a special session. Therefore, the focus was on persuading President Hoover to call such a special session or, if he was unwilling to do so, making him pay the political price.

The PL generated as much activity as it could with a view to persuading opinion leaders of the need for a special session. These included strategy sessions with other left and labor groups,[71] meetings with congressional leaders (of both parties) and the chairs of the Democratic and Republic national committees,[72] letters to the president,[73] and letters to members of Congress.[74]

It circulated a petition for presentation to the president,[75] garnering 1,200 signatures—an indication that the PL was more than just Dewey, Marsh, and a mimeograph machine.[76] A veteran reporter, used to Marsh's publicity techniques (and therefore discounting some of Marsh's claims), was impressed nonetheless. In a column, Rodney Dutcher described the petition as "an impressive record of sentiment" that reflected an authentic "mass movement."[77] A delegation of leaders descended on Washington for a promised meeting with the president to deliver the petition. On the day it was scheduled, the White House at the last minute notified Marsh that the meeting would be with a presidential assistant, not the president. Then that, too, was canceled. After waiting in the White House lobby, they were left with handing the petition for a special session to the assistant's clerk. Edmund Wilson, then an editor at the *New Republic*, was a member of the delegation and wrote an evocative column describing the experience of the day (1996, 303–309). Later, Marsh even suggested a rent strike.[78] It was all for naught. Hoover consistently opposed a special session, and business lobbies supported that position.[79]

Another front in the battle was the role of local charities and the Red Cross. Hoover proposed that local volunteers and nonprofit groups be the focal point for helping those in need. The PL disagreed, saying that the federal government had the primary obligation to—at least—*fund* such efforts. The Red Cross, trying to be apolitical, found itself appearing to be on the side of the business establishment and the president. At one point, after being attacked by the PL for failing to meet basic humanitarian responsibilities,[80] the head of the Red Cross had (apparently) promised Marsh that his organization would at least investigate any documentation of starvation among miners' families in West Virginia.[81] He quickly backed down when local business groups howled that he was being manipulated by union propaganda. The Red Cross then reaffirmed its policy of not getting involved in "local economic depressions."[82] Getting personal, Dewey excoriated Hoover, given that a president was automatically the honorary president of the Red Cross: "It is typical of the character of the man whose duplicity with respect to the economic policies and situation in the nation has made him condemned of the informed and the suffering."[83]

Trying another tactic, the PL organized a delegation of mothers to come to Washington to press for help, making vivid and personal the suffering that their families were going through. It was a terrific news angle, even making the front page of the *Los Angeles Times*, a conservative newspaper whose editorial stance usually influenced news coverage.[84] Who could say no to a mother except a heartless and cold politician? Six women and five children came to Washington the week after Mother's Day. Hoover declined to meet with them, but one of his White House staffers did, as did an assistant secretary of labor and the assistant director of the Red Cross.[85]

Once the window for a special session had passed, PL shifted tactics. In November 1931, it instigated the creation of a new umbrella group to keep pushing for relief legislation, this time with emphasis on it being approved during a regular session of Congress. Called the Joint Committee on Unemployment, it was a coalition of labor, left, and socially liberal religious groups. Dewey served as chair. Its policy agenda reflected the PL's earlier programs and initiatives, including a large appropriation for relief ("sufficient to meet the needs of the masses"), mandatory unemployment insurance, a larger public works program, creation of jobs by limiting full-time jobs to six hours a day and five days a week (i.e., a thirty-hour workweek), forbidding hiring children younger than sixteen, and a pension program for all over sixty-five.[86] How would the Joint Committee pay for these programs? By increasing taxes on the wealthy (such as an income tax surcharge), higher taxation of estates, taxation of tax-exempt bonds, taxing corporate profits, and closing tax loopholes.[87]

Representatives of the organizations met in Washington in late November to refine their platform and went to Capitol Hill to lobby for it.[88] Dewey gave a talk that was broadcast on the radio. He said the federal government was the appropriate entity to deal with relief and unemployment. Echoing his views from *The Public and Its Problems*, he explained his approach, which, in contrast to laissez-faire economics, did not expect local charities to deal with unemployment and relief:

> Having undermined the spirit of neighborliness by fostering inequality, having adopted policies that make many the victims of exploitation by the few, they now appeal to brotherly love and neighborly kindness to help relieve the suffering which has been created, and to avoid recognition of their own responsibility. . . . What shall be said of the conduct of those who having fattened on privilege would now pass the responsibility for relief to private charity and to the impoverished who have been fortunate enough to retain some sort of a job?[89]

On behalf of the Joint Committee, Marsh testified three times at legislative hearings during the 1st session of the 72nd Congress to urge adoption of its proposals (US Senate 1931, 208–231; US Senate 1932a, 86–102; 1932b, 48–55). On one of those occasions, Marsh got into a public spat with the Republican committee chair. Marsh, in his testimony, had asked that other members of the Joint Committee be permitted to testify at a later hearing. Sitting in the back of the hearing room a few days later, he was startled to hear the chairman announce that it was the last hearing. Testily, he got up and argued with the chair for (apparently) maneuvering to wrap up the hearings on purpose and prematurely to prevent Joint Committee member Norman Thomas and others from testifying (US Senate 1931, 427–438). The chairman gave as good as he got. It was great copy for newspapers,[90] but more importantly it showed that Marsh was not cowed by those in power and did not hesitate to go toe-to-toe with *anyone*.

In another appearance, Marsh succinctly summarized the difference that remains to this day between right- and left-oriented economics: "Private industry will get a loan if bankers can see a profit. The Government is the only agency which can provide work on the basis of no profit for anyone, and I think, on the whole, it is as efficient as private industry" (US Senate 1932b, 54). This would have been just as timely to say during the Great Recession, when Democrats wanted stimulus programs to hire the unemployed and give loans to bankrupt car companies (which could no longer borrow from banks), while Republicans wanted to cut taxes for those they called job creators. Similarly, for Republicans, government by definition was inefficient (or incompetent), while for Democrats funding public-sector jobs was as good an economic stimulus as anything else.

The Joint Committee kept pressing for relief legislation throughout the spring of 1932. Marsh shepherded about a dozen people to testify on behalf of the organizations belonging to it at a congressional hearing on unemployment (US House 1932, 21–23). Then, at a meeting of the coalition in New York City in March, the Committee made two modifications to its agenda. Based on recent developments in Washington, the administration and conservatives in Congress were now talking about a new way to balance the federal budget, namely with a sales tax. The group attacked the idea as regressive in its impact, exactly the opposite of the Joint Committee's focus on progressive taxation, such as a surcharge on higher incomes. Second, given the timing of the political calendar, the focus was inevitably shifting from presidential and congressional action to the party platforms of the presidential nominating conventions. The Committee sought to have each party take a side concerning sales taxes versus income taxes. Dewey, as chair of the Joint Committee, addressed the meeting and acknowledged political realities. He said, "We are especially interested in the Democrats [platform]. Hoover's record speaks for itself, and he probably feels by this time anything he says or does only makes it worse."[91] The group met again in Washington in April, still pressing Congress to do *something*.[92]

While these proposals for social and labor legislation were controversial with Hoover and Republicans, Sautter credits Dewey and the PL, along with other reform voices from the left, with "the broadening recognition of the nationwide—and therewith federal—aspect of the matter" (1991, 128; see also 226–228, 325). In the short run, measured by congressional action in 1931–32, the PL and Joint Committee's work was unfruitful, but in the long run it was quite successful. Most of their legislative agenda eventually became mainstream ideas and enacted into law, except its proposal to redefine full-time work to fewer hours. Even the thirty-hour workweek bill almost passed Congress in 1933. It was approved by the Senate and had the necessary votes for passage in the House. Only the passage of the National Recovery Administration (NRA) bill successfully co-opted it (Alter 2006, 300–301).

Even when Hoover did take action, such as with the creation of Reconstruction Finance Corporation (RFC), Dewey and Marsh were critical, especially if the RFC would be viewed as in lieu of policy proposals for unemployment insurance, direct relief, and increasing taxes on the rich.[93] The PL first criticized the slow pace of the RFC's allocation of its available credit to the point of condemning its "penny-pinching policy" when it should have been aiming for maximal spending.[94] From the other direction, the PL also criticized RFC's approved projects as "salvaging at public expense the financial hi-jackers [*sic*] who have been depressing the nation."[95] Marsh acerbically noted that RFC loans were going to borrowers who were turned down by commercial banks, demonstrating not only the failure of the for-profit financial markets to right the economy, but also the high risk involved in using public funds "on those rotten securities."[96] Seventy years later, these points were echoed in the criticisms of the 2008–09 federal bank bailouts, known as TARP.

The theme to which Dewey and Marsh consistently returned throughout these years was a focus on who had and had not benefited from the 1920s prosperity versus who was and was not now suffering from the Depression. Given their left-based critique of the American economy, they flagged the disproportionate benefits to the capitalist class of the prosperity in contrast to the minimal impact of the Depression on them. This kind of heads-I-win-tails-you-lose was embodied in an exchange of letters with Assistant Secretary of Commerce Julius Klein, often the administration spokesman on economic policy (especially after Treasury Secretary Mellon's star began fading). Dewey pointed out that banks had made good money before the crash *and* after. Banks made big profits during the easy-credit policies of the market's rise in the 1920s. Then, after the crash, the impact of deflation had a positive benefit for banks, as the money they were being repaid by debtors was now worth more than when they had lent it (Dewey 1985, 346–354).[97] Again, before and after the crash of 2008, this was a similar criticism of the banks. They made money in the housing bubble, then kept making money after the crash, notwithstanding the defaulted mortgages in their portfolios. It was as though they were the house at a casino.

Other Domestic Issues

Besides these central economic issues, during 1931–32 the PL lobbied on many other related subjects and developments, including testifying at the Interstate Commerce Commission (ICC) against approving a rate increase requested by the railroads (Dewey 1985, 368–371, 504), urging federal takeover of coal mines to prevent further violence and labor unrest, belittling the administration's antihoarding campaign (379–380), which was a major problem during the interregnum (Alter 2006, 150–151), and supporting a veterans' bonus as a way to inject money into the economy.[98]

One political issue that dominated American politics in the late 1920s and early 1930s was Prohibition. Comparable to the abortion issue in American politics in the early twenty-first century, it was an emotional issue that was often linked to a person's religious affiliation; it had no middle ground, and each party was predominantly on one side of it. Both sides went at it hammer and tong. The PL was exasperated with the inordinate amount of time and attention Prohibition was getting as a policy and political issue compared with the serious and pressing economic problems of the country. What was being accomplished by all this Sturm und Drang? it wondered. Actually, almost nothing, but that did not make a difference for an issue that cut so deep for so many Americans.

Ever so delicately, the PL waded into these never-ending arguments about Prohibition. Without taking sides between the drys and wets, it condemned how much congressional floor time was wasted on debating the subject, given the Great Depression. At one point, it suggested that Congress limit the daily debate on Prohibition to half an hour and then get on to the important public business that was pending.[99] Another time, when Congress was seemingly devoting inordinate amounts of time to debating whether to permit 3.2 beer, Dewey complained that liquor interests were dragging "the red herring of beer" across the trail and distracting Congress from vital actions to prop up the economy. A reporter characterized Dewey's statement as "sharp."[100] Considering the kind of hot rhetoric that the PL generally used to frame its positions and criticize its opponents, this description helps to convey the intensity of Dewey and Marsh's dislike of how much the Prohibition issue was continually deflecting the attention of policy makers. This was pure irrationality. But, showing a sense of humor, in its last newsletter before the 1932 elections, the PL was glad to point out that "among the few things in this election to be grateful for, is that neither major party even dares discuss booze as a major or even important issue."[101]

Foreign and Military Policy

As during the first half of Hoover's presidency, foreign policy had been of little interest to Washington's politicians and to an isolationist country—notwithstanding WWI or perhaps because of it. The international issues that got a modicum of attention were those intertwined with domestic economic issues, such as reparation payments by the defeated WWI nations and repayment of war loans by the winners. When a US senator pontificated against forgiving some of the interallied debt, Dewey replied that this would be a mistake economically as well as for the cause of long-term peace. He said opposing renegotiating the debt would be selfish on the United States' part, especially because "our gross national debt is an insignificant percentage of our national wealth." Carrying the debt was not a major drag on the American economy, he said. (Here, again, were echoes of the argument in 2009–12 if the federal deficit was a major problem in and of itself and if cutting it in a recession was a good idea.) Dewey noted that, contrary to the American economic situation, the war debts held by US allies were a very large proportion of their wealth, and they would suffer significantly if forced to repay the debts in full (1985, 364–367).

The PL continued to oppose American intervention in Latin American countries, whether economic or military. Many times it tried to draw public attention to the presence of marines in Nicaragua and Haiti. It distributed two brochures addressing in detail the situation and the lack of any legal or international justification for the continued US control of the governments of the two countries.[102] It signed a petition to Hoover from nine US organizations opposing the Haitian policy (Chap. 2) and wrote several letters of protest to Secretary of State Stimson on the subject.[103]

The United States also routinely meddled in Liberia because it was settled by American ex-slaves who dominated the country's government, even though the descendants of the slaves were a small minority of the entire population. In 1931, Stimson condemned the existence of vestiges of slavery in Liberia (of indigenous Africans). Marsh jumped in, pointing to the hypocrisy of the Hoover administration condemning harsh living conditions in Liberia while seeming to tolerate de facto slavery in Cuba.[104]

Risking the usual attacks that it was a Communist sympathizer (or fellow traveler), the PL actively sought to reply to rhetorical and policy attacks on the SU. It formed a Committee of One Hundred to offset the "hysterical propaganda" aimed at it by some conservative Americans, including the AFL. Almost predictably, a letter to the editor in the *New York Herald Tribune* accused the PL, Dewey, and Committee members of being "Socialists, whose objective is, despite its Utopian ideals, a despotic collectivism such as now prevails in Russia."[105] Replying to the attack with a statement released by Columbia, Dewey said he and the Committee were neither "Red nor anti-Red.[106] Instead, he called for "a fair and friendly policy toward Soviet Russia, both as the proper attitude toward a great social and economic experiment and as a means of furthering international understanding and peace" (Dewey 1985, 322). He noted that the United States had its own economic problems and should focus on solving those before spending time and effort criticizing similar situations in other countries. On another occasion, Marsh criticized Hoover for opposing food aid to Russia, even though Hoover had generally urged food shipments to starving populations notwithstanding political issues (such as to Germany right after the armistice ending WWI, but before the signing of the Versailles Treaty).[107]

The Lobby also continued its role as a peace organization, calling for antiwar policies, outlawing war (a major Dewey interest), an economic boycott of Japan for its military conquests in Manchuria and parts of

China, and other efforts to promote international peace.[108] Contradicting the impression that it always opposed the Hoover administration, the PL supported the US position for an international treaty to ban *use* of chemical weapons during war.[109] But, typically, it urged going further by banning even *possessing* such armaments.

One of the military's initiatives after WWI was to promote planning for a better mobilization of the national economy in case of another war (Lee 2005, chap. 4). Marsh testified against it at a hearing of the War Policies Commission in 1931. He said he opposed the premise, because it assumed another war. Secretary of War Patrick Hurley, chairing the hearing, got into a heated argument with Marsh. Hurley tried to pin Marsh down: Was he was a revolutionary opposing the current constitutional regime? Was he was a Bolshevik or, at least, a socialist? Marsh replied evenly that he and the PL believed in orderly change, not revolution, and that he was not a socialist (US House 1931, 323–338). The headline exchange was a flip comment by Marsh that Hoover was on a Caribbean cruise on a Navy vessel "to see if any other country is in worse condition than our own." Hurley protested vociferously. Marsh replied that he was joking and (uncharacteristically) withdrew the comment.[110] (Here was an early example of media coverage focusing on minor and nonmaterial matters over seemingly boring substance.)

In a sense, 1932 ended on the November election day. Once FDR was the president-elect and Hoover a lame duck, the focus quickly shifted to lobbying the nascent administration and the incoming Democratic Congress, even though the presidential inauguration was not until March. Hence, this chapter concludes at this point, and a presentation of the PL's legislative program for FDR begins in the next chapter, even though it began in 1932.

Chapter 4

Lobby Operations and Conservative Attacks, 1928–1932

Advocacy Strategy: PR to the Max

The preceding chapter described the public policy positions for which the People's Lobby advocated and, indirectly, the broad definition that Dewey and Marsh gave to the concept of lobbying. In the narrower sense of it, their activities were the same as those of special interest groups: testimony at congressional hearings, correspondence with legislators, meetings with executive branch officials, and meetings with White House staff. That was lobbying in the formal meaning of the term. But they also viewed the act of lobbying as equally oriented to influencing the broad public opinion on the issues of the day. That was the rationale for dedicating so much of their efforts to publicity, as the concept had evolved during the Progressive era. The PL's publicity efforts were seemingly of a PR mega-mall. Their modus operandi very much paralleled the motto of one of the major Prohibition advocacy groups: "Do Everything" (Okrent 2010, 18). Dewey and Marsh tried to do anything and everything they could think of to get their message out, to reach and convince the public that there were policy alternatives to what the Republican and Democrats offered and that the non-Communist and progressive left had a concrete agenda of potential actions in which the pallid left of the Democratic Party was uninterested. Paralleling Dewey's (organizationally separate) interest in a third party, the PL's communication doctrine was to promote a third way in Washington's stale policy debates.

Earlier discussions provided extensive documentation of the media relations efforts in which Dewey and Marsh engaged. If coverage roughly reflected what reporters and editors thought was newsworthy, then the PL was newsworthy. Marsh could create a sharp turn of phrase and relate different developments to each other—thus being able to ride the news du jour to get publicity for another matter altogether. Similarly, Marsh showed a sophisticated understanding of the news business. He understood that releasing a letter to the president was more newsworthy than merely a press release and that releasing something late in the day would often make his "news" the most recent of developments and therefore the most newsworthy. While Marsh understood the mass media as a way to reach the populace at large, he also was aware of the benefit of dealing with publications oriented to specific demographics. So the PL's activities in certain subject areas of particular interest were often covered more extensively in African American newspapers than the majority press, as were labor-oriented statements in the labor press and Latin American–related positions in Spanish-language newspapers.[1] The Lobby's general statements on the economy were sometimes covered in German and Italian newspapers because of the interest of its readers, often immigrants in unskilled work.[2]

For the times, Marsh and Dewey also had a relatively sophisticated perception of the ebb and flow of news, often timing releases for the big Sunday papers or slower news days. For example, Marsh realized that the week between Christmas and the New Year was very slow politically in Washington. Congress was out of session, many people were on vacation, and generally little governmental news was generated. But the maw of the media was still wide open, needing to fill the news hole of the daily newspaper. So, for example, on Christmas Day of 1929, Marsh issued a press release.[3] Later that week he released another, and then a third (all on different subjects) on New Year's Eve.[4] The PL's publicity offensive even triggered a sarcastic editorial note in the *New York Times*. On Christmas Eve, the editorial writer compared the tranquil mood of a white Christmas with the "red-hot, steaming, parboiling Christmas it undoubtedly is for the People's Lobby." In particular, the writer criticized the tone of the Lobby's denunciations of US policies. "After reading in some of the longest and sputteringest sentences ever penned how many kinds of a crook he is, the one thing Uncle Sam will want to do is to jump off the deck."[5] Undoubtedly, Dewey and Marsh did not mind being criticized by the very proper and dignified newspaper of the Establishment. At the very least, it indicated they had broken through and attracted attention.

They also understood the benefit of having a news peg for PL statements, an early permutation in mass communication that Boorstin later dubbed pseudo-events (2012). Sure, press releases and public letters were fine sometimes. But in the eyes of a reporter, statements to an audience at an external event were that much more in the nature of traditional and legitimate news. They provided the when and where of the who-what-when-where mantra of journalism. Reporters felt they were covering something that *happened*. Therefore, Marsh and Dewey often convened what they called conferences on specific policy areas and with major civic or public figures as speakers. They refined an approach Marsh had experimented with during the PRL's existence (Chap. 1). These PL sessions took place either in New York or Washington. The media sometimes reported them as conferences, giving a somewhat misleading impression of their nature, size, scope, and tilt because these events were usually more in the nature of open public meetings or symposia, with several prominent speakers on one topic. Whether a real conference or not, these sessions often garnered press coverage for PL's views on issues. Dewey sometimes attended and chaired them (whether in New York or DC); at other times he sent messages to be read to the audience. Occasionally, at the end of the day's sessions, the attendees would vote on proposed policy resolutions (prepared in advance by Marsh) reflecting what public policy goals the PL should pursue.[6]

The first conference was in May 1928 in Washington and served as a kickoff for the new organization, with Dewey speaking as the headliner.[7] Many others were convened, including in June 1930 (New York), July 1930 (New York), October 1930 (New York), and September 1931 (DC). At some of the initial conferences, the PL made an effort to provide a somewhat balanced program, with at least one speaker representing an organization on the other side of PL's positions. For example, a staffer from the National Association of Manufacturers spoke at the conference on unemployment insurance, explaining in great detail why his organization opposed it (Sargent, 1930). Julius H. Barnes, the chairman of the US Chamber of Commerce, was invited to speak at one. He declined because the topic of the session he was to address was "Why Has Business Broken Down." Barnes said such framing of the subject was "manifestly an exaggeration and thus unfair to a great section of business leadership that is devotedly trying to improve progressively and stabilize business, particularly in its aspect of employment."[8] Gradually the conferences became increasingly one-sided, representing a kind of public gathering of people who agreed with the PL's viewpoint.

Generally, these events attracted a respectably sized audience, enough to give a kind of stamp of approval to the validity of the event. In one case, despite a relatively impressive roster of speakers, the initial attendance was so small that "the speakers at first were in the majority. The conference withdrew into a corner of the auditorium."[9] For the *New York Times*, this did not diminish the newsworthiness of the speakers' comments. It ran two stories the next day on what the speakers said.[10] This hinted at the power of such conferences as news events. Also, the architecture of these conferences permitted speakers to make relatively controversial statements without the PL being seen as endorsing those views, but as merely giving them a platform.

Beyond providing the benefits of press coverage, these conferences were organizing tools—ways to reach potential supporters, recruit new members, and generally disseminate the ideology and policy alternatives of the Lobby. The discussion in the preceding chapter noted other activities that were simultaneously organizing and publicity mechanisms, including a mass petition to the president with an effort to present it to him personally, a mothers' delegation to meet with the administration, meetings with congressional leadership, congressional testimony, and speaking to other organizations and conferences. These all put the PL on the map, and, if publicity indeed was a rough measure of importance and persuasion, then the PL had made itself a player on the public policy issues facing the nation.

When it came to other forms of public relations, Marsh did everything he could think of. He was a jack of all trades, comfortable with just about every imaginable avenue for promoting the Lobby's views. He was a kind of perpetual-motion lobbyist and tireless word machine. Along with media relations, the Lobby's monthly *Bulletin* was the main communication venue. Marsh was its author, editor, and publisher. It will be recalled that in 1931, Mrs. Ethel Clyde had offered to underwrite the costs of a professional-looking monthly with the proviso that it be widely circulated, such as to college libraries and potentially interested faculty (Chap. 2). In 1932, she followed up by offering a donation of $4,500 to cover the costs of a print run of 6,000 copies of the *Bulletin* and mailing costs.[11] This was, to use twenty-first-century argot, a force multiplier, permitting the Lobby to reach a much larger, but targeted, audience and as a recruiting device for more members and subscribers. If media relations was indirect wholesale communication to a mass and undifferentiated audience, the Clyde contribution facilitated direct retail communication toward a likely interested category of the population.

Marsh also traveled to give public talks and lectures. In that respect, he understood the maxim of American politics that all politics is local. If he wanted to cultivate a grassroots base for the PL, it was not enough to make pronouncements in Washington to politicians and reporters. He wanted to talk to rank-and-file citizens and convince them that there was a third way to approach public policy problems and that the anemic leftish orientation of the Democratic Party overlooked many possible populist and progressive policy alternatives.

Therefore, when Congress was out of session, Marsh frequently traveled. Sometimes these were one-shot trips, such as a luncheon speech to the Civic Club in Manhattan, the National Conference of Social Work in Philadelphia, and a symposium at the University of Virginia.[12] More often, especially in the summer, he went on extensive speaking tours. In mid-1929, for example, his engagements included Salt Lake City and Los Angeles.[13] In the summer of 1931, he was on the road from July 21 to August 27, speaking in twenty-three cities. His itinerary took him from Washington through the upper Midwest, to the Northwest, down the Pacific Coast, and then back across the United States through the Great Plains and border states.[14] On such trips, in each city he met with local officials to inquire of conditions and then gave a talk to civic groups and local PL members on his take on national developments. Most speaking engagements were covered by the local press, sometimes before, sometimes after, sometimes both.[15] (These trips also gave him credibility in his congressional testimony when he talked about the real conditions of the economy.)

Not all of Dewey and Marsh's communication goals came to fruition. An example of a false start was Marsh's plan to write a short book on the PL's proposal for unemployment insurance. A popularly priced mass pocketbook would help add wind to the sails of the campaign for public opinion support. The plans were advanced enough for Dewey to write an introduction, but the book project was never completed (Dewey 1985, 399–400). Nonetheless, the public relations activities of the Lobby in its first four years displays an impressive array of modes of communication, venues and platforms, all aimed at direct lobbying of national legislators and indirect lobbying by using publicity to influence public opinion.

When Dewey and Marsh cofounded the Lobby in 1928, they were determined to shape the organization so that it would not be a wholly owned subsidiary of the Democratic Party. They wanted an authentically independent organization that would pursue a progressive policy agenda regardless of whose ox they were goring. They were equal opportunity critics, always zeroing in on whom they disagreed with, regardless of party affiliation. As part of this approach to lobbying and PR, the PL exhibited an intensity in public communication that often clashed with the more muted and polite exchanges of political Washington. The Lobby had a kind of take-no-prisoners organizational culture, a political version of a scorched-earth approach. Dewey and Marsh used vehement language to make their points. But above all, they were willing to criticize anyone with whom they disagreed no matter the consequences. They did not care that an attack on a politician one day might reduce their lobbying effectiveness with him (as they were mostly men at the time) the next. This was the opposite of insider lobbying, obsessed with access, niceness, and credibility.

This approach to public communication as a form of lobbying was epitomized by how the PL characterized Senator Robert Wagner (D-NY) over a period of less than a year. In April 1930, it vehemently criticized his employment and relief legislative proposals as inadequate to the situation and reflecting "obstruse economic ratiocination." The headline in the *New York Times* was "Wagner Bills Hit by People's Lobby."[16] Then, in March 1931, it praised his later unemployment insurance bill and urged enactment. The sub-headline in the *Times* was "People's Lobby Asks the Senate Committee to Heed Wagner's Proposal in its Inquiry."[17] Marsh and Dewey would "call 'em as they saw 'em." That was its PR and lobbying strategy: communicating to the max and damn the consequences.

In Operation

It will be recalled that the final action in the creation of the People's Lobby was its incorporation in Delaware in October 1931 as a non-stock corporation (Chap. 2). The next year provided a first time around for the PL to operate under Delaware's corporate law. First, it was necessary for the temporary board of directors, which had been established in October by the incorporators (the professionals in Wilmington who did this routinely), to be succeeded by a permanent board. The meeting took place in Dewey's apartment in Manhattan on November 10, 1931. This process necessitated following a formal legal process, almost comical considering that only a handful of people were present.

First, they approved a waiver of notice for the initial formal meeting.[18] Then they formally convened the meeting and elected temporary officers for that first meeting, followed by an agenda of the necessary business required by Delaware law.[19] These initial actions included adopting an official seal of the corporation to be embossed in all minutes of subsequent meetings, authorization for issuance of official organizational memberships (these would be stocks in for-profit corporations), authorization for a treasurer to open a corporate bank account, authorization for the treasurer to disburse funds from that account for the expenses of the corporation, establishing a location of a principal office (in Washington), authorizing the president of the board of directors to call meetings of the board, and permission to file all corporate reports required by law. Each motion had to be moved, seconded, and voted on. With that done, the People's Lobby, Inc. could now "transact its business" and "maintain its corporate existence."[20]

Having complied with this legal mumbo jumbo, they got down to real Lobby business. The officers of the corporation were Dewey as president, Ethel Clyde as vice president (the donor who kept the PL solvent; see Chap. 2), and Harry Hunt as treasurer. The three officers were deemed to be the PL's Executive Committee. They promptly authorized Marsh to continue as executive secretary, with an annual salary of $5,000. The officers approved a policy agenda for the coming year (essentially continuing what the PL had been doing up to the incorporation), including the efforts of the Joint Committee on Unemployment and for a moratorium on farm mortgage indebtedness.[21]

The first extensive business meeting of the new corporation occurred on April 25, 1932, again at Dewey's apartment.[22] It was a mix of required legal procedures and approving the ongoing public policy agenda for the rest of the year. The three officers appointed Marsh and Harry Laidler (a longtime labor activist who had worked extensively with Dewey and Marsh in the past) to the Board of Directors and designated that the executive committee would consist of Dewey, Clyde, and Marsh. They also voted to create a Council to serve in an advisory capacity to the small board of directors (and be listed on the stationary letterhead and newsletter masthead). The directors appointed seventeen members; almost all had been on the preceding Advisory Council that had existed before the incorporation.[23] The Board also amended the corporate By-Laws, mostly to make it easier for the small group of PL activists to function in an official and legal manner.[24]

While fulfilling all the legal requirements for corporations registered in Delaware, including some of the largest in the United States, the PL was a modest organization. As of late 1932, it had an annual income of about $15,000 and expenditures of about $9,000. There were two employees, Marsh and a secretary, both modestly recompensed. In terms of membership, Marsh reported to the officers that the PL had about 1,430 members. While 350 members were in arrears in annual dues (and perhaps not planning to renew), they were roughly replaced by 270 new members.[25] At one point, Marsh claimed publicly that he was organizing ten PL chapters around the country to oppose the Smoot-Hawley tariff bill, but that appears to have been a gross exaggeration.[26]

Media Characterizations and Conservative Attacks

The template of objective journalism made it hard for reporters to convey to readers exactly who or what the People's Lobby was. Most often they did it indirectly, by reminding readers that Dewey was the PL's president. For most followers of public affairs, his prominence on the left was an adequate enough signal. But other reporters sought to be more direct in identifying the politics of the PL. Given that Dewey and Marsh never used ideological self-characterizations, reporters had to venture beyond the just-the-facts writing style and assert their own conclusions about the PL's place on the political spectrum. During these first four years of the Lobby's existence, newspapers used various adjectives and did not seem to be able to settle on a universal one.

In chronological order, it was variously described as "a liberal organization,"[27] "consisting partly of 'radicals,' "[28] "a nation-wide organization for tax reduction,"[29] "a force outside of Congress,"[30] "a group of Progressives,"[31] "claiming to represent the liberal viewpoint in foreign affairs,"[32] "a left-wing group of the Progressive faction,"[33] a "decidedly 'left wing' organization,"[34] "socialistic,"[35] "anti-administration,"[36] and "an organization of progressives."[37] The Joint Committee on Unemployment, which the PL organized and Dewey chaired, was described as a "Socialist, labor and liberal" coalition.[38] Without using a specific label, one columnist made his point by stating that Marsh was critical "sometimes even [of] most progressives."[39]

Some newspapers, such as the *Chicago Tribune* and *Los Angeles Times*, injected an overt conservative editorial slant into their news articles and coverage. Their characterization of the PL's politics was much more explicit. The *Tribune* identified the organization as "the radical people's lobby" and a "propaganda agency."[40] The *Times* described it as "the so-called People's Lobby."[41] It was not just conservative newspapers raising flags about the PL. During its initial four years of existence, the Lobby already attracted the attention of conservative red-hunters in America, official or otherwise. While accusations about radical revolutionaries plotting against the country were common long before the Russian Revolution in 1917, overt claims or indirect insinuations of Americans who were Communists and were in league with the SU quickly became common. Almost from the start, the PL was categorized by these conservatives as un-American and a threat to the American way of life.

In 1929, Alice Ames Robbins attended Marsh's speech to the League of Women Voters in San Francisco. She promptly wrote to the Intelligence Division of the US Justice Department to inform it of what he had said. Robbins said he had given a "seditious" speech, especially about American economic intervention in foreign countries. She primly noted that most of the women had not appeared to be in agreement with Marsh's comments, "but there were some Levantines in the audience who cheered vociferously at each anti-American statement he made." (This was likely a reference to Jewish women, with "Levantine" probably a euphemism used in polite WASP society.) Robbins hoped the department "can run him out of the country as an undesirable citizen." An assistant attorney general replied legalistically that the department had no legal authority to do that.[42]

Possibly triggered by that letter, the PL was now squarely in the sights of the US Justice Department. On behalf of the attorney general, early in 1930, his Special Assistant Paul Chase asked the department's Bureau of Investigation for a report. Specifically, "what can you tell me about the People's Lobby, its Sec[retar]y Mr. Marsh and its President John Dewey"? FBI Director J. Edgar Hoover[43] combed the bureau's files on subversives and radicals for information on the PL. He also sent an undercover FBI agent to PL office "in a very confidential manner" to collect written materials, observe what was going on in the office, and read the office building directory.[44] This was quite different from the approach the bureau had used in 1921, when it openly sent an investigator to interview Marsh about the PRL (Chap. 1).

In late January 1930, the FBI submitted three reports to the attorney general with information it had on the PL, Dewey, and Marsh. However, the reports were all ostensibly presentations of documented information and drew no conclusions. Hoover let the attorney general do that. Generally, the reports were summaries of PL publications, press coverage, Marsh's congressional testimonies, and credit bureau reports. The only nonpublic information was collected when FBI agents "interviewed under pretext" at least four sources, three on Capitol Hill and a woman who had worked for Marsh for ten years. She said that he "disseminated propaganda" but was "conscientiously for the people." She also said that Marsh's writings, especially about disarmament, were "socialistic in tendency" and that he was "a great friend" of Roger Baldwin, a co-founder of the ACLU. The report also noted that two of the press clippings in the Bureau files were coverage of PL activities "in foreign tongue."[45]

The FBI files on Dewey all predated the PL and focused on his political and social involvements. Most documented his friendly contacts with the SU, including a trip there, as well as his involvement in various left causes, such as the case of Sacco and Vanzetti. The FBI file included a letter in Russian that the FBI had obtained and then translated.[46] Oddly, an article Dewey had written in a Christian pacifist magazine (*The World Tomorrow*) was sourced to "a confidential bulletin . . . the origin of which is not disclosed." Given that the magazine was in public circulation, it was unclear why the article needed such circuitous and secret sourcing. The FBI prominently quoted from the accusation by Matthew Woll of the AFL that

Dewey was a "Soviet Apologist" and that the Russians felt he was "doing more for the Soviet case than all of the avowed Communists the country has ever sheltered or produced."[47]

Marsh and Dewey figured that the FBI continued to be interested in the PL, as it had been when Marsh was interviewed about the PRL. With a wicked sense of humor, Marsh added FBI Director Hoover to the mailing list of PL's monthly *Bulletin*.[48] It was a gesture indicating that the PL had nothing to hide, that Marsh knew Hoover was keeping a file on the organization, and that he was not intimidated by such official surveillance. He and PL would continue following the path and ideology it had set and would do so without fear or defensiveness. Being popular was not particularly important to the PL, Dewey, or Marsh. They were not in high school, and they stood by their principles, even if that put them under some kind of suspicion as disloyal citizens. Still, FBI surveillance, Hoover's campaigns against subversives and radicals, and the nearly hysterical tones of politicians against communism prompted the PL to oppose giving additional police powers to the FBI. In a statement, Marsh strongly condemned a suggestion floated by Elihu Root (something of the voice of the establishment) that such powers were necessary to combat domestic communism.[49]

Communist hunters on Capitol Hill quickly took note of the PL. A senator published a letter he received from a woman in Alabama who claimed that there were "interlocked lobby groups" of radicals on the left trying to sway the confirmation of a judicial nominee. She included the PL (and, separately, the PRL) as part of that organizational infrastructure.[50] At a September 1930 hearing of the House Special Committee to Investigate Communist Activities[51] (which eventually became the House Un-American Committee [HUAC]) in Chicago, a Farm Bureau official submitted information he had received from the American Vigilant Intelligence Federation. One characterized a PL conference held in July 1930 in New York City. It stated that "Revolution was the outstanding solution offered by the participants," and "this certainly indicates unity of objective, to us—and that is a socialist state" (US House 1930a, 93–94). A few months later, a reporter for the conservative *National Republic* journal (not to be confused with the liberal/progressive *New Republic*) submitted a report to the committee on several left groups. It identified the PL as "composed of pacifists, internationalists, and socialists"; claimed that it "receives funds from the same source as do the reds" and stated that President Dewey was "communist-sympathizing" (US House, 1930b, 284). A different article from the *National Republic*, submitted for the record at a hearing on naturalization of WWI alien conscientious objectors, stated that the PL was an "organization for the formation of a new socialist party" and that it had received a $1,000 grant from a foundation that was "communist-socialist controlled" (US Senate 1932c, 73–74).

Conservative activists seeking to ferret out Communists now had the PL on their radar. Former Assistant War Secretary Charles Burton Robbins tried to pin down the individuals involved in what he called "a well-organized movement to overturn our Government and replace it with one founded on the communist form." In a speech to a woman's patriotic group in 1931, he listed thirty people serving on "a series of interlocking directorates," including two affiliated with the PL.[52] The next year, at a House hearing on unemployment relief legislation, a representative from a small conservative group called the Woman Patriot Corporation strenuously opposed one of the bills before the committee. She said, "[T]his bill is full of politics—third-party politics, People's Lobby politics, Children's Bureau politics, socialist and communist politics, [and] wage-for-mothers feminist politics" (US House 1932, 179).

The right-wing attacks on the PL and, more generally, on the left, along with the intensity of the economic crisis facing the country, sometimes prompted Dewey and Marsh to see the mirror image of what they were being accused of. In 1932, they twice raised the specter of what extreme conservatives seemed to be wanting, based on their rhetoric and in the context of the rise of fascist and antidemocratic movements in Germany and Italy. In January, Dewey predicted that "we shall have a full-fledged fascism in America." That sounded quite over the top. What triggered the observation? He said that this kind of fascism would be the result of the "state capitalism" promoted by the Hoover administration, such as, apparently, the RFC and other initiatives that undergirded the existing private-sector economic elite with official governmental support.[53]

This was no onetime slip (or a Marsh statement without Dewey's approval). Dewey made a much more alarmist statement a few months later in late May. Just as the right was continually warning of anti-American subversion by the left and a secret plan for a Communist revolutionary takeover (akin to Russia), now Dewey invoked the possibility of a coup d'état by the right. He saw straws in the wind of "the establishment of some form of fascism or extra-legal control, in view of the widespread distress and consequent unrest." Several developments triggered this alarmist view. He noted "the deliberate drive of newspapers and interests that represent concentrated wealth and privilege to discredit the law-making body," calls by some urging the president "to usurp the function of initiating Federal legislation," and suggestions to reactivate the WWI-era Council of National

Defense, thereby triggering presidential emergency powers. In a letter to seventeen senators whom the PL considered to be progressives, Dewey said that "it is of vital importance that there should be present in Washington whenever Congress is not in session, two or three Senators who can call attention to any overt act on the part of the Chief Executive of the Nation, subversive of popular rights" (Dewey 1985, 393–394).

These extreme observations seem, in the perspective of history and knowing what really happened subsequently, to border on the paranoid at worst and to be silly exaggerated rhetoric at best. But the sense of living during an unprecedented economic crisis—of the weakness of American democracy and the policy gridlock in Washington—led to such perceptions of doom and of possible collapse of a democratic form of government. Conversely, beginning in 1933, one of the long-running attacks by the right on FDR was that he wanted to be a dictator and to destroy the republican form of government. While Dewey and the PL twice made such an accusation against the right during a Republican presidency, the counteraccusations by conservatives were a near-constant theme for the entire duration of the Roosevelt administration. Here, too, was another parallel of politics during the Great Depression and the Great Recession. The Democratic criticisms of Republicans paled compared to the Republican attacks on President Obama. They accused him of being a socialist and a threat to free market economics; they claimed that his health care legislation was a threat to personal liberty and that the health care law was a government *takeover* of the entire health care system. Bureaucrats would now decide what treatment your doctor could give you. There even would be government death panels to decide if a senior citizen could get care or should be left to die.

In all, the first four years of the PL's existence from 1928 to 1932 had mirrored the country's economic roller coaster. The Lobby went from advocating for the populations that were not benefiting from the economic prosperity during the Coolidge administration to promoting policies to lift the economy out of the Great Depression during the Hoover administration. For Dewey and Marsh, their left-progressive political ideology provided a consistent source of policy prescriptions for economic, domestic, and foreign policy. They engaged in a broad effort to promote their alternatives, not only to Republican policies, but also to those of the Democratic Party. They were showing that the progressive left was a rich source of public policy ideas, further to the left than the Democrats, but not Communist either. If ideas and publicity were the coins of the realm of the public policy debates in Washington, Dewey's People's Lobby was in the thick of it.

Chapter 5

Policy Advocacy during FDR's First Term

Criticizing the First New Deal as Too Conservative, 1933–1934

Now it was a whole new ball game. Democrat Roosevelt had defeated President Hoover in the November election. Roosevelt had been relatively opaque during the election campaign, seemingly promising change ("Happy Days are Here Again"), but skimpy on the details. On one hand he advocated a balanced budget, on the other seemed more open to federal government intervention to help those suffering from the Great Depression (Ritchie 2007). Dewey and Marsh were unimpressed by FDR's campaign promises and viewed the election results as "not determining anything except discontent" (US Senate 1933a, 202).

Interregnum, November 1932–March 1933

The transition from the presidencies of Herbert Hoover and Franklin Roosevelt was more important historically than most others. This because, substantively, the economy seemed to be nearing a standstill and runs on banks were threatening the entire financial system. Politically, there were substantial policy differences between the outgoing and incoming presidents (with FDR noncommittal about nearly everything). Hoover was trying to maneuver FDR into a commitment to maintain Hoover's central economic principles. Finally, there was the matter of time. These events were occurring during the last presidential cycle that would have such a very long interregnum, with inauguration day on March 4, 1932. (For 1936–37 and after, it was moved up to January 20, specifically to limit the duration of the uncertainty between administrations.)

Economic Policy

It will be recalled that in October 1932, Dewey had criticized FDR's economic views quite sharply (Chap. 3). It was a national story and carried by newspapers around the country. Some headlines included "John Dewey Hits Roosevelt Views on Federal Aid" and "People's Lobby Head Criticizes Roosevelt."[1] This did not endear them to the candidate. Undeterred and unapologetic, Dewey and Marsh now wrote several letters to the president-elect with their advice. In December, Dewey urged a farm policy that would lower the value of farmland.[2] (This reflected Dewey and Marsh's continuing support for Henry George's single land tax plan.) Louis Howe, an aide to FDR, responded with a bland thank-you.[3] Then they urged FDR support for a Federal Trade Commission study of private electric power versus public power, urging greater federal focus on government facilities to generate electricity.[4] (FDR, as governor, had been relatively supportive of public power [Alter 2006, 81, 84].) Another noncommittal thank-you from Howe.[5]

In some of their public statements, Dewey and Marsh were much more pointed about their lack of enthusiasm for a Roosevelt administration. An article in the *Bulletin* wondered how Roosevelt and the congressional Democrats could pass significant relief legislation given "their efforts to serve two masters—privilege that paid the piper and is calling the tune—and the people whom the Democratic Party betrayed in the world's worst war" (i.e., the way President Wilson brought the United States into WWI). In a not very veiled criticism of FDR's somewhat amiable relations with New York City's Tammany Hall political machine, the article alluded to the "Tammany hordes of hungry hi-jackers" as nominal Democrats with little interest in major economic or political reform.[6] Marsh also criticized FDR's lack of action as governor on the need for governmental assistance to provide housing, especially for the unemployed. The president-elect, he said, "should attend to this situation in his own state and in New York City before coming to Washington."[7]

Roosevelt was keeping his own counsel, not tipping his hand before the inauguration. President Hoover had been so repudiated in the election that he was now largely marginalized in any policy-making that might occur in Washington. Dewey and Marsh turned their attention to Congress.[8] The lame duck session of the Congress elected in November 1930 extended from December 5, 1932, to adjournment sine die on March 3, 1933. They hoped that the shock of the election results to congressional Republicans might break the policy, political, and ideological logjam that had largely paralyzed Washington since the market crash.[9]

They scheduled a two-day conference of the Joint Committee on Unemployment in Washington just days before Congress reconvened. Their program remained mostly the same as it had been since creating the Joint Committee in November 1931, focusing on direct federal funding of relief. Originally the Joint Committee had suggested appropriating $500 million for relief. Now, based on increasingly dire circumstances of the economy, it was doubled to $1 billion. Three of the talks at the conference were broadcast on a national radio network. Dewey's comments focused on expanding the modest precedents of the last few years of some federal responsibility for alleviating economic suffering. He called for a "new social responsibility," namely that "there is at least a minimum standard of living which must be maintained," even if federal spending was necessary to do so. Dewey criticized the views of the business and conservative establishment, which still opposed that principle. In particular, he noted the work of "active publicity agencies, duly inspired and greased, have so far scared the American public by repeating like a parrot 'dole, dole.' "[10] (Dole was the political attack term that was used to condemn relief proposals as merely giving people money for not working.)

During the congressional session, Marsh testified on behalf of the Joint Committee at a hearing on a bill to reduce the definition of full-time employment to thirty hours a week. By reducing the workweek, proponents thought more jobs would be needed to do the same amount of work now accomplished in a forty-hour workweek. Marsh's testimony pointed to the increased productivity of the American worker, partly due to technology and automation. Given that salaries were not increasing with productivity, employers were benefiting and workers were not. By shifting to a thirty-hour workweek, Marsh argued, workers would be paid a salary commensurate with their earlier productivity, thus creating new jobs as productivity increased. Marsh also alluded to the hushed fears of a revolution in the United States, as had occurred in Russia and just recently the Nazi revolution in Germany. To prevent a revolution here, he said, Congress needed to enact major social legislation quickly (US Senate 1933b, 234–243).

Besides leading and speaking for the Joint Committee, Dewey and Marsh pushed for other specific policies to reverse the effects of the Depression, consistent with the policy positions they had adopted before the election.[11] They called for financing federal relief with increases in taxes on the wealthy rather than of deficit spending, opposed enacting regressive taxation such as sales taxes, urged redistributing income to have "a semi-intelligent reorganization of our economic system," writing down debts, and dealing with the economic status quo of idle productive capacity in some sectors and over-production in others (US Senate 1933a, 184–202). As to farm policy, Marsh opposed solutions that focused on increasing prices. That, he felt, would merely make it harder for the unemployed to buy food. Instead, the focus should be on reducing costs farmers incurred so that they could still prosper with low prices. He blasted an idea circulating on Capitol Hill to finance agricultural aid with a consumption tax. "Genuine sympathy for farmers' plight does not justify compelling underpaid or unemployed workers to foot the bill. It would be just as logical to commandeer farm products to feed and clothe the destitute unemployed," he said with his usual bite (US Senate 1933c, 472).

During that winter, the Senate Finance Committee held hearings on the causes of the crash and depression. Dewey was one of dozens of national leaders invited to provide his views. In a letter, he listed what he thought the causes were, including

- "Speculation in land values;"
- "Our banking and credit system, which is run not primarily to foster needed production and investment, but to promote speculation and make profits;"
- A taxation system that, in relative terms, put a larger burden on "those of small incomes" than on those with "surplus incomes," i.e., the wealthy;
- Wages not keeping up with worker productivity; and
- "irresponsible sale of foreign securities issued in boom times for speculative profit" (US Senate 1933d, 961–962).

This list is nearly perfectly aligned with the widely accepted causes of the 2008 crash. The only tweak necessary to make them identical would relate to the last item. Stock speculation up to the 2008 crash was not being limited to equities of foreign corporations, rather to almost all equities and bonds available to American investors.

Foreign and Military Policy

While foreign policy was of little interest to outgoing and incoming Washington policy makers, the PL continued advocating for its international agenda. As a peace organization, it participated in a call for controlling the sale of arms, which it saw as contributing to the potentialities of war. Reflecting the progressives' belief in the power of publicity, one of the polices the PL and other groups urged was for Congress to "ratify the 1925 convention providing for *publicity* in export of arms, and adopt an American system of licensing with *full publicity* of exports, both as an aid to control and that the public may be able to obtain reliable data."[12] As part of a book review on arms merchants, a reviewer in the *New Republic* praised Marsh's combative and argumentative appearance at the 1931 hearing of the War Policies Commission (Chap. 3).[13]

Marsh was also on the road during the presidential transition spreading the PL's gospel. At a conference in New York City in late November, he characterized American economic policy up to now as "establishing and maintaining special privileges . . . , building up a class of multimillionaires too rich and too polite to be taxed."[14] In Boston in early February he talked about the importance of the principle of direct federal funding of relief, rather than the Republican doctrine of leaving it to state and local governments and to charities. He "denounced Congressmen and Senators in general, *and the coming administration at Washington in particular*" unless they took bold action including putting appropriate tax burden on the rich. Otherwise, he said with his usual knack for a sound-bite, "Al Capone is a New England deacon beside your Congressmen at Washington."[15] Later that month, he gave a similar talk in Syracuse, New York.[16]

In the last issue of the *Bulletin* before the inauguration, Dewey addressed what was paralyzing the country at the moment, bank runs and collapses. The economy was practically at a standstill. While some criminal wrongdoing was being exposed, Dewey tried to keep the focus on systemic issues, some related to banking practices (such as speculation), some to government inaction (such as inadequate relief), and some to basic inequities in the economic system. He concluded by deprecating emergency interventions that did nothing to correct the injustices and imbalances within the economy as a whole: "Making the President a banking dictator in a crisis is not a solution—it is merely a postponement of the inevitable remaking of our profiteering banking system" (Dewey 1986, 254–255). Dewey was throwing down the gauntlet to the incoming president. Are you going to go for minor reforms and patches to a broken economic system or for major reform to accomplish social and economic justice? This was the People's Lobby gauge for grading the new president.

FDR's One Hundred Days, March–June, 1933[17]

Roosevelt's first hundred days in the White House are correctly remembered as a kind of crack in time, when the economic emergency was so severe that Congress seemed willing to pass just about anything FDR proposed. In at least one case Congress voted on a bill before a printed version was available (Alter 2006, 251). Just as Roosevelt understood that a crisis was an opportunity for new policy, so did Dewey and Marsh. They were eager to evaluate what the president was proposing in relation to the systemic and left social reforms the PL had been urging since the 1929 crash. Dewey and Marsh were hoping that they could ride the same policy wave as FDR was. Even if not successful at passage, they wanted to be sure to make known that there were substantive reform ideas from the non-Communist left, even if not endorsed by the new administration. The difference between FDR and the PL was that FDR was at this point a pragmatic, nearly nonideological politician, while Dewey and Marsh had a fixed field of political values.

Economic Policy

Dewey invited members of the Joint Committee on Unemployment to a summit in Washington in March to review the committee's pre-FDR proposals to Congress.[18] At the meeting, the representatives of the organizational members of the joint committee slightly reoriented its focus. Now they shifted away from a primary focus on relief to a more comprehensive redistribution of income through the tax code as the way to stimulate employment. Specifically, the committee urged Congress to reduce consumption taxes (which disproportionally affected lower- and middle-income people) and increase taxes on the wealthy.[19] Members of Congress were invited to sit in on the sessions and about twenty-five new members attended. Some of the talks at the conference were broadcast on a national radio network.[20] The focus was its program, not the administration's legislative proposals.

Dewey sent several letters to Roosevelt urging him to promote redistribution of income, higher taxes on the rich, and other PL items. Each time, Howe, now secretary to the president, replied warmly ("My dear Mr. Dewey"), but without any substantive comment.[21] The era of good feelings lasted less than a month. In early April, a newspaper report referred to the PL as "a hitherto friendly Roosevelt organization."[22] No longer. It began vociferously and loudly criticizing the policy proposals of the administration as either too minor, too status quo, or giving too much power to the president vis-à-vis Congress. (Notwithstanding its persistent criticisms of the administration, Marsh wrote a friendly letter to Interior Secretary Harold Ickes urging him not to drop his subscription to the *Bulletin*. Ickes, an old-line Theodore Roosevelt Progressive, responded in kind with an invitation that Marsh rarely got from Cabinet members, Democrats or Republicans: "I hope some time you will come in and we can talk it all over, whether we agree or not."[23])

At a mid-April conference of political scientists, Marsh criticized the administration for seemingly greater interest in protecting property than people.[24] At the five-week anniversary of the new administration, the PL found little that it liked in the various legislative proposals so far requested by the president and passed by Congress. The banking moratorium bill? "The Administration miffed [*sic*] the opportunity to make banking and the creation of credit a Federal non-profit-monopoly." The bill to cut government spending? Cutting wages of federal employees "is thoroughly unjustified." The Civilian Conservation Corps? It "may be very helpful to a limited number, but the military control involved is not appropriate." The farm bill? A "precarious experiment" that "comes as near being an octopus farm price regulation bill as anything well could be." The securities and stocks regulation bill? It "is a cheerful gesture at reassuring owners of stolen mules by locking the stable door after the mules have been taken out." The only positive comment related to the relief bill, which vaguely implemented what the PL had been urging since the crash, praising the rumor that Harry Hopkins would be its administrator. "He is well qualified for this task, by sympathy and training."[25]

In early May, Dewey drew a line in the sand. Federal spending should be financed by increasing taxes on the wealthy, not by deficit spending (1986, 259–260). He wrote the President saying that property values should be permitted to drop and inflationary pressures to be avoided (1986, 265–266). All this may have been good economics and justified by the principles of public finance, but it was a losing political argument. Clearly, Dewey and Marsh had decided that they needed the PL to stay true to its progressive policy principles, Democratic president or not. They were to be consistent critics of FDR from the left. This was authentic reflection of their policy agenda since founding the PL. But it was also, more subtly, recognizing that in politics the squeaky wheel gets the grease. This was especially true of FDR, a politician and compromiser par excellence, who could be expected to calibrate his positions by carefully balancing the predictable criticism from the right with those of Dewey and like-minded people on the Left. In that sense, Dewey and Marsh were trying to prevent Roosevelt from drifting too far to the right in a natural political inclination to reduce criticism and controversy. They were anchoring him in the middle, in a vaguely but softly liberal political stance. Not satisfactory, but better than Hoover.

Now that the PL had broken with FDR, Marsh's congressional appearances were much more pointedly critical of the administration, along with the rest of the economic establishment. His testimony on behalf of the PL at a hearing on emergency railroad legislation was typical of his approach to lobbying. He was alternately funny, self-effacing, quick to reply, ideological, detail oriented, easy to quote, well prepared, and had carefully read the bill. No dilettante was he.

The issue at hand was whether the railroads would be given some special privileges to help improve their financial status, which had suffered due to the economic slowdown. Marsh took several swipes at the proposal in the context of Roosevelt's two-month-old New Deal. He said of the bill: "This is not part of a new deal when you do it at the expense" of stakeholders other than stockholders, such as employees. Further, in a highly quotable line, he said the bill "is not a new deal or part of a new deal; it is just a new steal." He also quipped and got a laugh when he said he was appearing against the bill even though for his retirement, he owned a small amount of railroad stocks. "I regret that I have appeared against my own financial interests. [Laughter.]"

Marsh explained that the PL opposed the bill on ideological grounds, namely that the right way to go would be the PL's objective of public ownership of utilities and monopolies. Once he got that on the record, the senators politely interrupted and asked that he focus on the bill at hand. Now he turned to the economics of the railroad companies, providing facts and researched background information that contradicted the narrative the railroads were trying to create to justify the bill. He provided an independently reported balance sheet of the financial condition of the railroads and asked to have that data included in the hearing record. Then, the members asked him if he had any specific comments on the bill itself? Yes, he did. Indicating how carefully he had read it, he suggested the need for several highly detailed amendments to clarify language and close loopholes. One of the members tried to pin him down on a specific (an authorized interest rate); he repeatedly declined to get caught in the political trap of endorsing any specific number.

It was a masterful performance and quintessential Marsh; an authentic political, policy, and publicity tour de force (US Senate 1933e, 205–210). (He was quoted in the *New York Times* coverage of the hearing.[26]) What is especially impressive is that this was a *routine* appearance for him; one of the more than *150 times* he testified at congressional hearings on behalf of the PL from 1928 to 1950. Most of those appearances were as sharp as this one.[27] He could hold forth on dozens of disparate policy areas and speak to them with sharp analytic observations. (A few weeks later, the House held its hearing on that bill. Notwithstanding his request to testify, the committee chair maneuvered to prevent Marsh from appearing [US House 1933a, 230]. This may have, in part, reflected the Democratic majority's newly found discomfort at being the targets of the PL's barbs, even though they had enjoyed the preceding years when Marsh aimed his criticism at Republicans. The bill reached FDR and he signed it [Alter 2006, 305].)

Throughout the spring of those One Hundred Days, Marsh continued spoiling the party by testifying from the left with criticisms of New Deal bills. He raised questions about the constitutionality of a minimum wage bill and of legislating about wages without counterpart controls on other aspects of the economy, such as prices and rents (US House 1933b, 979–980). He opposed an omnibus industrial recovery bill (which authorized creating the NRA) because it had only been released two days earlier, delegated too much power and discretion to the president, permitted Congress to avoid taking sides on dozens of thorny economic issues, and, most importantly from the PL's legislative agenda, did nothing to redistribute incomes, tax corporations, close loopholes or increase taxes on the wealthy. Marsh's quotable quotes from his testimony were that the bill created a "dictatorship" and "the Lord have mercy on you if you do not do something for the American people in addition to simply passing the buck to the President. Make it mandatory, and tell him what to do" (US House 1933c, 156). The AP coverage picked up the latter quote.[28] When the bill reached the Senate, he criticized the incipient NRA as a "morganatic or common-law marriage of the Federal Government and trade associations" (US Senate 1933f, 315–329). The bill did not bode well for the PL's goal of taxing the wealthy and opposing taxes that were regressive. Marsh also pointed out the bill would have an unintended consequence. Because of its tax treatment of partnerships, successful businessmen could evade taxes simply by restructuring their corporations into partnerships. Conservative Senator Harry Byrd (D-VA) seemed startled and wholly unaware of it when Marsh pointed that out. Marsh submitted a six-page amendment, drafted at his request by Joseph Wechsler, a CPA in New York, to close some of the loopholes in the bill as well as shift to a more progressive tax burden. The document's central argument was that the conventional wisdom was wrong that it would be unconstitutional for Congress to tax the tax-exempt bonds issued by state and local governments. If the PL and Wechsler were right, then the (better off) buyers of such bonds would contribute to the federal government's tax revenues, thus shifting the tax burden. Given how much Wall Street banks and higher income people had a stake in continuing this tax break, the idea went nowhere.

Foreign and Military Policy

Somewhat lost to history were Roosevelt's foreign policy activities in his first term, which usually reflected his domestic economic policies. The PL disparaged the initial meetings the president was having with foreign representatives, but excluding the SU. After the 1917 revolution, the United States had not diplomatically recognized the Communist government. American politicians did not want to appear to be soft on communism and atheism. (FDR finally did at the end of 1933.) Discussions about international matters without the USSR, Marsh bitingly wrote, was "a good example of Hamlet with Hamlet left out."[29]

Other foreign policy matters were highlighted by the Lobby. In April 1933, it called attention to the maltreatment and oppression of Jews in Germany. These "cruel and vicious" actions may have troubled Americans, but the PL complained that the US government merely took "cognizance" of them and little more. Marsh speculated that the State Department would not protest these actions vociferously to Hitler's government because that might give him an excuse to cease payment of international debts.[30] Marsh protested to Secretary of State Cordell Hull after Congress approved a bill requested by the department to restrict release of secret information. He felt this was a threat to what today is called freedom of information and transparency.[31] At the request of the PL, Senator Wheeler introduced a resolution calling for an investigation of foreign concessions to American corporations.[32] (It did not pass.) Marsh criticized the administration's low priority for international cooperation, prompting a tart response by USDA Secretary Henry A. Wallace.[33]

By the end of the Hundred Days, Dewey summed up the primary rationale for the PL's disenchantment with Roosevelt. The policies of the New Deal were a "superficial treatment" of systemic economic problems. Emergency solutions, by definition, would not be long-lasting. Also, he was concerned about the geo-centrism of the New Deal, with policies "settled on a narrow nationalistic basis. Every major economic issue of every nation is international," he wrote (1986, 261–264). Marsh topped that with even more aggressive criticism at a labor conference on Long Island, New York. The president's policies were "futile," and that the NRA-style approach would hand over power to business, "if corporations will promise to divide their swag with the workers." Regarding foreign relations, FDR's policies were "hypocritical," because "we tell Europe not to arm, to submit Ghandi-like [*sic*] to exploitation by American citizens. We call this 'ending isolation.' "[34]

During this period, the PL continued its aggressive publicity efforts. On May, it convened a panel of speakers to discuss economic policies on debt, interest and taxation. Speakers were not ideologically or politically balanced, instead all were critical of FDR's policies so far. The event was covered live on a national radio network, got newspaper coverage and the transcript was inserted in the *Congressional Record*.[35]

Marsh was on the hustings for two weeks to whip up support for the PL's domestic economic policy proposals. He spoke in fourteen cities, with the purpose of organizing local groups to support the PL's legislative program.[36] For example, in Atlanta he called for funding relief through a redistribution of incomes. This would entail "reducing exorbitant standards of living on a few scores of thousands, and increasing the living standards of many millions of families." Excessive (and unspent) wealth should be "commandeered through taxation to make possible increased consumption." The audience consisted mainly of social workers and at the end of his appearance they organized a committee to press local Congressmen for the PL's goals.[37] At a talk in New York City, he claimed that the Lobby was in the process of organizing such committees in all 48 state capitals as well as 160 other cities.[38] (There is no archival documentation of this claim.)

Finally, early in the fall, Marsh was one of the speakers at an international ecumenical conference in Chicago. Summing up the PL's view of the Hundred Days, Marsh pointedly enumerated the failures of the New Deal, including that "labour [*sic*] has been coded [i.e., with NRA codes], but not employed. Farmers have been given pep but not made prosperous. We have learned we can't drink ourselves into prosperity" by repealing Prohibition (Weller 1935, 240). Like a party pooper at a party, Dewey and Marsh did not see much to celebrate with the results of the Democratic sweep in the November 1932 elections.

To the Midpoint of FDR's First Term, Mid-1933 to the November 1934 Elections

After the crisis of the first hundred days and the near-miraculous stabilizing of the economy, the normalcy of politics and ideology gradually resumed. Contrary to the romantic myth of FDR's New Deal as a liberal's fantasy come true, Roosevelt was a cautious politician. And in American politics, caution almost always meant being conservative about actions and conservative in ideology. This accurately captures the first half of FDR's initial term and, in a more limited extent, to his budget balancing effort up to 1938 (Zelizer 2012, chap. 6). The NRA emerged as a kind of freeze-in-place approach to economics, of industry-wide production codes to bring consumption in line with supply; namely by limiting production in all sectors, not just agriculture. It was a corporatist and syndicalist approach to controlling the economy down to the smallest details. While depicted as voluntary, it was a de facto centralized command-and-control model of the political economy.

Economic Policy

The People's Lobby had organized the Joint Committee on Unemployment in 1931 as an umbrella group to press for congressional passage of unemployment related legislation (Chap. 3). Notwithstanding all the new laws passed during the Hundred Days and policies initiated by the Roosevelt administration, the members of the Joint Committee were still unhappy. For starters, in September 1933, as chairman of the joint committee, Dewey sent a letter to Harry Hopkins, head of the Federal Emergency Relief Administration, of the inadequacy of the relief funding up to now and the excessive dominance of employers on the official local relief bodies handling the federal funding to the detriment of the unemployed (1986, 271–272).

In December, the Joint Committee held a full day of panels in Washington on the economic situation and to decide on an agenda for the future (or, impliedly, to dissolve). Speakers were from labor, religion, academe and nonprofits (the latter including Leon Henderson, then with the Russell Sage Foundation). Dewey gave a talk on "Government and Children." He summarized information on the state of public education since the crash. Total spending on public schools had dropped significantly, teachers were being laid off, and the secondary curricular topics of art, music and phys ed were being discontinued, as well as health services to students. (These were nearly identical to funding of public education in the years after the 2008 market crash.) In some places, the school year was shortened by one or two months to cut spending. Dewey called for a significant increase in *federal* spending to rescue the schoolchildren who were suffering. Any federal funding of public education was a controversial subject in Washington then (and to this day, with conservative calls to abolish the US Department of Education). Directly linking the economic emergency with his long-standing views on education and its role in democratic citizenship, Dewey sought funding to cover educational costs, food, and care "to maintain future citizens in sound body and mind."[39]

At the end of the day, the members of the Joint Committee approved staying in existence notwithstanding the record of Congress and President Roosevelt in 1933. They adopted a comprehensive platform of policy proposals dealing with unemployment and such related issues as writing down debt, child labor, construction, and taxes on the rich. This agenda was virtually the same as the PL's. Significantly, the updated platform began with the statement that "no marked improvement in economic conditions has been recorded during the nine months since the new Administration took office."[40] Some other Democrats, labor union leaders, and liberals may be satisfied with FDR or afraid to criticize him publicly, but not this group. They were not trimming their sails for a Democratic president, no matter how much he had accomplished already.

In early February 1934, a delegation of the Joint Committee met at the White House with presidential aide Marvin McIntyre to present its proposals for presidential endorsement. He only promised to convey the material to FDR.[41] Marsh testified at three congressional hearings on behalf of the Joint Committee: in favor of increasing taxes on the rich to help fund unemployment and relief programs (US House 1933–34, 327–342) and to urge that the federal government take over direct marketing of farm products as a way of helping both farmers and consumers (US Senate 1934b, 37–49; US House 1934a, 30–34).[42] Trying to get more support for the latter idea, the Lobby publicly called on the NRA's Consumers Advisory Board to endorse the idea because of the benefits it would have for all consumers.[43]

In April, with the administration now in office more than a year, the Joint Committee held a public session with leading progressive legislators to continue pushing for more vigorous unemployment initiatives. Dewey said the main constraint on improving employment was that so much of the national income was in the unearned category (as opposed to wages), specifically revenue from property, such as dividends on stocks, rent on real property, and interest on loans. This meant the propertied classes were receiving a percentage of the national income "out of all proportion" while wage-earning classes (including farmers) "do not get much more than a subsistence income on the average." To Dewey, a major reason for the excess in productive capacity in the economy and high unemployment was because the propertied class could not realistically expend all their income on consumption and instead were saving it. If income were redistributed, then the wage earners would regain their "mass purchasing power." They would be able to afford consumer goods, thus stimulating the economy and increasing employment. Dewey gently warned that such economic redistribution was necessary; otherwise "radical change in the whole system" would be necessary.[44] He was showing himself to be a social democrat, strongly preferring to create a more fair social system through constitutional and democratic means than those more radical than he who were calling for revolution and dictatorship. Sensing the passing of the crisis mood of the nation and openness for new reform ideas, the PL and Joint Committee feared that, essentially, this was it. No more major economic initiatives. By staying active and visible, they did not want to let such an assumption go unchallenged.

Separate from its leadership role on the Joint Committee on Unemployment, the PL also focused on advocating for several other policy items related to the economy. In particular, Dewey and Marsh decided to promote public ownership of natural monopolies, utilities, and other strategically important economic functions as a way to improve the economy, especially as it would lower costs to consumers. They had pushed for this goal since laying out their original policy agenda in 1929 (Chap. 3). However, there was a particular tactical benefit to pushing it now. FDR *liked* public power, first as governor and now as president. In May 1933, he had proposed creating the Tennessee Valley Authority (TVA), partly for lower-priced power (Alter 2006, 84, 287–288). Dewey and Marsh hoped that promoting a mere expansion of the president's already existing support might be like pushing on an open door. In modern marketing parlance, they were aiming for a brand extension. Marsh organized two public symposia in Washington in February and May 1934.[45] Speakers reviewed the possibility of further public ownership of electrical generation, now a relatively noncontroversial topic to New Dealers and Democrats. Then the topics moved to public ownership of much more controversial activities, including railroads, banks, coal mines, and natural resources. While those areas of endeavor might be relatively new in the traditions of the American political economy, the PL could rightly argue that the precedent of government-owned dams generating power had already been firmly set, so they were merely applying the identical principle to related and comparable activities.

Dewey set the tone at the February session. He made the case that extending public ownership to some natural monopolies and other key areas made sense economically as well as historically, based on the recent record of performance of private companies in those areas. But Dewey also framed the case in political terms. He argued that the New Deal policies enacted up to now were "patchwork measures" and needed a more comprehensive approach and organization. He suggested the economic problems had not been solved in any systemic and permanent way:

> The one great question before the American public is whether it is going to trust to various measures of hocus-pocus to ensure against an even more tragic return of our present abominable and unnecessary calamities, or whether it has the intelligence and courage to take over the basic agencies of public welfare and manage them for the welfare of all the people. (1986, 285–286)

Two senators spoke at the May 1934 event. Bronson Cutting (R-NM) called for nationalizing the banking system and promised to introduce a bill doing that. Gerald Nye (R-SD) criticized the private capital markets which "by manipulation, can make existing money and banking credit create fictitious values upon which a return [on investment] must be paid by the American consumer such as creates profit on value that does not exist."[46] He said that the benefits of the pre-1929 crash went disproportionately to investment bankers and bonuses to corporate leaders (also a familiar refrain after the Wall Street crash in 2008). Marsh arranged for newspaper coverage before and after the sessions as well as a live national radio network broadcast from both events.[47] Trying to keep the idea of expanding public ownership beyond the TVA alive, in the summer of 1934, the PL sent questionnaires to all members of Congress running for reelection for their views on the subject.[48]

In terms of the administration's overall economic program, Dewey and Marsh continued criticizing Roosevelt from the left and the administration continued its polite and noncommittal responses. In November 1933, Dewey wrote the president criticizing his agricultural policies. Howe thanked him for the letter.[49] The next month, Dewey sent the White House a letter urging much more forceful policies for the benefit of wage earners over property owners. He described the administration's policies as positive but largely "one-sided" (1986, 277–279). Howe thanked him again.[50]

(Not all administration officials were as restrained. The director of housing wrote Marsh that "in view of your assumption that the honesty of the Administration is open to question, further explanation or argument is hardly possible or necessary."[51] On the other hand, another middle-level official was friendlier than Howe. The Interior Department's top lawyer, in reaction to a letter from Marsh, replied that he would "like very much to have a personal discussion with you" and invited him to make an appointment for a meeting "sometime next week."[52])

The Lobby's public criticisms of policies enacted to promote economic recovery were sometimes quite pointed and, either explicitly or implicitly, criticized the President. In September 1933, Dewey said that the program adopted so far "failed to recognize that the basic causes of our depression are the maldistribution of the national income between various classes, especially the inequitable distribution of the national income between property and producers." Furthermore, he feared that inflation would be triggered by some of the extant programs and that inflation was "the most volatile of all nostrums, and as difficult to control as escaping gas" (1986, 276–268).[53] On New Year's Eve, Dewey said that Congress needed to become more active in overseeing and refining economic policy. In particular, it needed to evaluate the impact (or lack of) of the "legislation known as the 'New Deal' so that it may know what is needed to prevent disaster." Congress needed to decide "the real and possible benefits of the measures the President has sponsored," given that payrolls were lower than a year earlier.[54] Marsh used sharper language, saying that after a year of the new administration "the same old set of forty thieves are in charge of the nation."[55]

Besides these general criticisms, the PL also zeroed in on problems with specific New Deal programs. It criticized the Agriculture Adjustment Administration (AAA) because, said Dewey, it "mulets consumers to increase unearned profits of farm-land speculators."[56] The Lobby maintained a running attack on the NRA, for example describing "the auto-intoxication of their belief that humanity can lift itself by its bootstraps."[57] Dewey asked FDR to refuse the request by the head of the NRA to abolish its review board and Marsh was one of the NRA's most critical voices at a congressional hearing.[58] They described the NRA and AAA as "childish efforts artificially to support an impossible capital structure."[59] Still, Dewey cheered when the Supreme Court ruled in *favor* of NRA-style price fixing of milk by New York State (Shesol 2010, 70–72). He said the decision to approve government intervention in the economy as constitutional "answers many fictitious objections to the program of the People's Lobby."[60]

In an effort to avoid an impression of negativism and of coming across merely as kibitzers and critics, the PL released in the spring of 1934 a position paper analyzing the state of the economy and enumerating specific policy actions it was *for*. It liked the principle of "the war on poverty." But in lieu of FDR's policies, it suggested a "profits tax and a tax on liquid assets of corporations," as well as a gifts tax and an estate tax. The key, from the ideological perspective of Dewey and Marsh, was to reformulate the federal revenue system so that it would be based on the principle of the ability to pay, including repealing all consumption taxes, which were inherently regressive. The Lobby's economic plan was to capture unearned and unused capital held by owners of property and, through taxation and spending, redistribute it to the purchasers of goods and services and the unemployed.[61] The Lobby's critique of FDR's relatively conservative economic and tax policies during the first New Deal was on point. His proposals did not seek to overturn the built-in regressivity of the existing tax code (Thorndike 2013).

Marsh continued promoting the Lobby's views on the economic recovery efforts on Capitol Hill. He testified at four congressional hearings in March and two in May 1934. On behalf of the PL, he supported additional regulation of the stock market because "stock exchanges are the inevitable product of an economic system under which rewards go to legalized robbery and honest labor, like virtue, is its own punishment" (US Senate 1934c, 7148). He criticized a revenue bill for being a "war on poverty by taxing poverty" instead of the rich (US Senate 1934d, 15). As an indication of the relatively unusual perspective Marsh brought to such hearings and the seldom-cited data on which he based his testimony, in a floor debate a sympathetic senator quoted Marsh's statistics as a reliable source to buttress his own position.[62] Marsh criticized a tariff bill because it delegated too much discretion to the president, was based on the premise of protecting certain special sectors of the economy, and generally raised prices for the average American. Members of the committee were exasperated that he called for "fundamental changes in our economic life in America," a broader subject than the bill (and therefore not before the committee) and that he was so negative about everything Congress and the president were doing (US House 1934b, 431–437). He criticized a bill to guarantee housing bonds as protecting the interests of creditors over debtors (US House 1934c, 131–141). This theme, too, was echoed in the post-2008 crash, when some argued that federal bailouts protected creditors by making them whole, such as in the AIG bailout, instead of forcing creditors to take a haircut.

At another hearing, Marsh called the premise of a National Housing Act "absolute stupidity" if it focused only on guaranteeing housing bonds without at all controlling the costs of home building (US Senate 1934e, 144). This would have the effect of incentivizing providers of home construction materials to keep raising prices on the assumption that no matter how much housing costs increased, the federal government would continue issuing guaranteed bonds at those inflated prices. Such ill thought-out actions would be "a farce," he said.[63] In contrast to his perceived knee-jerk negativity, in May 1934, he testified in support of additional spending for public works (but could not resist a swipe against more spending on armaments) because "things are worse in America today than on March 4, 1933" (US Senate 1934f, 293). Congress would be "committing moral treason" if it adjourned without passing further stimulus legislation and funding.[64] In all, those six instances of congressional testimony in a three-month period cemented the PL's reputation as a persistent, but well-informed and detail-oriented, critic of FDR's New Deal from the nonrevolutionary left. To Marsh and Dewey, the glass was almost always half-empty and needed to be filled further based on their progressive ideological leanings. They focused on what was still needed instead of what had been accomplished.

Other Domestic Issues

The economic crisis was certainly the 800-pound gorilla dominating Washington in 1933–34. But, other, more routine domestic policy issues were also being considered. At one point, trying to explain the mission of the organization, Dewey wrote that "the People's Lobby represents the public welfare" (1986, 275–276). It was trying to be the voice of the relatively unorganized public, which often had no professional representation in Washington compared to special interest groups. Consumer protection was one of those areas of an imbalance between economic interests and the consumers-at-large. This continued to be one of the priorities of the PL.

To pursue this mission, for example, Marsh gave a fiery testimony at a hearing on regulating food, drugs, and cosmetics. He minced no words in telling the chief sponsor of the bill to his face that the bill "is in large measure a swindle" because it gave the impression of consumer protection but in reality provided little strict regulation and many protections from liability to business. Legislators who supported the bill were "murderers on the installment plan," giving "practically an immunity bath" to manufacturers. Not just legislators, but also Roosevelt, who, said Marsh, "lost his nerve in fighting these big interests." Having given the bill a close read, he noted that the federal government would only be able to declare a product a "public nuisance" if there were "repetitious" violations of the law. This was, in his view, condoning multiple initial violations without any consequences, and, by the way, how many violations needed to occur to be repetitious? The author of the bill sitting at the committee table, of course, took umbrage at Marsh's attacks and tried to defend his bill. Comically, at one point in the hearing, they reversed roles, with Marsh intensely interrogating the defensive senator in a series of rapid-fire and pointed questions (US Senate 1934g, 475–490). Another indication of the Lobby's credibility and record as a voice for the consumer occurred when, during this period, a coalition of consumer groups appointed Marsh to be its legislative lobbyist and requested him to speak for all of them on Capitol Hill.[65]

Foreign and Military Policy

Generally during his first term, Roosevelt wanted to put foreign affairs on the back burner. Brands describes FDR as having a political and policy "allergy" to foreign policy (2008, 479). The Lobby tried to prevent that from happening or, at least, to make the president pay the political price for doing so. Marsh traveled to London for a long-planned international economic conference and submitted to the US delegation the PL's program for international cooperation.[66] However, the president, without warning, issued a statement in July that essentially torpedoed any chance of success (Alter 2006, 307–308). The Lobby criticized him severely for doing that.[67]

Dewey and Marsh also tried their best to prevent the right from being successful in its efforts to treat the SU as a pariah nation. For example, Marsh visited Russia in 1934 and then criticized the isolationist and red-baiting attacks on it. Russia, he said, had the right "to try out its experiments in achieving the greatest good of the greatest number of their people."[68] This stance, awkwardly, put the PL in the position of sometimes defending or even praising FDR and his administration. In April 1934, Marsh complimented Secretary of State Hull for his softer line on dealing with the Soviets.[69] On another occasion, Marsh ridiculed attacks on FDR by red-baiting conservative members of Congress. They were, he said, "insulting Russia, through an investigation of the fool charge there is anything Communistic in this Administration."[70]

The PL also continued its role as a peace group relating both to international and domestic policy. It was intent on promoting antiwar initiatives, opposed increases in armaments, was suspicious of weapons merchants, and was anticolonialist and anti-imperialist. It tried to call attention to the increasingly militaristic rhetoric and policies abroad, especially in Hitler's Germany and Mussolini's Italy.[71] The PL called for a Pan American conference to promote arbitration of international disputes,[72] opposed intervention in Cuban politics,[73] supported a congressional investigation of the arms industry,[74] and opposed larger appropriations for the US Navy.[75] In early 1934, the Lobby's Board of Directors passed a motion praising FDR for his policy of nonintervention in the affairs of other nations and praising Secretary Hull's promotion of freer trade and lower tariffs.[76]

These activities could give the impression that Dewey and Marsh never met a peace cause they didn't like. Not true. They wanted to retain a reasonable, if idealistic, stance and also wanted to be careful not to be ensnared in what later might be viewed as a Communist-controlled coalition. So, for example, a few of the PL's leadership participated in an antiwar congress in New York in the fall of 1933, attended by 2,000 people. However, by the conclusion of the conference, they decided "that because of some items included in the program adopted, [the PL] was compelled to notify the [Anti-War] Congress that it could not endorse that program."[77] Even socialist-leaning idealists had their limits.

Heading into the 1934 mid-term elections, the Lobby discerned that the administration's policies would "almost certainly be toward the right." Looking back over FDR's actions since assuming office, the PL discouragingly concluded that the administration was "quite definitely committed to oppose any form of socialization."[78] Nonetheless, Dewey and Marsh were optimists, hoping that the next battle might be won. They were not giving up on the future direction of the country. The fight over what economic philosophy should govern anti-Depression policies was far from over. From the PL's perspective, its mission was to provide a comprehensive "substitute" for the administration's seemingly conservative policy agenda.[79] The Democratic Party's way—whether the White House or Capitol Hill—was not adequately liberal. Therefore, it was up to the Lobby to show policy makers that there were constructive alternatives from the non-Communist left that deserved to be considered in the competition for ideas within Washington's policy machinery.[80] There were more choices than merely the Republican and Democratic platforms.

Chapter 6

Policy Advocacy during FDR's First Term

Criticizing the Second New Deal as Too Conservative, 1935–1936

For purposes of reexperiencing history as it was unfolding, it is important to remember that FDR's wildly successful and historic political career as president was unknown during his first term. All that lay in the future. During these first few years of his presidency, no one knew if he really was a good politician or a good president; certainly no one knew if he would be reelected in 1936 (let alone be elected to third and fourth terms). With the economy only mending slowly and some of the early New Deal programs (especially the NRA) overturned by the Supreme Court, was that *it*? Did he have any other ideas to offer? And would Congress approve them? If adopted, would they work? Even if they worked, would the country still be experiencing an economy that was mending so slowly that the voters would lose patience and try the other guys? Maybe FDR would be a failed one-term president like Hoover and Taft (both Republicans) or Carter and Cleveland (both Democrats)?[1]

Similarly, a comparison of FDR's first term to Obama's is compelling. In the first half of Obama's first term (2009–10), he was very successful in passing major legislation relating to rebuilding the economy, including stimulus spending, tax cuts, and health care reform. The midterm elections in 2010 changed the political landscape, with the majorityship in the House shifting from Democratic to Republican. Then the second half of Obama's term was less productive in terms of policy, and the economy was repairing very slowly. No one knew if he would be reelected in 2012.

In the fall of 1934 (but before the elections), Dewey announced that the PL had adopted a new economic policy agenda for the upcoming 74th Congress (to be elected in November) and covering the second half of FDR's term. At that time, of course, no one knew what the results of the midterm elections would be. As a rough rule of thumb in American politics, generally the party of the president does poorly in these elections. Dewey and Marsh at this point did not know if that would hold true in 1934, and if so, to the point of flipping the majorityship in each house to the Republicans. By releasing their platform and program before the election, just as they had done in the fall of 1932 (Chap. 3), Dewey and Marsh were demonstrating their consistency and credibility. In most of political Washington, where one stood depended on where one sat. Not so for the PL. It did not trim its sails for Democrats or increase its stridency when Republicans were in power.

Economic Policy

Dewey announced that the central theme and slogan of the PL's new economic program was to balance consumption and production by "elimination of profits" (1986, 289–290).[2] Here was, at its clearest, a central tenet of the political ideology Dewey and Marsh brought to the People's Lobby, whether either of them openly self-identified as a socialist (or Communist) or not. To convey how central this principle was to the work of the lobby, it was incorporated into the masthead of the monthly publication for all issues through to the end of 1935: "To balance consumption and production by eliminating profit."[3] No one could miss it. The goal of eliminating profit was the equivalent of ending a market-based capitalist system. In reality, the specific elements of the new program were little changed from the preceding policy agenda: taxing the rich, public ownership (which the PL rather opaquely called "socialization"), government marketing of agricultural goods, and international cooperation "through increased freedom of exchange and allocation of natural resources."[4] One topic to which the PL had dedicated major efforts ever since the crash in 1929 had been the establishment of a comprehensive unemployment insurance program largely funded by the federal government. However, in its new program, unemployment insurance had completely been deleted from the agenda. This reflected the change in Dewey and Marsh's thinking. With their increased focus on eliminating profit, including government socialization of all basic industries, banking, natural resources, and utilities, they did not expect much need for unemployment insurance (US House 1935a, 478; 1935b, 155). Government would employ everyone who wanted a job.

As it turned out, the 1934 election was a smashing success for Democrats. The voters did not agree with the message of Republican candidates that the Democrats had had two years of control in Washington and clearly had not solved the economic problems of the Great Depression. Instead, going against the tradition of midterm elections, the voters *increased* the Democratic majorities in each house. The Senate went from 59 to 36 to 69 to 25 and the House from 313 to 117 to 322 to 103.[5]

Having announced in 1934 its policy agenda for the 74th Congress, the PL engaged in vigorous lobbying in 1935–36 to promote these goals. As before, they did so mostly through congressional testimony and news media publicity. Dewey continued to be the public face and the front office man of the Lobby. Generally, statements made in his name were usually accorded more importance and significance than those by the PL (without any proper names) or by Marsh. After the election, in December 1934, Dewey traveled to Washington to be the headline speaker at a PL conference that was also broadcast live on a national radio network. He praised the administration for successfully persuading Congress to pass legislation creating the TVA as "the most promising enterprise of the New Deal" but noted that many of its benefits, such as cheaper power, would "be absorbed by those who monopolize the land and the machines that are made out of the products of the land." That led to his overall judgment about FDR's policies as being "compromised, prejudiced, yes, nullified by private monopolization of opportunity." From there, Dewey segued to the theme he and Marsh had decided on for the PL for the year, namely the elimination of profit. Applying the principles of his writings about society as well as his socialist leanings, Dewey focused on the need to implement them concretely: "Why not go to the root of the matter and give the unemployed an opportunity to work by socialization of the land? Why not pay the bills that are mounting by social appropriation of the values socially created?"[6] At the end of the year, Dewey gave another talk at a Lobby luncheon in Washington (also broadcast) on "Government and Youth."[7]

Throughout 1935, Dewey engaged in activities to advocate for the goals of the PL by using his prominence to increase attention to its policy agenda, mostly relating to economics. He wrote about the Lobby's economic goal of eliminating profit, but chastised some of those who agreed with that goal who were "over zealous." Members of that camp "are prone to deplore any reliance on taxation as part of the program of socialization. This I believe to be a mistake." Dewey argued that a tax system based on the ability to pay was one of the effective ways to promote a more fair society, not only because the wealthy paid more, but also because such taxation could be used as revenue to cover welfare programs instead of deficit spending. He also disagreed with other socialists by acknowledging openly that any government expropriation of private property "cannot be made without some payment to owners." The key was that the money raised by the government for such compensation come from progressive taxation; otherwise, the working class would be directly paying out of its own pocket for the costs of nationalization. Dewey concluded by blasting business for "inhuman and futile opposition to the necessary use of Federal funds for relief."[8]

Other Dewey activities in 1935–36 to promote the PL's economic platform included a letter to each of the forty-eight governors urging state laws to promote housing (public or otherwise) and consideration of the Henry George idea of taxing only land, not property on it.[9] He wrote Secretary of State Hull complimenting him on a speech supporting lower tariffs and other actions to increase international trade. Dewey praised the stance (which did not necessarily reflect FDR's consistent views) as "removing some of the causes which engender rivalry and conflict between nations." Hull replied warmly.[10] For Dewey, improving the economy through international trade also meshed nicely with his internationalist political ideology. Reflecting that, he gave a radio talk promoting international cooperation, including the importance of trade.[11]

(While not directly linked to the PL, Dewey gave an address in mid-1935 to the American Philosophical Association. He explained what he thought liberal social philosophy stood for in the current economic circumstances. In particular, he denounced those who used ends to justify means, for example, Communists and fascists justifying violence to accomplish a revolution. This would always fail in the long run, he said. Only intelligent action could have a long-lasting impact on achieving social reforms, even relatively radical ones. By these comments, Dewey was explaining his work since 1928 in the PL, calling for major social reforms, but through peaceful democratic means.[12])

In addition to Dewey, other officers of the Lobby also played public roles as advocates and lobbyists for the Lobby's agenda, especially in the area of economic policy. John H. Gray, the PL treasurer, was a past president of the American Economic Association. He testified at a congressional committee considering a revenue bill and urged adoption of "an entirely new tax plan headed by a Federal land tax."[13] Gray proposed higher taxes on speculators and the wealthy and opposed the commonly mentioned suggestions of regressive consumption taxes to finance federal relief programs (US House 1936a, 574–579). Gray also spoke at several of the PL's public events on the inadequacies of current economic policy and against the popular Townsend plan (which proposed a social security system, but without a sound actuarial basis [Alter 2006, 310–311]).[14]

Colston Warne, a professor of economics at Amherst (later one of Dewey's successors as PL president), wrote several essays on the economic platform of the Lobby and spoke at a PL event on the radio.[15] (Earlier in FDR's first term, he had testified on behalf of the Lobby at a congressional hearing [US House 1933–34, 342–349].) Gardner Jackson, also an officer of the PL, discussed problems of agricultural economics and tenant farmers in the South and spoke on behalf of the PL at a May Day rally in Washington.[16] (Marsh and Jackson were also hoping to create a major public and legislative campaign on behalf of sharecroppers. In February 1936, the PL hosted a private dinner with legislators interested in this cause to develop a strategy for an effort to improve conditions [Auerbach 1966, 45–46].[17] However, this initiative never blossomed in the way they had hoped.) In March and April 1936, Warne and Jackson accompanied Marsh on a one-week speaking tour to promote the PL's economic program. They had nine events in six cities, including Pittsburgh, Cleveland, Detroit, and Chicago.[18]

Similarly, other activists contributed to PL's efforts to promote and enact its economic program. In early 1936, the Lobby published a ten-page position paper arguing that government monopolies *were* constitutional. It was written for the Lobby by Irving Brant, who was the chief editorial writer for the liberal *St. Louis Star-Times*. Brant made historical arguments about the Constitution and the writings of the framers to demonstrate that the kinds of monopolies the PL advocated would withstand challenges to their constitutionality. No constitutional amendments would be required for the socialization of the major elements of the political economy.[19] A congressional ally of the PL liked it so much that he inserted it in the *Congressional Record*, thereby expanding its reach and ease of access.[20] As briefly mentioned in the preceding chapter, Joseph Wechsler, a CPA, compiled some statistical information about corporate taxation that Marsh had used in his testimonies to document his assertions about taxing business, especially cash reserves (US House 1933c, 156; US Senate 1933f, 318).

These public efforts by Dewey and others to promote the economic policies of the Lobby demonstrate that the PL was not at this time an organization with a misleading letterhead camouflaging that it was a one-person operation. Marsh was not a one-man band. No one could put words in the mouths of these intelligent activists if they disagreed with the statements they contained. That said, Marsh continued to be the workhorse of the Lobby in promoting its economic policy platform. As earlier, he did most of the heavy lifting in terms of lobbying Congress directly and indirectly through press relations and public events. Between January 1935 and the November 1936 elections, Congress was in session for about fourteen months. Marsh testified about seventeen times, thus more frequently than once a month.

For his congressional testimonies, Marsh had a knack for uncovering facts that almost always seemed to clash with conventional wisdom. He was a careful researcher, successful in tracking down obscure but reliable statistics that contradicted the morning line of whatever legislators were comfortable with and assumed was true. Through his many congressional appearances, he stitched together a nearly comprehensive counternarrative to interpret current developments. Demonstrating the credibility Marsh had generally garnered in spite of his argumentativeness, in at least one case, a congressman credited the PL with the statistics he was using in a floor debate.[21] Another time, a senator quoted from the PL's position on a bill as contributing to the case he was making on a bill being debated.[22]

Marsh was an aggressive, even provocative, presence at hearings on the Hill. He testified against the NRA for undermining antitrust principles (US Senate 1935a, 1401–1405).[23] The next month, on May 27, 1935, the Supreme Court issued its *Schechter* decision, essentially invalidating the legal and constitutional underpinnings of the NRA (Shesol 2010, 134–143). Marsh adapted to the new legal situation quickly. Testifying against a regressive taxation bill, he criticized the court's decision as being covertly intended to *help* the administration politically to get out from under a policy that was clearly failing. This tossed-off observation (which was catnip for reporters[24]) had the effect of getting under the skin of some legislators. The committee chair demanded that Marsh strike from the hearing record such insulting comments about the court, saying that he should be ashamed of himself. Marsh refused, then doubled down by comparing the nine justices with "any nine radicals." At least these judges followed election results, he said, compared with the "intelligentsia" (US House 1935c, 107–108). The chairman got no satisfaction. Marsh was willing to go toe-to-toe with him and refused to back down or be intimidated by the setting. On another occasion, he stood up at the end of a hearing to complain that he was not being permitted to testify. He got into an angry exchange with the chairman, saying that the so-called hearings were really "star chamber dictatorships" (US House 1936b, 489). He stomped out and released his testimony to the press, probably gaining more attention for the PL's views than if that unplanned contretemps had not occurred.[25]

On other occasions, Marsh criticized an early proposal for social security as actuarially unsound and recommended the approach used in Scandinavian countries (US Senate 1935b, 961–974). He critiqued the Works Progress Administration (WPA) as well as the inadequate funding of the

National Youth Administration (US Senate 1936b, 246–249). At least once, because of scheduling conflicts, he was unable to be present to testify against a banking bill and instead submitted a written copy of his planned testimony for inclusion in the record (US Senate 1935c, 1005–1006).

While his sharp criticisms of proposed legislation and administration actions gave him an image of negativism, Marsh sometimes *supported* pending legislation on behalf of the Lobby, including a particular approach to social insurance (US Senate 1936c, 80–82) and an administration proposal in an omnibus tax bill to tax undistributed corporate surpluses (US Senate 1936a, 388–415). Hearings on tax bills were usually dominated by special interest groups opposing any tax increases that would affect them. Marsh's support for the tax bill exemplified the PL's desire to advocate for the point of view of the broad public-at-large, which was usually unrepresented on Capitol Hill, especially at tax hearings. A reporter noted how unusual Marsh's testimony was by flagging for the readers that "the Committee yesterday heard its first favorable testimony for the bill, aside from the Treasury's own statement."[26]

Other Domestic Issues

The preceding discussion indicates that the PL's major efforts in 1935–36 were, as would be expected, on Topic A of Washington's policy makers, the state of the economy and efforts to ameliorate the Great Depression. While somewhat related to the overarching economic issues, several subtopics were sometimes dealt with slightly separately. These included housing, agriculture, and consumer affairs. Marsh and the PL engaged in active lobbying on these discrete economic policy areas.[27]

Ever since his activism in urban planning in New York City at the beginning of the century, Marsh considered himself something of an expert in housing policy. Marsh and Dewey were critics of proposals for housing legislation that had the effect of rewarding creditors over lenders, trying to prop up pre-crash property values, and rewarding those who speculated in land (and thus had driven up land prices and values). At a hearing on creating low-rent public housing, he criticized the bill and its author (Senator Robert Wagner [D-NY]) as "useless" because it did not get to the core issue of inflated land values. He also took a quotable shot at FDR, saying the bill would subsidize land speculators, including "the President's boon companion, Mr. Vincent Astor, and the Secretary of the Treasury and his family" (US Senate 1935d, 141). However, as was the case most of the times he testified during this period, Marsh was not merely negative. He followed up his criticisms with positive alternatives that the PL supported. In this case, in addition to describing the housing policies that the Lobby endorsed, he also introduced a draft of a bill accomplishing precisely that policy. It was a fully fleshed out bill to create a National Housing Corporation (145–147).

When Marsh testified on a similar housing bill the next year, he provided specific amendments to the bill under consideration (US Senate 1936d, 255–256). He clearly had read the bill carefully before the hearing.[28] Still, the PL should not be seen as a knee-jerk criticizer of FDR from the left. In a backhanded compliment of the president's existing housing policy, in 1936 the PL criticized a proposal by the administration to close down its public housing program. The Lobby said the continuation of that program was needed because it was "the most important single field for large-scale employment of non-professional workers" and because the ending of the program would lead to a resumption of "private exploitation" of people seeking housing.[29]

As with housing policy, based on his past, Marsh also held strong opinions on farm policy, the latter from his pre-PL lobbying in Washington. He actively promoted alternatives to the conventional wisdom of the time. An indication that the PL had some standing in Washington agricultural policy debates occurred when USDA Secretary Henry Wallace accepted an invitation to speak on the administration's farm policy at a PL luncheon. Wallace discussed one of Marsh's favorite subjects, speculation in land values as hurting farmers.[30]

At congressional hearings on agricultural policy, Marsh continued advocating for the PL's idea of creating a federal corporation to market foodstuffs. By eliminating the middleman, farmers would be able to increase their incomes, and the consumer would benefit from lower prices (US Senate 1935e, 349–357). After all, he argued, a consumer buying food "does not care whether he is gypped by a chain store or by a retailer," but rather prefers lower prices, which would be accomplished by government marketing (US Senate 1936e, 115). Preemptively reacting to the standard criticism from the right of direct government marketing, he said he expected that this idea would be attacked as socialistic—that anything that even remotely "interferes with sanctified property rights and grants" was always denounced as socialistic or unconstitutional. His exasperation with such ad hominem red scare attacks was apparent. At that congressional hearing, in advocating for the joint interests of farmers and consumers, Marsh made a suggestion that can be seen as a very early conceptualization of what became food stamps three decades later. He suggested that "milk must be made a public utility as well as the other basic foodstuffs" (US House 1935d, 348).

An example of Marsh's effort to build a political coalition of farmers and consumers outside the venue of congressional hearings was a joint statement by the PL and a consumer group criticizing processing taxes on agricultural products.[31] Not all his efforts to build such a political coalition panned out. He tried to convene a "Consumer's Conference on Farm Programs" for late January 1936 but failed to draw adequate advance support, and the conference never occurred.[32]

Some of the PL's advocacy for consumers was unrelated to farm policy, such as when Marsh testified against a food and drug bill as a sellout by the Senate's Democratic majority to corporate interests. A supposed consumer protection bill was, he said, "a swindle and a farce on the American public." As sometimes happened when he spoke so pointedly, the chairman warned him that comments on "personalities about members of the Senate, or anybody else, will not be received." Marsh shot back that his comment was not an attack on any senator's character, and "I am very sorry if skins are so thin that they cannot stand facts." Continuing his riposte, he linked it to the subject of the hearing, saying, "We ought to have some of what you may call 'curatives' for thin skins, which are advertised" but likely not restricted by the bill (US Senate 1935f, 142–143).[33]

Foreign and Military Policy

With the comfortable twenty-twenty perspective of hindsight, the initial events that portended WWII occurred in 1935–36. Nazi Germany was rearming and the Saar region voted to rejoin Germany. Hitler denounced the Versailles treaty, withdrew from it, said he would not be bound by its limitations on Germany's military, and sent troops to remilitarize the previously demilitarized Rhineland. Italy invaded Ethiopia, the League of Nations was impotent despite the dramatic personal appeal of Emperor Haile Selassie, and the Western world declined to intervene. Hitler and Mussolini signed a pact allying Germany and Italy in foreign and military activities. The Spanish Civil War began, and the SU quickly intervened on the side of the Republicans while Germany and Italy aided the rebels led by Franco. Japan began extending its military control from Manchuria into northern China and Mongolia.

American policy makers may have been preoccupied during this period with domestic economic matters (and the upcoming presidential election), but Dewey and Marsh not only lobbied on behalf of international matters, they also saw links between the economy and foreign policy. In late 1934, PL was already raising concerns about "the powder keg in Europe" caused, in part, by the inequities of the Versailles and other post-WWI treaties (a reminder that Dewey had supported US involvement in WWI, while Marsh had opposed it). They noted the rise in dictatorial governments in central Europe and that "popular movements are being suppressed."[34]

In mid-1935, Marsh organized a delegation of peace groups to call on the under secretary of state to protest Italy's invasion of Ethiopia. However, for pacifists like them, there was no option of supporting a threat of the use of force or military intervention. They were limited to calling for diplomatic solutions and upholding the Kellogg antiwar treaty they had supported after WWI.[35] A few months later, the Lobby was asking its members to write letters *opposing* the use of economic sanctions to punish Italy. Instead, it supported a global settlement on fair access to natural resources by all countries. This approach fit in nicely with the PL's views on public control of natural resources and the importance of international cooperation.[36] In the fall of 1935, another delegation of peace groups delivered a joint statement to the State Department on the need to resist war, promote peace, and seek international cooperation to reduce tensions and conflicts.[37] In late 1936, Dewey was asked by the Church Peace Union to involve the PL in a potential international economic conference to promote peaceful cooperation and economic growth, rather than armaments and militarism.[38]

As they had done earlier, Dewey and Marsh tried to defend the SU without being apologists for it. As non-Communists, they had a credibility that American Communists did not. Dewey and Marsh were willing to praise some developments in Russia as interesting revolutionary experiments, urge patience before coming to definitive negative conclusions about Communism in Russia, and generally give it the benefit of the doubt that Americans would routinely grant to regimes in other countries. At the same time, Dewey and Marsh were willing, when events dictated, to criticize the SU. For example, in early 1935, the PL's monthly publication condemned the mass executions and political assassinations then ongoing as part of (what we now know as) Stalin's reign of terror. An unsigned article (probably written by Marsh) said that "no thoughtful person can approve the execution of 103 counterrevolutionists in Russia without a trial" but then quickly softened the condemnation with the qualifier of "except on the ground that the revolution is still on in Russia." He also asked readers to judge the SU in the context of violence in other European countries at the time and the general turmoil, militarism, and sabre rattling going on there. Ending on a pro-Russia note and a larger PL theme, he distinguished between the capitalist European countries "devoting their efforts to maintaining systems which foment war instead of creating economic systems in which war would be an anachronism," like the SU.[39]

As a peace organization, the Lobby was increasingly alarmed about the seeming slide toward war at home and abroad. Presciently, an article in its newsletter in late 1935 (also probably written by Marsh) predicted war within two years.[40] The Lobby also denounced the release of several revised iterations of the Army's Industrial Mobilization Plan. Ostensibly, it was an effort to learn from the mobilization mistakes of WWI, but it was also a blueprint for what to do in any coming war (Lee 2005, chap. 4). This was an abhorrent planning premise for Dewey and Marsh. They wanted national planning for peace and full employment, not war.[41]

Attempting to change the focus of attention from war to peace, Marsh tried to organize a national conference on "The Real Program for Peace" in the fall of 1936. His goal was to create a revitalized coalition of labor, women, church, civic, and farm organizations to promote a comprehensive pro-labor international economic platform. He received about three dozen endorsements of this effort from prominent activists, including A. Philip Randolph, Harvard history professor Arthur Schlesinger (Sr.), and Chicago professor Paul Douglas (later a US senator). However, the response and interest were inadequate, and the conference never occurred.[42] Another peace-related effort involved the United States joining the World Court. In 1935, FDR had submitted the protocols for joining to the US Senate. At a meeting of the PL's Executive Committee, the officers decided to support approval of the treaty and directed Marsh to lobby for it in the Senate.[43] (It was defeated.)

In mid-1936, Marsh spoke to a conference at Wellesley College. He provided a *tour d'horizon* of contemporary developments, closely linking domestic and international events. In his view, despite the best efforts by Secretary of State Hull (whom Marsh praised), the Roosevelt administration gave little encouragement for international cooperation. What was needed, said Marsh, were reductions of tariffs and barriers to free trade, such as the anticompetitive policies of the NRA and AAA. Further, there was a need to tamp down on the "chief inciters to war," such as munitions makers and steel producers. Finally, he denounced British imperialism, especially in India.[44] At another conference, Marsh again linked the goal of socialization of natural resources in the United States and abroad as "a necessary step toward peace."[45]

As the chief spokesman for the PL, these lectures demonstrated how integrated the various elements of the Lobby's 1935–36 policy platform were. Peace, international cooperation, public ownership of monopolies and basic industries, taxation of property owners, and assistance to the economically deprived were pieces of a whole. This was a distillation of the interwar worldview of pro-labor and socialist activists like Dewey and Marsh. They knew there were alternatives not only to the conservative politics at home and abroad, but also to the mild leftist tilt and inherently incrementalist policies of the Democratic Party and its counterparts abroad. From Marsh's perspective, the gradual convincing of American public opinion of the rightness of the PL's worldview would make its internationalist policy platform a political force to be reckoned with.

The policy-oriented aspects of the second half of FDR's first term came to a conclusion in mid-1936, when the 74th Congress adjourned sine die and the two parties began drafting their platforms in advance of their presidential nominating conventions. Given the PL's advocacy orientation to influencing public policy, Marsh testified evenhandedly before both platform committees.[46] In each case, he presented the Lobby's policy program, explained it, and urged consideration of its components in the official Republican and Democratic presidential platforms.[47] (Furthering this non-partisanship, Marsh also made a presentation on the PL's views to the platform committee of the new Left Party being organized by students of George Washington University in Washington, DC.[48]) Certainly, the Lobby's ideology would hold little interest to Republicans, so his presentation to its platform committee could be viewed as a fool's errand. Similarly, the PL's further-to-the-left viewpoint and sharp criticisms of FDR gave Marsh's testimony little appeal to Democrats. Again, Marsh was not expecting much. Nonetheless, he made the effort, if only to demonstrate the Lobby's narrow view of its role as "a non-political organization" engaging only in policy advocacy.[49] The PL's board and Marsh were careful to adhere to IRS guidelines regarding nonprofits not engaging in partisan activities, which qualified it for the tax-deductibility of contributions. The Lobby was completely divorced from political campaigns. (Dewey's involvement in presidential campaigns, usually tilting to a Socialist or other third-party candidate, was wholly separate from the PL.)

Being careful to be neutral in terms of explicit partisan and campaign involvement did not inhibit the Lobby from expressing its views forcefully. It would not pull its (policy) punches, presidential election year or not. The PL continued to be a fierce and consistent critic of FDR's policy record from the left. In the summer of 1936, surveying the record of the administration as the president was preparing to run for reelection, Marsh made a "scathing denunciation" of the New Deal. Unintentionally agreeing with conservative critics of FDR, Marsh said the debt taken on by the federal government would be an unfair burden that the next generation would have to carry. Today's politicians were robbing from the future, he said. But he quickly parted company with the right. Marsh condemned the increase in the national debt instead of financing the New Deal with additional taxes on the property-owning and wealthy classes. For all that spending (and debt) for relief bills, New Dealers "have not insured security, because security can be guaranteed only through participation of all in adequate consumption out of current production and income." He predicted that eventually, the United States would repudiate those debts as unsustainable, just as European nations had done with their WWI debts.[50]

Chapter 7

Lobby Operations and Conservative Attacks during FDR's First Term, 1933–1936

Advocacy Strategy: PR to the Max

As they had from the start, Dewey and Marsh believed in the power of publicity. Information was power, and the more they could communicate with the public-at-large, the better their chances of success in Washington's policy-making world. They were publicity hounds with a purpose. Their philosophy about publicity was nicely captured in a mailing to PL members in the winter of 1932–33. It was titled "Government Responds to Headlines—The People's Lobby Gets Its Share." The flier was a pastiche of headlines of coverage of PL statements, mostly focusing on Dewey, given his standing and fame. The introductory text claimed that the Lobby's public criticisms of the RFC "helped induce" the agency to change its policies.[1] This was the simple two-step process that Dewey and Marsh believed in about the power of publicity and its role in lobbying. Bad publicity then triggered those being criticized to change their behavior, the classic view of publicity by Progressive-era reformers. This particular example confirmed to Dewey and Marsh that their standard operating procedure of maximal PR was a successful template of lobbying for policy changes in Washington.

However, it would be incorrect to associate the hyperattention to publicity solely to Dewey and Marsh. For example, at a 1935 meeting of the PL's Executive Committee, the officers discussed strategy for dealing with artificially high property values (notwithstanding the Crash) that might be paid to sellers under a new federal homesteading plan being discussed in the Capital. Marsh asked if he should use judicial tactics to stop the plan, such as filing a lawsuit or an injunction. No, said the officers. Rather, they directed him "to use all possible publicity methods" to defeat the plan.[2]

This consensus was an indication of the broader support within the PL's leadership for Dewey and Marsh's publicity-centric lobbying tactics.

One of the major developments in the PL's public relations activities in 1933–36 was that it perfected the formula for publicizing its regular public events. As discussed in Chapter 4, from the PL's start in 1928, Marsh planned its meetings with a view to maximizing media coverage. Now, during FDR's first term, he figured out a way to amplify the PL's views much more. He gradually developed relationships with radio networks to broadcast (sometimes live) talks given at PL events on some Saturdays in Washington. It was an enviable triple play. First, given that Saturday was a slow news day in Washington and newspapers were hungry for news to place in their large Sunday papers, the print press coverage of these Saturday events was unusually high. Second, radio networks welcomed public affairs programs on Saturdays because it was a lower audience day (compared with weekdays) and therefore had lower advertiser demand for time. Further, these free broadcasts helped station managers document that they were using their federal license in the public interest. Third, Marsh often invited politicians friendly to the PL's views to speak on the broadcasts. They welcomed such opportunities for publicity and national exposure, which would give Marsh some goodwill for lobbying them in the future. And all this for free!

By 1934, Marsh could boast that NBC had made a commitment to broadcast a series of half-hour programs on Saturday on its national Red network and that the World Wide broadcasting company had similarly promised the PL a series of fifteen-minute broadcasts on Sundays.[3] By early 1935, NBC had committed fifty minutes for the talks at some Saturday PL fora plus another fifteen minutes for Marsh to present an update on Washington developments.[4] During the year, the allotted time was expanded from fifty minutes to an hour. Later, the CBS network agreed to broadcast some PL meetings.[5] Dewey occasionally participated in these broadcasts, giving them further luster.[6]

Marsh was ecstatic. He estimated the national audience for each broadcast at about 150 to 160,000 people. He told PL members that he had received about 1,700 requests for additional information from people who had heard the broadcasts. These people were perfect for future mailings and for potential recruitment as PL members. Marsh made a point to ask current PL members to write to their local radio stations and the national networks to praise them for broadcasting the PL meetings or, if they did not carry them in their media market, to ask local station managers to do so. Ever the political organizer, he also urged them to consider inviting friends over to listen to the broadcast and then discuss what was said afterward.[7]

If anything gave the PL stature above its size, it likely was Marsh's success at having PL meetings in DC broadcast nationally for free. It was a PR man's dream.

Marsh also hoped that the Lobby's monthly *Bulletin* could be an intermediary platform for further publicity. For example, its masthead prominently included the statement "NOT Copyrighted."[8] This was an invitation to readers to republish any of the contents in other publications they might be affiliated with, such as the newspapers of union locals or labor councils, church bulletins, and newsletters of civic groups. It was a primitive version of what came to be called a force multiplier. The more the PL's copy was reused and reprinted, the more people it reached. In turn, that would increase the potential of persuading public opinion of the policy alternatives the Lobby was generating. Marsh was using every angle he could to extend the voice of the Lobby.

In the PL's initial years, Marsh sometimes had gone on speaking tours to give public talks (Chap. 4). During FDR's first term, the amount of time he was on the road seemed to increase. He usually made a western swing in September or October of each year that lasted about a month.[9] Most of his talks were on domestic policy, although occasionally he addressed foreign policy.[10] These trips always had tightly packed schedules, aiming for at least one talk a day. For example, in 1933, he was on the road from October 7–27, with twenty-four appearances at luncheons or evening events.[11] In Salt Lake City, Marsh provocatively pronounced that FDR's program "was doomed to failure."[12] Then, "on his return from a tour of 19 States," he promptly issued a press release summarizing his (self-fulfilling) observations of what he had found, particularly the need for increasing taxes on the wealthy to expand relief for the unemployed.[13] He then headed back out for New England. In all these appearances, Marsh was the consummate organizer, urging audiences to meet with their member of Congress and US senators to "be questioned on their stand on the Lobby's program in Congress."[14] In at least one case, he made a winter swing through the Midwest, appearing in Madison, Wisconsin; Milwaukee; and Chicago.[15] Closer to home, Marsh made frequent one- and two-day trips to northeast corridor destinations, including speaking at a New York synagogue, a Harvard student group, a Boston civic club, and in Hartford, Connecticut.[16]

In a year-end summary to the Board of Directors of his activities in 1933, Marsh said he had given talks at 143 meetings in 31 states, testified at 11 congressional hearings, had 111 meetings with legislators and 22 with executive branch officials, written 17 articles for magazines (not counting the *PLB*), issued 43 news releases, and been interviewed 103 times by reporters.[17] Two years later, he reported roughly the same level of out-of-town speaking engagements (122) and meetings on Capitol Hill (more than 100). As for his media relations activities, he estimated that during 1935, the PL had reached 10 million readers of "the capitalist press."[18]

Marsh seemed to have an inexhaustible supply of energy and enthusiasm. He applied himself to implement a strategy of public communication and advocacy to the max. It is hard to imagine something he did not do—or at least try to do.

In Operation

Marsh continued to be punctilious about adhering to the formal requirements for ongoing operations of corporations chartered in Delaware. Following its first full year as an incorporated entity (1932), from 1933 to 1936 the Lobby settled into a detailed annual routine and cycle for meetings, elections, officers, audits, and reports. There generally were two sets of meetings, those of the Executive Committee and annual meetings of the membership of the Lobby, the latter mostly to elect officers for the upcoming year and receive the accountant's annual financial report. Each meeting required comprehensive documentation of the minutes of the meeting, including attendance, compliance with quorum and advance notice provisions, proxies submitted for the meeting, reading or dispensing of reading of minutes, motions made, name of the mover of the motion and the seconder, and the resulting vote on each motion.[19] Humorously, these highly ritualized meetings sometimes had as few as three people present: Dewey, Mrs. Clyde, and Marsh.

From 1933 to early 1936, there were eighteen such meetings (some back-to-back of the Executive Committee meeting and followed by the annual membership meeting), all occurring in Dewey's apartment in Manhattan. As president, Dewey chaired every meeting. Based on standard American parliamentary procedure, that meant he played a neutral role in meetings and did not make or second motions.[20] Complying with that protocol, Dewey's voice was not often reflected in the formal minutes of these meetings. Nonetheless, he was actively involved in the business at hand. For example, at an Executive Committee meeting in 1935, he participated in an extensive discussion of the specifics of the position the PL would take on a proposal for a federal housing corporation. He presented an amendment (which he had apparently drafted before the meeting) on how the corporation should calculate rents and that the corporation should have the power of eminent domain. It was adopted.[21]

Invariably, the agenda for each gathering included financial reports (especially the annual report by the public accountant who audited the books), adoption of budgets, revisions to the bylaws to facilitate smoother governance, acceptances of resignations (especially from officers and the Advisory Council), new appointments to same, discussions of policy matters, guidance on invitations for the Lobby's involvement in projects of other organizations (usually declined), reports by Marsh, and decisions on revisions in the policy agenda for the Lobby or, at the turn of the year, adoption of a policy platform for the upcoming calendar year.[22]

The PL continued to be a modest organization. As of 1936, it had an annual income and expenditures of about $10,000.[23] As in earlier years, Mrs. Clyde's annual commitment was a major pillar in the Lobby's financial stability, sometimes as much as half of its annual budget.[24] As before, there were only two employees, Marsh and a secretary, both with low salaries. Marsh's pay for 1933 was $4,000.[25]

In terms of membership, in early 1934, Marsh reported to the officers that the PL had about 1,200 paid up members and about 500 in arrears. There were also about 600 paid-up subscribers to the *Bulletin* (i.e., not PL members) and another 300 in arrears.[26] A year and a half later, he reported that the Lobby was getting about 125 to 150 new members or subscribers a month, evidently a rate that was greater than that of lapsed members and subscribers.[27] While publicity was a major motivation for his speaking tours, membership was also. The aim of an appearance in Hartford was explicitly to help organize a local PL chapter there.[28] After his western tour in 1935, Marsh said he enrolled about sixty new members.[29] A few months later, he said that he had increased the membership by nearly 50 percent in 1935, but provided no detailed statistics.[30] One impressive indication of the high level of activism and interest of the members was that more than 581 had filled out and sent in their proxies for the 1936 annual meeting.[31] Depending on what the membership was at that point, this could be a response rate of one-fourth or even one-third of the entire membership.

The partnership between Dewey and Marsh during 1933–36 remained strong, but there was one recurring problem that they tried to clarify, not always successfully. It will be recalled (Chap. 2) that Dewey reviewed all drafts of PL statements that were issued in his name. Helpfully, he had suggested that Marsh feel free—without preapproval from Dewey—to issue releases that either were in Marsh's name or were attributed to the PL in general, without any proper names in the statement. This was a clear and logical guideline. However, reporters sometimes inserted into their stories the identifier about the PL along the lines of "of which Professor John Dewey is President." While accurate, this could imply that a statement was Dewey's when it was not. For example, in March 1934, Marsh issued an intemperate release in the name of the Lobby attacking FDR's latest proposal regarding the economy. It called FDR's expected plan "a farce" and asked Congress to "stop the President's favorite indoor pastime of playing new deal politics with human misery."[32] The way the *Washington Post* edited the story, it sounded like the quotes came from Dewey. They did not. Dewey got a complaint for his (supposedly) over-the-top language.[33] In reaction, Dewey wrote Marsh, suggesting the need to be clear *who* in the PL was making a public statement and reminding him of Dewey's practice of avoiding personal attacks and instead focusing on the substantive policy matter at hand. Gently chiding Marsh, Dewey displayed a tactical sense of political combat. Such an attack "alienates persons who would otherwise be glad to support the Lobby. We don't get anywhere, we go backwards, on the basis of personal attacks, especially on Roosevelt who still has the confidence (whether rightly or not) of the great mass of the American people. . . . Anyway you don't analyze his actual policies but call them names."[34] Dewey told Marsh that he (Dewey) did not want to insist on clearing all statements made in the name of the PL, but wondered if that might be necessary to avoid such misattributions in the future.

Accepting Dewey's suggestion, Marsh was more careful to include his own name in PL statements so that they would not be linked to Dewey. However, even when he did so, Dewey at least once got a complaint about *Marsh's* attack on a bill. Replying to the complainant, Dewey defended Marsh, saying Marsh was "scrupulous" about not invoking Dewey's name without advance approval.[35] It was a strong vote of confidence. Advising Marsh about the exchange, Dewey carefully noted that Marsh's statement had not even implied Dewey had approved it, but nonetheless "even intelligent writers interpret action that seems to come officially from the People's Lobby" with Dewey. Dewey again was more tactically political than Marsh, noting that the bill in question (which Marsh had attacked) at least "*may* have a much needed positive effect."[36] Still, in the context of working closely together between 1933 and 1936, these problems were minor. Other exchanges between Dewey and Marsh continued to demonstrate a close working relationship, Dewey's trust in Marsh, and Dewey's ongoing and active behind-the-scenes involvement with the PL's policy positions and publicity efforts.[37]

Media Characterizations and Conservative Attacks

During the PL's first years of existence, reporters had struggled with how to characterize what the PL stood for without violating their professional norms (Chap. 4). By then, they had largely settled on radical.[38] The conservative *Chicago Tribune* also used it sometimes,[39] but its characterization of the PL tended to be situational. For example, when strongly disagreeing with the PL, the *Tribune* described it as a "Socialistic" and "propaganda" organization for the left.[40] However, when Marsh and Dewey criticized FDR, coverage was different altogether. Without the usual adjectives, the paper prominently ran Marsh's condemnation of the New Deal's farm program.[41] Another Marsh attack on FDR described the PL this way: "Dr. John Dewey of Columbia University is head of the People's Lobby, which is a nonpartisan organization."[42]

Communist hunters in Congress and elsewhere were not as ambivalent as the *Tribune*. They saw the People's Lobby more clearly and without doubt of what it really was. They *knew*. For example, the American Legion viewed the People's Lobby as one of the spokes of the wheel of interlocking associates of "the Third Internationale as the hub of a wheel of communism."[43] A Congressman said the PL was "pacific" (i.e., pacifist) and "actively engaged in breaking down proper preparedness in the United States."[44] A congressman and a far right conservative activist both labeled the PL as "Socialist."[45] Other smears were slightly more dainty, but equally condemnatory. One called the PL a "left wing group,"[46] while another said that "the People's Lobby may not be subsidized by Moscow, but it has the same effect as if it were."[47]

Some epithets were damning by faint clarification. One confessed that Dewey was a "non-Communist," but that the PL was nonetheless one of the "so-called 'liberal' or 'progressive' groups."[48] In a radio speech, a conservative congressman accurately stated the PL's mission as his rationale for criticizing it. It was, he said, "against the profit system and in favor of Government ownership."[49] This labeling of the left as opposing the profit system emerged as a standard charge by conservatives after 1932, directed not just at the PL and like groups, but also at FDR and the New Deal. When the Liberty League was founded in 1934 to oppose Roosevelt, a leading *raison d'être* was that the New Deal violated private property rights.[50] Humorously, Dewey jumped to the defense of the president. He fired off an indignant letter to the head of the League challenging him, among other items, to cite any specific instances of confiscation of private property by the New Deal without due process and fair compensation.[51] Given the toxic politics of the times (and again in the 2010s), the two sides were living in separate political realities, and one's truth was the other's falsity. It was like shouting at each other across the Grand Canyon.

The PL and other left-of-center organizations were occasionally defended from such common red smears. At the annual conference of the American Library Association in 1936, Leon Carnovsky, a faculty member at the University of Chicago's library school, read a paper on "The Worst Periodical Usually Found in Library Reading Rooms." It was an attack on the *National Republic*, a magazine dedicated to "Fundamental Americanism." One of Carnovsky's examples justifying his characterization was the magazine's attack on the People's Lobby. He detailed and dissected the publication's carefully stated insinuations that the PL, Dewey, and Marsh were Communists and participants in a Moscow-based anti-American plot, but without ever quite saying it explicitly. After documenting his case, Carnovsky concluded that "the writer, you see, is very careful to avoid identifying Mr. Marsh with the poison plot, but there is just sufficient cleverness to suggest a casual connection to the gullible reader" (1936, 739). While a well-constructed analysis, it hardly counterbalanced the many attacks from the right on the Lobby.

In 1936, a conservative congressman tried a different and seemingly nonideological tack in fighting the PL and its ilk. Congressman Howard Smith (D-VA) complained that "in recent years there has grown up a different system of government in this county; I may say a government by propaganda." He introduced a bill requiring lobbies (groups trying to influence legislation) and political groups (trying to influence elections) to disclose their sources of money and their expenditures. At a quickly called hearing (where he was the sole testifier), the only specific example he cited was a letter from the PL urging members of Congress to oppose a farm bill and to replace it with legislation following the PL's principles. Smith said that the purpose of his bill was "to get at all this kind of propaganda. . . . I won't say what organization it is, but you probably all know about it. . . . What I want to do is get at those birds" (US House, 1936c). The bill did not pass.[52] While his was an attack by the right on the left, the issue of transparency in political spending by nonprofits continued long after. At the time of writing (2014), it had transmuted to being mostly the left against the right, but the principle was the same: Who was spending what, how much, for what purpose, and where did they get the money? *Plus ça change, plus c'est la même chose.*

After Eight Years as President, Dewey Semi-Exits

During the winter of 1935–36, the Lobby touted its continuing uniqueness. While explicit substantive victories were relatively sparse, it could rightly boast that it was accomplishing its goal of being a countervoice to the well-funded lobbies of special interest groups in Washington. If something was better than nothing, then the PL was making its mark. Now, entering its ninth year of existence, it was "*still* the only organization in Washington working on a general program of economic justice at home—and cooperating in the peace movement."[53]

There were other straws in the wind from 1933 to 1935 indicating that the Lobby had established itself. A mainstream and nationally syndicated columnist who routinely referred to the PL as "radical" made an unusual point in a 1934 column. In most of his congressional appearances, Marsh routinely spoke (his) truth to power, with Committee members wholly ignoring him. "Yet a surprisingly large number of conservatives on Capitol Hill concur in expressions of their opinion that Marsh 'said a mouthful' the other day." Marsh's point in that testimony had been relatively de rigueur, saying that the way out of the Depression was not by propping up prices and property values, but rather by a large write-down of the values of major industries. Conservatives took note, wrote the columnist, and for a change saw that minor policy initiatives might not be enough to get out of the Depression. Surprisingly, "they indorse [*sic*] Dr. [*sic*] Marsh's diagnosis. When it comes to accepting his prescription they balk, and prefer palliatives. 'We haven't the courage to face facts,' I have heard many of them confess."[54] It was a backhanded compliment to the PL's economic program and to Marsh's insights, but a favorable mention nonetheless, and it reached a national readership.

Another gauge of the status that the PL attained in this period was demonstrated by two reader features in newspapers. The *Boston Globe* routinely published on its editorial page a quiz on public affairs as a test of the readers' familiarity with recent news. It was called "The Knowmeter." The first of six questions on October 17, 1933, was this: "Explain the boldface word in this news item: 'The forces backing inflation collided head on with the **people's lobby**.' " The answer was provided on the back page: "Voluntary organization of citizens formed for the purpose of influencing legislation by bringing public opinion to bear upon proposed measures. They have representatives at committee hearings who present the case for the public."[55]

About two years later, the PL was the subject of a reader's query in a nationally syndicated daily feature from Washington called "Questions of Readers Answered." One was a request for more information about "an organization known as the People's Lobby." The answer was that the PL's purpose was "to represent the common interests of the common people in relation to federal legislation. Its recent interests in matters related to the field of social work include advocacy of a federal relief board for children and unemployment insurance."[56]

These depictions of the PL were *exactly* what Dewey had in mind when he cofounded it. He and Marsh would speak for the nonorganized public-at-large. Based on its appearance in these two features, the PL had made it as a player in Washington news. Yet the descriptions of the PL were incomplete. Yes, the PL had a general good-government mission on behalf of the public interest. But both had omitted the PL's distinct ideological place on the political spectrum. It was not just on the left, but quite significantly to the left of FDR and the Democratic Party.

For Dewey, such milestones of public awareness of the PL's work and role would likely have been sources of great satisfaction. With little money and a small membership, the People's Lobby had confirmed its necessity, filled a vacuum in Capital lobbying, and played the role he had wanted for it. Now seventy-five, he felt a need to reduce his public obligations. But he did not want to do anything to harm the PL or give the appearance that he was backing away from its mission and views.

Indicating careful succession planning, Dewey shared his desire to retire as president but to continue to convey his support for its work. At the annual meeting in early 1936, as usual in his Manhattan apartment, he declined reelection to another one-year term as president.[57] He said he wanted to dedicate his time to writing. However, "I retain my full confidence in [the PL's] program, its methods of works and its officers, and am glad to think that my resignation as President will not cut me off from all association with its activities."[58] He accepted election to the newly created office of honorary president. To emphasize his continuing support for the Lobby, his status as honorary president was routinely displayed on the masthead of the monthly *Bulletin* and on the letterhead of the Lobby's stationary. Humorously, the headline of the *Washington Post*'s story of the news made it sound like Dewey had been dumped: "Dewey Out as Head of People's Lobby."[59]

Professor Colston Warne, professor of economics at Dartmouth, who had been active in the Lobby previously (Chap. 6), was elected president in Dewey's place. Warne quickly picked up where Dewey left off, signing a membership-recruiting letter in April 1936 titled "The Unorganized are Victims" and authoring the lead article in the Lobby's monthly newsletter a few months later.[60]

Part III

Dewey as Honorary President of the People's Lobby and After

Chapter 8

Policy Advocacy during FDR's Second Term, 1937–1940

The omniscience of history telling usually conveys an "of course" about FDR's reelection in 1936. It is difficult to reconstruct that this was not so. Republicans were quite optimistic, even confident, that the electorate would decide that Roosevelt had failed to revive the economy in any permanent way during his term. Naturally, then, the voters would turn to the other guys and give them a chance, just as long as they had not renominated Hoover (who was interested in a rematch). In more recent times, the same political situation of a perhaps weak first-term president running for reelection occurred in 1980—President Carter against Ronald Reagan (with Republicans being right about the political dynamic this time)—and in 2012, President Obama against Mitt Romney (wrong). To increase their chances of victory in 1936, the Republicans nominated Alf Landon, the moderate and likeable governor of Kansas. But, to appeal to the party's base of FDR haters, as VP they named conservative Frank Knox, an influential newspaper publisher. He made slashing attacks against the New Deal and Roosevelt, undercutting Landon's authentic position and political strategy.[1] No one, not even FDR, foresaw quite the landslide that it would be (Shesol 2010, 234–240; Brands 2008, 451–455).

While the People's Lobby was careful to avoid any open partisan or political role, as a private citizen Dewey endorsed Norman Thomas for president in 1936 (just as he had in 1932). Here was an indication where the political hearts of most of the activists in the PL lay. They were further to the left than FDR and the mainstream of the Democratic Party. Many were Socialists (or, at least, social democrats) in ideology, and some were openly so in partisan affiliation. But they were not revolutionaries in the sense of supporting a violent or nondemocratic overthrow of the American constitutional regime. Nor were they divided in allegiance to their country.

Many were sympathetic to the Communist Revolution in the SU, but they were neither members of the Communist Party nor followers of the dictates of the SU-controlled Comintern. Therefore, with FDR so overwhelmingly reelected, what now for the Lobby?

Dewey as Honorary President, 1936–40

John Dewey was the PL's marquee name. He was the person who gave the views of the organization instant credibility and gravitas, and he knew it. As will be recalled (Chap. 7), when he stepped down as PL president after serving from its founding in 1928 to 1936, he wanted to be sure to continue giving such standing to the organization even though he was bowing out of the day-to-day involvement he had had during the eight years of his presidency. For that reason, the Board created the new position of honorary president, which Dewey agreed to hold. His name continued to be prominently displayed on the masthead of the PL's *Bulletin* and the letterhead of its stationery. At congressional hearings, when Marsh explained what the organization he was speaking for was, he mentioned Dewey prominently. A 1939 letter to the editor from a PL member urging readers to join similarly referred to Dewey's central relationship to the lobby, even though by then he was only its honorary president.[2]

While Dewey was more remotely connected to the organization, he still sometimes was involved. For example, in 1938, he issued a statement in support of federal funding of public education in rural areas to boost a coalition the PL had organized to lobby for that goal.[3] On another occasion, the PL hosted a policy briefing in New York City, partly to recruit new members and partly to raise its profile. Dewey came to the event and spoke of the importance of the PL's continuing existence. He told the audience, "There has never been a time when the work of the People's Lobby had so much significance. It has a non-partisan program of measures that are fundamental for the future."[4] His talk (and several others) was broadcast on WNYC, the city government's public radio station.

When Marsh testified against a bill to expand the navy, he stated in his prepared remarks that Dewey, even though he was merely the PL's honorary president, had specifically endorsed the views that Marsh was about to present (US House, 1938b, 2445). Highlighting Dewey's continuing link with the Lobby, Marsh also reprinted a Dewey piece first published in a 1933 issue of the *Bulletin* as the lead article in the July 1938 issue. He wrote he was doing so "at the request of some subscribers." It was titled "Superficial

Treatment Must Fail" and related to Dewey's argument about the need for national economic programs that would systemically solve problems, rather than just the above-the-surface symptoms. In an editorial note, Marsh wrote that Dewey's column was "as true then—true now."[5]

Dewey was no figurehead in the sense of not following the work of the Lobby. For example, he was a careful reader of the monthly *Bulletin*. In October 1939, he threatened to resign as honorary president if an article quoting from a book that appeared to praise Stalin accurately reflected the PL's views. By then, it was twenty years after the Communist Revolution in Russia, and Stalin's abuses and dictatorship were clear. In the early years, Dewey and Marsh often defended the SU, believing the experiment deserved the benefit of the doubt, at least for a few years. The depredations of the SU and Stalin were now evident to clear-eyed observers like Dewey. Furthermore, only two months earlier (in August 1939), Hitler and Stalin had signed a nonaggression pact and the next month jointly invaded Poland. The lead article in the October issue of the *Bulletin* (unsigned but written by Marsh) tried to provide a unified interpretation of the war in Europe.[6] Marsh saw events as interconnected, largely reflecting the interests and manipulations of bankers (especially the House of Morgan), American industry (such as DuPont), and British propaganda. This was generally the perspective that Socialists had before and after WWI. For Marsh, events in the 1930s were either the inevitable outcomes of the failed Versailles treaties or an exact rerun of the Great War. In the article, Marsh quoted liberally from a book by a writer using the pen name "The Unofficial Observer" (Carter 1935). (The author's identity was only thinly disguised. It was John Franklin Carter, who also wrote a syndicated column from Washington.[7]) The book, *Our Lords and Masters: Known and Unknown Rulers of the World*, was a readable pastiche of gossipy personality profiles, European politics, and trenchant observations, but wholly lacking in a consistent political perspective. The author seemed to be critical or snide toward just about every public figure he mentioned.

Dewey took great offense at Marsh's quotes from the book about the potential domination of Europe (and Asia) by the SU and characterization of the SU's political ideology as Socialism. In an uncharacteristically brusque letter, Dewey accused Marsh of "going Stalin at this day and date." The accusation is a bit opaque, but likely reflected unhappiness with the depiction of Stalin's dictatorship as Socialism. Whatever point Dewey was making, he wrote that he was resigning as honorary president of the PL.[8] Alarmed, Marsh (who was on his annual western speaking tour) apparently wrote a placating and (also uncharacteristically) apologetic letter to Dewey.[9]

Dewey genially accepted Marsh's explanation for the quotes from the book and withdrew his resignation. He said, "I didn't suppose you had really gone Stalin but the last paragraph of the Bulletin quoted would give readers the impression you approved that as well as the rest."[10] The crisis was averted.

But only a month later, in November 1939, Dewey again was unhappy with Marsh. A friend of Dewey's had told Dewey of a conversation with Marsh. Marsh apparently had outlined his conspiracy theory of "a Jewish-Catholic war affiliation."[11] Evidently, after the signing of the German-Soviet Nonaggression Pact and invasion of Poland, Marsh was seeing a harmony of interest by Jews and Catholics in favor of war against Germany and the SU. In his view, Jews were motivated by opposition to Hitler because of his anti-Semitism, and Catholics opposed the SU because of its general suppression of organized religion, but especially its repression of Catholics after its partial occupation of Lithuania in September and October 1939.[12] Dewey was appalled by such an insinuation but carefully asked Marsh for an explanation, clarification, or confirmation. Marsh again replied in a conciliatory way.[13] Dewey accepted Marsh's explanation and general observation that it was hard to know what was happening. Dewey agreed with the latter point and wrote that he was baffled by the latest developments. He saw "the complete bankruptcy of the isolationists as represented by 'America First'—new Interventionists in reverse." Dewey was also surprised by "the build-up of destructive communism." Now, with Hitler and Stalin in alliance, "the outlook here is not a pretty one."[14] For good measure, Dewey enclosed a personal check of $5 as a donation to the PL. He was back in the fold. The Lobby and Marsh could continue to work under his imprimatur.

Economic Policy

As it had done in the past, to avoid accusations of political expediency, partisanship, or favoritism, the Lobby's Board of Directors approved a legislative agenda for 1937 before the November 1936 election. Meeting in October in Mrs. Clyde's Manhattan apartment, they endorsed a platform that was largely a continuation of the policy goals the PL had pursued when Dewey was president.[15] It called for increasing progressive taxes on the wealthy; reducing regressive taxes; government-run public housing and marketing corporations; nationalization (called socialization) of utilities, banks, natural resources, steel, textiles and car makers; social security; and international cooperation.[16]

Many of the New Deal programs were scheduled to expire in 1937; and congressional approval would be necessary to continue funding them.[17] In a report to the Board of Directors in early 1937, Marsh assessed the chances of adoption of the PL's goals of comprehensive and systemic reforms of the political economy versus the incrementalist and more status quo–oriented ones of FDR. He optimistically concluded that "the breakdown or retardation of many New Deal measures, and continued widespread unemployment are turning attention to more basic measures. It is a strategic opportunity for the People's Lobby to develop and organize sentiment for such measures in its program of legislation."[18]

In 1937, the economy started slumping. By 1938, it was clearly in recession. Presciently, in spring 1937, Marsh predicted a major economic downturn during FDR's second term.[19] Facing reality, Roosevelt had to give up on his goal of a balanced budget (which may have contributed to the economy's decline) and reverted to priming the pump and relief spending (Brands 2008, 489–494). Given that new or reinvigorated programs were needed to save the New Deal, the Lobby hoped this would provide an opening for its advocacy of major and systemic economic reforms, such as paying for relief programs through higher taxes and government control of major sectors of the political economy. In this context, Marsh continued trying to crash the (Democratic) party with reminders that there were plenty of policy options to the left of FDR that populists and progressives supported.

In an open letter to President Roosevelt, the new PL president, Methodist Bishop Francis J. McConnell, enumerated the failings of the New Deal and outlined a comprehensive economic recovery program, which, instead of raising prices and property values and relying on debt, would provide relief to low-income families and increase taxes on the wealthy.[20] In a speech, McConnell said that capitalism existed only by the consent of the public. If the economic impacts that a market-based society create are "too great a social cost, society has a right to proceed with any measures that seem wise."[21] The PL was making it clear that there was a third way—that it had constructed a multifaceted program against the recession that was neither the moderate Democrats' way nor the Republican alternatives.

In particular, Marsh and the PL developed a new prism for political and economic analysis. They focused on how the New Deal had given many previously suffering segments of the population distinct economic benefits. Now some groups, such as portions of the labor movement and farmers, liked the status quo and opposed any fundamental reforms that might threaten their improving condition. Parts of the traditional coalition on the left had moved to the center, even becoming conservative about major change. And now that their income was improving, they certainly did not want to see their taxes raised. In Marsh's view, they had been bought off. He was losing allies who had long supported the more radical thrust of PL's policy goals.[22] Behind closed doors, he told the leadership of the Lobby that in 1938, "a discouraging feature of the year's work has been the non-cooperation of other organizations on the Lobby's program, even on the moderate taxation plank."[23] He had sent a PL position paper on revising the tax code to make it more progressive to 7,000 leaders of labor, farm, religious, and civic organizations requesting their endorsement.[24] The (relative) silence he heard back was deafening and a clear signal of how much FDR and the New Deal had changed the political landscape.

Nonetheless, Marsh and the PL continued pushing for major reforms, such as government control or ownership of important economic sectors, tax increases on the wealthy, and major increases in federal expenditures to provide real relief to real people (as opposed to property owners). The title of a statement by President McConnell identified the policy goal succinctly: "Congress must tax more and borrow less."[25] Marsh testified that "America has reached the limit of trying to manipulate economic laws, instead of establishing economic justice" (US Congress 1937, 549) and that an emergency relief spending bill was inadequate (US Senate 1937a, 248).

Despite its relatively radical platform, the Lobby continued to have access to major legislators. A delegation organized by the PL and led by President McConnell met with both majority leaders and the Speaker to push for more social welfare legislation.[26] The Lobby also released several reports it had prepared analyzing economic data to buttress its policy positions. One, prepared by McConnell's predecessor, Colston Warne, focused on high-income taxpayers and how much of the nation's wealth they controlled.[27] Another, a few years later, confirmed the continuing validity of that economic trend.[28] Marsh was able to locate progressive legislators who supported some of the Lobby's goals. One called for federal control of the iron and steel industries, another for federal ownership of natural resources and railroads.[29] None of the bills even received a public hearing.

Undeterred, Marsh continued his indefatigable presence as a witness at congressional hearings. More often the tart and quotable critic than the praiser, he criticized the administration for its "inane policy of inflating prices and profits so as to attempt to get by on low tax rates" (US House 1938, 197), that it "has sold out to predatory interests" (US Senate 1938a, 1267), and of "pump-priming to enrich property owners at the expense of those least able" to pay (US Senate 1939a, 251). He tepidly praised a tax bill for slightly tightening corporate taxes.[30] He testified that he was "recognizing when an admirable thing is done, and I am glad to do that," but then quickly turned to what was wrong with the bill (US House 1939a, 274). He was more fulsome in supporting a bill for federal licensing of corporations, even admitting the need for pragmatism, because "perfection" could not be achieved immediately, rather requiring gradual legislation in that direction (US Senate 1938b, 431).

Marsh did not hesitate to insult legislators. When he finished denouncing a tax bill that he considered a giveaway to special and corporate interests as well as to the detriment of low-income families, he wrapped up his testimony with a self-righteous comment. When the senator chairing the hearing parried it somewhat lightheartedly, Marsh didn't hesitate to amplify the original insult:

> MARSH: I thank you for your courtesy; may God have mercy on you if you do not follow as to our recommendations.
>
> CHAIRMAN: I hope God will have mercy on us anyhow.
>
> MARSH: I am not sure you are entitled to it. (US Senate 1938c, 426)

It was exchanges like this that made him somewhat unwelcome and a bit feared at congressional hearings.

Other Domestic Issues

Through congressional testimony, public forums in Washington and New York, radio broadcasts, articles in the PL's *Bulletin*, and sundry other public venues, the PL continued vigorously advocating for the goals of its (non-economic) domestic legislative agenda, mostly a continuation of the public policies developed during Dewey's presidency. Marsh testified at several hearings in favor of government-owned and -run housing projects, emphasizing the difference between low-cost housing and public housing. The former, he said, "is a swindle" benefiting primarily property owners (US Senate 1939b, 57). Similarly, he testified against New Deal farm programs, urging that they be replaced with direct aid to farmers (US House 1937a, 161–173), and for a federal role in the purchase, marketing, and sale of agricultural products (US Senate 1937b, 41–50; 1939c, 355–358). This would aid not only farmers, but also consumers, he emphasized. Separate from such advocacy that would benefit consumers as well as farmers, the PL continued to view consumer protection as one of its distinct missions. For example, it urged more representation of consumers on relevant government bodies and, generally, consideration of consumer interests in policy making in the executive and legislative branches.[31]

Marsh also continued advocating for the PL position of government ownership of the railroads and, more generally, against railroad rates, profits, and self-inflicted indebtedness. He condemned a bill to subsidize railroads as "a dangerous tendency to pyramid plunder on posterity. . . . In the case of the railroads the rod, not the yardstick, is the proper method of achieving conduct compatible with public welfare" (US Senate 1939d, 2). Pragmatically, the obscure senator chairing the hearing, Harry Truman (D-MO), did not rise to the bait and instead tried to keep Marsh on task, welcoming specific comments on the bill while avoiding unnecessary arguments. Testifying at the House hearing, Marsh reiterated the PL's position on government takeover of the railroads.[32] However, the member of Congress chairing the session took the opposite approach of Truman, trying to argue with Marsh and undermine the credibility of his typically acidic testimony. The chairman wanted to pin Marsh down on who he was claiming he spoke for, what the PL was, and how many members it had. In response to the congressman's question on the amount of dues for PL members, this pointed exchange ensued:

> CONGRESSMAN ALFRED BULWINKLE (D-NC): What are their dues?
>
> MARSH: Well, they are trying to survive the New Deal, and it constitutes a very difficult task.
>
> BULWINKLE: That has not answered my question.
>
> MARSH: Well, I will answer your question in my way, and you will ask your questions in yours. (US House 1939b, 1361)

At a major rate case before the Interstate Commerce Commission (ICC), Marsh again testified (as he had in 1931, see Chap. 3) in opposition to the request for an across-the-board 15 percent rate increase. Instead, he said, the government should take over the railroads (as it had in WWI) and create an integrated national transportation system.[33] This time, Marsh was aided by research and testimony by Eliot Janeway. Later famous as an economic and financial author, in the 1930s Janeway was working both sides of the street. He was a professional (and ostensibly objective) journalist and, behind the scenes, an activist and economics researcher for the New Deal and other progressive causes (M. Janeway 2004, 96). For the PL's position at the rate case hearings, Janeway wrote a research paper examining in detail economic data about the railroads and documenting issues that undercut the rate increase request. Janeway submitted it at the ICC hearing on behalf of the PL.[34]

In addition to these now-traditional and continuing issues, there were three new and major domestic issues that captured Washington's attention: court packing, executive branch reorganization, and federal aid to education. Marsh, of course, was in the thick of it.

As a result of the US Supreme Court striking down as unconstitutional several New Deal laws and programs during his first term, in 1937 the president sought to capitalize on his landslide reelection to change the number of justices (which is not set in the Constitution) to create a pro–New Deal majority on the court (Shesol 2010). This was a major showdown between the administration and the majority-party Democrats on Capitol Hill. Predictably, supporters of the New Deal generally tended to endorse the president's bill (as a means to an end), while conservative Democrats and minority Republicans who opposed the New Deal were naturally against it. However, within the liberal and progressive movement, there was a different kind of split focusing largely on the merits of the issue. Given that the PL was to the left of FDR and felt that the New Deal did not go far enough in terms of systemic societal reforms, what position would it take? At its Board meeting in February 1937, Marsh asked the directors to give him clear direction. He said that based on his one-on-one discussions with members of the Board, it appeared to him that there was "a difference of opinion." What, if any, position should he take at the congressional hearings on the court-packing bill? After a lengthy discussion, the only consensus the Board of Directors could reach was that the PL "should not take any position on it."[35]

Typically frustrated by inaction and neutrality, Marsh testified against the bill. At the beginning of his comments, instead of merely introducing himself as a private citizen expressing his personal views, he unnecessarily reminded the senators that they knew him as the PL's executive secretary. This confused whom he was speaking for. Further, he said the PL's president had permitted him to testify, compounding the implication of mild agreement with Marsh's views. Marsh proceeded to rip the court-packing plan. He said the president's rush to pass it was "a race between appointments and constitutionality, instead of advocating sound measures, a constitutional amendment, or limiting the power of the Supreme Court to invalidate legislation, be it ever so damn foolish" (US Senate 1937c, 1827–1828).[36] Understandably, reporters from two major newspapers misattributed this pointed criticism as on behalf of the PL instead of merely by Marsh personally.[37]

Further fuzzing up the distinction between his personal and the Lobby's official views, Marsh wrote a bylined article in the PL's *Bulletin* excoriating the court-packing proposal.[38] In the article, he made no mention of the views being his own and not the Lobby's. This was egregiously misleading. Most articles in the monthly were unauthored and therefore, at least impliedly, representing the views of the organization. Similarly, the occasional bylined article by Marsh routinely reflected the Lobby's viewpoint.[39]

Also in 1937, Roosevelt asked Congress to approve a major reorganization of the executive branch based on the recommendations of the Brownlow Committee, which he had appointed to study ways to improve the management of the government. Triggering almost the same intensity of pitch as the court-packing bill, opposition was fierce and alarmist. Many accused the president of seeking to become a dictator, Marsh included. This time speaking in the name of the Lobby, Marsh released a press statement that was in league with the over-the-top chorus of critics. He said the bill was "futile fascism," claiming that it would give the president powers similar to those of dictators like Hitler and Mussolini who used those powers to advance the interests of "the exploiting classes."[40] The rhetoric of opponents such as Marsh became so heated that Roosevelt felt compelled to release a public statement saying he had no desire to be a dictator and that the bill would not lead to that. In a more tempered explanation in the PL's *Bulletin*, Marsh feebly admitted that the bill had some "admirable" elements (such as expanding the civil service system to more positions in the executive branch), but that did not change his mind overall. In particular, he attacked a small piece of the committee's recommendations, namely to create a central federal agency for public information. Such an agency "is the first step to Fascism and to control of the press and radio," Marsh said as one of the justifications for the PL's overall opposition to the bill.[41] Two years later, in 1939, with barely a political whimper, Congress passed a somewhat watered-down version of the bill.[42] Marsh was still against it, agreeing with a new book that was a "not too flattering appraisal of the proposed plans to make national administration work."[43]

The third topic that loomed large in this period was federal aid to education. This goal—the belief that the federal government had a role in elementary and secondary education, in particular to help level the playing field between schools with high proportions of students in poverty and those of middle-class–dominated schools—became a touchstone of liberalism. Conservatives saw no role for the federal government, arguing that public education was clearly a local issue directed by elected school boards. The People's Lobby was a strong supporter of federal aid to public schools but equally an opponent of tax funds going to religious schools.[44] This position was explicitly adopted by the PL Board of Directors, then presided over by Methodist Bishop McConnell (US Senate 1939e, 252). Its two-part position, for a change, was relatively widely held by liberal and progressive reformers. It also represented a split between old-line Protestant good government activists and the Catholic Church, which sought tax aid to its parochial schools. Marsh and the PL were prominent in supporting the legislation and insisting on the separation of church and state (Mitchell 1949, 139). Typically, Marsh testified that the funding level proposed in the bill was too low and that more should be appropriated (US House 1937b, 427). Nothing came of the effort at the time.[45]

The PL also led a coalition lobbying for federal funding to schools through the back door. It urged that some existing WPA appropriations could logically be spent as relief to schools in poor rural areas. McConnell led a large delegation meeting with the WPA's deputy director.[46] As mentioned at the beginning of this chapter, Dewey, as the PL's honorary president, provided a statement of support for the group to use in its lobbying. Dewey questioned the relatively widespread support for federal funding of good roads (in this case in rural areas) and contrasted it with the absence of financial support for public education in the same places. He wrote, "[P]ublic schools are the road to democratic institutions as well as to enlarged opportunities for the young."[47] Nonetheless, understandably, the agency was not interested in bashing that beehive, nor was Congress. There was no political consensus supporting federal aid to education.[48] More than a quarter of a century later, the issue was largely settled with the passage of the 1965 Elementary and Secondary Education Act as part of LBJ's War on Poverty, and it continues to reverberate to this day in American politics. Calls by conservatives at the time of writing (2014) to abolish the US Department of Education represent this continuing political battle.

Foreign and Military Policy

Brands noted that FDR's second term "centered increasingly on foreign affairs." The problem was that "in 1937 foreign affairs polarized American politics more strongly than ever" (2008, 479). For the president, this presented a political tightrope, but not for the Lobby. It knew whose side it was on: peace and voluntary international cooperation. As the tide of war was gradually rising, the PL was trying its best to rally its fellow peace organizations at home and abroad.[49] This gave the PL some strange bedfellows, as it found itself in agreement with conservative isolationists, who strenuously opposed any military role for the United States in the war as absolutely as lefty pacifists did.

The first major issue was the American role (or non-role) in the Spanish Civil War, which had begun in 1936. Generally, the left supported aid to the legitimate Republican side, while some conservatives and many Catholics supported Franco's rebel side. However, Roosevelt and the dominant public opinion opted for neutrality.[50] In 1937, Congress passed an even stronger Neutrality Act. At its annual meeting that year, the PL's Board of Directors discussed what position to take. On one hand, the PL was a peace group against all wars. On the other hand, its political sympathies were with the (Spanish) Republican side. There were strong differences of opinion on which direction to go in, and an extended discussion ensued. Finally, as it had on the court-packing controversy, the only consensus it could come to was not to take a position. Informally, it urged some of the umbrella religious peace groups to convene a conference to discuss it, but that was hardly a policy position.[51]

That gave Marsh very little maneuvering room. He occasionally included references to neutrality in general, and Spain in particular, in the issues of the *Bulletin*, but in the form of observations rather than positions.[52] He tiptoed close to expressing a position in the April 1937 issue with the theme of "When Does Unneutrality Start?" He argued that declarations of war were increasingly anachronistic, given the multiple wars going on at the time. If so, it "challenges our present conception of neutrality." But then he murkily ended with a question: "Can the conclusion be escaped that neutrality today is merely a figment of the imagination?" Still, he was careful not to cross the line and instead tepidly restated the PL's long-standing principle of promoting international cooperation instead of war.[53]

As the war continued, the issue continued. In 1938, the Senate Foreign Relations Committee faced a resolution to permit a temporary lifting of the Neutrality Act in order to provide arms to the Republican side. At the last minute, the committee voted against the action. Marsh, barely concealing his personal opinion, wrote that the killing of the motion was "one of the most gruesome stories in Washington." He urged all PL members to contact their US senator to push for another committee vote, but carefully did not state explicitly which substantive side he hoped the letter writers would take.[54] But it was clear.

Taking a position on the Spanish Civil War continued to roil the leadership of the Lobby. The only way to break the deadlock on the Board of Directors was a decision to conduct an unprecedented referendum of all PL members. In late 1938, Marsh sent a questionnaire to all paid-up PL members asking what views they thought the Lobby should take on the Spanish arms embargo and on a few domestic issues (mostly related to New Deal programs allegedly propping up inflated property values and encouraging speculative buying). The vote on the Spanish question was 479 to 9 in favor of lifting the embargo to provide arms to the Republican side.[55] The referendum had been timed so that the results could be discussed at the PL's annual meeting, which traditionally convened at the beginning of the new year. The issue was discussed at the January 3, 1939, meeting, but even with the results of the referendum, it still "was discussed at length." Eventually, the motion to favor lifting the Spanish arms embargo passed.[56] However, this was for naught because events quickly made this policy decision moot.

The first opportunity to unveil the new policy was a hearing in Congress on the Neutrality Act in April 1939. By then, the Spanish Civil War had ended with the complete victory of Franco's rebels. Given that the referendum of the members had related exclusively to an exception to the neutrality act for the Spanish case, Marsh could not base his testimony on it. Therefore, he was compelled to emphasize that "I speak chiefly for myself, although I think that I shall represent largely the viewpoint of our members" (US House 1939c, 294). This phrasing purposely left the impression that he was somewhat speaking for the organization, or at least a majority of its members. As a result, the hearing record mistakenly, but understandably, identified him as representing the PL. The takeaway from his testimony was that neutrality was impossible and that the United States should not—however indirectly or unintentionally—find itself supplying arms to the side of imperialist, colonialist, and warmongering powers like the United Kingdom and France. In particular, because of FDR's unilateral efforts at neutrality in the beginning of the Spanish Civil War, Marsh "opposed giving discretionary power to the President to deal with problems of neutrality."[57]

International developments also affected domestic decisions about the military. Actions by Japan, Germany, and Italy prompted Roosevelt to call for increased spending to strengthen national defense and hemispheric defense to maintain the Monroe Doctrine. It was an adroit political move. Even isolationists felt that international events justified increasing the defense of the country and being able to enforce the Monroe Doctrine. Who could reasonably be against improving the capability of the Navy to protect a country bounded by two oceans, with war-making countries on the opposite shores of those oceans? Isolationists could not, but pacifists and Socialists could and would.

Marsh testified at a hearing by the House Committee on Naval Affairs against FDR's request for increased funding for naval construction to build a two-ocean navy instead of the current fleet, which was adequate for only one.[58] He unloaded with both barrels, saying, "[W]e won't be attacked on both coasts simultaneously, and if we were, we need coast defenses, not two marauding navies. We have no more right to run South America than Japan has to rape China. . . . It is true the President in his naval message proclaimed that a state of war scare existed, but he is worse scared over the inevitable failure of the esoteric economies which are called a New Deal. America's only real enemies are here at home; the war against poverty here is being lost, so it is natural to beat the tom-toms, for a war to make America safe for lynching" (US House 1938b, 2410). In his prepared statement, Marsh made a point of saying that Dewey, while then only the PL's honorary president, had specifically endorsed the views Marsh was presenting (2445).

Marsh's provocative comments triggered such negative reactions in the room that committee chairman Carl Vinson (D-GA) had to interrupt and pound the gavel for order. When Vinson told Marsh a few minutes later that his time had expired, Marsh kept talking. After a few more minutes, Vinson again told Marsh that his time was up. Marsh objected, talked a bit more, and then said he wanted to insert some additional material in the record of the hearing to document his position. Vinson agreed, but only if the submissions were no more than 10,000 words. Marsh refused to accept that. Vinson then called for a committee vote on whether to hold Marsh to 10,000 words. The vote was a tie (eight to eight), so the motion failed. Marsh promptly inserted fifty-four dense pages of additional material to underscore his arguments (2414–2468). Writing in the 1970s, a historian cited Marsh's combative testimony as emblematic of the anti-imperialist movement in the United States in the 1930s (Papachristou 1974, 66, 69).

After the bill passed the House, Marsh testified against it again at the counterpart Senate hearing. He was equally vehement in his opposition. Early in his testimony, he said that "the real reason for the present naval-expansion scheme is to cover up the fact that the present administration is the most stupid since the World War [I] profiteers skinned the people out of many billions under the protection of Bernard M. Baruch" (US Senate 1938d, 288). He concluded with the statement that comprehensively captured the PL's worldview of domestic and foreign policy being interrelated: "We prefer an economic democracy to the conscription of men; and if you will kill this bill and enact legislation to end unemployment at home you will have very little demand for such measures as you have before you" (302). (This time the chairman was lenient about letting him insert published material into the record.)

For a bill funding fortifications in the Pacific as public works, Marsh again testified against it. He said, "No fortifications of Guam, the Philippines, Hawaii, or any submerged islands are needed, until the American people defeat the special privileges at home, which have routed them, and left 10,000,000 unemployed" (US Senate 1939f, 163–164). Marsh also made the unusual argument that missionaries abroad had no right to call for the United States to intervene diplomatically and militarily to protect them. "Missionaries have no ethical right to insist that their Government protect them when they are trying to convert other people against their will," he said (170). This position had the potential of offending some of the religious denominations that were often sympathetic to the PL's policy agenda but were also active in missionizing in Asia.

The PL also objected to the administration's use of international conditions as the justification for a more muscular so-called hemispheric defense and more interventionist policy toward Latin America. Marsh applauded Mexico for nationalizing property owned by US corporations and individuals. From the PL's perspective, this was precisely what it was advocating for the United States: socialization or public control of natural resources, monopolies, and other major industrial sectors. Marsh praised the actions on the grounds that the Mexican government was "doing something for its people instead of to them." But the Roosevelt administration decided to intervene on the side of private property owners by sending quite threatening notes to Mexico about the necessity of full and fair compensation or undoing the confiscations. It was a not-so-veiled threat to intervene militarily if necessary to protect American commercial assets in a foreign country. Marsh said that the United States was acting as "a collection agency for the unsavory Rockefeller-Hearst looters of Mexico."[59] In reply, a coalition opposing the confiscations called the PL's criticisms "insulting and brazen."[60]

Marsh later accused the United States of trying to establish a "protectorate" over Latin America, even though those countries did not ask the United States to "save" them. He claimed that the new interventionist policy toward the Americas was motivated by the president and Democratic Party seeking to distract the electorate's attention away from the failures of the New Deal at home, which, in turn, would lead to a major defeat in the 1940 elections.[61] It was a far-fetched and paranoid-sounding accusation, but logical in the context of the PL's persistent criticism that the New Deal was on the verge of failing because it was too status quo–oriented and too solicitous of property owners.

In the retrospect of history, Marsh said even worse on other occasions. He wrote that the British government was dominated by a triumvirate of landowners, bankers, and businessmen. Based on that control, the British government in turn was "operating" Hitler, that is, acquiescing to his "stupid treatment of Jews and of liberals" just as long as he protected the principles of a for-profit economy and private property ownership.[62] Another time, in just plain bad taste, he headlined the lead article in an issue of the *Bulletin* with "Heil, American Property Rights!"[63] He was not alone. In another issue, PL Treasurer John Gray wrote that "the Jews the world over have influence, particularly in finance, out of all proportion to their numbers."[64]

The odd coalition of conservative isolationists and left-wing pacifists came to a culmination by rallying around a proposed constitutional amendment requiring a national referendum before the United States went to war. It was introduced in late 1937 by Senator Robert La Follette, Jr. (R-WI). The PL instantly endorsed it and urged its members to convey their support to their state's congressional delegation.[65] After intense lobbying by the administration (and internationalist interest groups), the referendum version in the House, called the Ludlow Amendment, was defeated in early 1938 by a vote of 209 to 188. That was pretty close and gave some encouragement to peace groups like the PL as well as isolationists.[66]

In May 1939, Marsh represented the PL at a Senate hearing on the referendum idea. He presented several reasons to justify having a war referendum, including that it was merely an extension of the approach that "farmers vote on crop control and labor on the union to represent them" (US Senate 1939g, 82). Surely going to war was as important? He packaged the PL's entire critique of the economic failures at home in an adjective-filled sentence. The United States needed even more now than at the beginning of the New Deal "an economic system that will work in soil-eroded, monopoly ridden, privilege-entrenched wealth and poverty stricken and slum-cursed United States" (83). Some senators on the committee also supported the resolution, but not this kind of depiction of the country. For them, Marsh stepped over the line when he counted Roosevelt as one of "four great messianic monomaniacs in the world today." (The other three were Hitler, Stalin, and Mussolini.) When several objected to that characterization of the president, Marsh refused to back down, saying, "I emphatically do make that statement, and you are entitled to your opinion, as I to mine" (87).

Until Hitler and Stalin's invasions of Poland in September 1939, the PL was still advocating against war. It used its public fora broadcast on national radio networks to promote its antiwar stance. For example, one of the featured speakers at a June event was isolationist and conservative Senator Gerald Nye (R-ND), no friend of socialists he. His address was considered important enough to be published in *Vital Speeches of the Day*.[67] Marsh traveled in Europe in the summer of 1939 and came back with his set views intact. The United States should stay out of a war that seemed imminent, likely over Poland. In a pacifist's and anti-capitalist's last plea before the apparently inevitable coming war, he said, "The world needs another example of making peace work, more than winning any war, and America's greatest service will be to provide that example."[68] This was the last issue of the Lobby's *Bulletin* before Hitler's invasion of Poland on September 1.[69]

Between 1937 and autumn 1939, regardless of developments, be they the Japanese-Russian war, Japanese incursions in China, or Hitler's threats to Czechoslovakia and Poland, the PL clung to its pacifist views that neutrality and international cooperation were the solutions to all violent global problems. Those wars were imperialistic, colonialistic, and focused on saving the capitalist system, which was on its deathbed. The victory of socialism and world peace was just over the horizon. With the twenty-twenty hindsight of history, it seems myopic, naive, and wholly disconnected from reality. But for these peace and left activists, WWI had been a mistake, and to learn from history meant to resist the siren calls for another American military role in wars abroad, especially in Europe.

Chapter 9

Lobby Operations and Conservative Attacks during FDR's Second Term, 1937–1940

Advocacy Strategy: PR to the Max

By 1937, the publicity orientation of the People's Lobby had settled into a comfortable and recurring template. As during FDR's first term, Marsh and the officers focused on maximal publicity of the Lobby's views, including public meetings, radio broadcasts, press releases, and speaking tours (see Chap. 7).

Marsh was especially pleased with the reach and impact of the radio broadcasts. An on-air forum in mid-February 1937 prompted 1,300 mailed requests for more information in the first ten days after the program.[1] Three years later, a broadcast on unemployment led to 1,029 requests for more information (evidently for hard copies of the talks). Marsh was especially delighted by the latter, because some requests were from non-members and residents of cities where the PL had little to no presence. He was glad to note they came from 44 states and 539 localities.[2] This was a concrete demonstration of the power of publicity and its ability to increase the base and potential influence of the PL.

The Lobby's mastery of free radio prompted a complaint by a media critic. In a blast at the amount and sources of public service broadcasting of radio stations, media critic Silas Bent made a few general complaints, but then specifically criticized only one organization. He wondered why "Socialists and Communists get more time on the air than they get space in newspapers, [and] that the People's Lobby has its say" (1937, 121). For Bent, these were examples of excessively easy access to free airtime. That he mentioned only the PL specifically indicates how prevalent its radio talks were—sometimes almost every Saturday.

Another successful venue for publicity was the distribution of reprints of the *Congressional Record*. Sometimes these were the texts of talks that senators and congressmen had given on the floor of their house, sometimes at PL events, sometimes inserts of items written by Marsh or reprints of articles in the *Bulletin*. Members of Congress could send out for free the reprints of something they had inserted in the *Record*. This was known as the frank. While that approach was ideal, Marsh was equally happy to reprint those inserts at the PL's expense and mail them out, whether by request or to a mailing list of potential interested citizens. In 1938, Marsh reprinted about 10,000 copies each of about half a dozen different congressional speeches promoting PL policy goals and mailed out copies as widely as possible.[3] Marsh estimated that he had mailed out about 320,000 copies of PL materials in 1939 and had increased that to 450,000 in 1940.[4]

Marsh also continued his annual speaking tours to the west. He was usually on the road for about a month. For example, a pastiche of local coverage of his 1938 trip included clippings from Pittsburg, Cleveland, Milwaukee, Minneapolis, St. Louis, Topeka, Bismarck, Kansas City, Seattle, Indianapolis, Cincinnati, and Butte.[5] He was a publicity hound *par excellence*. On several occasions during these trips, he gave the sermon at Sunday services.[6] Upon his return from these trips, he would convey his impressions of conditions. After his 1937 tour, he claimed that a "growing fear of fascist coups were expressed by the liberal ministers of many denominations, based partly on the retreat to conservatism of the wealthy lay members of their churches."[7] After his 1939 trip, he said his audiences were "at least five to one against sending American boys abroad."[8] A year later, he said he encountered groups "working to provide in America an economic setup here, which shall be a moral equivalent for imperialism and war."[9] Marsh made shorter visits to New England and elsewhere on the East Coast giving public talks.[10] In general, he wrote, "one of the most pleasant features of lobbying is discussing the program of the people's lobby every year from coast to coast" (Marsh 1938, 82). Here was a classic formula of his PR strategy: grassroots organizing plus publicity equals lobbying.

In Operation

Based on the precedents and meeting cycles established when Dewey was president, the Lobby continued having annual meetings early every calendar year to approve the slate of officers for the year, name members of the Executive Committee, review the proposed annual budget, and approve the lobbying and policy agenda for the year. Sometimes these were membership meetings, as opposed to of the Board of Directors or the Executive Committee. In those cases, as he had done when Dewey was president, Marsh would mail out proxies to all members and ask them to sign and return the proxies before the meeting.[11] Also, as a corporation, the Lobby was always meticulous about having an independent public accountant audit the Lobby's books and submit a report to the officers.

While these formal meetings sometimes had only about half a dozen people present, they nonetheless demonstrate an organizational commitment to regularized and routine operations. This may have been a small coterie of activists, but they were maintaining a viable nonprofit corporation in all respects.[12] Yes, Marsh was the engine of energy for the Lobby after Dewey stepped partially aside, but Marsh was not speaking in the name of a fictional paper organization or a letterhead. This was a working organization of people committed to the cause of public policies further to the left of FDR. They may have been few, but they were some. And they were not led around by the nose by Marsh.

One indication of the existence of a working organization was the involvement of Bishop McConnell as the Lobby's president. McConnell was not merely a name on a letterhead. He had standing and credibility as an activist for social justice before his involvement in the PL (Steinkraus 1957). The previous chapter detailed some example of his personal participation in the PL's ongoing work. He also spoke at meetings in New York and Washington, led delegations, gave talks on the radio, and signed statements of PL policy positions.[13] McConnell, no lackey he, would not have expressed those views and given of his time unless he agreed with them and felt the Lobby as an organization had already approved those policy positions.

Another manifestation of an independent board overseeing Marsh were the occasions when the leadership prohibited Marsh from testifying on certain matters in the Lobby's name. Given that Marsh was so familiar to legislators from having testified dozens of times on behalf of the PL, he had to bend over backward so that it would be clear in the record that he was only speaking for himself. (As mentioned in the preceding chapter, Marsh testified against the court-packing plan somewhat on his own, but permitted the impression that his views semi-represented those of the organization.) Some of those non-PL issues included his appearances on legislation to create farmer crop insurance because the Lobby preferred a federal marketing corporation (US Senate 1937d, 128) and to revise the tax code of the District of Columbia, as the Lobby had no position on that (US Senate 1937e, 22; US House 1939d, 36).[14] These examples are another indication that Marsh did not dominate the Lobby's board or policy positions.

The Lobby's commitment to neutrality in US foreign policy caused it to have at least one notable resignation in principle. Rabbi Edward Israel of Baltimore had been active in the PL and a member of its advisory Council. His name was listed on the letterhead of the Lobby and the masthead of the monthly *Bulletin*. Marsh praised Israel, saying that "the most active support for our tax program" was from Israel as chair of a social justice committee of the national association of reform rabbis.[15] But things began looking different to Israel after Hitler and Stalin's invasion of Poland in September 1939. At that point, the Lobby's Board had reaffirmed its position of promoting American neutrality and criticizing any US support to France and the United Kingdom that could possibly be used to maintain those countries' empires and colonies. Israel was understandably affected by the fate of his co-religionists under Hitler, but more generally to the apparent ascendancy of fascism in Europe and the general threat it posed to the principle of democratic government. For left-leaning activists, the German-Soviet Nonaggression Pact (just before the invasion of Poland) was a jarring event causing significant dissonance. In reaction, Israel submitted a forceful letter of resignation, stating:

> I by no means condone the imperialism represented by the allied governments, but I think that it is a case of moral myopia to be unable to distinguish between the potentialities for some decent civilization as represented by such democracy as exists on one side and the impossibility of any such realization through the totalitarianism on the other side. . . . I cannot without absolute horror contemplate a world in which the cause of Hitler and Stalin would be victorious. With all the rottenness of democracies, there is hope of constant improvement and inner re-generation. . . . I, therefore, cannot be neutral in the present crisis. Nor can I be part of any organization which looks upon both sides as similar from a moral point of view.[16]

Here was a good example of the split occurring in the non-Communist left in the period before Pearl Harbor. Was the lesson of WWI to stay neutral and not reward French and UK colonialism, or was the lesson a justification for another internationalist role for the United States (as had been Dewey's position)? The PL's leadership and its political ideology did not doubt it was right in opposing the war, but Israel's resignation indicated the diminishing base of the PL's potential support and membership. And, at least in the current retrospect of the conventional wisdom of American history, Israel was right about the US role and the PL was wrong. Still, this minority opinion held by the PL is an interesting documentation that the opposition to a US role in the war was not only being advocated by isolationists on the right, but also by socialists on the left. It held those views regardless of defections and general unpopularity with increasing segments of the liberals.

The PL maintained active membership drives to expand its base and spread its gospel. It frequently engaged in mailings to lists of activists in the left's causes, hoping to recruit new members and strengthen the PL's grassroots reach and always-tight finances. Mass mailings with catchy headlines included "We Can Win a War on Poverty Here But Not a Foreign War" (October 1939), "Strength Needs Sense" (November 1939), and "Why Not Look Before We Leap Into—?" (May 1940).[17] Marsh was also quite proactive in pursuing members with lapsed dues, urging them to re-up for the next year. Showing a good sense of customer relations, he was also prompt in sending thank-you letters to those who renewed. Another source for potential new members was a routine solicitation of renewing members for suggestions of names of other people they knew whom the PL could contact.[18]

A special effort to recruit new members was a dinner meeting in New York City in April 1937. It featured all of the Lobby's stars to discuss the policy agenda it was pursuing that year. Topics included government housing, socialized waterpower, federal licensing of corporations, and public ownership of natural resources. In an effort to attract as large a crowd as possible, the flier was mailed out widely (with a "Please Post" stamped on it), with a promise that no speech would last longer than eight minutes and that "no financial appeal will be made at this dinner."[19] As mentioned in the previous chapter, Dewey was one of the speakers, and his speech was broadcast on the radio.

One unusual membership activity during this period was the publication of a list of some of the members of the Lobby. Published in 1940 in a formal typeset format, it contained a listing of about 150 prominent members, including their titles and home city.[20] It is unclear what prompted the issuance of the list. It is possible that it was viewed merely as part of an ongoing recruiting, indicating to potential members that the Lobby was a major organization given the impressive list of its members. In that case, it conveyed a kind of message that one would be in good company if one joined. Given the timing, it is also possible that the publishing of names was for a different (or second) purpose. One of the manifestations of the increasing anti-Communist hysteria whipped up by the right, especially after the German-Soviet Nonaggression Pact in August 1939 (to be discussed in more detail in the next subchapter), related to *names*. HUAC was holding hearings on subversives in the United States and routinely pressed for people to "name names" of the supposed vast left-wing conspiracy in the United States. In parallel, the FBI was actively investigating all political radicals and potential subversives. They were sometimes on the right (such as pro-Nazi groups), but traditionally Director Hoover was more suspicious of the left and especially interested in its subversive and anarchist potential (dating back to the bombing of the home of Attorney General Palmer in 1919). If this *tour d'horizon* is roughly right, then a purpose of the publication may have been to reduce fear by openly advertising the names of major members. The message would have been along the lines of "These important people are not afraid to be publicly associated with the Lobby." Hence, the list may have been trying to indicate to potential members that there was nothing to be afraid of if they, too, joined the PL.

Despite these membership recruitment drives, the PL continued to be a modest organization. For most of the years between 1937 and 1940, it had an annual income and expenditures of about $10,000. There continued to be only two employees, Marsh and a secretary, both with low salaries. Membership in 1940 was slightly more than 2,000, with about an additional 500 subscribers to the *Bulletin* (US Congress 1940, 389).

Marsh liked to emphasize why it was difficult to recruit new members or to retain existing ones. That was because the Lobby was not a special interest group; rather—based on Berry's typology—it was a public interest group. The PL was not lobbying on behalf of the self-serving economic interests of its members, as was so nearly universal in Washington at the time. Even some of the groups lobbying for noneconomic matters were still pursuing self-interested (if abstract) benefits, as had the Prohibition and Suffragette organizations. In fact, the Lobby was often advocating for economic policies that explicitly went against the self-interest of its members. For example, in advocating for a more progressive tax system and for increasing taxes to pay for relief and military expenditures (instead of deficit spending), Marsh reveled in saying that the PL wanted to increase the taxes its members would pay. This, of course, made Marsh a standout at the routine Washington hearings with typically long lists of special pleaders. Such a political anomaly went to the heart of precisely what Dewey and Marsh were seeking to have, namely an organization that pursued the public's best interest even if it was not in the economic self-interest of its own dues-paying members.

In his annual report for 1937, Marsh frankly said this unique organizational mission made it especially hard to maintain membership levels.[21] He was not complaining, but was highlighting one of the reasons why the size of this national organization was so modest. At a congressional hearing, for example, he tried to make the most of this unusual (for Washington) situation: "If I were here pleading for exemption for our members I would be ashamed of myself. If members of the People's Lobby want to resign because I have advocated our program they will resign, but I think they are all of them loyal enough to want to pay more taxes" (US Senate 1940a, 452). In this way, the PL held the moral high ground in the me-me-me world of Washington politics.

Media Characterizations and Conservative Attacks

The media continued having trouble labeling the People's Lobby. In one story, it was described (along with some coalition partners) as "a group of liberals."[22] Similarly, the popular Washington Merry-Go-Round column described the PL as a peace group, "headed by that old liberal warhorse, Ben Marsh."[23] An AP story identified it as "an independent investigating agency."[24] The conservative *Chicago Tribune* placed the lobby's title in quotation marks (and lower case): " 'the people's lobby.' "[25] More ominously in terms of its standing and image, at least once the *New York Times* also placed its name in quotation marks, but in upper case: "the 'People's Lobby.' "[26] (This appears to have been a one-off, not routinely used.)

The Lobby was often smeared by conservatives as red. A Democratic politician in New York City accused the La Guardia administration of being linked to the Communist Party because an appointed department head was "a member of the council of the People's Lobby, a radical Socialist lobby maintained in Washington."[27] A conservative Democratic congressman noted that "Communism works under the most appealing titles known to tongue or pen" and then named the PL as one of them.[28] In 1939, a Republican congressman pooh-poohed the threat of pro-Nazi groups in the United States; instead, he claimed, "the danger lies entirely in communism." His list of un-American Communist organizations that should be banned included "the Peoples [*sic*] Lobby."[29]

Sometimes when Marsh testified at congressional hearings, his interlocutors tried to undermine his credibility by calling out the PL as red. At a Senate hearing in 1939, Marsh testified against additional naval expenditures, especially as supposedly public works. Naval Affairs Committee chair David Walsh (D-MA) tried to pin him down:

> MARSH: The conflict in the world today is . . . between two conflicting economic systems—the system of private profit and the system of attempting to meet the needs of the people.
>
> WALSH: What name did you call that system by? The system to attempt to meet the needs of the people; would you call that a socialistic state?
>
> MARSH: No; not necessarily. I would call it public ownership and common-sense protection for our people.
>
> WALSH: You are against the system that permits profits?
>
> MARSH: I am against a system which permits profit at the expense of the producers and the consumers. (US Senate 1939f, 166)

A more pointed attack on the PL occurred in 1939 during the Senate hearings on FDR's nomination of former Congressman Fred Amlie (Progressive-WI) to the Interstate Commerce Commission. The conservative coalition mounted a major effort to defeat the nomination by accusing Amlie, by virtue of his Wisconsin Progressive philosophy, of being far to the left, anti-railroad, and anti-corporation. Marsh testified in support of Amlie's confirmation. Ranking Subcommittee member Warren Austin (R-VT) was ready:

> AUSTIN: You have expressed your own views and the views of the People's Lobby in a hearing several years ago before a commission to promote peace and to equalize the burdens and remove the profits of war; is that not a fact?
>
> MARSH: Yes; and I was wondering—I do not remember the date. . . .
>
> AUSTIN: March 5 to 18, 1931 . . . On that occasion this transcript, on page 323, indicates that you testified as follows . . .
>
> MARSH: Am I being confirmed?

AUSTIN: Perhaps not, but the value of your testimony is under consideration. . . . Did you represent the sentiment and beliefs of the People's Lobby in so expressing yourself?

MARSH: I do not just know what that has to do with Mr. Amlie's confirmation . . .

AUSTIN: On that occasion you prefaced those remarks, which I have read, apparently, with this statement [that Marsh had cleared his testimony with John Dewey and that his testimony was on behalf of the PL]. That was probably correct, was it not?

MARSH: Yes. . . . Now, I do not want Mr. Amlie to be blamed for anything I have said. . . .

AUSTIN: The People's Lobby publishes a bulletin, does it not?

MARSH: Yes . . .

AUSTIN: And you consider that that bulletin truthfully represents the thoughts of the People's Lobby, do you?

MARSH: I am responsible for anything in there unless some article that is signed.

AUSTIN: . . . [reads long except from *PLB* on supporting government ownership of railroads.] The question is, "Do you adhere to those views now?"

MARSH: In substance, but I cannot conceive how the confirmation of Mr. Amlie will affect that. He cannot take the railroads away from their private owners. (US Senate 1939h, 157–160)

Austin was going for a two-fer. He then grilled Marsh about a person who had testified before Marsh, also in favor of the appointment. Was it true that the person was indeed affiliated with the Lobby? Yes, said Marsh, he had served on the Board of Directors and then, as he got older, shifted to the advisory Council (160–161). That was exactly what Austin was looking for. He could use the PL to discredit the earlier witness, too. Eventually, facing defeat, Amlie asked the president to withdraw his nomination. The red-baiters had won. Marsh angrily observed that "whenever a fellow is losing an argument he just accuses somebody else of being a Communist" (156). It worked.

Several self-proclaimed Communist hunters and activists similarly labeled the PL as red and dangerous. A. Cloyd Gill said its "program is in accord with the Socialist-Communist system of Russia."[30] Testifying at a HUAC hearing, Walter Steele repeatedly identified "John Dewey's People's Lobby" as the affiliation of many of the people he was naming. Steele explicitly identified Marsh as a socialist and a writer for a "Communist organ" (US House 1938c, 690). For Marsh, never afraid of authority and officialdom, HUAC was the gift that kept on giving. He enjoyed sending public letters to its chair, Martin Dies Jr., ridiculing the committee's so-called investigations, baiting Dies and the committee, and pointing out the committee's absurd activities.[31]

Much more serious was an FBI report on Marsh in 1941 (but before Pearl Harbor). Based in part on its own investigation and partly from the Special Investigations Division of the Washington Police Department, it stated that Marsh "has taken an exceptionally active part in communistic activities in the District [of Columbia]." An undercover police officer had attended some public meetings that Marsh addressed over the years and had taken verbatim notes. Marsh was quoted as expressing vehement criticisms of FDR and some positive comments about the SU. As a result, the FBI classified Marsh as a "probable radical." Ominously, it recommended him "as a fit subject for custodial detention in the event of a national emergency." The FBI categorized Marsh in the classification "Internal Security–C."[32] This meant he was a threat to internal security as a Communist and was listed on the FBI's Custodial Detention Index.

An important detail that stands out in this FBI file is that all of Marsh's careful parsing of his utterances over the years was for naught. On different public occasions over the years, he had said he was not a revolutionary, not a Communist, and did not even belong to the Socialist Party. The FBI did not care about such, to it, minor and irrelevant distinctions. A radical lefty of whatever tint of red was a Communist and a security threat to the United States in time of war. Criticizing the president in strong terms and praising the SU in mild terms were all it took. It is also interesting that the FBI categorized Marsh not as a Communist, but as engaging in "communistic" activities. To the FBI, this was apparently a distinction without a difference. Evidently, holding communistic views was enough to classify someone as a Communist, even if they were not members of the Communist Party. Yet, there *is* a clear difference between holding views and *being* something. The FBI did not care. This is a good example of the times—that

Marsh proclaimed his left-leaning views at public events loudly, clearly, and repeatedly, yet he never indicated a support for a violent takeover of the US government or of having a fidelity to a country other than the United States. In those days, one's views were enough to make one dangerous. (As it turned out, the FBI's detention of subversives in the first few days after Pearl Harbor was limited to Germans and Italians. Because Marsh was not in that category, he was not taken into custody.)

These political and governmental attacks on the left in general, and the PL specifically, left their mark. Around the country, people were afraid of being called a Communist. In mid-1941, Marsh went on his annual western speaking tour. There were committed (but small) groups of supporters of the PL and its political ideology in every city he visited who served as an audience for his public talks. But, he noted, "few people talked as frankly in open meeting, as they did privately!"[33] This poignantly conveys that even before Pearl Harbor, people were afraid of being outside the political mainstream. No matter how loyal they were to the United States, were non-Communist in their politics, and committed to political change only through constitutional means, they were scared. Marsh's observation was a powerful hint of the impact of the use of anti-Communism by conservatives—this at a time when the SU was now fighting Hitler as vigorously as the United Kingdom (and the United States was not). No matter. It was a dangerous time to be further to the left of the Democratic Party, even a little bit.

Dewey Steps Down as Honorary President

Late in 1939, Dewey received a letter complaining about the positions of the PL. The letter writer, a professor (not an acquaintance of Dewey's), accused Dewey and the PL of having Communist ideology, especially because it espoused public ownership of key economic functions. Dewey replied at length defending the PL's policy platform. He noted that the Post Office, highways, and public schools were all economic activities owned by the government. Surely no one considered these as examples of Communism at work? Then, extending his logic, if public ownership of highways was OK, why would ownership of railroads not be? Here was a cogent and low-key way to make a point, typical of Dewey's style in contrast to Marsh's slash and burn rhetoric. Dewey also noted that, as its honorary president, "I have no active share in forming the policies of the Lobby." Nonetheless, he was more than willing to defend its (and his) long-standing views. He concluded with the underlying premise of the work of the PL since he and Marsh had cofounded it in 1928. The lobby supported changes in public policies only "by democratic methods." This approach was "not only non-communistic but is in all human probability the best means of forestalling attempts at violent change in our institutions."[34] This letter was the last time Dewey wrote of the Lobby. It presents an apt summary of the political ideology he and Marsh had crafted more than a decade earlier.

At the PL's annual meeting on January 8, 1940, Dewey was reelected as the Lobby's honorary president for the year.[35] Evidently, he accepted, given that his name continued to be displayed on the Lobby's stationery letterhead and the masthead of the monthly *Bulletin*.[36] While there is no archival record, Dewey retired from the Lobby in mid-1940. It is possible that was triggered by a policy difference regarding the US role in WWII (pre–Pearl Harbor), but the absence of any correspondence on the subject suggests that he resigned quietly and for nonpolicy reasons. His departure was probably due to age and limited energy. In June 1940, he was eighty years old (and three months shy of his eighty-first birthday). Withdrawal from even an honorary position with the Lobby would be understandable. It was now four and a half years since he had stepped down as president. Dewey had delayed severing his last ties with the PL as long as reasonably possible. He had accomplished what he wanted, namely that there was never any doubt about his continuing agreement with the Lobby's work. (Later that year, Dewey left little doubt how he felt about FDR's campaign for an unprecedented third term. He endorsed Norman Thomas again [Bullert 1983, 162].)

After stepping down as honorary president, there were a few vestigial or implied links between Dewey and the PL, but they were minor. For example, even though he was no longer connected to the Lobby (except as a rank-and-file member), the issue of the *Bulletin* for April 1941 reprinted a Dewey column that had first been published in the *New Republic* in February.[37] Also in early 1941, Marsh wrote Eleanor Roosevelt complaining that, contrary to something she had said and that was quoted in the *New York Times*, some organizations like the People's Lobby had not been given an opportunity to testify at the Senate hearing on Lend-Lease. In his letter, Marsh invoked John Dewey's name and views, implying that denying the PL the right to testify was tantamount to denying it to Dewey.[38] This was a stretch, especially given that Dewey no longer had any formal leadership role in the PL. Mrs. Roosevelt declined to get involved, saying she had great respect for Dewey, but that it was her impression that an adequate number of peace groups opposed to Lend-Lease had been given a chance to testify at the Senate hearing. She felt the PL's side was fully expressed at that public forum, even if the PL's specifically was not.[39]

With Dewey stepping down as honorary president, how would the People's Lobby fare without any link to him?

Chapter 10

Policy Advocacy and Lobby Operations after Dewey

World War II and Postwar America, 1941–1950

With John Dewey stepping down as the honorary president of the People's Lobby in 1940, the organization lost its marquee name and the celebrity who had given it credibility and standing. Without Dewey, the Lobby was less distinguished, less distinctive, and less of interest. Indeed, while it survived Dewey by a decade, the Lobby was in a long, slow fade-out.

Dewey had always served as a kind of balance to Marsh's combative instincts. Dewey was gentler, did not like attacking a person's character, especially not with personal insults, and generally—philosopher that he was—tried to keep the PL's focus on higher, abstract public policy goals. Dewey had sometimes restrained Marsh when Dewey felt Marsh was going too far. They were a good team. Even when Dewey was merely the honorary president of the Lobby, his presence and tutoring of Marsh kept Marsh from following his worst instincts. Now, without Dewey, Marsh was much less restrained. Yes, the Lobby had a real and working Board of Directors, officers who took their role seriously, and a prestigious president (Bishop McConnell) who had standing and credibility preceding his involvement in the PL. Nevertheless, none of them had the status, patience or counterweight to rein in Marsh that Dewey had had. So, in the post-Dewey decade of the Lobby, Marsh's statements hewed to the same political ideology and the same emphasis on public relations but sounded increasingly shrill and personal. His self-righteousness was an asset in that he never got discouraged, but it seemed that his statements were becoming so far to the left of the liberal mainstream that he was hurting his own ability to be paid attention to, let alone to influence policy making.

World War II: Criticizing Federal Policies

The PL's first comment on the Japanese attack on Pearl Harbor came in its December *Bulletin*. In the lead story, Marsh grudgingly accepted the need for a declaration of war against Japan in reaction to the attack. He quickly segued to the federal government's wartime emergency powers. These could lead to some of the Lobby's policy goals, such as government control of the railroads and major industrial manufacturers. Here was a chance to finally defeat the economic royalists (whom he felt the New Deal had kept in power) and facilitate unhampered federal access to natural resources, the Army's ability to control some land uses, lifting of tariffs, and closing of the stock markets. If the latter kinds of scenarios were to occur, he concluded, they would be conducive to a true national "spirit and purpose, essential [to] create a dynamic unity in America."[1]

Later in the issue, Marsh pointedly drew attention to the potential of disparity in the war effort. "Our efforts to get armaments under private enterprise has shown that private enterprise must be abolished or subordinated to public need, for the duration of the war. We cannot maintain national unity with a double standard—voluntary cooperation for property [i.e., armament manufacturers], and conscription for the youth of America."[2]

He also pivoted quickly to his traditional animosity to FDR. He applauded early post-declaration initiatives in Congress to monitor and investigate the way the government would be prosecuting the war. Criticism was healthy, in his view. This approach should also be extended beyond Congress to the public-at-large. Even in wartime, "private citizens have an equal right to suggest methods of making America's war policies more efficient, to criticize, and to insist upon efficiency in government."[3] In that sentence, Marsh defined precisely how he expected the PL to behave during the war.

Pearl Harbor occurred just a month before the PL's annual meeting, which always decided on the policy platform for the coming year. The meeting, which had already been scheduled for January 12, 1942, would be the venue for determining the PL's wartime legislative program. First, the approved program for 1942 replaced a general call for socializing (i.e., nationalizing) key sectors of the economy with the goal of "profitless defense" with direct government control of all military production and with those plants and factories operated by technicians and engineers, not owners and managers. Second, it replaced the principle of funding for the New Deal and relief through progressive taxation instead of deficit spending with the goal of "paying most costs of defense by current taxation, of ability to pay." Third, it maintained the goal of increased federal funding of public education and protection of civil rights. Finally, it replaced the general principle of international cooperation with the goal of planning for a "post-war world organization as will reduce the danger of another war to a minimum."[4]

The political constant of the PL's views during WWII was to be critical. Explicit statements of support for the United States in the war were tepid, when expressed at all. This again paralleled the isolationist right. For example, conservative leader Senator Robert Taft (R-OH) "only faintly supported the war" (Weintraub 2012, 61). Oddly, the clearest expression of the PL's support for the US war effort by Marsh was in a letter to the editor two years after Pearl Harbor. Marsh had attended a meeting of the strongly pacifist National Council for the Prevention of War. In its coverage, the left-leaning New York City newspaper *PM* listed the PL as sending a delegation to the conference, implying support for the organization's endorsement of overt action, including encouraging soldiers not to fight. Marsh, pedantically, insisted on clarifying that he was an observer, not a delegate. He then claimed that when the idea of encouraging soldiers not to fight came up, he said at the meeting, "[T]his should be done only after German and Japanese troops were withdrawn from occupied areas."[5] Here was a clear indication of the careful positioning of the PL during the war. It had been against the United States participating before Pearl Harbor (as a rerun of WWI) and criticized the United States' conduct in the war once in it. But the PL never openly opposed the war after the declaration by Congress. Such a position would clearly be unpatriotic, maybe even treasonous in a time of a declared war. The Lobby would not advocate for any activities that were in overt opposition to or behavior against the war itself. This permitted Marsh to assert that the PL was not a pacifist organization for the purposes of WWII once the United States declared war, that it was loyal to the United States, that it was not supporting civil and soldier disobedience, and that all of the PL's statements critiquing the prosecution of the war were intended solely to *improve* wartime policies and actions.[6]

Nonetheless, the focus of the PL in 1942–45 was on all the things that were *wrong*. This created a mirror image of what the conservative coalition on Capitol Hill was saying. They were incessantly criticizing how the administration was prosecuting the war. Ditto for the People's Lobby. The similarities between the right and the left during WWII are striking, not only in the continued focus on the negative, but also in the ideological underpinnings of those criticisms. The right feared that FDR would use the war to further enact New Deal policies under the guise of wartime conditions. The left, at least as represented by the PL, was complaining that FDR wasn't being liberal enough and that the war was an opportunity to increase the role of the federal government in the political economy, but that FDR (and the dollar-a-year men) were opting instead to maintain the status quo of private property and profit-based economics in pursuit of victory. This was incisively captured by a columnist, who noted that a plan for postwar social policies was attacked not just by conservatives as "socialistic," but also by the PL as "nowhere near socialistic enough."[7] A political scientist, observing the complaints by the right of the president during the war, commented that they seemed to be "damning him for not being perfect" (Hart 1943, 31). The same could be said of the PL on the left. For it, good enough was not good enough.[8] Whichever direction these criticisms were coming from, they were catnip for reporters. They were news. Success, like a dog not barking, was not news; negativity was.

Wartime Advocacy Strategy: PR to the Max

The Lobby's focus on maximizing publicity to influence public opinion continued into the war with many of the PR devices it had refined before Pearl Harbor. For its regular national radio broadcasts, the PL quickly pivoted its themes to fit the new war situation. For example, only a month after Pearl Harbor, the theme of one of its broadcasts was "Can war be ended under the system of free enterprise?"[9] Another, "Why food shortages and high prices?," focused on a subject of broad interest to listeners.[10] These broadcasts often featured talks by officers of the Lobby, such as McConnell and Warne, and by its allies on Capitol Hill. (This also documents that the PL at this point was an organization of more than just Marsh).

The PL also continued its focus on holding one-day and half-day conferences on major subjects, with talks by multiple speakers. The list of speakers was not balanced, but while most were left of center (such as from labor), not all were supporters of the PL agenda. These conferences were usually in Washington, but at least one was in New York City.[11] The themes of the conferences similarly reflected efforts to tie the Lobby's legislative program to broad public interests. They included "War Taxes and War Economics," "Maximum Food for Rationing," "Shall it Be [the] Century of the Common Man or Century of Cartel Control?," and "The People's Stake in War Production." These conferences were sometimes covered by the news media, further expanding the reach of the underlying views of the PL.[12] One of the refinements of its publicity orientation was that the PL now published the texts of the talks at these conferences and mailed them out broadly, hence getting a second bang for the buck by reaching new audiences and providing alternative sources of information for researchers, such as high school and college students. These booklets and pamphlets ranged from twelve to thirty-six pages.[13]

Marsh also tried to expand the mailing list of the PL so that he could reach more people. He asked members to send him the mailing addresses of friends and relatives serving in the military. He wanted to "get facts" to them (echoing the old slogan of the PL: "We get and give the facts"), especially "the necessity for a socialized economy to prevent postwar collapse, and another war."[14] He also received permission from the US Bureau of Prisons to send the monthly *Bulletin* to the libraries of all of the federal penal institutions.[15]

Ever the master of publicity, Marsh once crashed a press conference sponsored by a rare coalition of business and labor. Sensing that anything big business and big labor could agree on would not be a good idea, he interrupted the press conference to question how consumers would be affected by this economic combination. Would it not violate antitrust laws? The speakers politely tried to ignore him, but reporters did not, mentioning it in their stories.[16]

During the war, Marsh initiated a new lobbying method. Every issue of the *Bulletin* when Congress was in session would have an assignment for the members. It would request them to write a letter on a specific issue of PL interest to their federal legislators. While Marsh could not expect that every member would write a monthly letter, it was a technique to demonstrate to the members of Congress that they had *constituents* who supported the Lobby's positions. Voters in their states or districts were much harder to ignore than a pesky lobbyist roaming Capitol Hill. This also gave Marsh a modest amount of added credibility when he lobbied them and testified at hearings. The first subject of this new effort was a January 1943 request to write letters supporting full funding of domestic welfare program, notwithstanding the budget demands of the war.[17]

There was a downside to Marsh's knack for publicity. His sharp rhetoric occasionally prompted complaints. A University of Wisconsin sociology professor objected to the consistent negative tone in the Lobby's statements about the war. In particular, he urged that "unifying ideas need to be stressed rather than divisive ideas."[18] He had accurately identified the theme of PL public communications. The author of a widely circulated newsletter complained that Marsh had falsely characterized the thrust of a story in a private and subscription-based newsletter when he testified at a congressional hearing.[19] (This was a common complaint: that Marsh characterized his *conclusions* about something as though that point had been explicitly stated in the piece.) An officer of the International Ladies' Garment Workers' Union objected to Marsh calling labor-management cooperation a "racket."[20] In general, these examples reflected the price that Marsh would pay over the years for his hyperbole and purple rhetoric. He was making enemies and pushing some supporters away. If it bothered him at all, he did not show it. And he certainly did not change his behavior in response.

One of the high-water marks of the PL's publicity orientation was a flattering profile of Marsh in a feature distributed by Associated Press for the Sunday newspapers. The column dubbed Marsh Washington's "No. 1 Hell Raiser" and described his honesty and tireless work for leftist causes. It said that people in Congress cringed when he entered a hearing room and that he was able to dig out and present documentable facts that no one else had noted. He lived modestly and took a streetcar to Capitol Hill. It was an admiring profile of an irascible, yet loveable, character who was sincere and respected, even if his views were so far to the left that they were rarely adopted.[21] On another occasion, the AP included in a column on Washington a saying Marsh made famous: "Democracy as practiced in America is the art of passing the buck to providence and the bill to posterity."[22] Marsh was the perennial cynic-optimist-humorist, positive that any day now everyone else would see the light and the PL's ideas would be enacted.

Counterbalancing such complimentary and widely published coverage was an article in *Harper's Magazine* during the war. The author surveyed the Office of Price Administration's (OPA's) relatively unsatisfactory track record in using price controls as a tool against inflation. At the end of the article, he wondered what actions could be taken to overcome the reasons for OPA's failings. He asked, "Why is there no People's Lobby?"[23] Such an organization, he felt, could make a major difference with OPA by lobbying to counter that of special interest groups. The author, editors, and fact-checkers of a quality national magazine evidently did not know that there indeed was a People's Lobby in existence. Nor did they know from their research that it was involved in trying to represent consumers' interests and balance out the pressures on OPA from self-serving lobbying groups and their allies in Congress. Here was an indication that for all of the publicity and coverage Marsh and the PL had attained, the organization was still largely unknown, even to the well informed.

In Operation during the War

The routine organizational operations of the Lobby continued during the war. Late in the calendar year, Marsh sent notices of the annual meeting to all members. He invited them to attend, but, if they could not, to please submit a proxy permitting one of the directors to cast votes on their behalf. He also solicited their views on issues and suggestions for the priorities for the PL policy platform for the coming year. The meetings always took place in Mrs. Clyde's apartment in Manhattan. They usually started with a Board of Directors or Executive Committee meeting. Marsh submitted minutes of the previous meeting, summaries of his activities in the preceding year to advocate for the policy platform for that year, a financial summary, and suggestions for the future. A slate of officers and directors was finalized and forwarded to the membership meeting. Upon adjournment, they immediately reconvened as the annual membership meeting. Marsh and other officers usually received about two hundred proxies to cast in the names of nonattending members. Sometimes, a few weeks later, Marsh sent the members a notice of the results of the annual meeting, especially focusing on distributing the new (or revised) policy platform for the calendar year.

These were always small meetings, usually with fewer than a dozen people. Nonetheless, these gatherings continue to document the existence of a traditional nonprofit corporation with members of a Board of Directors who actively fulfilled their fiduciary duties. The PL was in full compliance with the reporting requirements for corporations under Delaware law. During the war, the officers of the Lobby continued without change, especially Bishop McConnell as president and Colston Warne as vice president. Even though McConnell retired as a clergyman in early 1945, he retained his involvement as president (just as Dewey had when he retired from Columbia). Mrs. Clyde, always the hostess (and major donor), was usually a member of the Board of Directors, but not an officer.

Further indicating that the post-Dewey board continued overseeing Marsh's public statements occurred when he testified at a congressional hearing on the reorganization of Congress (eventually leading to the Legislative Reorganization Act of 1946). At the beginning of his comments, he said he was testifying "as an individual and not on behalf of the People's Lobby" (US Congress 1945, 1023). He then proceeded with a pointed and impolitic critique of everything he felt was wrong with Congress, ending with a criticism of a pay raise under consideration. The officers were right to insist on Marsh separating himself from the Lobby on this occasion, if only because the reorganization of Congress was not on the PL's policy platform for the year. Marsh was respecting the organization's democratic process by venturing beyond the platform only as an individual. He could not toss around the name of the Lobby willy-nilly.

The Lobby lost some individual members over some of its stances or, at least, over how Marsh articulated those positions. Alfred Baker Lewis, a prominent New York lefty, objected to Marsh continuing to blame WWII on American and British economic elites and the Vatican for supporting the Spanish rebels and opposition to Communism.[24] A doctor in Massachusetts canceled his membership in reaction to Marsh's sharp criticisms of labor unions.[25] More serious was the resignation of Harvard Professor Kirtley Mather from the PL's Advisory Council and cancellation of his membership. Mather was particularly unhappy with the consistent tone that Marsh used to put the actions of the SU in the most positive possible light and, conversely, those of capitalist democracies in the most negative.[26] Even Dewey's son, Frederick A. Dewey, wrote Marsh complaining about one-sided use of statistics to prove a point about concentration of wealth. Dewey *fils* wrote that the selective statistics were "a gross distortment [*sic*] of realities" and "partisan beyond partisanship."[27]

The PL's stance on immigration of Jewish refugees from Nazi Europe to British Mandatory Palestine was also controversial internally. It began oddly, with an article in the *Bulletin* that softly endorsed lifting British limits on admission of additional Jews to Palestine (which had been imposed by the UK in its 1939 White Paper). In lieu of the name of the author (or no authorship, meaning Marsh) was this disclaimer: "(A member wishing to be anonymous, submitted this statement.)"[28] This indicated the fierce emotions then going on over the arguments on the left regarding whether the British WWI commitment to establishing a Jewish National Home in Palestine was colonialism by another name or a worthy and justified goal. The article quickly prompted a fierce letter of objection from a professor of Semitic languages at the Duke University's School of Religion. He took the pro-Arab position and opposed further Jewish immigration to Palestine. It was a world problem that needed a world solution, he wrote, rather than imposing the full weight of the solution on the Arabs in Palestine.[29] Another complaint from a member in Vermont said that "[t]here's lots of room in Australia" and, anyway, most Jews would prefer living in New York than Palestine.[30] (This argument was a foreshadowing of the later division on the American left between liberals and labor generally supporting Israel and the New Left supporting the Palestinians.)

These noisy resignations and complaints by members may have been relatively small in number, but they highlighted the continuing struggle to maintain a membership size that could sustain the organization. Marsh was always exploring ways to recruit new members. In the winter of 1943–44, he sent a mailing to more than 20,000 people urging them to join the Lobby.[31] The cover letter was titled "*You* Need the People's Lobby." It explained the *raison d'être* of the PL, namely that business, farmers, and labor had their own lobbies, but the people did not. He summarized the Lobby's legislative program and the rationales for the positions it was taking. In particular, he focused on the government not giving up ownership of the plants it paid to construct during the war.[32] These mass mailings were sometimes effective in bringing in new members. Famed leftist reporter I. F. Stone joined, and equally famous Kansas editor William Allen White sent in a few names of potential members.[33]

During 1941, the Lobby's membership had dipped below 2,000. The United States joining the war prompted increased membership: 2,274 in 1942, 3,512 in 1943, and a peak of 4,280 in 1944.[34] Marsh was realistic about how high the membership could go, acknowledging to the Board that the organization "is not, and probably will not, be a mass movement" because it was "pioneering" in its stances and therefore could never appeal to the masses.[35]

Notwithstanding modest success with membership drives, the Lobby's financing was always tight. In 1942, Marsh voluntarily reduced his salary by 40 percent, but even then the deficit for the year was $400. While Mrs. Clyde continued her subsidy for the *Bulletin*, the Lobby was never able to obtain ongoing or major support from other foundations and grantors. For example, in 1942, such large contributions dropped by $1,200.[36] At one point, Marsh appealed to current members for urgent donations because "not even economic reformers can make bricks without straw."[37]

In an interesting gesture to underlie its commitment to increasing taxes to pay for the war, in early 1945, the Board of Directors decided to discontinue its tax-exempt status with the IRS. As a nonpolitical nonprofit (nowadays called a 501-c-3), the PL qualified for tax deductibility of donations to it. It will be recalled that in 1929, the newly formed organization was contacted by the IRS to clarify its tax status, leading to incorporation in Delaware (Chap. 2). The Board decided in 1945 that from then on, donors to the Lobby would *not* qualify to deduct those payments on their personal tax returns. For the leadership of the lobby, this was a relatively minor financial decision, but one made on principle. If the Lobby were to continue advocating for a pay-as-you-go financing of the federal budget, especially through a more progressive tax system (i.e., higher tax rates on the wealthy), then it should put its money where its mouth was. The motion passed by the directors at its January 1945 meeting (preceding the annual membership meeting) stated that the Lobby "would not seek to get contributions to the Lobby deductible for income tax purposes" in order to be faithful to its policy program.[38] (The decision was unilateral; there was no change in organizational or legal status of the PL vis-à-vis the IRS or Delaware.)

Politically, the PL continued to be isolated from the liberal and labor movements supporting the New Deal and FDR's war policies. In January 1945, in his formal annual report, Marsh acknowledged that "no major farm, labor or church organization has endorsed our social control program."[39] This confirmed the Lobby's placement on the ideological spectrum somewhere between liberalism and Communism.

Another indication of how much had changed politically was the 1944 presidential election. The given narrative is that this was not even a real race—that FDR's reelection was inevitable and that FDR did not even break a (political) sweat. After the election, Marsh wrote that the results were "a forgone conclusion."[40] This was incorrect. It was a real race, especially because winning the war looked guaranteed, because Thomas Dewey's campaign platform *supported* the war, and because of FDR's increased absence from the political circuit (Weintraub 2012; Jordan 2011). FDR was already quite ill, and the widely spread rumors about his health were largely accurate. While the PL, as a nonpolitical nonprofit, expressed no preference in the election, the increasingly shrill attacks on FDR's war policies made clear where Marsh and the PL stood regarding FDR's presidential record. Yet, significantly, John Dewey endorsed FDR—the first time he had ever done so (Jordan 2011, 247). That meant the PL post-Dewey was to the political left of Dewey himself, paralleling Dewey and Marsh's differing views on President Wilson and WWI.

Wartime Conservative Attacks

During WWII, the FBI, HUAC, and conservative activists maintained ongoing monitoring of the People's Lobby, Marsh, and even Dewey. None seemed aware that Dewey had stepped down as president in 1936 and as honorary president in 1940 and no longer had any leadership association with the PL. The PL, Marsh, and Dewey still were all under suspicion of being either Communists, fellow travelers or, in some manner or another, un-American. The anti-Communism of the FBI and HUAC went on unabated even though the United States and SU were allies against Hitler and the two governments cooperating closely. As it turned out, there was a basis for suspicions that some American citizens were so sympathetic to the SU and its political ideology that they engaged in spying. During the war, the SU treated the United States as an inevitable postwar adversary. It maintained a very aggressive espionage operation in the United States, including successfully stealing the secrets of the nascent atomic bomb. To the most strident in the anti-Communist establishment, there was little differentiation between those holding political views on the left and those who were actively spying for the SU. Temporary allies or not, anyone on the left was a *potential* traitor, subversive, or spy.

The FBI occasionally received letters from citizens forwarding materials published by the Lobby and raising concerns about its patriotism. All their enclosures were added to its files and the citizens thanked for the submissions. One letter writer was active in conservative women's organizations. She wrote that some of the names on the PL's letterhead "have been connected with fellow travelers' organizations." They did not deserve the protections and liberties of "the present American form of government."[41] The FBI also added to its files information from HUAC and from the anti-Communist *National Republic* magazine.[42]

When Marsh spoke in the state of Washington during his annual western speaking tour in late 1942, the FBI's Seattle office collected information about his talk. As reported to Director Hoover, Marsh said that "President Roosevelt is corrupt, is seeking to be a dictator, and is responsible for the present war." Marsh also allegedly said that Hitler's "treatment of the Jewish people is no worse than the Poles had treated them." Hoover replied that there was "no active investigation" going on about the PL or Marsh, but invited submissions of any additional information that the Seattle office might come by.[43] Meanwhile, the FBI's field office in New York City subscribed to the PL *Bulletin* for $2 a year, an expenditure that the assistant director in charge of the office felt was "justified." As a subterfuge, the FBI used a PO box for receiving PL mailings.[44]

In 1943, the FBI's field office in New York City conducted a de novo review all the information it had on Dewey to decide what his status in the "Custodial Detention–C" (for Communist) list should now be. This was similar to the report it had prepared on Marsh in 1941 (Chap. 9). The review listed all the organizations in which Dewey had been active, most of which were sympathetic to the SU's Communist revolution and domestic left-wing causes. It noted that he was "a Communist recommended author" and also listed him as still president of the People's Lobby. However, the report also discussed Dewey as being openly critical of the show trials in Moscow and supportive of Trotskyites (who broke with Stalin) in the United States. These causes were in sharp disagreement with the Party line.

The report also was interested in Dewey's personal life, including his home address and his visitors when he was hospitalized. Two informants noted that he lived in an eight-room apartment in Manhattan but paid very low rent, somewhere between $150 and $260 a month. (The low rent may have been because it was a rent-controlled building.) The report also highlighted that he was living in such a large apartment either alone or with only one other person, his adult daughter. Given that he was retired, Dewey had no visible means of support, traveled a lot, and wrote a lot. Without stating it explicitly, it raised the suspicion that he had some covert financial support, perhaps from enemies of the United States. But when he was hospitalized for an operation, he had few visitors, mostly former colleagues from Columbia. So that was not a promising line of further investigation. The report concluded that the current FBI files "failed to disclose Communist affiliations" by Dewey or any current activity "inimical to the best interests of the internal security" of the United States. Therefore, the investigation and case were closed.[45]

HUAC's interest in the People's Lobby around the same time was less ambivalent than the FBI's. Marsh deserved ongoing attention because he was "a free-lance 'reformer,' who has cooperated with some Communist front organizations and campaigns." As the chief funder of the PL, Mrs. Clyde was described as a sponsor or director of several Communist front organizations and member of the Advisory Board of another organization "dominated by the Young Communist League." Another donor to the PL was the Garland Fund, described by HUAC as also funding explicitly communist publications and organizations. Finally, many of the officers and Board members of the PL were also "associated with Communist front organizations," including Bishop McConnell.[46] HUAC's (closed) files also justified attention to the PL because it "advocates government ownership."[47] HUAC had no doubts that the PL was an un-American organization. In a public document, HUAC was slightly more restrained. It named Marsh as active in Communist front organizations, but did not categorize the PL (US House 1944b, 381, 383).

HUAC was much more alarmed about Dewey than the FBI. It (inaccurately) listed Dewey as the "leader" of the PL. Also, "it is a well-established fact that he is an atheist" and that his influence on public education was so significant that it was "a matter of no small concern to the religious interests of America." The HUAC files included a physical description of Dewey, including that he had "carelessly combed gray hair," dressed in a "disheveled" manner, and spoke in a "monotonous drawl."[48]

In addition to HUAC, other conservative power centers on Capitol Hill were interested in exposing the PL. One of the major conservative projects at the time was the House Special Committee to Investigate Executive Agencies. When Marsh testified in support of the OPA, the Committee's general counsel, Aaron Ford, tried to undercut his testimony by questioning him closely about the PL's political ideology. Ford asked Marsh point blank, "Do you believe in the capitalist system of this country?" Typically, Marsh refused reply in a yes-or-no manner, instead saying that the PL's long-term goal was "a socialized economy." However, he quickly emphasized, "that doesn't mean any revolutionary method, of course" (US House 1944a, 2393–2394). It was enough of an admission to confirm for conservatives whose side the PL was on.

Criticizing Postwar and Cold War Policies, 1945–50

The United Kingdom held a general election in July 1945. To everyone's surprise, despite his heroic and winning role in defeating Nazi Germany, Winston Churchill and his Conservative Party lost to the Labor Party led by Clement Attlee. (The results came in during the Potsdam summit conference of the United Kingdom, United States, and SU in July and August 1945. Attlee quickly replaced Churchill in talks with Truman and Stalin.) Marsh was ecstatic. The Labor Party's platform nearly duplicated the PL's. At last, there would be a real-life example of the policy goals of the Lobby. Indeed, through 1950, the Attlee government pursued the domestic and economic goals that the PL had promoted lo those many years in the United States, including a greatly enlarged system of social services, the nationalization of major industries and public utilities (including coal mines, railroads, airlines, and the Bank of England), the expansion of legal rights of workers, and the creation of the National Health Service. In terms of foreign policy, Attlee's government also delighted Marsh and the PL. It reversed the deeply embedded colonialist and imperialist policies of the country, giving independence to India, Pakistan, Burma, Ceylon, and Jordan. It withdrew from Palestine, leading to the creation of Israel.

These developments gave new energy to Marsh and the PL, given their long-standing program of government ownership of utilities, railroads, and natural resources; more worker rights; expanded social services and health care programs; and anticolonialism. Maybe it *was* possible for the same to occur in the United States? Sometimes it seemed that Truman would be more liberal than FDR. His Fair Deal agenda as a follow-up to the New Deal contained many ideas that the PL should like, national health insurance being the most prominent. Shifting from proposals to actions, Truman did many of the things the PL promoted, such as supporting civil rights and desegregation, vetoing the Taft-Hartley antiunion bill (overridden), vetoing tax cuts (also overridden), expanding public housing, and supporting public power. Later (in 1952), Truman tried to nationalize the steel industry, which would have thrilled the PL.

But, in general, the Truman presidency and the postwar policies were not wins for the Lobby. It was almost as if Marsh preferred to criticize than to praise. Finding fault was his métier. Marsh was rarely one to compliment something as a step in the right direction. Rather, to him, it was unacceptable because it was too short a step. Only perfection deserved praise, apparently. So, for example, in a press release in 1950, Marsh could find only negative things to say about Truman. During the president's whistle-stop series of speeches, Marsh called Truman's statements "whistle-up-the-wind" and "a masterpiece of bamboozle." He concluded that Truman and Hoover were in the same category.[49] The PL became an increasingly discordant voice urging policy goals that had little to no support on Capitol Hill.

The end of WWII had little impact on the PL's policy agenda. Its first postwar program in early 1946 called for pursuing long-standing goals such as government ownership of natural resources and basic industries, a steeper progressive tax system, opposition to deficit spending, government controls over the economy, opposition to a peacetime draft, and increased US participation in international cooperation including of atomic energy, over which the United States briefly had a monopoly.[50]

Postwar Advocacy Strategy: PR to the Max

Now into his fourth decade of testifying on Capitol Hill and issuing press releases, Marsh's previously successful formula for maximal public relations was wearing thin. His testimony at congressional hearings was rarely quoted in the news coverage, and PL press releases were rarely picked up. When he testified, committee members seldom asked him questions, even when they sharply disagreed. Better to get it over with. The template for his testimony had also ossified. He had a few extreme quotes, rarely took a position on the bill at hand (unless asked point blank), focused on the negative, and mostly described the PL's socialist alternatives. He often repackaged that testimony into press releases, but they, too, were usually ignored.

Only occasionally would the old approach work when multiple papers ran a release. When the PL had to vacate its office because the building was about to be torn down, Marsh put out a release saying the PL deserved an office in the White House because it was doing the people's business. That got attention.[51] So did an accusation by Marsh that the chairman of the Joint Economic Committee was anticonsumer.[52] Otherwise, coverage was few and far between. When the PL called on Truman to veto the Taft-Hartley Act, the *Washington Daily News* (a Scripps Howard afternoon paper) picked it up.[53] A PL call for nationalizing the coal industry prompted a lead editorial in a Texas paper denouncing the idea.[54]

Similarly, in past years, holding policy conferences in Washington with multiple speakers on issues the PL supported had routinely garnered significant media coverage. In the postwar years, that format received less reportage than earlier.[55] Sometimes coverage was limited to a notice of an upcoming event, not spot news of what the speakers said.[56]

Some journalistic attention to the PL was negative. Syndicated columnist Marquis Childs wrote that the PL "never has had much influence," but qualified that assessment by noting the PL's lack of funding compared with most lobbies.[57] Another wrote of Marsh as "the one-man crusader for lost causes."[58] An editorial in a Montana newspaper said of the PL that "its activities have never been very effective."[59] Marsh and the PL had been so marginalized by the *Washington Post*, the most important media outlet in the capital, that he was reduced to writing letters to the editor as the only way to publicize the PL's views. In 1948–49, the *Post* published seven letters.[60] Other leading papers read within the capital, the *Times* and the *Sun*, also published a few of Marsh's letters to the editor.[61]

Three factors likely contributed to the diminished coverage. Marsh was largely repeating the same talking points he had for years, merely trying to tie them to the crisis du jour. Also, it became clearer how few members the PL had and, therefore, what little legitimate claim it could assert to be speaking for the public-at-large. Finally, Dewey's absence was major. He had given the PL credibility because of his own prominence. No longer associated at all with Dewey after 1940, the Lobby's voice was not considered as important as when Dewey was behind it.

Marsh did himself no good with his constant barrage of overheated rhetoric. Attacking potential allies may have felt good, but it undermined the possibility of working together in the future. For example, Marsh issued several releases severely criticizing Americans for Democratic Action (ADA), an important group of anti-Communist liberal Democrats. In one, he said ADA's positions were "unwitting allies of fascism."[62] Another time, he criticized a major civil rights lobby for supposedly "trying to bamboozle people" by excluding economic issues from its goals.[63] Probably the low point was a press release after President Truman's 1949 State of the Union address. Marsh said Truman's policy plan "sounds like Hitler's National Socialism."[64] This was truly offensive and probably destroyed what little credibility he may still have had.

One event was a publicity bonanza for the PL, somewhat reversing its declining public profile. After debating lobbying regulation for decades, in 1946 Congress passed the Legislative Reorganization Act, which included a requirement that all lobbyists register with the clerk of the House and the secretary of the Senate and then be required to file quarterly reports. Marsh was delighted. He and Dewey had reveled in the name of their organization as a kind of thumb in the eye of all the well-heeled special interest lobbyists who had been protecting special privileges for all those years. Marsh loved to identify himself as a lobbyist because he was so much the exception to the rule.

With the law signed by President Truman on August 2, initial registration would begin at the end of the month. Marsh wanted to be the first. That would be a way of creating a splash about the work of the People's Lobby, reflecting Dewey's original idea in 1928 (Chap. 2). The first day of registration was set for August 21. But the new registration forms were not available beforehand. Therefore, based on his reading of the legal requirements for registration as stated in the law, Marsh listed all the required information on the stationery of the PL and had it notarized. Then he handed it in as early on the first day as possible. By doing that, he was the first to file. His earliest registration was prominently mentioned in the press coverage of the implementation of the new law.[65] (The Women's Christian Temperance Union, not Marsh, was the first to file using the new form. Media coverage dubbed both the first.)

The next day, Lowell Mellett, former FDR aide and now syndicated liberal political columnist based at the afternoon *Washington Star*, highlighted the wonderful irony of Marsh as first. "So the first person caught in the dire business of lobbying is one who has proudly proclaimed himself as a lobbyist for the past quarter of a century," he noted, praising the People's Lobby for its work.[66] That was followed by more feature-style coverage, including the weekly newsmagazine *United States News* and the Boston-based newspaper *Christian Science Monitor*.[67]

As a result of his coup, Marsh now routinely referred to himself as Washington's "No. 1 Lobbyist," a catchy though misleading moniker. Reporters loved it and used it often. In particular, the title fit well with Marsh's evolving into something of a character in Washington after all these years. He was depicted as ornery, opinionated, and out of the mainstream, but still loveable—an authentic American type of the old-fashioned kind. Over the next few years, he became the subject of many profiles in columns, syndicated features, and periodicals. The *Post* profiled him (with a photo) on his thirtieth anniversary as a lobbyist, King Features Syndicate released an article on him, and two United Press reporters wrote profiles.[68] Even a business magazine tipped its hat to him.[69]

His standing also made him a frequent presence in news articles about the excessive influence that lobbies had in Washington.[70] (After the initial registration day, Marsh was also punctilious about filling out and filing the quarterly reports required of lobbyists, just as he was regarding paperwork to maintain the PL's standing as a Delaware corporation.)[71] Topping it off, Marsh was interviewed by a periodical for advertising and PR professionals. He was profiled in its public relations section, an indication of his accomplishments in the field of PR.[72] If PR professionals thought he had made it in the practice of PR, then he surely had.

In Operation after WWII

From 1945 to 1950, the size, budget, operations, and Board leadership of the PL continued largely unchanged from its earlier years, with stable membership levels, tight budgets, and a functioning Board of Directors and officers. Membership rose as high as 4,000.[73] However, the bulk of those were for $1 and $2 annual memberships, so the increases in membership did not significantly increase income. Marsh reported a $700 deficit at the end of 1945 and appealed to members for contributions above and beyond their membership dues.[74] In late 1949, he said that income for the year was only about two-thirds of the previous year's, and despite his efforts to cut expenses, there still was a deficit.[75] Given the postwar inflation and an aging membership, Marsh concluded that "our members seem to be getting hard up."[76]

At the end of 1946, retired Bishop McConnell asked not to be reelected to another term as president. This was apparently due to age and other commitments, not dissatisfaction, because McConnell agreed to continue serving on the Board of Directors.[77] He was succeeded by James H. McGill, an industrialist in Valparaiso, Indiana. Despite his capitalist credentials, McGill supported the leftist program of the PL and welcomed becoming president.[78] He wrote the lead article in the February 1947 issue of the *Bulletin*, endorsing government ownership of natural resources, monopolies, and basic industries.[79] However, McGill was in ill health and died in April 1948.[80] He was succeeded by Broadus Mitchell, an economics professor at Rutgers University in New Jersey.[81]

Two major themes dominated organizational activities during the postwar years, one relating to Marsh's slashing rhetoric, the other over the legal exclusivity of the PL's name. Marsh had always had supporters and critics. Examples of the former included a member who was a congregational minister in Cleveland,[82] a Portland, Maine, member who hoped Marsh was training a successor,[83] and a letter from Senator Arthur Capper (R-KS) stating (in its entirety), "I hope you will stay in the lobby business for many years. You have always been for the best interests of the people."[84]

But Marsh received more negative reviews than positive ones. Some were from members, such as C. H. Coyle of Illinois, who complained to McConnell about at a talk Marsh gave in Chicago. Marsh's blanket criticisms of organized labor would "foster distrust and hostility" with potential allies.[85] Another (a member of the PL's Advisory Council) was unhappy about Marsh's "pacifist attitude" during the war.[86] Some complaints came from union officials, generally sympathetic to the PL's causes, who took offense at Marsh's blanket denunciations of organized labor as a racket and an increasingly conservative force.[87] Marsh was unrepentant in his replies.[88]

Much more serious were complaints from Harry Laidler. Laidler was a longtime labor activist in New York and friend of Dewey's. He was also executive director of the League for Industrial Democracy, an organization of American socialist intellectuals (Westbrook 1991, 277–278).[89] Significantly, in 1950, Dewey was *still* the honorary president of the League, although he had stepped down from that role with the Lobby a decade earlier. Laidler had been a supporter of the PL from the beginning. In the late 1940s, he was still a member of the Board of Directors and a diligent attendee at annual Board and membership meetings. In 1948, Laidler wrote Marsh of his unhappiness with what Marsh was writing about the SU in the *Bulletin*. He objected to Marsh's "very one-sided presentation of Russian foreign policy" and pointed out that such opinions did not reflect the policy platform adopted by the Board.[90] Two years later, Laidler complained about unauthored *Bulletin* articles denouncing the United States for an imperialist foreign policy, but not the SU's parallel activities. He also noted Marsh's persistent criticisms of the labor movement.[91]

Laidler was especially concerned about Marsh propagating a sinister and rabid anti-Catholic interpretation of world events. Writing in 1945 just after WWII ended, Marsh claimed that "the Vatican's powerful influence was exerted in Europe—from the Armistice" (i.e., the end of WWI) to the present.[92] Another time, he wrote that "America's foreign policy has, since 1933, been dictated more by the Vatican . . . to control the world."[93] In multiple fora, Marsh elaborated on his conspiracy theory. The Vatican supported Hitler's ascent to power as a way to check Communism, which the Vatican viewed as a major threat. It then sided with Franco in the Spanish Civil War and used its influence in the FDR administration to promote the policy of neutrality and an arms embargo, which had the effect of undercutting the loyalist side.[94] Marsh pointed to Postmaster General James Farley's Catholicism (during FDR's first term) as proof. Then, in the post-WWII world, the Vatican was anti-Communist and worked for an aggressive US foreign policy to confront Stalin. Marsh said that the State Department was "largely manipulated by reactionary Catholics."[95] In addition to its supposed influence on American foreign policy, Marsh talked of a "Catholic conspiracy" at work in Western Europe promoting an economic union.[96] Furthermore, he said, the Church was exercising a veto power on Capitol Hill to prevent federal aid to education from being enacted unless its parochial schools were eligible for federal funding, too. It was all bizarre, offensive, incredible, and paranoid. Marsh was becoming the mirror image of Communist hunters of his time, like Senator McCarthy, who perceived a secret red conspiracy so vast that it was everywhere and omnipotent. For Marsh and McCarthy alike, the conspiracy was so pervasive, subtle, and sneaky that even seemingly persuasive facts contradicting the narrative could be explained away and disregarded.

In his 1950 letter to Marsh, Laidler expressed unhappiness with Marsh's anti-Vaticanism, specifically when Marsh insinuated that the Catholicism of a senior State Department official was the sole explanation for the official's hard-nosed and negative attitude toward the SU. In this case, Laidler's role on the Board carried the day. The Lobby's leadership imposed a change on Marsh.[97] From then on, the masthead of every issue of the *Bulletin* would be required to carry the disclaimer "The Editor is solely responsible for unsigned articles."[98] Here was another example of the leadership structure of this nonprofit holding the staff accountable and imposing internal policies that were not initiated or recommended by the staff. The PL's officers and Board members were generally supporters of Marsh, but they were not his lackeys.

The second organizational issue that had increasing frequency during the postwar period was the need to protect the group's legal ownership of its title. During all of its existence, there were various organizations around the country that called themselves a People's Lobby.[99] But their proliferation and higher-profile activism seemed to increase after the war. They included the very conservative People's Lobby of California,[100] a largely African-American group in Chicago lobbying for a law to establish a state Fair Employment Practices Commission,[101] and a Communist-leaning group in New York City.[102] Probably the most disappointing to the PL was a call by Socialist Norman Thomas in 1948 to create in Washington a group to lobby for the people's interests.[103] Thomas surely knew of Dewey and Marsh's group and had had minor contact with them over the years. So either he had forgotten or, with Dewey out of the picture, felt the Marsh group was fading to insignificance. Either way, it was an insult to what remained of the PL in New York and Washington.

Marsh tried his best to stem the tide and protect his organization's monopoly over the title. At the first Board meeting after VJ Day, Marsh told the members he had received an inquiry from a lawyer in California seeking a copy of the PL's By-Laws because the lawyer wanted to determine if the PL held exclusive rights to the term "people's lobby" and if a local organization could use the term without legal complications. The Board directed Marsh to reply that the PL "does not wish [to have] local organizations affiliated with the People's Lobby because of differences on state and local issues, while the People's Lobby confines itself to national issues."[104] A few years later, Marsh wrote a short article in the *Bulletin* about the proliferation of other organizations using the term. He said that the PL had legal ownership of the name "People's Lobby" (without a modifier after the term) and "People's Lobby, Inc." To prevent any confusion, he said that other organizations could use the term, but only if they added to the formal titles of the organizations the "name of [the] state or city in which operating." Otherwise, "use of our name is probably actionable" in a lawsuit.[105]

Still, he had to keep swatting down copycats. In 1948, when a group of businessmen talked of creating a people's lobby to promote their interests, Marsh roared back at the irony of the situation. This idea, he wrote, would be "that the lion can be the voice of his prey" and, besides, the PL already owned the term.[106] (Apparently, the idea never came to fruition.) Later that year, Marsh protested when *New York Times* reporter James Reston claimed to have told then–Vice President Henry Wallace that there was a need for "a lobby for the people." Reston wrote that Wallace had agreed with him and, liking the phrase, said he might use it in future speeches. Marsh pointed out that there already was a lobby for the people and that Wallace was very familiar with it, having participated in several of its conferences and radio broadcasts. So Reston must be wrong in his recollection and, impliedly, a lousy reporter with a poor memory for the participants in Washington's policy debates.[107]

In 1948, Marsh wrote a letter to the editor of the *New Republic* to clarify that a reference in an earlier issue was to the (conservative) People's Lobby of California. While using a title with a modifier was legally permissible, he wanted to emphasize to the readers that it was wholly unaffiliated with the national left-leaning PL. He said he had publicly repudiated the work of that group several times.[108] In 1949, a freshman congressman from

Massachusetts announced his desire to create a People's Lobby in his district and in Washington to lobby for the public interest.[109] This prompted a PL member living in Boston to write a letter to the editor pointing out that there already was a People's Lobby and that it had existed for more than thirty years.[110] But the editors titled the letter "Earlier People's Lobby," which gave the impression to casual readers that this previous PL no longer existed, and therefore the congressman had no need to rename his group.

In summary, although Dewey was no longer associated with it, the PL largely continued Dewey's socialist policy platform. Without Dewey, though, Marsh become the center of gravity of the group and dominated its rhetoric and positions. However, the PL was not a paper organization or false letterhead for Marsh to do and say whatever he wanted. During the 1940s, the Lobby continued as a modest but functioning organization. It had officers and a Board of Directors who met at least once a year (usually twice) to vote on the annual policy platform, deal with suggestions made by its leaders, and decide on new issues that Marsh brought to its attention. They usually approved of what Marsh proposed, but occasionally reined him in.

Postwar Conservative Attacks

From its beginnings, the PL was attacked as a Communist and un-American organization (Chap. 4). These accusations continued persistently from the right through the FDR years (Chaps. 7 and 9). However, the fear of Communism reached new heights in the aftermath of WWII. Abroad, the antidemocratic actions by Stalin and the SU in Eastern Europe, its support for domestic Communist rebellion in Greece (leading to the Truman Doctrine in 1947), and exploding of an atomic bomb (in 1949) were catalysts for the Cold War. Domestically, American Communists were accused of loyalty to the SU above the United States, of supporting an armed revolution to take over the country, of spying for the SU, and all other manner of subversive activities.

The hunt for traitors lurking in the United States became a cottage industry. The jargon was deliberately vague, such as subversive, fellow traveler, known associate, and parlor pinko. These all implied being a traitor to the country, but were neither automatically nor largely so. The number of actual spies who were caught (such as the Rosenbergs) was relatively small. People who had been members of the Communist Party at some time in their lives were considered security risks and, if employed by the federal government, fired. Lefty Hollywood writers were accused of planting near-subliminal pro-Communist messages in their screenplays, deliberately trying to brainwash audiences. They, too, were fired. Marsh called HUAC's hearings in Hollywood a "Spanish Inquisition."[111]

In this atmosphere, the PL was a clear target. It did not matter how many times Marsh stated that he and the membership supported socialism, *not* Communism, or that the PL only supported constitutional means of changing government policy. Criticizing the economic status quo; calling for government takeover of industrial subsectors, as was happening in the United Kingdom after a free election; and saying anything about the SU that was not a denunciation were enough to make one suspect.

An indication of the times came from Professor Harold U. Falkner of Smith College's History Department. Falkner was a friend of longtime PL officer Professor Colston Warne. That led to Marsh inquiring of Falkner in 1947 if he would accept the PL's treasurership. Falkner replied that he indeed agreed with the platform of the Lobby and, in fact, had been a member of the Socialist Party in the 1930s. However, a substantial portion of his income came from royalties for textbooks he wrote or edited for high school and college. (In those days, the salaries of professors were quite low—hence the stereotype of a professor with elbow patches on his sports jackets—and royalties from textbooks were for some a necessity to attain a middle-class income.) He told Marsh that already several times his books had been attacked by the National Association of Manufacturers (NAM) and others because of his socialist background. He had "managed to survive" those attacks, but "I hate to go through the experience again during these reactionary days." Accusations of "any appearance *even of liberalism*" could be fatal in terms of the acceptance of a textbook. Falkner declined Marsh's request.[112] His letter captured how frightened the left was, regardless of the unfairness or lack of merit to wild accusations. Merely to be accused was enough to kill a career.

It was in this environment that the PL's officers, members, and Marsh tried to soldier on. Never one to shy away from a fight, Marsh relished being controversial as a way to obtain a platform to promote the Lobby's views, but it was a big price to pay. For example, in 1946, racist and demagogic Senator Theodore Bilbo (D-MS) denounced the Lobby in a floor speech as a "socialistic organization" because, he said, it was "espousing Government ownership of industry and redistribution of wealth by confiscatory taxation."[113] The next year, Congressman Alvin O'Konski (R-WI) denounced someone for speaking at a PL conference because the theme of the event was "for the consideration of Socialization of Natural Resources, Transportation and Banking."[114] In both cases, the PL was not accused of being Communist, but merely of promoting socialistic goals. But that was all it took.

HUAC continued to monitor the PL and collect information about it. For example, when a subscriber to the PL's *Bulletin* received in the mail a pro-Russian publication (with no link to or sponsorship by the PL), he or she anonymously complained to HUAC.[115] Congressman James Davis (D-GA) forwarded a PL publication to HUAC. Its chief investigator thanked him and wrote that "your suggestion that an investigation be made of this organization will be brought to the attention of the Committee."[116] On another occasion, the same committee staffer thanked a citizen for forwarding PL material and praised the sender for "your interest in the suppression of subversive activities."[117] A local elected official in New Jersey wrote to HUAC chair J. Parnell Thomas (R-NJ) complaining that the local public high school library was receiving unsolicited mail from the PL. He enclosed a copy of the PL's October 1946 *Bulletin* and complained about its "subversive approach." Thomas responded that he was glad to have it for the committee's files and that "this matter will be brought to the attention of the Committee at an early date."[118]

HUAC prepared summaries of the information in its files on the PL in 1947 and 1949. Congressman Robert Chiperfield (R-IL) inquired about Marsh in 1947. Using a standard committee form titled "Information from the Files of the Committee on Un-American Activities," he was informed that Marsh had many "Communist front affiliations."[119] Two years later, Senator Virgil Chapman (D-KY) asked HUAC about the PL. Senior Investigator Louis Russell replied with a three-page summary of the information on the PL in HUAC's files. He said that HUAC "has never made an investigation" of the PL, and the staffer was merely summarizing what was in its files. Based on that information, he noted that several of the PL's officers "have openly defended the Communist Party, in one way or another." Also, the PL's leaders "have been affiliated at some time or another with various Communist-front organizations."[120]

Marsh loved tweaking HUAC and other professional commie hunters. When they became interested in so-called subversive books (an activity later made infamous by Senator McCarthy), Marsh gave the books on economics he had accumulated in the PL's office (largely, of course, left leaning in content) to the library of the National Press Club. He sent the list to HUAC member John Rankin (D-MS) and said in a cover letter that if Rankin wanted to examine any of the PL's economics books for un-American tendencies, he was confident the Press Club would loan them to Rankin. Marsh then issued the letter and list as a press release.[121] At the beginning of testifying at a Senate hearing in 1947 on food supplies, Marsh made a point of saying with great mirth, "I hope it is going to be safe to announce I am not a Communist, I have never been a Communist and I do not expect to be a Communist in spite of the House Committee on Un-American Activities" (US Senate 1947, 69). In a press release, he sarcastically noted that when stocks and the economy went down, spy scares from Communist hunters went up.[122] He suggested that spy scares were a deliberate distraction from the reality of the economy—practically bread and circuses for the masses.

More seriously, Marsh emphasized that the term "subversive" was often hurled at "progressive organizations seeking economic changes by legal methods," but that the term was wholly undefined legally and therefore lacked any authoritative weight.[123] He took on the FBI, too, for its conservative political leanings. Its director, J. Edgar Hoover, had piously told the press that the FBI never *initiated* loyalty investigations, but only carried them out in reaction to receipt of credible material submitted to it. That was false. (Similarly, for years, he said the FBI did not engage in PR and had no staff paid to do PR.) But Hoover's public standing and credibility at the time were very high, including his representations that the FBI was punctilious about upholding a citizen's constitutional rights. That was good enough for the *Washington Post* editorial board. In response, Marsh wrote a letter to the editor citing a column by one of the *Post*'s columnists that specifically related an instance when the FBI did initiate a loyalty investigation.[124] Marsh was flummoxed by the paper's willful ignorance and lack of skepticism when covering Hoover.

Marsh vociferously attacked the two politicians most closely identified with the hunt for Communists, Senator Joe McCarthy (R-WI) and Congressman Richard Nixon (R-CA). A few months after McCarthy's infamous Wheeling, West Virginia, speech in February 1950 accusing the State Department of employing known Communists, Marsh denounced "McCarthyism" (then a relatively new term, invented by *Post* cartoonist Herblock at the end of March). He criticized "the wondrous exhibition stunt" by McCarthy in his subcommittee hearings and on the floor of the Senate, both venues giving him immunity from defamation lawsuits. Marsh viewed McCarthy as "not an isolated phenomenon" because of the tacit support McCarthy was getting from respectable and moderate Republican senators, who saw political benefits to McCarthy's attacks, even if they disagreed with his tactics.[125]

Marsh also blasted a bill promoted by Nixon to create a Subversive Activities Control Board and then require Communists to register with it. If a Communist did not do so, that would be a crime. Marsh tried to testify at a public hearing on the bill but was refused the opportunity.[126] In a statement that he asked to be published in the record of the hearings, he called the bill "one of the most subversive and futile efforts to create a crime" and suggested it was likely unconstitutional. Typically, he saw the bill in the larger context of creating a fake hysteria about the threat of Communism and using that sentiment "to get billions for jobs producing armaments" (US House 1950a, 2362–2363). On another occasion, he called the Nixon bill "a very red herring to cover up" the conservative economic policies that were to the detriment of the average income earners.[127] (A slightly different version of Nixon's bill became law in 1950.)

Chapter 11

Denouement and After

Demise, 1950

By the end of the 1940s, with Marsh and many of the PL's leadership getting quite old, a different question arose: Was there a next act? All his life, Marsh had been intense, hyperactive, and a whirlwind. From the preceding chapters, it is clear that he seemed to have boundless energy and passion for his projects—he was a true workaholic. And he was a man on a mission. Marsh was out to save the world, and he was convinced that he was right—that his and Dewey's mild brand of socialism would inevitably win out. That he was seemingly the only person advocating this perspective at scores of congressional hearings, year after year, decade after decade, made no difference to him. His cause was right. He never thought of himself as utopian or unrealistic. Regardless of domestic and international developments, he was always sure that a socialist America was just around the corner.

This high-strung person would sometimes try to do too much and ignore other physical and emotional needs. It sometimes caught up with him and he had no choice but to stop. During his regular fall trip to the West Coast in 1945, he had to be hospitalized in Oregon for bronchitis and pleurisy and had to cancel some of his planned appearances. Wanting to minimize the cancellations, he left the hospital as soon as he could to pick up on his planned schedule in Los Angeles. But he had returned to the road too quickly and had to be admitted to a Los Angeles hospital with virus pneumonia and additional complications. He canceled the rest of the trip and returned to Washington.[1] In early November, he was still in frail condition and had to cancel a speech in Boston.[2]

PL President McConnell wrote to wish him well and expressed amazement that Marsh had even been able come back to decent health from such a serious condition. "What are you made of to get through virus pneumonia—steel and flint?"[3] It was both a compliment about Marsh's seeming indestructibility and ferocity and an acknowledgement of how much Marsh had constantly pushed himself to the utmost during all those years.

Monitoring Marsh's health became a permanent subject for the leadership's attention. At a March 1946 meeting of the Board of Directors, Marsh raised for discussion the topic of whether he should commit to his usual trip to the coast that fall. The Board members decided he had "better not do so." Going one step further, they adopted a motion that he should take six months off with pay to recuperate.[4] Even though he took some time off (it is unclear if he took the full half-year; probably not), the Board revisited the subject in January 1947. The members decided that "in view of Mr. Marsh's illness," he should take another three months off with pay.[5]

Even while resting, he continued working, especially writing and editing the monthly *Bulletin*. The regular financial statement for registered lobbyists also came due while he was off. Marsh wrote the House clerk with an explanation of why he could not make the deadline and asked if he could have a postponement. The clerk replied that the lobbying registration law did not give him (the clerk) discretion to waive the reporting deadlines for any reason (Zeller 1948, 257). When he finally returned, Marsh testified in July 1947 at a House hearing. He explained, "I was ill and away a good deal last winter." House Ways and Means Committee Chairman Harold Knutson (R-MN), no fan of the PL's political philosophy or of Marsh's preternatural abrasiveness at hearings, gently replied, "We have missed you. . . . The Chair was happy to see you in the room this morning" (US House 1947, 1832).

At a Board meeting in the fall of 1947, the members discussed the possible need for Marsh to have an "understudy" given that it now looked like he would have to take every winter off to be in a warm and dry climate.[6] (Nothing came of it.) Nonetheless, for the half-decade between 1945 and 1950, Marsh and the PL soldiered on. The Board had regular leadership meetings, Marsh continued testifying at congressional hearings, he edited and largely wrote the contents of the monthly eight-page *Bulletin*, and he engaged in the usual publicity efforts to promote the policy program of the Lobby. Yes, the pace was a bit slower, but otherwise there was no change in the PL's efforts.

In mid-1950, the PL was functioning as it always had. The annual meeting of members took place in May. (To increase attendance, in 1947 the annual meeting was permanently shifted from January to May.) The Board had a routine meeting prior to the membership meeting. It nominated a slate of officers and Board members for 1950–51.[7] The membership meeting—largely the same people, along with the proxies that members sent Marsh—took place immediately afterward. The officer slate and a policy program for 1950–51 as recommended by the Board were adopted,[8] and the meeting was adjourned. None of the attendees knew or expected it was the last. In fact, planning for future activities, later that month Marsh wrote the directors suggesting "that early in the fall, we can have a two or three hour meeting of the Board to discuss our program, and how to get more support for it."[9]

Two documents indicate that just before its dissolution, the PL had an active leadership cadre and membership. In May, Marsh prepared a biographical summary of the PL's leadership.[10] For 1950–51, in addition to its president and vice president, there were four members of the Board of Directors (not counting Marsh, who was an officer and Board member), and the Advisory Council (which did not have regular meetings) had twelve members. In addition to Mrs. Clyde (the wealthy widow and admirer of Dewey) and Laidler (the labor activist who objected to Marsh's over-the-top writings against unions and Catholicism), many of the PL's leadership were faculty, mostly emeriti, but some still working. A few were lefty and union activists in New York, while others included a labor leader in Montana, a lawyer and a PR man in California, a retired military officer in Chicago, and several clergy.

Also, for the annual membership meeting in May 1950, 646 members had signed and returned proxies to be cast at the meeting. In all, this indicates a small but functioning nonprofit organization, not in any sense a Potemkin Village of just Marsh. In mid-1950, it had an adequate number of volunteers willing to serve as officers, board members, and council members as well as an active and attentive membership. Furthermore, the Lobby continued being in compliance with all annual reporting requirements for Delaware corporations. Its books were annually audited by an accountant who then issued a formal written statement of his conclusions. The People's Lobby was a very small national organization, but a real and authentic one in all regards.

After the annual meeting in May, Marsh resumed his standard routines in Washington. In early July, he testified at a congressional hearing on a tax bill and for the umpteenth time urged a steeper progressive income tax and opposed deficit spending. When he concluded, none of the members had any questions, leading Marsh to quip, "I am delighted to find such complete agreement." According to the stenographer's official transcript, that was followed by "[Laughter.]" (US Senate 1950, 81). For a House hearing in late July on agricultural policy, Marsh submitted a statement of the PL's position, but without testifying (US House 1950b, 224–225). Also routinely, he dashed off letters to prominent committee chairs calling on them to investigate what Marsh thought were unfair policies and laws.[11] Complying with lobbyist registration requirements, he filed the quarterly financial and activity report through June 30, 1950.[12] He also continued writing the monthly *Bulletin* as well as engaging in media relations. In late May, he issued a release on international poverty and hunger and in early September a statement denouncing the 1950 tax bill.[13]

However, by late summer, Marsh's health was so bad and he was so weak physically that he could not continue. His doctor ordered him to stop active work. Marsh (uncharacteristically) accepted the advice and notified the Board of Directors of his resignation effective October 31. The directors needed to decide if to try to continue after Marsh's retirement. They quickly agreed to close the People's Lobby completely. In an act of genuine generosity, Mrs. Clyde quickly volunteered to cover Marsh's full salary for the entire year, a bonus for the office's equally dedicated and poorly paid secretary, and whatever additional sums were required to close the books without any unpaid obligations.[14]

Characteristically, Marsh was punctilious about the paperwork necessary to close the PL. He notified the landlord, closed the bulk mail account with the Post Office, and filed a final financial report.[15] Carefully, he obtained letters of resignation from officers and Board members so that there would be a clear legal record that the PL no longer existed, and no one could claim to speak or act in its name afterward.[16]

On September 30, the Board wrote all Lobby members and *Bulletin* subscribers of Marsh's retirement and its decision to dissolve the PL because Marsh and the organization "are one and inseparable."[17] If any member or subscriber wanted a refund for the portion of his or her payments that would be unused, he or she was invited to submit such a request. Almost no one did. Still, for those who did, Marsh prepared a form letter enclosing the refund and carefully requested the person sign a receipt and return it to him for the files.[18]

Instead of requesting refunds, there was an outpouring of touching letters from loyal members throughout the country to Marsh waiving the refund offer (some enclosing an additional small contribution) and expressing appreciation for all he had done over the years:

- "We shall miss you more than we realize at the moment."

- "Your devoted and unselfish service is an inspiration and an example to thousands of people."
- "You have been for many years an effective and statesman-like servant of the people."
- "More than anyone I know you have voiced the will of the people in today's struggle of man against wealth."
- "You have fought the good fight . . . It may be that the results of your efforts have not always been directly evident, but you may rest assured that what you have done adds up to a real achievement, and a big one."
- "We who have known you down through the years will always think of you as a devoted, patriotic American who passed up the temptation of material reward to labor for National Justice that the great majority of our citizens have let deteriorate from their own indifference."
- "You have fought a long and good fight. We are all indebted to you."
- "Washington will be the poorer as the result of your resignation and the folding up of the People's Lobby."
- "Though you have probably had moments of despair at the blind determination of our people to destroy a great heritage, you must also know that your efforts have not been in vain."[19]

Marsh issued a press release on October 12 announcing his retirement and the dissolution of the People's Lobby.[20] It was widely covered and uniformly positive, largely soft pedaling his very leftist political ideology. He was called the "dean" of Washington's lobbyists, having been in that role for thirty-two years, longer than anyone else in the current lobbying corps. An AP story (and photo) described him as "lean, twinkly, scraggly-haired" and always with a pipe on hand. For all those years, he "has been busy tossing out ideas and opinions."[21] The *Post* profiled him as a "lean, hawk-nosed, white-haired man with the look of a retired farmer [who] admits to being a radical in economics, but insists on the democratic process."[22] Another paper described him as a "foe of special interests" and opaquely characterized the PL's goal as "a cooperative instead of a competitive economy."[23] An editorial in the *Portland Oregonian* lauded him for being the exception to the rule regarding lobbyists: he was not well paid, did not have money to spread around, focused on the merits of his ideas, and relied on small contributions.[24]

The last issue of the *Bulletin*, the 234th of its twenty-year run, was largely devoted to substantive issues, such as foreign policy, taxes, and the British Labor Party. It also included the usual recommendation of a suggested topic for the monthly letter from the member to Congress. In a short article on the second-to-last page, Marsh wrote of the Lobby's closing. He concluded with the hope that the members would continue to be active in other organizations espousing PL-type ideology because it was "never more needed."[25]

The last day of operations was October 31, 1950.

Postlude: Dewey and Marsh

Marsh retired to Florida to rest and write his autobiography. After so many decades lobbying day in and day out, he could not quite stop so abruptly. Somewhat amusingly, in January 1951, he felt compelled to submit a written statement for a congressional hearing on whether to extend reciprocal trade agreements. Having supported them for so many years and knowing of all the special interest groups that opposed free trade as harming their economic self-interest, Marsh felt obliged to try to balance the record. He wrote that "although the People's Lobby, Inc., with which I was associated, has been terminated, and I have retired," he still wanted to contribute his voice in support of renewing the agreements. To the last, he was true to his belief in international cooperation, anti-militarism, and socialist economics:

> [I] have tried to understand some of the problems of the rest of the world, and feel that to foster lasting peace, we must pay vastly more attention to helping the peoples of the world to achieve themselves a higher standard of living, instead of relying so much on either arming or alming them; and the reciprocal trade agreements seem to me an important measure in such a program. They may involve adoption of more efficient methods of production and distribution here, which would also benefit American consumers. (US House 1951, 624)

It was a fitting self-epitaph of his entire career.

John Dewey died in June 1952 at age ninety-two. The *Times*' obituary noted that "later in life Professor Dewey devoted much time and thought to reform of government. . . . He referred to the major political parties as 'the errand boys of big business,' and he championed new thought, actively through his connections with the People's Lobby, of which he was the president."[26]

Marsh died in Florida seven months later on December 31, 1952.[27] (Publicist and propagandist extraordinaire to the end, he died on a slow news day.) He was seventy-four. The United Press' Washington bureau distributed a sentimental and nostalgic profile, clearly written by a veteran reporter who had known him for a long time:

> Benjamin C. Marsh, voice of the "People's Lobby" for 22 years, is dead and the capital will never be quite the same. Old Ben, whose tall, stooped frame was a familiar sight in the halls of government during three decades . . . Old Ben was almost a legend in Washington, and in a sense his death symbolizes the end of an era—an era of reform, of the rise of labor in politics, of the uphill fight for the "little man." . . . He cursed Communists and capitalists alike. . . . Many of the newcomers to town won't remember old Ben, or his piercing gaze shooting from atop a stooping, six-foot-one frame. But something has gone in the capital with old Ben's death. The old timers won't forget.[28]

A few days later, Congressman John Dingell (D-MI), chairman of the Ways and Means Committee, eulogized Marsh. In a similarly warm tribute, Dingell said that Marsh was a "noble old soul who was always on hand to champion the cause of the lowly and underprivileged. Though not always in accord with his views, I could never challenge his honesty or sincerity of purpose, nor did anyone else so far as I can recall who listened to his testimony before my committee."[29]

Marsh had finished his autobiography before his death. *Lobbyist for the People* was published in mid-1953 (Marsh 1953). The only major paper to review it was the *Post*, which praised the book as "fascinating and provocative."[30] A syndicated service distributed an editorial that praised the book but skipped lightly over Marsh's political ideology. It concluded by assigning Marsh an honorary title from Roman days—"Tribune of the People."[31]

In academic journals, the reviews were mixed to negative. A social history journal perceptively noticed that Marsh's approach was not just direct lobbying of Congress, "but also through the medium of oral and written propaganda." Notwithstanding those who would disagree with his leftist ideology, the reviewer concluded that Marsh "deserves our attention, his ideas often having a touch of originality" (Bibliography 1955). The *Annals* applauded Marsh's "many shrewd observations" but wondered if the main benefit of the book was as "a psychological study of a professional do-gooder" (Myers 1954). Two other political science reviews were more negative. The *Western Political Quarterly* wondered if Marsh "seems more concerned with his personal successes and failures than with the causes which he espoused," such as his focus on "getting his name in the headlines of the press" (Outland 1954). Similarly, while praising Marsh's "remarkably active and courageous" work, the reviewer for the *Journal of Politics* wrote that "at times, I suspect that his actions gratified his love of being an iconoclast more than they aided his causes" (Strong 1954).[32]

Dewey and Marsh may have been deceased, but that did not stop Communist hunters from chasing them. In late 1952, a school superintendent in West Virginia had received a citizen complaint that the school district's report cards carried a Dewey quote. The citizen claimed Dewey had been branded a subversive and the quote should be deleted. The superintendent wrote the FBI to ask if that indeed was the case. Hoover replied bureaucratically (and falsely) that the FBI was "strictly a fact-finding agency" and that it did not "make evaluations or draw conclusions as to the character or integrity of any organization or individual." On the internal copy of Hoover's letter was the notation that the FBI's earlier investigation "failed to disclose Communistic affiliations." However, Dewey was "a member of numerous front organizations."[33] The FBI was apparently unaware that Dewey was dead.

The apex of Senator McCarthy's Communist-hunting influence occurred during the winter of 1953–54, when he investigated alleged Communists at the Army's Fort Monmouth, New Jersey, base. His investigation re-raised the issue of whether the PL was Communist or not. However, oddly, it was not an accusation by McCarthy, but rather a finding by the Army. In a convoluted series of developments, the Army reacted to McCarthy's investigation by seeking to demonstrate that it was as vigilant against Communists as the senator. One of its actions was to resuspend and fire Aaron H. Coleman, a radar engineer and civilian employee under suspicion of being a Communist. One of the specifics of the Army's charges to justify the firing was that Coleman had been a member of the PL. The Army characterized the PL as "a coalition of groups including many Communist, Communist-front and left-wing groups." (As worded, the accusation could not have been true because the PL had individual members; it was not a coalition of other organizations.) Coleman appealed, confirming that he had been a PL member for a year or two, but that the organization was "wholeheartedly and intelligently anti-Communist," even though it supported public ownership of natural resources.[34]

Marsh's son, Michael, who was a Washington-based reporter for a union publication, promptly protested the Army's smear. He said it was "ridiculously untrue" that the PL and his late father had been Communist. He wrote the secretary of the Army (a presidential appointee) and—showing his father's flair for the turn of a phrase—asked the Army to withdraw "this false and fraudulent advertising-in-reverse." Marsh *fils* also pointed out that "Army's hysterical hawkshaws are just as bad as Senator McCarthy."[35]

After going through an internal administrative process, Coleman was eventually fired by the Army secretary on general grounds of national security, but without any specific charges. After a long court battle, in 1958 the US Court of Appeals overturned the Army's action precisely because of the lack of any specific evidence. (The administration declined to appeal to the Supreme Court.) Coleman was reinstated with back pay. The long litigation never addressed the original Army charge that the PL was Communist because the eventual firing was on general grounds.[36] That the Army chose to finesse its original specific charges probably indicates that it knew it had a weak case overall, including regarding the PL.

From the mid-1950s to the mid-1960s, HUAC continued to track and keep files on Dewey, even though he was deceased. In response to a 1954 request from a member of Congress, it summarized the information in its files with the disclaimer that "the individual referred to is *not necessarily* a Communist, a Communist sympathizer, or a fellow-traveler," conceding that Dewey had sometimes been critical of the SU.[37] In 1956, former Chairman Martin Dies Jr. asked for all information in HUAC files on Dewey. As the request did not refer to Dewey as deceased, it is possible Dies thought Dewey was still alive.[38]

In 1965, a far-right organization opposed the Post Office's plan to issue a stamp honoring Dewey (and several others) as part of a new series of commemorative stamps of Prominent Americans. It claimed that Dewey's educational philosophy "initiated the down-grading of Nationalism and love of country, a contempt for American traditions, and the ever shrinking regard for morality, decency, ethics, self discipline, and eternal truths." More specifically, they said he was a supporter and/or member of several "Red fronts" (but did not specifically list the PL).[39] Receiving a letter opposing the Dewey stamp from a constituent, a congressman asked HUAC what it had on Dewey. An internal report confessed that regarding Dewey and the others up for stamps "none has been identified as a CP [Communist Party] member," a very narrow perspective, that HUAC had never used before as the central criterion to judge Dewey.[40] Replying even more cautiously to the congressman, HUAC stated that "while John Dewey was at one time associated with some front organizations, he had by the late 30's, become actively anti-Communist"—an exculpating perspective for the last twenty years that HUAC had never heretofore thought important to highlight.[41] The Post Office disregarded the extreme rightist campaign and issued a thirty-cent Dewey commemorative stamp in 1968 as part of its Prominent Americans series. It was issued on his 109th birthday from his birthplace of Burlington, Vermont.

1968 Dewey stamp, United States Postal Service, © United States Postal Service.

Conclusion

The moniker "People's Lobby" has lived on long after Dewey. It was just too good a phrase to forgo, precisely for the same reason Dewey had insisted on it when creating the PL. The nonprofit Common Cause, founded in 1970, has consistently described itself as a "people's lobby" (McFarland 1984, 7, 95), including on its Web site.[1] Reporter Neal Peirce called Common Cause "the first broad-scale 'people's lobby' of U.S. history" (Peirce 1972, x). This characterization indicated either an ahistoricism on his part or that he viewed Dewey's PL, with 4,000 members at its height, not counting as broad scale. In recent years, a dizzying array of other groups used the title. They included a liberal group in California,[2] a Green Party chapter in Florida,[3] a self-characterization of a Tea Party group,[4] a small political action committee (PAC) in Minnesota,[5] a socialist group in the United Kingdom,[6] and a political group organized through social media.[7]

So the name Dewey decided upon lives on, but without necessarily the meaning he tried to give it. The term was merely an empty vessel without specific meaning, somewhat akin to the many meanings of "efficiency" (Lee 2008, 199–202). The meaning that Dewey and Marsh tried to give the term was two-pronged and somewhat contradictory. First, the PL was like the current-day Common Cause, lobbying for the broad public interest when there was no other voice to call out special interest groups. Examples included the promotion of free trade and arguments against tariffs when the congressional hearings were dominated by special interest groups seeking preferential treatment and protection. The same happened on most tax and revenue bills, with economic self-interest dominating the hearings to obtain targeted benefits or to block losing them.

The PL was often the sole voice at those hearings for the broad public interest in opposition to special interest groups. Marsh especially enjoyed pointing out at tax hearings that the PL was advocating increasing taxes on its own members and that those members were in support of doing that.

Federal revenues should be based on income taxes, not consumption taxes (which were regressive), and the rates of an income tax should be steeply progressive. No one else at those hearings ever called for increasing taxes on themselves. This is one of the characteristics that make the PL nearly unique. There are few other examples of it in American politics, perhaps none before the PL's efforts.

Another good government issue was congressional regulation of lobbying, with the PL welcoming the minimal requirement of lobbyist registration and Marsh maneuvering to be the first one licensed.

Mostly, though, the meaning Dewey and Marsh gave to the term "people's lobby" was the leftist bent of "people's," such as the later common People's Republic of ______ formulation for post-WWII Communist countries. The PL stood for social democratic and socialist ideas because Dewey and Marsh were convinced that a collectivist political economy was better for the mass public than a market-based economy. They not only wanted to redistribute income, but also wanted public ownership of monopolies, utilities, natural resources, railroads, and major heavy industries. They felt that, for example, all minerals being extracted from the land should be deemed public property, and the profits from any utilization of it should inure directly to the public-at-large. In general, they saw modern society as a conflict between capital and labor, imperialism and self-government, autocracy and popular democracy. Internationally, they opposed war and peacetime conscription, seeking nonviolent solutions to the world's problems. This leftist ideological meaning that Dewey and Marsh gave to the PL was likely what ghettoized its appeal and gradually degraded its effectiveness and perceptions of how broad a swath of the citizenry it actually spoke for.

A few years after the PL disbanded, there were two editorial pieces in newspapers that concisely got to the heart of why lobbying for special interest groups usually succeeded and why the PL usually lost. In 1954, a Scripps-Howard reporter mentioned that dynamic in the context of mounting concerns over the disproportionate influence of special interest groups and lobbyists in the capital. Fraser Edwards reminded the readers that there had been a good lobby in Washington. "Folks might think a 'people's lobby' would have solid support," given that most Americans were rank-and-file citizens, not associated with any well-funded special interests. That was not the case, he wrote. "The late Ben Marsh was the People's Lobby for two decades and he nearly starved to death. He fought every bill favoring special interests and most statesmen scorned him."[8]

Similarly, an editorial in a Montana newspaper in 1952 cut to the quick of why the PL had been weak compared to special interest groups:

> This is a big country with different powerful groups whose interests conflict at different points. But the biggest group of all is the great unorganized middle section of our citizenship. Too often, the members of this group find themselves squeezed between the organized groups. About all they can do is to complain but their protests seldom have much effect simply because they are voiced by individuals rather than organizations speaking through paid representatives. For many years, there was a fine old gentleman from Iowa who maintained in Washington what he called a "people's lobby" but since he had no credentials showing that he was authorized to speak for the millions whom he tried to represent, his influence didn't carry very far when opposed to highly paid lobbyists who were there to press the views of organizations numbering hundreds of thousands or millions of voters.[9]

These two commentaries incisively identified the fatal flaw of American politics: the salience of economic interest over broad sentiment. Fehrenbacher had analyzed why in pre–Civil War politics slavery always won in legislative and policy showdowns. Slavery was an *interest*, while abolition was merely a *sentiment* (2001, 28). The intense involvement by those who benefited from slavery consistently trumped the more amorphous moral commitment of abolitionists. A small group that cares immensely about a single issue for economic reasons tends to win over widely held views of a large amorphous public. An additional factor in this asymmetry of power is that a special interest group tends to care only about one or a handful of issues, while the broader public-at-large is affected by many, if not all of them. Public opinion, which is a mile wide and only an inch deep, does not win out over a special interest deeply concerned about a narrow slice of the pie.

That dynamic was true for the PL and continues to be true to the present time. Trying to decipher the logic of seemingly irrational decisions by American elected officials, a *New York Times* analysis in 2014 captured the political math of the intense few versus the inattentive many:

> While a few small interests have a lot to gain, the costs are spread out over a large group of people (that is, taxpayers). The concentrated group of beneficiaries is much more motivated to lobby for their desired outcome than the more diffuse, disorganized group hurt by it. This is a classic political economy problem that occurs with many public policy decisions.[10]

This is a good description of where Marsh found himself vis-à-vis the lobbying of well-funded interest groups and corporations. He was one against many, with the many focusing on just one issue while he had to spread himself thin to cover dozens of like issues.

This history of the People's Lobby is also a good reminder of *plus ça change, plus c'est la même chose*. The pressing issues on the public policy agenda that decision makers in Washington were faced with, and the alternatives proposed by the PL, bring into stark relief the continuity of American political and economic history. It seems like the issues that were argued about during the PL's existence have often been eerily echoed in the arguments in Washington in the first two decades of the twenty-first century. They included controversies over maintaining or restoring prosperity, too-easy credit, reckless loans, speculative bubbles, anti–Wall Street, excessive influence of and deference to banks, bankruptcies by home and farm owners, disproportionately large tax cuts to the wealthy, the expanding economic gap between the wealthy and working classes, investment portfolios of members of Congress, domestic poverty, chronic unemployment, hunger, and the suffering of children.

In the international sphere, the arguments then and now have been over American intervention in other counties and projecting military power to protect what were claimed to be American interests. At times the opposition to intervention was due to the too-close relationship between US economic interests (i.e., of large corporations) and meddling in other countries. One of those countries was Nicaragua, with Dewey speaking vociferously against US intervention, as did the left during the Reagan presidency (leading to the Iran-Contra affair). Assertions that the two Iraq wars of the two Bush presidents were partly motivated by control of oil can be seen as extensions of what the PL said of US intervention in Mexico. Even modern references to a peace movement hearken back to the era of the PL, as it was identified as a peace organization or peace agency.[11]

Overlapping as both a domestic and international issue, the subject of tariffs is still alive and well at the time of writing (2014), although the nomenclature has changed. Now the subject is usually identified as free trade, indicating what the default position is. Whatever it is called, arguments about free trade, fair trade, dumping, or anything else are still about the same subject. Free trade agreements with other countries are increasingly controversial and difficult to pass on Capitol Hill. The ones debated during the Obama administration largely squeaked through with vociferous opposition, sometimes from the left, sometimes from the right, sometimes both. Conferences of the World Trade Organization invariably attracted protests, usually by the left.

In terms of the strength of democracy, there were then and still are now serious concerns about the apparent capture of the policy-making institutions by moneyed special interest groups, trumping those who spoke for the un-moneyed interests, the unorganizable public interest, and the marginalization of policy stances of those further to the left of the Democratic Party.

Not all issues of the PL's era are still alive nearly a century later. For example, the controversy over ownership of power and utilities has ended, with a victory by the proponents of investor-owned (i.e., for profit) utilities, even if subject to state and federal regulation of profits. The approach of public power advocates—that the people (i.e., the government) should own natural monopolies and power companies like the TVA—has been defeated. It no longer resonates as an ongoing area of political controversy. The private sector won.

Yet, from the longer perspective of history, one must judge that the policy ideas the PL proposed and lost on have nonetheless been largely vindicated by developments since. Some examples include raising taxes on the rich to reduce income inequality and enhance progressive taxation based on the ability to pay, criticisms of the influence of Wall Street, balanced budgets, civil rights, free trade, international cooperation, reducing deference to the military, anti-colonialism, and avoiding armed entanglements abroad. Its major historical error was opposing deficit spending as a way to combat economic recessions. (Another was the US role in WWII, but that occurred after Dewey had stepped down as honorary president.)

Hansen viewed the PL as a "prototype" of leftist public interest groups (1987, 193), and that is an apt description. The PL was an early version of a lobby in Washington that was advocating neither for economic self-interest nor for more abstract, but still self-benefiting, social causes, such as suffragettes. The Lobby was seeking to promote the interests of the public-at-large with leftist and socialist goals even when its proposed policy solutions went against the economic interests of its members.

As mentioned earlier in this chapter, the PL also lobbied for some good government goals, making it similarly a prototype for the less overtly ideological advocacy groups now so common in Washington, such as in the areas of environmentalism, human rights, and animal welfare.

In terms of its mode of operations, the PL was a harbinger of the new style and structure of nonprofit advocacy now so prevalent in Washington. These generally consist of a centralized office of professional activists and experts being financed by a relatively passive membership whose main role is to pay annual dues. Marsh was similar to the nonprofit entrepreneurs of today. Yes, he encouraged members as volunteers to write letters to their members of Congress, but volunteers were not central to the PL's modus operandi, as they are not in today's national policy advocacy nonprofits. Now, as then, these are self-perpetuating nonprofit corporations, owned by no one and ostensibly controlled de jure by a board of directors (which usually appoints successors, directly or indirectly), but de facto by the professional, full-time staff. These organizations often have the appearance of being democratic, but are not in actual practice.

Another strand of modern nonprofit advocacy that can be found in the PL was an early example of what Jenkins called the "protest business," namely Marsh and Dewey always being dissatisfied with the current state of affairs, always pushing for new actions and altering of policy (2006, 326). They were agitators of change. Berry and Sobieraj have suggested this approach to advocacy now be called the "outrage industry" (2014). If anyone was a precursor to that contemporary phenomenon, it would be Marsh. He had a nearly unlimited capacity to express outrage and to use it as a device to promote the PL's advocacy goals.

Tobin described the PL as providing "constant prodding" of the New Deal (1986, 236), an apt description of modern-day nonprofit advocacy, too. Given the multiplicity of influences on eventual policies (which tend to be combinations of compromises), this prodding role is difficult to measure in terms of degrees of influence. Tobin called efforts to assess the PL's (and sister groups') impact as "unresolvable" (236) and focused instead on a slightly different scale of measurement: "I believe it is a mistake to dismiss them as the progressive footnote . . . Their contribution extends far beyond their organizational enthusiasm and lobbying skills . . . They organized and wrote, debated and complained" (250).

In particular, the legacy of the PL is probably its do-everything approach to nonprofit advocacy, sometimes manifested as direct lobbying, other times as indirect lobbying through publicity. Marsh and Dewey were masters of political advocacy, advancing a template that became common only decades later. They knew how to create news, how to generate publicity, how to focus the spin of coverage on the perspective they wanted, and generally how to appear to be players. They were promoters and propagandists par excellence, evolving a kind of mega-mall approach of doing just about anything they could think of to advocate for their ideas. Leff called the PL "an efficient publicity machine" (1984, 104).

In terms of how it implemented its policy advocacy mission, the PL engaged in a broad range of direct lobbying tactics that help depict the world of the lobbyist circa the 1920s to the 1940s. In addition to the obvious venue of testifying at congressional hearings, which Marsh did frequently, his tactics included meetings with individual members of Congress; meetings with groups of legislators; arranging for delegations to meet with legislators; submitting statements for inclusion in congressional hearings without testifying; mailings to all legislators; requesting a legislator to insert some material in the *Congressional Record*; inviting legislators to speak at PL meetings, especially those broadcast live on a national radio network; participating in coalitions (including sometimes organizing them, such as the Joint Committee on Unemployment); asking friendly legislators to conduct an informal hearing; and petitions.

In the arena of publicity, the PL was an innovator at media relations and press coverage, including press releases (especially on slow news days), public letters to senior officials, radio interviews, speaking tours, and letters to the editor. The PL also sent its newsletter to opinion leaders and university libraries as a way of further disseminating its public policy ideas and attracting new supporters. Here was an early instance of what in the twenty-first century came to be called convergence, namely the use of all techniques of publicity, PR, advocacy, marketing, and promotion as a comprehensive approach to communication.

In terms of its role in the emergence of nonprofit advocacy, the People's Lobby probably deserves some credit for discernibly contributing to the evolution toward the contemporary world of policy networkers in Washington. Through its structure, modus operandi, and PR-centric efforts, the People's Lobby was an early iteration of the modern advocacy nonprofit group. This truly was a prototype for nonprofit policy advocacy, a kind of "all of the above" approach.

On the other hand, in terms of its substantive political ideology, if success means enactment, then the PL would be judged a failure. However, while America loves winners, this study of one of the losers helps bring back into sight the power of ideas. So much of Washington—whether then or now and claims to be pragmatic—interested only in ideas that are politically viable and is quick to declare some proposals as dead on arrival. The story of the People's Lobby reminds us that our cynicism about politics has the effect of pulling our attention away from the substance of ideas and policy alternatives. There is a value to considering unorthodox thinking and nonmainstream proposals. History should not only be about the winners, but also needs a focus on the ideas that were not adopted. That helps us see the larger panoply of policy thinking, the ideas that perhaps were DOA, but why? What was wrong with them? What made them so unthinkable? Dewey's persistence (and Marsh's after Dewey left the PL) shows the excitement of nontraditional ideas, of trying to broaden the horizon of policy making.

That Dewey, Marsh, and their PL were history's losers does not mean their ideas were. The iconic line from the movie *Mr. Smith Goes to Washington* was "The only good cause is a lost cause." There may come a time in the United States of disenchantment with the results of market-based economics and market-oriented public policies. If and when that happens, the social democratic ideas of Dewey, Marsh, and the People's Lobby may make a comeback. They put their ideas into the permanent historical record, ready for serious consideration should circumstances ever change. Ideas don't come with expiration dates, and the cycles of policy invariably turn. Either way, ideas matter.

And what of Dewey's dream? That the PL would be an example of a concrete step toward realizing the society he envisioned in *The Public and Its Problems*? It will be recalled that Dewey's book provided a philosophical and theoretical underpinning to the PL (Chap. 2). Specifically, he wanted to help transform American society and its democracy by engaging in maximal publicity to reach the citizenry, using such publicity efforts to give a larger coherence to the episodic nature of news, disseminating information and alternatives that the economic and political oligarchy may be suppressing, and providing relevant and credible new knowledge that may contribute to a public debate about policies. Dewey and Marsh implemented these goals through the work of the People's Lobby. Nonetheless, their efforts did not revolutionize American politics as Dewey had hoped for this specific initiative. The politics of knowledge was a worthy goal and well thought out by Dewey, but much, *much* harder to actualize. As one of Dewey's efforts to implement his philosophy, this one fell short of his hopes.

Dewey had aimed very high—for a utopian modern democracy. It was not to be, at least for the PL as platform toward an end. Once again, the United States proved how hard she is to change significantly. And, especially, how powerful vested special interest groups are and the public—as a policy and legislative force—is not. Dewey's optimism and idealism crashed on the rocks of reality. Yet it would be incomplete to describe the People's Lobby merely as a failure. Perhaps noble effort and good idea get somewhat closer. Dewey's ideals for democracy, citizenship, and the public interest continue to have validity, and they may well prompt future tries that may be more successful in having concrete impacts. In the meantime, Dewey's ideas as a philosopher-lobbyist for improving democracy and the role of the People's Lobby as a factor to help attain that remain a worthy if hard-to-reach goal.

Notes

Preface and Acknowledgments

1. "The War Lords of Washington," *People's Lobby Bulletin* 18:8 (December 1948), 5–6. In a nice bit of historical symmetry, as a syndicated columnist in 1933 (before becoming a federal public information officer), Catton had written about overzealous Communist hunters who were smearing perfectly respectable organizations, mentioning the People's Lobby as one of his examples (Bruce Catton, "When Patriotism Goes Too Far" [syndicated column], *Olean [NY] Times-Herald*, February 3, 1933, 14).

Introduction

1. This abbreviation was used routinely by the Lobby's president, John Dewey. For example, see letters from Dewey to Marsh: April 15, 1931, and August [n.d.], 1931, Nos. 05139 and 05151, *The Correspondence of John Dewey* (digital database). Hereafter references to this database will be limited to the number assigned to the letter. The abbreviation has also been used in the subsequent historical literature (e.g., Bordeau 1971, 68–69).

2. The Center for Dewey Studies, retrieved February 4, 2014: http://deweycenter.siu.edu/.

3. Thirteenth Annual Meeting, January 8, 1945. File: Minutes, Stockholders and Directors 1931–1950, Box 3, Benjamin C. Marsh Papers, Manuscript Division, Library of Congress. Hereafter all archival references are from the Marsh Papers unless otherwise identified.

4. SUNY Press Web site, retrieved January 8, 2014: http://www.sunypress.edu/searchadv.aspx.

5. Michael Beschloss, Review of *Pacific Crucible* by Ian W. Toll, *New York Times* (hereafter *NYT*), November 27, 2011, Sunday Book Review, 30.

Chapter 1

1. Based on ProQuest Historical Newspaper databases, searched on July 2, 2012.

2. Based on EBSCOhost *New Republic* Archive, searched on July 17, 2012. The magazine began publication in 1914, and his first piece was in 1915.

3. This text was omitted from their 1932 revised edition (Dewey and Tufts 1961).

4. Some of the subsequent printings of the book formally subtitled it *A Sequel to "Public Opinion"* (Lippmann, 1927). Also, the pagination is slightly different (195 pages versus 205), but there does not appear to be any change in the text.

5. Great Society was a term coined by British academic Graham Wallas, which came to be (mis)used during the 1920s to convey the benefits of the seemingly permanent economic prosperity.

6. Disappointingly, Lippmann did not review Dewey's book. E-mail from William R. Massa Jr., Archivist, Manuscripts and Archives, Yale University Library, July 11, 2012, author's files. Yale's Archives hold the Lippmann Papers and the Robert O. Anthony Collection of Walter Lippmann's writings. The *New Republic* review was by Robert Morss Lovett and was favorable ("A Real Public," August 24, 1927, 22–23). In the book, Dewey also took a shot at his former idol, Woodrow Wilson, for "enormous ineptitude" in Wilson's effort to lay out a philosophical basis for his economic and governmental reform proposals (93).

7. One of the anonymous SUNY Press reviewers suggested the need for a clearly stated caveat that the People's Lobby should not be viewed as Dewey's only effort to implement his philosophy. Rather than rephrasing the suggestion and blending it into the text without proper acknowledgement, I'd rather let the external reviewer's excellent observation be presented directly to the reader firsthand:

> "In fact it [the PL] was one facet of a much broader program. That program included:
>
> (1) 'democracy as a way of life,' in all institutions and settings: democracy in the workplace, the school, the family, the religious congregation, the neighborhood, etc.—direct democratic participation in small face-to-face settings as a training ground for the character and skills needed to participate in national representative government in the 'Great Society.'
>
> (2) Basic and applied research in all the human sciences: e.g.
>
>   (a) economics for a counter cyclical theory and practice;
>
>   (b) psychology for fundamental improvements in child rearing and teaching;
>
>   (c) education, child development and cognition, urban development, etc.

(3) progressive education to create a competent citizenry (which the author does allude to in passing)—in order to foster inquiry and problem solving; and also substantive knowledge, with historical comparative perspective, of economic production, distribution, and consumption."

I appreciate the reviewer's broader perspective and hope that this history of the PL is indeed seen in a proper and larger Deweyian context.

8. Several sources misspell his middle name as "Clark" (Frumkin et al. 2011, 19; Bromley 2005; LeGates and Stout 1998, xxi).

9. "Greenwich Milking Almost Waterloo," *New York Tribune*, May 31, 1914, 12; "Marsh Expelled from City Club," *New York Tribune*, March 4, 1916, 3.

10. "Benjamin C. Marsh," FBI file, January 28, 1930, 1. File: John Dewey, No. 61-HS-6611, Central Records System, Federal Bureau of Investigation (hereafter FBI).

11. John Dewey, "Why We Are at War," *Chicago Tribune* (hereafter *CT*), September 9, 1917, D4.

12. Letterhead, letter to President Wilson, October 3, 1918. File: Correspondence 1913–1922, Box 1.

13. Letters to President Wilson, October 3 and 28, 1918. File: Correspondence 1913–1922, Box 1; "High Taxation Is Urged to Curb Excess Profits," *CT*, June 8, 1918, 5.

14. Letterhead of Marsh letter to Coolidge, July 15, 1924. File: Correspondence 1923–1928, Box 1.

15. "Federal Ownership of Railroads Asked by Farmers' Council: Lower Rates and Cessation of 'Looting' Are among the Reasons for Stand Given by B. G. [sic] Marsh," *New York Tribune*, September 21, 1919, 17.

16. Marsh letter to President Coolidge, July 15, 1924. File: Correspondence 1923–1928, Box 1.

17. "Farmers Council Plan Is Outlined," *Christian Science Monitor* (hereafter *CSM*), January 8, 1921, 4.

18. "Farmers Ask Wilson to Veto Shipping Bill," *CT*, June 6, 1920, 10.

19. "Benjamin C. Marsh," FBI file, January 28, 1930, 4. File: John Dewey, No. 61-HQ-6611, FBI.

20. Arthur M. Evans, "Party Leaders Wakening Up to Hi [sic] Cost Issue," *CT*, June 5, 1920, 3.

21. "Farmers Criticize Party Platform," *CSM*, June 16, 1920, 2.

22. "Harding Taking Rest," *Washington Post* (hereafter *WP*), June 27, 1920, 1.

23. "Asserts Wall Street Leads Farmer Bodies," *New York Times*, January 30, 1920, 15.

24. "Another Bill for Packer Control," *CSM*, April 10, 1920, 4.

25. Ibid.

26. "This Week," *New Republic*, March 3, 1920, 3.

27. Leading to some confusion, the People's Legislative Service was sometimes colloquially referred to as a "People's Lobby" ("'People's Lobby' Is Source of Much Congressional Lore," *CSM*, June 21, 1922, 6). This was an informal appellation and was, organizationally, wholly unrelated to the People's Lobby, Inc. that Dewey and Marsh founded in 1928.

28. This use of "People's" preceded (and had a softer leftist meaning) than the later Communist formulation in the mid–twentieth century century of "People's Republic of ____."

29. "People's Reconstruction League" (introductory pamphlet), probably early 1921, 4. Pamphlet Collection, Wisconsin Historical Society.

30. Letterhead, letter from Marsh to Attorney General Harry Daugherty, June 30, 1921 (Naison 1989, reel 18, frame 408).

31. Ibid. At the time, "reconstruction" had a specific and negative political meaning, namely the supposedly failed and misguided federal effort to reconstruct the South after the Civil War, including providing political rights to the freedmen. This politicization (and perversion) of history was promoted by Southern Democrats as a rationale for Jim Crow laws, reversing the political rights of African-Americans. The 1915 movie *Birth of a Nation* was the apotheosis of this racist propaganda. Marsh instead wanted to convey the earlier and more positive meaning of the term—a sense of the need to reconstruct the country after a war (this time WWI), in part because of the unintended consequences of a war, the social upheaval it created, and the political initiatives that were put on hold for the duration of the war. Also, the seemingly endless and sometimes violent labor-management conflicts were another obvious phenomenon justifying the need to reconstruct the basic building blocks of American society.

32. "People's Reconstruction League" (introductory pamphlet), cover page.

33. Westbrook dates its founding to "shortly after World War I," which—while technically accurate because of its vagueness—conveys a misimpression about a close temporal linkage of the two events (1991, 445).

34. "Plan to Save Workers $6,000,000,000 a Year: Farmers and Unions Form Non-Partisan Organization to Get 'Economic Justice,'" *NYT*, January 28, 1921, 5.

35. "Farmers to Meet Unions," *NYT*, April 4, 1921, 3; "Farm and Labor Men to Meet Here," *WP*, April 4, 1921, 10.

36. John Skelton Williams, "What Congress Should Do," Address before the People's Reconstruction League, April 15, 1921 (apparently a self-published pamphlet; OCLC Accession No. 21251235); "Increased Tax on Privilege Sought," *CSM*, April 15, 1921, 5; "Ex-Comptroller Williams Criticizes Reserve Board," *Wall Street Journal*, April 16, 1921, 5.

37. "Nonpartisans Pay Visit to Congress," *CSM*, April 16, 1921, 2; "Conference Drafts 'People's Program,'" *NYT*, April 16, 1921, 16.

38. "Enactment Urged of Packer Bill," *CSM*, February 11, 1921, 5. This was a long-running issue with more hearings at which PRL testified and more public statements Marsh released.

39. Transcript in *Congressional Record* (hereafter *CR*), December 22, 1921, 719–720; "Grills Tax Witnesses," *NYT*, May 20, 1921, 11.

40. Federated Press, "14 Billions Cost of U.S. Congress," *New York Evening Call*, February 25, 1923, 5; "Farmers' Ills Blamed on Special Privileges," *WP*, June 21, 1926, 4; "The Standard Oil and Mexico," *CR*, March 4, 1927, 5952–5953.

41. "Joint Brief to Minority Members of the Ways and Means Committee," *CR*, June 30, 1926, 12310–12312.

42. Associated Press (hereafter AP), "22 Senators Ask for Mergers Inquiry," *CSM*, July 12, 1926, 4A.

43. "Hungarian Group Heavily Guarded; Pickets Arrested," *WP*, March 20, 1928, 24.

44. Letter from Commerce Secretary Herbert Hoover to Marsh, January 25, 1922. File: Correspondence 1913–1922, Box 1.

45. "The People's Part in Congress," *The Survey* 46:3 (April 16, 1921), 73.

46. "People's Reconstruction League Organizes Branch in Boston," *Machinists' Monthly Journal* 33:8 (August 1921), 633.

47. "Poor Man's Lobbyist Plans Protest Meet on Foreign Policies," *Waterloo [IA] Evening Courier*, May 19, 1927, 1.

48. Ibid.; "Benjamin C. Marsh Gets Cold Reception in Oregon," *[Portland] Oregonian*, August 17, 1921, 10; "City Club Speaker Fights for Farmer," *Los Angeles Times* (hereafter *LAT*), July 17, 1925, A10; "Imperialism Talks Planned," *LAT*, April 29, 1927, A2. Clippings in the Marsh Papers include coverage of his talks in other cities (File: Scrapbooks, 1924–1926, Box 5).

49. "Attacks City Help in Housing Relief," *NYT*, September 14, 1927, 18.

50. "Tariff Conference to Open Tomorrow," *WP*, December 27, 1925, 5; "Tariff Attacked as Unnecessary," *NYT*, December 29, 1925, 11; David J. Lewis, "Methods in Tariff Making," *CR*, July 1, 1926, 12465–12471; *The People vs. the Tariff; Proceedings, Conference, The People's Reconstruction League* (mimeograph, not paginated). The only copy of the proceedings in OCLC/WorldCat is at the Steenbock Memorial Library, College of Agricultural and Life Sciences, University of Wisconsin-Madison.

51. "Meeting Will Discuss Mexican Intervention," *WP*, April 26, 1926, 4.

52. "U.S. Economic Claims Held as Inviting War," *WP*, July 24, 1926, 8. Prominent leftist Norman Thomas was one of the speakers.

53. "Americans' Concessions Abroad," *CR*, January 5, 1927, 1108–1112.

54. "Coolidge Would Stifle Criticism, Says Speaker," *WP*, July 7, 1927, 4; AP, "Concession Inquiry to Be Sought," *LAT*, July 7, 1927, 7; "U.S. Action in Nicaragua Called 'Exploitation,'" *WP*, July 8, 1927, 4.

55. "League Outlines Program," *NYT*, September 30, 1921, 13.

56. Memo from R. E. Vetterli, Special Agent in Charge, Washington Field Office, to J. Edgar Hoover, director, FBI, January 28, 1930, re: People's Lobby, 2. File: Dewey, John, No. 61-HQ-6611, FBI.

57. Transcript: "Interview by Mr. Stowell of the Department of Justice, with Mr. Marsh of the People's Reconstruction League, June 24, 1921" (Naison 1989, reel 18, frames 409–413).

58. "Benjamin C. Marsh," FBI file, January 28, 1930, 1–2.

59. Letter from Marsh to Attorney General Harry Daugherty, June 30, 1921 (Naison 1989, reel 18, frame 408).

60. Reply from Attorney General Harry Daugherty to Marsh, July 11, 1921. File: Correspondence 1913–1922, Box 1.

61. "Benjamin C. Marsh," FBI file, January 28, 1930, 2–3.

62. "Radical Aim Is Exposed: 'Domestic Reds' Whet Claws," *LAT*, January 29, 1923, 1–2.

63. "Carlo Tresca," *CR*, December 19, 1925, 1219.

64. *CR*, February 23, 1927, 4596.

65. "Conference Drafts 'People's Program,'" *NYT*, April 16, 1921, 16.

66. Sillars mistakenly attributed the 1921 editorial reference to Marsh of the People's Lobby, which was not founded until 1928.

67. "Anti-Monopoly League Formed in Washington," *CSM*, November 30, 1927, 7.

68. "Anti-Monopoly League" (typeset four-page introductory flier), n.a. (probably Marsh), n.d. (probably late 1927). File: Printed Matter 1916–1918 and 1930–1935, Box 4.

69. "Policy in Cent[ral] America Rapped," *Coshocton (OH) Tribune*, December 9, 1927, 10; "Antimonopoly [sic] League Hears Admiral Rodgers," *WP*, December 10, 1927, 11.

70. Rodney Dutcher, "New League Fights Monopoly on Oil, Gasoline, Electricity and Anthracite," *Manitowoc [WI] Herald-News*, December 3, 1927, 5.

71. "Anti-Monopoly League" (editorial), *[Emmetsburg, IA] Palo Alto Tribune*, December 14, 1927, 4.

72. "Congressmen Aiding Profiteers, Is Claim," *WP*, December 26, 1927, 14.

73. "A People's Lobby to Watch Congress," *NYT*, September 18, 1906, 6; "A People's Lobby" (editorial), *The Independent* 61:3017 (September 27, 1906), 761–762.

74. "The People's Lobby" (editorial), *CT*, September 24, 1906, 8.

75. "People's Lobby Organizes," *NYT*, October 23, 1906, 3.

76. "Plea for a 'People's Lobby,'" *CT*, October 29, 1907, 3.

77. "The People's Lobby" (editorial), *CT*, October 30, 1907, 8.

78. J. O. Hammitt, "The First Lobby for the People," *The Independent* 62:3038 (February 21, 1907), 411–414; "A Lobbyist—For the People," *World's Work* 15:1 (November 1907), 9599–9601.

79. "The New Lobbyist: He Works for the People Instead of for the Corporations," *New York Tribune*, December 16, 1906, A3, A5.

80. Massachusetts: Joseph Lee, "A People's Lobbyist," *The Independent* 62:3051 (March 23, 1907), 1203–1206. Illinois: "People's Lobby to Start," *CT*, April 23, 1907, 2. Nebraska: "People's Lobby Planned," *CSM*, January 20, 1921, 4.

81. "Boss or No Boss?" (editorial), *LAT*, December 17, 1910, II–4.

82. "Broad Community Plan Announced," *CSM*, September 29, 1920, 11; "Community Board Locates Here," *WP*, September 27, 1920, 6.

Chapter 2

1. Pinchot said he had invented the term "conservation" as a variant on conservative so that it would be seen as a policy goal reflecting the values of conservatism rather than as a new and radical idea.

2. "Public Utilities Senate Target," *Wall Street Journal*, November 28, 1927, 4; Kenneth Clark, "Former Governor Pinchot Locates in Washington; House Political Mecca," *New Castle [PA] News*, November 30, 1927, 1–2.

3. For example: " 'People's Lobby' Newest in Ranks at Washington: Former Governor Pinchot Heads Group at Capital," *Alton [IL] Evening Telegraph*, November 19, 1927, 2; "Pinchot Fosters 'People's Lobby': It Is Outgrowth of Idea Generated by Former Governor Who Went to Washington after Retirement," *Altoona [PA} Mirror*, November 22, 1927, 12.

4. Marsh knew Pinchot from their mutual involvement in progressive causes in Washington (Marsh 1953, 195–196). Also, Pinchot's brother, Amos, was similarly a progressive reformer, active in New York City politics. He had worked side by side with Marsh on many issues before Marsh moved to Washington (Tobin 1986, 21, 45. 48, 77, 105). Therefore, it is almost certain that Marsh knew of Gifford Pinchot's trial balloon about creating a people's lobby.

5. In a press release in early 1928, Marsh described the Anti-Monopoly League as "often called the 'People's Lobby' " ("Lobbying Now a Virtue, Says 'Champion of People,' " *New York Herald Tribune*, March 19, 1928, 2).

6. The word was routinely capitalized then and was shorthand for special interest groups and their concomitant lobbying efforts. For example, this headline: "A.F.L. Condemns Schools in Pay of 'Interests,' " *CT*, November 29, 1928, 16.

7. An indication of the negative meaning of the terms "lobby" and "lobbyist" occurred in 1931. By then, the People's Lobby was up and running. Marsh publicly criticized President Hoover as a "White House lobbyist" who promoted only the economic interests of the wealthy. This startling and disrespectful characterization was catnip for the press ("President Hoover Called Lobbyist: People's Lobby Claims Chief Executive Working Only for Wealthy Few," *BS*, September 27, 1931, 6).

8. Westbrook was in error in ascribing Dewey's association with PL as beginning in 1929 (1991, 445).

9. "B. C. Marsh to Lecture," *WP*, April 22, 1928, 7. Typically, he attacked ("Borah's Nicaraguan Stand Is Assailed," *WP*, April 23, 1928, 16).

10. "Monroe Doctrine Change Proposed: Co-operative Policing of Unstable Latin-American Republics Is Advocated," *CSM*, May 16, 1928, 3.

11. Notwithstanding his political preference for a third party, Dewey endorsed Governor Al Smith (D-NY) for president over a more ideologically leftist minor

party candidate ("Prof. John Dewey Declares for Smith," *NYT*, November 1, 1928, 22). Again, Dewey kept such political endorsements clear of his leadership of the PL.

12. "Organizations to Talk on Legislative Topics," *WP*, November 26, 1929, 9.

13. "Anti-Monopoly League" (typeset four-page introductory flier), n.a. (probably Marsh), n.d. (probably late 1927), 4. File: Printed Matter 1916–1918 and 1930–1935, Box 4.

14. Letterhead, letter from Marsh to Attorney General Harry Daugherty, June 30, 1921 (Naison 1989, reel 18, frame 408).

15. "Questions and Answers on Imperialism," n.d. (probably late 1928 or early 1929). File: Printed Matter 1916–1918 and 1930–1935, Box 4.

16. "Tugwell Is Conservative He tells Stormy Hearing; Confirmation Now Likely," *NYT*, June 12, 1934, 1, 15.

17. At the time, Wheeler was an FDR and New Deal supporter. However, he is most remembered for a later role as a vocal isolationist and a central opponent of a US role in WWII (before Pearl Harbor).

18. Norris knew Dewey. They had worked together on some progressive political causes. In 1930, Dewey had publicly called on Norris to run for president in 1932 as a third-party candidate. Norris declined (Laurence M. Benedict, "Norris's Hat Not in Ring," *LAT*, December 27, 1930, 1–2).

19. Presumably, this was a sarcastic remark by Norris trying to help Tugwell. It was aimed at commenting on the histrionic efforts by conservatives during the hearing to pin *something* controversial on Tugwell and their increasing frustration due to Tugwell's adeptness at not rising to the bait or being successfully provoked to make an impolitic remark.

20. Apparently, after Tugwell had accepted Dewey's initial invitation to serve on the advisory committee when PL was founded, Tugwell forgot about the matter, assuming his term of service had expired. Even after forming a formal board of directors, the PL continued to list a "council" as a kind of continuation of its initial advisory committee, but never doubled back to Tugwell to confirm or remind him of that.

21. Marsh, "The Peoples' Lobby" (letter to editor), *New Republic*, April 3, 1929, 202.

22. Dewey letter to Villard, January 16, 1929, No. 04991.

23. Dewey letter to Lindeman, June 18, 1931, No. 07634.

24. Lindeman letter to Dewey, June 23, 1931, No. 05146.

25. "Describes Plans of People's Lobby: Dr. John Dewey Explains Aims of Group and Raps Use of Armed Force in Haiti," *Philadelphia Evening Bulletin*, December 14, 1929.

26. Dewey letter to Marsh, April 15, 1931, No. 05139.

27. When Dewey's (first) wife died in 1927, Clyde wrote him a touching condolence letter, even though she had had little personal contact with Dewey before that (Clyde letter to Dewey, July 30, 1927, No. 05658).

28. I was unable to locate any examples of any of PL's pre-Clyde stenciled newsletters, neither in the Marsh Papers nor elsewhere.

29. Dewey letter to Marsh, June 24, 1931, No. 05148.

30. Dewey letter to Marsh, August __ (n.d.), 1931, No. 05151.

31. Letter from David Burnet, deputy commissioner of Internal Revenue, Treasury Department, to Marsh, December 23, 1929. File: Correspondence 1929–1933, Box 1.

32. Reply from Marsh to Burnet with notarized affidavit, December 24, 1929. File: Correspondence 1929–1933, Box 1.

33. Affidavit of Benjamin C. Marsh, March 4, 1931. File: Correspondence 1929–1933, Box 1.

34. Marsh, "Other Lobby" (letter to editor), *New Republic*, September 6, 1948, 31.

35. For reasons that are unclear, the title of the PL file with corporate minutes and records was "*Stockholders* & Directors" (Box 3). It is possible that this was a standard phrase and category for records kept by all Delaware-based corporations and that Marsh, no rebel when it came to legalities, simply wanted to follow standard procedures and titles.

36. Certificate of Incorporation of the People's Lobby, Inc. File: Minutes, Stockholders and Directors 1931–1950, Box 3.

37. The People's Lobby, Inc., By-Laws, ibid.

38. Inspector's Certificate, ibid.

39. "New Incorporations," *NYT*, October 14, 1931, 45.

40. John Dewey, "Full Warehouses and Empty Stomachs" (transcript of radio address on NBC, April 13, 1931), *People's Lobby Bulletin* (hereafter *PLB*) 1:1 (May 1931), 1–3.

41. "Dewey Will Lecture on Unemployment Relief," *Harvard Crimson*, May 12, 1931.

42. Letter from Herbert A. Seligmann, director of Publicity, NAACP (national office in New York) to Sallie Stewart, president, National Association of Colored Women, Washington, DC, December 3, 1931. Records of the National Association of Colored Women's Clubs, 1895–1992, Part 1, Reel 7, Folder 117, ProQuest History Vault. In the end, nine signed ("Nine Organizations Ask End of Control in Haiti," *New York Amsterdam News*, December 16, 1931, 9).

43. Dewey letter to Marsh, January 11, 1929, No. 05133.

44. Dewey letter to Marsh, April 26, 1931, No. 05142.

45. Dewey letter to Marsh, June 29, 1931, No. 05149.

46. Dewey letter to Marsh, June 24, 1931, No. 05148.

47. "Criticizes President for Indiana Speech: Dewey Charges Hoover with 'Tragic Failure' to Appreciate Gravity of Unemployment Crisis," *NYT*, June 28, 1931, 7.

48. Dewey letter to Marsh, June 13, 1931, No. 05144.

49. Dewey letter to Marsh, June 17, 1931, No. 05145.

50. Dewey letter to Marsh, July 3, 1931, No. 05150.

51. Dewey letter to Marsh, April 25, 1931, No. 05141.

52. Dewey letter to Marsh, April 1, 1931, No. 05138. Marsh followed the advice, releasing the letter in his name and adding two more prominent wealthy New Yorkers as addressees ("Urges Special Session of Congress," *NYT*, April 27, 1931, 14).

53. Dewey letter to Lewis Stiles Gannett, November 27, 1928, No. 04917; Dewey letter to Marsh, April 25, 1931, No. 05141. The latter meeting had to be rescheduled because on short notice Dewey went to Chicago to attend the funeral of his friend George Herbert Mead (Dewey letter to Marsh, April 27, 1931, No. 05143).

54. "Foes of Imperialism Will Meet in London," *NYT*, July 7, 1929, 3; "Prof. Dewey to Address Anti-Imperialism Rally," *New York Herald Tribune*, July 8, 1929, 10. Marsh arranged for a discounted group fare on the White Star Line and invited interested citizens to join the delegation of the PL to the conference (Marsh, "A Conference on Imperialism" [letter to editor], *New Republic*, May 1, 1929, 309). I could find no record of Dewey's talk in his collected papers, so it is possible he canceled at the last minute.

55. "Monroe Doctrine Change Proposed," *CSM*, May 16, 1928, 3.

56. " 'Positive Mischief' Seen in Tariff Bill," *NYT*, June 7, 1930, 4; AP, "Urges A.F. of L. Indorse [*sic*] Unemployment Insurance," *Boston Globe* (hereafter *BG*), October 7, 1930, 15.

57. Dewey letter to Marsh, March 12, 1929, No. 05134.

58. Dewey letter to Marsh, February 11, 1931, No. 05137.

59. Dewey letter to Marsh, August __ (n.d.), 1931, No. 05151. In the same letter, Dewey shared the tragic news that his granddaughter had died in Vienna and that he was hurrying over to be there. That Dewey would give such a compliment to Marsh while preoccupied with a family death adds to of the authenticity of the comment.

60. Dewey letter to Oswald Garrison Villard, January 16, 1929, No. 04991.

61. "Program of the People's Lobby for 1929," n.d., last page. File: Dewey, John, No. 61-HQ-6611, FBI.

62. This version began appearing above the title of its monthly publication beginning with *PLB* 4:7 (November 1934), 1.

Chapter 3

1. "Uniform Rate Is Expected," *NYT*, July 13, 1928, 23; "Federal Reserve Action Attacked: People's Lobby Charges Federal Board Helps 'Freeze Out' Small Investor," *CSM*, July 21, 1928, 2; "Federal Reserve Board under Fire," *Baltimore Sun* (hereafter *BS*), August 13, 1928, 5.

2. "Attack Farm Plank of the Republicans," *NYT*, June 17, 1928, 2.

3. "Queries 6 Candidates on Foreign Policies: People's Lobby Asks Their Position on Draft of International Relations' Plank," *NYT*, May 31, 1928, 8.

4. "Call Up Oxenstierna!" (editorial), *North American Review*, 226:2 (August 1928), 246–247.

5. June 4, 1928: "Coolidge Quizzed by People's Lobby," *[Xenia, OH] Evening Gazette*, 1; "Question Coolidge," *[Sandusky, OH] Star Journal*, 1.

6. Reply from Assistant Secretary of State W. R. Castle Jr. to PL, August 9, 1928; letter from Marsh to Frank Kellogg, chairman, American Delegation to the Conference on Conciliation and Arbitration, State Department, December 15, 1928. File: Correspondence 1923–1928, Box 1.

7. "Says U.S. Groups Looting Bolivia: People's Lobby Avers Nation Milched by Avaricious Corporations," *Bakersfield Californian*, December 17, 1928, 1.

8. *La Prensa*, August 24 and 27, 1928, 1.

9. "Program of the People's Lobby for 1929," n.d. File: Dewey, John, No. 61-HQ-6611, FBI.

10. To shorten the interregnum, during FDR's presidency, inaugurations were moved up from March to January 20.

11. "Says Gunmen Rule Leather Bags Trade," *NYT*, June 30, 1929, 22.

12. "Hoover Tries Pressure in Senate Crisis," *BS*, May 13, 1929, 2; International News Service (INS), "People's Lobby Head Assails Finance Policy," *Indiana [PA] Evening Gazette*, July 18, 1929, 2.

13. "Attorney-General Mitchell Attacked: Dr. Dewey Assails His Action in Packers' Consent Decree Matter," *BS*, August 26, 1929, 4; "Proposed Modification of the Meat Packers' Consent Decree: Statement of People's Lobby," *CR*, June 19, 1929, 3093–3094.

14. "Reserve Rate Rise Now Held Unlikely," *NYT*, March 27, 1929, 2.

15. This was, of course, before the FDIC was created, so depositors' money was truly at risk when a bank failed because of uncollectible loans.

16. "To Scan 'Amazing Document,'" *NYT*, October 14, 1929, 19.

17. AP, "People's Lobby Asks 'Credit Octopus' Probe," *BS*, January 27, 1930, 2; Marsh letter to Senator Caraway, January 20, 1930. File: Correspondence 1929–1933, Box 1.

18. "Inquiry on Lobby Begins Tomorrow," *BS*, October 14, 1929, 2. The PL continued pressing for such legislation after the 1932 election. At its request, Senator Lynn Frazier (R-ND) reintroduced the proposal in 1933 ("Publicity on Federal Employees Stock Holdings," *PLB* 3:2 [June 1933], 7).

19. "Urges Lobby Inquiries," *NYT*, September 30, 1929, 24.

20. Thomas L. Stokes, "Maze of Senatorial Probes Recalls Oil Scandal Days; Three to Open this Week," *Atlanta Constitution* (hereafter *AC*), October 14, 1929, 4.

21. Anne O'Hare McCormick, "Light on the Elusive Lobbyist," *NYT Sunday Magazine*, November 3, 1929, 18.

22. Frederic J. Haskin, "Our Washington Letter" (syndicated column), *Chester [PA] Times*, November 2, 1929, 6.

23. n.d. (probably early 1929). File: Printed Matter 1916–1918 and 1930–1935, Box 4.

24. Richard V. Oulahan, "Vote on Peace Pact Likely This Week," *NYT*, January 7, 1929, 7.

25. "Coolidge Will Sign Kellogg Pact Today," *NYT*, January 17, 1929, 6.

26. n.d. (probably late 1929 or early 1930). File: Dewey, John, No. 61-HQ-6611, FBI.

27. "A.F.L. Condemns Schools in Pay of 'Interests,'" *CT*, November 29, 1928, 16.

28. "Leading Progressives Tell Why the Peoples' Lobby," n.d. (probably mid-1929), emphasis added. File: Dewey, John, No. 61-HQ-6611, FBI.

29. La Follette's running mate was Senator Burton Wheeler (D-MT), who subsequently was sometimes friendly to the PL.

30. Marsh, "The Peoples' Lobby" (letter to editor), *New Republic*, April 3, 1929, 202.

31. "President to Sign Tax Cuts at Once," *NYT*, December 16, 1929, 4.

32. "Robinson Blames the Republicans," *NYT*, October 31, 1929, 3.

33. "Asks Rich to Spend as Spur to Trade," *NYT*, December 30, 1930, 27.

34. "Holds Government Must Aid Jobless: B. C. Marsh of People's Lobby Warns that Survival Depends on Taking Responsibility," *NYT*, December 29, 1930, 4.

35. "$250,000,000 Fund to Aid Idle Urged: People's Lobby Votes to Back Demonstration in Washington for Insurance Program," *NYT*, October 7, 1930, 31.

36. Louise Joseph, "L.I.D. [League for Industrial Democracy] Winter Conference Held during Vacation," *[Poughkeepsie, NY] Vassar Miscellany News*, 15 (January 17, 1931), 4.

37. Radford Mobley, "Only Eighth of U.S. Families Earning $2,000," *[Madison, WI] Capital Times*, November 14, 1929, 6.

38. Dewey letter to President Hoover, May 8, 1930, No. 22261; "They Say—" [Dewey letter to President Hoover], *NYT*, July 27, 1930, Section 9, 2. See also a pastiche of press coverage of the PL in the summer and fall of 1930 ("The People's Lobby Made Public Unemployment Insurance an Issue. Won't You Help Make It a Fact?" File: Printed Matter 1916–1918 and 1930–1935, Box 4).

39. "Wagner Bills Hit by People's Lobby," *NYT*, April 7, 1930, 5.

40. Marsh Letter to President Hoover, December 8, 1930. File: Correspondence 1929–1933, Box 1; "Five-Day Week in Government Jobs Is Sought," *CSM*, December 8, 1930, 4.

41. Nicholas Kristof, "Progress in the War on Poverty" (op ed column), *NYT*, January 9, 2014, A23.

42. PL, "Reasons for Direct Federal Child Relief," n.d. (probably late 1929 or early 1930). File: Dewey, John, No. 61-HQ-6611, FBI.

43. "Liberal Groups Urge Child Labor Reforms," *CSM*, December 2, 1929, 3.

44. "Child Relief Steps Urged on Congress: Professor Dewey, in Statement, Asks Popular Support for the Wheeler-La Guardia Bill," *NYT*, December 30, 1929, 17.

45. AP, "Asks Inquiry on Hearst: Peoples [*sic*] Lobby Wants Caraway to Investigate Publisher's Activities," *NYT*, December 7, 1929, 23.

46. "Hoover Hurries to Capital and Settles Tariff Snarl; Flexible Plan Agreed On," *NYT*, May 26, 1930, 2.

47. "Walker Ridiculed by People's Lobby," *NYT*, March 27, 1930, 21.

48. PL, "What the Smoot-Hawley Tariff Bill Does," *CR*, May 22, 1930, 9339–9340.

49. "Wheat Flares Up as Major Campaign Issue Next Fall," *BS*, July 14, 1930, 2.

50. United Press (hereafter UP), "Situation Is Called Grave," *[Madison] Wisconsin State Journal*, August 10, 1930, 4.

51. "Hoover Asked to Act on Consent Decree," *NYT*, February 10, 1930, 4.

52. "Sees Packers Favored: People's Lobby Asks Why Ending of Consent Decree Is Not Opposed," *NYT*, March 31, 1930, 17.

53. UP, "Further Probe of Shoals Lobby Is Senate Decision," *Dunkirk [NY] Evening Observer*, April 1, 1930, 15.

54. *CR*, January 15, 1930, 1678.

55. "Bonner Is Assailed by People's Lobby," *BS*, January 13, 1930, 2.

56. Dewey and Marsh letter to "Dear Friend," " 'No More Serious Government Question' Than Strengthening People's Lobby" (flier), February 1, 1930. File: Dewey, John, No. 61-HQ-6611, FBI.

57. *CR*, April 11, 1930, 6943–6950; AP, "Senator Walsh Scores Witness," *Reno [NV] Evening Gazette*, April 11, 1930, 12; AP, "Rejects Wilbur Offer on Flathead Power," *NYT*, April 12, 1930, 16.

58. Respectively: "Hoover Policy Attacked by Two Liberal Groups," *BS*, December 9, 1929, 1–2; AP, "Nicaraguan Quiz Aim of Lobby Head," *LAT*, December 3, 1929, 5; Letter from Dana G. Monro, chief, Division of Latin American Affairs, State Department, to Marsh, January 20, 1930. File: Correspondence 1929–1933, Box 1; Dewey letter to President Hoover, February 26, 1930, No. 07551; "$42,000,000 Sugar Loan Is Opposed: People's Lobby Demands Close Scrutiny of Cuba Deal," *WP*, November 24, 1930, 2.

59. Marsh letter to Secretary of State Stimson, July 15, 1930; reply from J. Theodore Marriner, chief, Division of Western European Affairs, July 23, 1930. File: Correspondence 1929–1933, Box 1; Pierce Miller, ""Russian Embargo Brings Conflict in Washington," *New Castle [PA] News*, July 30, 1930, 2. Stimson (a Republican) later served as FDR's secretary of war from 1940 to 1945. His acceptance of the appointment during the run-up to FDR's unprecedented campaign for a third term was considered a major political coup by Roosevelt and a blow to GOP nominee Wendell Willkie.

60. "Sees Treachery Here for Arms Delegates: People's Lobby Says They Will be Victims of 'Government Dishonesty' and Business," *NYT*, December 23, 1929, 5.

61. Charles P. Stewart, "Modern Arms Obsolete in Future Wars" (syndicated column), *Burlington [IA] Hawk-Eye*, November 12, 1929, 6.

62. "Delays Hearing on Naval Treaty," *BS*, May 5, 1930, 9; Marsh letter to President Hoover, February 17, 1930. File: Correspondence 1929–1933, Box 1.

63. Republicans were the majority party in both houses in the 71st Congress (1929–1931) and in the Senate in the 72nd Congress (1931–1933). While Republicans were initially the slight majority in the House in the 72nd Congress, Democrats became the majority party because of several deaths of Republican members.

64. Franklyn Waltman Jr., "Call for Stand on Prohibition Sobers G.O.P.," *BS*, March 9, 1931, 2; "Challenge to Progressive Senators to Act for Relief," *PLB* 1:2 (June 1931), 5.

65. "Democratic Tactics in Congress," *PLB* 1:10 (February 1932), 4–5.

66. "Democratic Double-Crossing," *PLB* 1:11 (March 1932), 5.

67. "The Progress of the Campaign," *PLB* 2:5 (September 1932), 2–3.

68. "Roosevelt Scored on Relief Policy: People's Lobby Says He Would Let Nation's 'Poor' Support Idle before Taxing Rich Here," *NYT*, October 24, 1932, 7; "Statements Issued by Campaign Committees and Kindred Groups," *BS*, October 24, 1932, 2.

69. PL, "National Employment Program," February 1932. File: Printed Matter 1916–1918 and 1930–1935, Box 4.

70. PL, "National Employment Program," October 1932, ibid.

71. "Borah Sees Need of Congress Call," *NYT*, March 22, 1931, 26.

72. "Urge Special Session for Relief of Idle," *NYT*, March 24, 1931, 6; Charles S. Groves, "Extra Session Plea Opposed by Watson," *BG*, March 24, 1931, 23; "People's Lobby Pursues Canvass," *NYT*, March 27, 1931, 13.

73. AP, "Dewey Letter Asks for Special Session," *BG*, April 16, 1931, 16; "Ask Hoover Again to Call Congress," *BS*, April 16, 1931, 7.

74. Dewey letter to members of Congress, July 1, 1931, No. 20880.

75. Marsh letter to Sidney Hillman, Amalgamated Clothing Workers, June 3, 1931. File: People's Lobby, Reel 16, Sidney Hillman Correspondence (Part A), Correspondence (Series VII), Amalgamated Clothing Workers of America (microfilm). Also: "To Petition Hoover for Extra Session: Group of Economists Led by John Dewey Will Press Employment Issue Today," *NYT*, June 1, 1931, 4; "Urges Extra Session," *Wall Street Journal*, June 3, 1931, 16. For unexplained reasons, Dewey did not come to Washington for the White House meeting ("Relief Lobby Is Discouraged by President," *New York Herald Tribune*, June 2, 1931, 9).

76. "1,200 Sign Appeal for Special Session: People's Lobby Proposes a Program of $3,500,000,000 Grant for Jobless," *NYT*, July 4, 1931, 4.

77. Rodney Dutcher, "Washington Letter" (syndicated column), *Frederick [MD] Post*, July 13, 1931, 6.

78. "Rent Strike Urged on the Unemployed: B. C. Marsh Also Advocates an Organized Refusal by Farmers to Pay Mortgage Interest," *NYT*, July 11, 1931, 8.

79. Robert S. Allen, "Hoover Rejects Every Plea for Special Session," *CSM*, May 23, 1931, 1; "'We Should Be Legislating'" (editorial), *Wall Street Journal*, March 25, 1931, 2.

80. "Hoover Backs $10,000,000 Red Cross Fund for Relief," *BS*, January 12, 1931, 7.

81. "Payne to Inquire on Mine Distress," *NYT*, April 5, 1931, 22.

82. AP, "Red Cross Refused Aid in Miners' Row," *WP*, April 5, 1931, M2.

83. "House Committee Rejects $25,000,000 Drought Fund, Backing Hoover's Stand," *NYT*, January 30, 1931, 14.

84. May 11, 1931: AP, "Mothers Seek Unemployed Aid," *LAT*, 1; "Mothers Will Ask Relief for Jobless," *WP*, 16; "Wives of Idle at Capital," *NYT*, 3; "22 Mothers to Ask Hoover to Aid Idle," *BS*, 18.

85. May 12, 1931: AP, "Women and Children Appeal to Hoover for Relief of Idle," *BG*, 8; "White House Help for Jobless Asked," *BS*, 18; "Fail to See Hoover," *NYT*, 29.

86. "Organized to Aid Nation's Jobless," *BS*, November 2, 1931, 12.

87. "Senate Fight on Import Tax Seen," *Wall Street Journal*, April 8, 1932, 2.

88. *NYT*: "To Offer Congress Relief Program," November 29, 1931, N38; "Urges Idle Insurance with Federal Backing," December 2, 1931, 26.

89. "Luncheon Speeches Broadcast," *PLB* 1:8 (December 1931), 5.

90. "Hearings Closed on Job Insurance," *NYT*, November 14, 1931, 3.

91. "Dewey Group Backs Fight on Sales Tax," *NYT*, March 23, 1932, 2.

92. "Joint Committee on Unemployment Demands Congress Act," *PLB* 2:1 (May 1932), 3–15.

93. Reflecting the Progressive-era view of publicity (as transparency), Congress attached to a bill expanding the RFC to include what was called a "publicity clause," i.e., the public disclosure of all loans the RFC made. This had the unintended effect of reducing confidence in the financial health of the borrowers (Alter 2006, 150). Learning from history, during the 2008 banking crisis, the Treasury Department insisted that the list of banks receiving bailout funding (called TARP) be confidential.

94. "R.F.C. Relief Loans Total $43,377,726," *NYT*, October 19, 1932, 34. Other PL comments on the RFC: "Criticism of Loans Draws R.F.C. Reply," August 8, 1932, *NYT*, 2; "Record of the Reconstruction Finance Corporation," *PLB* 2:6 (October 1932), 3–4.

95. Franklyn Waltman Jr., "California Loans Far Exceed Others," *BS*, October 10, 1932, 2.

96. "Executive Power over Congress Hit," *BS*, January 18, 1932, 5.

97. Dewey letter to Marsh, June 29, 1931, No. 05149.

98. "Railway Emergency before I.C.C.," *Railway Age* 91:4 (July 25, 1931), 133; "Shall We Pay Railroads Dividends on Unearned Increment?," *PLB* 1:2 (June 1931), 6; AP, "Lamont, Doak Seek Joint Mine Parley," *WP*, July 23, 1931, 2; "Wheeler to Press $100,000,000 Plan," *NYT*, March 2, 1931, 2.

99. UP, "People's Lobby Hits Wet-Dry Congress Debate," *AC*, January 6, 1930, 2.

100. "Wets Pressing Congress for Action on Beer," *CSM*, July 6, 1932, 4.

101. "The Progress of the Campaign," *PLB* 2:5 (September 1932), 3.

102. PL, "What Right Have We to Control Haiti and Nicaragua?," n.d. (probably 1931); "Why United States Marines Are in Nicaragua [and] Why the Marines Should Come Out," n.d. (probably 1931). File: Printed Matter 1916–1918 and 1930–1935, Box 4.

103. Marsh letters to Stimson, February 3 and May 22, 1931; letter from Maxwell M. Hamilton, assistant chief, Division of Far Eastern Affairs, State Department, to Marsh, January 5, 1932 (this letter also dealt with China and Japan). File: Correspondence 1929–1933, Box 1. Also AP, "People's Lobby Urges Stimson to Call Parley," *BS*, April 20, 1931, 2.

104. Marsh letter to Stimson, January 8, 1931. File: Correspondence 1929–1933, Box 1; Drew Pearson, "New U.S. Envoy to Liberia Instructed on Slavery Issue: Mitchell, Negro Diplomat, Confers with Hoover and Stimson—People's Lobby Taunts President on 'American Slavery,'" *BS*, January 9, 1931, 2.

105. "The People's Lobby" (letter to editor), *New York Herald Tribune*, July 25, 1931, 8.

106. "Dewey Denies Group Is 'Red,'" *New York Herald Tribune*, July 29, 1931, 2.

107. Marsh, "What He Would Do" (fragment, may be part of a letter or press release), n.d. (handwritten: January 6, 1932). File: Correspondence 1929–1933, Box 1.

108. "Japan, China, and Manchuria," *PLB* 1:9 (January 1932), 5–6; "Arms Cut Appeals to Be Made Today," *WP*, October 15, 1932, 9.

109. "Hoover Asked to Back End of Chemical War," *CSM*, January 18, 1932, 5.

110. AP, "Anti-Hoover Jest Arouses Hurley," *BS*, March 19, 1931, 11.

Chapter 4

1. "Federal Unemployment Insurance Is Sought," *Pittsburgh [PA] Courier*, November 8, 1930, A2; "Dewey Raps Weakness," *Labor's News* 20:11 (March 14, 1931), 3; "El 'People's Lobby' de Washington hace la historia del empréstito a Nicaragua," *Prensa*, August 24, 1928, 1.

2. From a pastiche of press coverage of the PL in the summer and fall of 1930: "The People's Lobby Made Public Unemployment Insurance an Issue. Won't You Help Make It a Fact?." File: Printed Matter 1916–1918 and 1930–1935, Box 4.

3. "Attacks Wage Disparity: People's Lobby Urges More Equitable Distribution of Wealth," *NYT*, December 26, 1929, 31.

4. "Child Relief Steps Urged on Congress: Professor Dewey, in Statement, Asks Popular Support for the Wheeler-La Guardia Bill," *NYT*, December 30, 1929, 17; "Stimson Queried on Marines' Use," *BS*, January 1, 1930, 6.

5. "Topics of the Times: Worst Wishes of the Season" (editorial), *NYT*, December 24, 1929, 11.

6. AP, "Urges A. F. of L. Indorse [*sic*] Unemployment Insurance," *BG*, October 7, 1930, 15.

7. "Monroe Doctrine Change Proposed," *CSM*, May 16, 1928, 3.

8. "People's Lobby Meets Today on Jobless: Unemployment and Poverty Topics of Conference Here—Julius Barnes Declines to Speak," *NYT*, July 22, 1930, 6.

9. "Calls World Bank a Mellon 'Scheme,'" *NYT*, June 8, 1930, 24.

10. Ibid.; "Would Let Bankers Decide Foreign Loans, *NYT*, June 8, 1930, 40.

11. Clyde letter to Dewey, January 29, 1932, No. 05154.

12. "Progressives to Get 4-Billion Relief Plan: People's Lobby Will Carry Fight to Washington, Marsh Tells Civic Club Here," *NYT*, September 3, 1931, 4; "Attacks on Hoover Stir Social Parley," *NYT*, May 20, 1932, 2; "British Tariff to Cut Tariffs Wins Approval: Institute at Charlottesville Hears Criticism of American Policy," *CSM*, July 16, 1932, 3. His talk at the social work convention was not part of the association's official program, but rather a rump session of left-leaning activists.

13. "People's Lobby Secretary Addresses Salt Lakers," *Salt Lake [UT] Tribune*, September 4, 1929, 13; "What's Doing Today," *LAT*, September 23, 1929, 18.

14. *PLB*: "Secretary's Trip to Coast," 1:3 (July 1931), 8; "Executive Secretary's Speaking Trip," 1:4 (August 1931), 5–6.

15. "Insure Against Unemployment," *Lincoln [NE] Star*, August 21, 1930; "Private Moratorium Urged: Peoples [*sic*] Lobby Secretary Would Call Halt to Paying Bills," *[Spokane, WA] Spokesman-Review*, August 4, 1931; "Marsh Lauds Harris, Scores George, Crisp," *AC*, March 12, 1932, 3.

16. April 7, 1930, 5.

17. "Urges State-Aid Plan for Work Insurance," March 30, 1931, 2.

18. "Waiver of Notice of the First Meeting of the Board of Directors," November 10, 1931. File: Minutes, Stockholders and Directors 1931–1950, Box 3.

19. First Meeting of Board of Directors, November 10, 1931, ibid.

20. n.t. (November 10, 1931, meeting), 28–29, ibid.

21. n.t. (November 10, 1931, meeting). File: Minutes, Board of Directors 1931–1950, Box 2.

22. Showing punctiliousness to legalisms, there was a short meeting on April 11 in Dewey's home to accept Clyde's contribution for specific purposes (discussed in the preceding subchapter). Viewing the donation and its conditions as a kind of contract, the short meeting gave official imprimatur to receiving the dedicated gift and the stipulations accompanying it (Minutes of Meeting of Executive Committee, April 11, 1932. File: Minutes, Executive Committee 1932–1936, Box 2).

23. Board of Directors, April 25, 1932. File: Minutes, Board of Directors 1931–1950, Box 2.

24. By-Laws, as Amended at Meeting of Board of Directors, April 25, 1932. File: Minutes, Stockholders and Directors 1931–1950, Box 3.

25. n.t. (November 10, 1931, meeting). File: Minutes, Board of Directors 1931–1950, Box 2.

26. "Hoover Hurries to Capital and Settles Tariff Snarl; Flexible Plan Agreed On," *NYT*, May 26, 1930, 2.

27. "Hoover Policy Attacked by Two Liberal Groups," *BS*, December 9, 1929, 1.

28. Charles Estcourt Jr., "New York Skylines" (syndicated column), *AC*, July 27, 1930, 6K.

29. "Declares City Fails in Aid for Jobless," *NYT*, January 4, 1931, 2. The subheadline identified Marsh as a "Socialist," but the term did not appear in the text of the article.

30. Arthur C. Wimer, "Tilson under Senate Fire for Opposition to Food Supply Bill," *Hartford [CT] Courant* (hereafter *HC*), February 3, 1931, 2.

31. AP, "Ask Extra Congress Session," *HC*, April 16, 1931, 2.

32. AP, "People's Lobby Urges Stimson to Call Parley," *BS*, April 20, 1931, 2.

33. Robert S. Allen, "Hoover Rejects Every Plea for Special Session," *CSM*, May 23, 1931, 1.

34. Charles P. Stewart, "Our Capitalist System Is Safe for Time Being" (syndicated column), *Burlington [IA] Hawk-Eye*, September 20, 1931, 1.

35. "Senate Group Hears Jobless Insurance Ideas," *CSM*, November 6, 1931, 3.

36. "Attacks on Hoover Stir Social Parley," *NYT*, May 20, 1932, 2.

37. Franklyn Waltman Jr., "California Loans Far Exceed Others," *BS*, October 10, 1932, 2.

38. "Organized to Aid Nation's Jobless," *BS*, November 2, 1931, 12.

39. Rodney Dutcher, "Washington Letter" (syndicated column), *Frederick [MD] Post*, July 13, 1931, 6.

40. *CT*: "Hope of Sales Tax Revival in Senate Fades," April 8, 1932, 10; Arthur Sears Henning, "Radicals Don't Conceal Lights under a Bushel: They're Clever and Busy with Propaganda," January 26, 1931, 6. In a letter to Marsh a few weeks later, Dewey commented on the latter article. He hoped it was "good advertising" and wondered if the article had been urged by the meat-packing industry (concentrated in Chicago) in reaction to the PL's efforts to block any weakening of consumer protections imposed on the industry in a court order (February 4, 1931, No. 05136).

41. Ashmun Brown, "War Blamed in Nation's Trend to Paternalism," *LAT*, April 29, 1931, 8.

42. Letter from Alice Ames Robbins to the attorney general, September 7, 1929; reply by Assistant Attorney General O. R. Luhring, December 18, 1929 (Naison 1989, reel 13, frames 525–528).

43. While he has gone down in history as "J. Edgar Hoover," the letterhead of the stationery he used for this 1930 memo to Chase lists him as "John Edgar Hoover," and he signed it "J. E. Hoover" (Memo from Hoover to Chase, January 28, 1930. File: Dewey, John, No. 61-HQ-6611, FBI).

44. Memo from R. E. Vetterli, special agent in charge, Washington Field Office, FBI to J. Edgar Hoover, director, January 28, 1930, re: People's Lobby, 1, FBI.

45. Ibid., 2–3. The names were redacted in the version released by the FBI, but one was a senator or congressman from Arkansas and the other two were apparently staffers of the Senate Appropriations and Agriculture Committees.

46. It was a thank-you note from Dewey on behalf of a delegation that had visited Russia to investigate its educational system. Presumably the letter had been drafted by Dewey in English and then translated on his behalf before he signed it.

47. Memo re: John Dewey, January 28, 1930, n.a. File: Dewey, John, No. 61-HQ-6611, FBI.

48. The addressee on the envelope was "J. Edgar Hoover, Dept. of Justice, Washington, D.C.," ibid. The example in the FBI files is undated, probably late 1929.

49. "Assails Root Project for Anti-Red Police," *NYT*, July 15, 1930, 3.

50. *CR*, May 6, 1930, 8436–8437.

51. In a sleight of hand, the formal House resolution creating the committee titled it the Special Committee to Investigate Communist *Propaganda* in the United States, but the title used on the covers of the published public hearing changed the title to Special Committee to Investigate Communist *Activities* in the United States—a major difference. Its chair at the time was Congressman Hamilton Fish (R-NY), representing a district in the Hudson Valley, including FDR's home. They loathed each other.

52. *CR*, January 31, 1931, 3674–3675.

53. AP, "Dewey Warns Congress of Fascism in America," *BS*, January 18, 1932, 7.

Chapter 5

1. *Macon [GA] News*, October 18, 1932; *St. Louis Globe-Democrat*, October 23, 1932. Both were displayed in a pastiche of PL newspaper coverage, "Government Responds to Headlines—The People's Lobby Gets Its Share." File: Printed Matter 1916–1918 and 1930–1935, Box 4.

2. Letter from Dewey to Roosevelt, December 10, 1932. File: Correspondence 1929–1933, Box 1.

3. Letter from Louis Howe to Dewey, February 2, 1933, No. 05156.

4. "Roosevelt Asked to Direct Valuation of Power Trust," *PLB* 2:9 (February 1933), 5.

5. Letter from Louis Howe to Marsh, February 28, 1933. File: Correspondence 1929–1933, Box 1.

6. "The Situation in Washington," *PLB* 2:7 (December 1932), 1–2.

7. "Marsh for Revival of Housing Body to Help Unemployed," *WP*, December 4, 1932, 20.

8. Dewey, "The Duty of Congress," *PLB* 2:7 (December 1932), 1.

9. This was a reasonable perception. Civil service reform, which had been vehemently opposed by conservatives of both parties, was finally passed by the lame-duck session of Congress in late 1882 in part because of the Republicans' shock at how badly they had done in the November 1882 elections.

10. "Speeches Broadcast," *PLB* 2:7 (December 1932), 7.

11. *NYT*: "Urge Writing Down Debts: Prof. Dewey Also Would Keep Interest Payments Low," November 17, 1932, 3; "New Taxes Loom in Beer Bill Delay," December 25, 1932, 2.

12. "Peace Groups Seek Arms Export Curb," *NYT*, February 6, 1933, 3, emphasis added.

13. Jonathan Mitchell, review of *Death and Profits* by Seymour Waldman, *New Republic*, January 18, 1933, 275.

14. UP, "Visions Disaster for Two Powers," *Bakersfield Californian*, November 26, 1932, 1.

15. "Marsh Seeks Support for Direct Relief Bill," *BG*, February 5, 1933, A30, emphasis added.

16. "Marsh to Be Civic Forum's Speaker Today," *Syracuse [NY] Herald*, February 19, 1933, 5 (second section).

17. Roosevelt used the term to cover the special session of Congress, March 9 to June 17, which was, somewhat coincidentally, exactly 100 days. Some historical writers begin the count on Inauguration Day (March 4) to the end of the congressional session, 105 days (Alter 2006, 273).

18. Dewey letter to Committee members, March 15, 1933, No. 18855.

19. "Income Redistribution through Taxation," *PLB* 2:12 (April 1933), 5–6.

20. "Joint Committee Conference on Unemployment," ibid., 6–9.

21. Dewey letter to President, April 6, 1933, No. 07689; Howe reply, April 12, 1933, No. 05157; AP, "Dewey Urges Roosevelt to Levy New Land Tax," *WP*, May 8, 1933, 2; Howe to Dewey, May 17, 1933, No. 05158. The last item acknowledged receipt of a May 15 Dewey telegram, but the Dewey papers project was unable to locate it.

22. AP, "Dewey Group Hits at Bill," *BG*, April 3, 1933, 3.

23. Marsh letter to Ickes, May 5, 1933; Ickes reply, June 15, 1933. File: Correspondence 1929–1933, Box 1.

24. "Sees City Deficit of $250,000,000," *NYT*, April 15, 1933, 15.

25. "Five Weeks of the New Administration," *PLB* 2:12 (April 1933), 2–5. The bill regulating securities was not the one creating the Securities and Exchange Commission (SEC). That bill passed in 1934.

26. "Asserts Rail Bill Slights Short Line," *NYT*, May 13, 1933, 17.

27. Based on the ProQuest database of congressional hearings, he testified for the PL about 164 times. Retrieved September 1, 2012. The figure is approximate because of some minor imperfections in the database, such as scans from poor-quality copies that garbled the text and typos in published hearings. The count can also vary slightly depending on how to categorize instances when March submitted written statements without testifying or when he testified on behalf of a coalition that the PL belonged to (or even led), such as the Joint Committee on Unemployment, versus testifying solely on the PL's behalf.

28. AP, "Labor and Industry Back Recovery Bill," *WP*, May 20, 1933, 2.

29. "The New Dealer," *PLB* 3:1 (May 1933), 6.

30. "The Hitler Boomerang on Wilson Policies," *PLB* 2:12 (April 1933), 12.

31. Marsh letter to Hull, April 5, 1933. File: Correspondence 1929–1933, Box 1.

32. "Wheeler Resolution to Investigate Foreign Concessions," *PLB* 3:2 (June 1933), 5.

33. Letter from Wallace to Marsh, May 31, 1933. File: Correspondence 1929–1933, Box 1.

34. "Roosevelt Is Assailed: People's Lobby Aide Calls Policy of Administration 'Futile,'" *NYT*, May 27, 1933, 9.

35. "For Business Men Who Listen In: On the Radio Today," *Wall Street Journal*, May 20, 1933, 3; "Tax Increase Urged for Higher Income," *WP*, May 21, 1933, 13; *CR*, June 7, 1933, 5148–5151.

36. "Executive Secretary Spoke in Fourteen States," *PLB* 2:12 (April 1933), 11–12.

37. "Marsh Advocates U.S. Relief Program," *AC*, March 31, 1933, 9.

38. "4 Billion Relief Plan Urged on Congress: Dewey Group Demands Vast Program of Public Works and Direct Help," *NYT*, March 18, 1933, 5.

39. Dewey, "Government and Children," *CR*, January 11, 1934, 435.

40. "Program of the Joint Committee on Unemployment," n.d. [late 1933]. File: Printed Matter 1916–1918 and 1930–1935, Box 4. Dewey referred to "the revised program of the Joint Committee on Unemployment" in a January 5, 1934, letter, No. 07714.

41. "Unemployment Delegation Warns Leaders Government Must Tax Wealth," *PLB* 3:10 (February 1934), 2–4.

42. Direct government marketing of farmers' products was no minor issue at the time. Populist and agrarian movements in the United States and abroad often pursued this idea going back to the nineteenth century (Foner 1983, 109).

43. "Lobby Wants NRA to Join in Marketing," *WP*, December 20, 1933, 3.

44. Dewey, "What Keeps Funds Away from Purchasers," *CR*, April 26, 1934, 7384–7385.

45. 1934 conference schedules: "America's Public Ownership Program," February 16; "A New Deal Public Ownership Program," May 19. File: Dewey, John, No. 61-HQ-6611, FBI.

46. *CR*, May 22, 1934, 9261. Excerpts of other talks at the session: *CR*, May 29, 1934, 9795–9796.

47. "Today on the Radio," *NYT*: February 19, 1934, 18 and May 19, 1934, 16; "Session Planned by People's Lobby," *WP*, February 14, 1934, 15; "Cutting Plans Bill to Create Federal Bank," *BS*, May 20, 1934, 2; AP, "Against Private Credit," *Wall Street Journal*, May 21, 1934, 4.

48. "Lobby Questions Candidates on Public Ownership," *PLB* 4:3 (July 1934), 5.

49. Howe reply to Dewey, November 11, 1933, No. 05161.

50. Howe reply to Dewey, January 27, 1934, No. 05163.

51. Letter from A. R. Clas, director of housing, Federal Emergency Administration of Public Works, to Marsh, July 23, 1935. File: Correspondence 1934–1935, Box 1.

52. Letter from Nathan R. Margold, solicitor, Interior Department, to Marsh, March 3, 1934. File: Correspondence 1934–1935, Box 1.

53. Coverage: "President Pushes Vast Credit Drive at a Night Parley," *NYT*, September 25, 1933, 2; UP, "Currency Inflation," *Wall Street Journal*, September 26, 1933, 10.

54. "Congress Warned to Assert Rights: Pay Rolls Cut and Elections Near, Says Prof. Dewey," *WP*, January 1, 1934, 3.

55. "Holds '40 Thieves' Still Rule Nation: B. C. Marsh Tells Fellowship of Faiths Conditions Are Worse Than in March, 1933," *NYT*, May 13, 1934, 30.

56. "Says AAA Works for Land Values," *BS*, December 25, 1933, 2. Now archaic, "mulct" meant to con someone out of money.

57. "Proponents Try to Defend NRA," *PLB* 3:7 (November 1933) 5.

58. "Inquiry into NRA Sought in House," *NYT*, May 23, 1934, 5; AP, "Johnson Reveals Plans to Revise Recovery Codes," *Salt Lake [UT] Tribune*, February 28, 1934, 2.

59. "Validating Stocks and Guaranteeing Bank Deposits," *PLB* 3:6 (October 1933), 7.

60. Dewey letter to PL members, March 31, 1934, No. 06689. This 1934 decision in *Nebbia v. New York* should not be confused with the major 1935 decision in *Schechter Poultry v. US* overturning the NRA's core powers.

61. PL, "Redistribute National Income by Taxation to Prevent Collapse," March 1934. File: Printed Matter 1916–1918 and 1930–1935, Box 4.

62. *CR*, August 5, 1934, 6086.

63. AP, "Pass Housing Bill, H. I. Harriman Asks," *NYT*, May 19, 1934, 5.

64. AP, "Waterworks Fund Urged," *NYT*, May 31, 1934, 17.

65. "Aid Consumer, People's Lobby Asks Roosevelt," *WP*, December 12, 1933, 10; "Lobby Asked to Represent Emergency Conference of Consumer Organizations," *PLB* 3:7 (November 1933), 6–7; Board of Directors, November 2, 1933. File: Minutes, Board of Directors 1931–1950, Box 2.

66. Second Annual Meeting, January 1, 1934. File: Minutes, Stockholders and Directors 1931–1950, Box 3. Marsh paid for the trip, not the PL.

67. "Roosevelt Ruins World Economic Conference," *PLB* 3:4 (August 1933), 4–6.

68. Marsh, "Russia—The Twentieth Century Challenge," *PLB* 4:4 (August 1934), 4.

69. Marsh letter to Hull, April 4, 1934. File: Correspondence 1934–1935, Box 1.

70. "Probe Refused in Accusations on Roosevelt," *WP*, April 1, 1934, 3.

71. "The European Volcano," *PLB* 4:6 (October 1934), 8.

72. "Recommendations on the Pan-American Conference," *PLB* 3:8 (December 1933), 7–8.

73. "Our Cuban Colony Remembers '76," *PLB* 3:5 (September 1933), 6.

74. "Investigation of Arms Industry," *PLB* 4:2 (June 1934), 4–5.

75. "Do We Need Big Navy to Bargain for Small One?," *PLB* 3:11 (March 1934), 8.

76. Board of Directors, January 1, 1934. File: Minutes, Board of Directors 1931–1950, Box 2.

77. "Lobby and War Congress," *PLB* 3:6 (October 1933), 4.

78. "Changed Emphasis in Washington," *PLB* 4:5 (September 1934), 1–2.

79. Third Annual Meeting, January 7, 1935. File: Minutes, Stockholders and Directors 1931–1950, Box 3.

80. Not everyone associated with the Lobby saw it as embodying mainstream leftism. In 1935, a member of the Lobby's Advisory Council resigned because of the Lobby's "alleged conservativism [*sic*]" (Eighth Meeting of the Executive Committee, May 20, 1935. File: Minutes, Executive Committee 1932–1936, Box 2).

Chapter 6

1. While Cleveland was defeated for reelection in 1888, he won the 1892 election, making him the only president to serve nonconsecutive terms.

2. Coverage: "Abolish Profit, Dewey Exhorts: People's Lobby Announces in Newly Adopted Program," *WP*, October 18, 1934, 5. Ostensibly, the news peg was an announcement of a membership drive. See also Marsh, "The People's Lobby" (letter to editor), *New Republic*, November 28, 1934, 74.

3. Masthead, *PLB* 4:6 (October 1934), 1. A year later, the Executive Committee removed it (November 11, 1935. File: Minutes, Executive Committee 1932–1936, Box 2). No reason for the change was listed in the minutes, and Marsh made the motion. It is possible that, without changing the general ideology of the Lobby, the slogan and its prominence were simply too provocative and conveyed a political philosophy seemingly further to the left than the Lobby wished to be seen as having.

4. "The Lobby's New Program," *PLB* 4:6 (October 1934), 1–2.

5. The 74th Congress was also the first to break with the long-standing pattern of congressional floor sessions, which included a major (lame-duck) session after the November elections and into the spring of the next year. The members of Congress elected in the previous November would not be sworn in until later in the odd-numbered year. The 74th Congress began in early January 1935, a tradition that continues to this day.

6. Paul W. Ward, "Norris Warns of New Attack Against TVA," *BS*, December 16, 1934, 2. For additional quotes from his speech: Dewey, "Socialization of Ground Rent," *PLB* 4:9 (January 1935), 1; AP, "Land Socialization Advocated by Dewey," *AC*, December 16, 1934, 2A.

7. "On People's Lobby," *Oakland [CA] Tribune*, December 13, 1935, 23.

8. Dewey, "Taxation as a Step to Socialization," *PLB* 4:11 (March 1935), 1–2. Dewey was arguing *against* the historical precedent. The most significant government seizure of property up to that point in American history was the emancipation of the slaves. It was done without any compensation to the former slave owners in the rebelling states. Early in the Civil War, Lincoln had clung to a long-standing

belief in gradual and voluntary emancipation that would include compensation to owners. He abandoned that policy when it was clear that it was not effective in drawing support for the Union cause from what passed as moderation on slavery.

9. "President Dewey Asks Governors Act on Housing," *PLB* 5:7 (November 1935), 4.

10. Dewey letter to Hull, April 3, 1935, No. 09362; Hull reply to Dewey, April 13, 1935, No. 05168.

11. Dewey, "International Cooperation or International Chaos," *PLB* 4:10 (February 1935), 6–7.

12. Dewey, "Future of Liberalism," *PLB* 4:10 (February 1935), 1–2.

13. Turner Catledge, "Treasury Counsel Turns the Tables on Tax Plan Foes," *NYT*, April 7, 1936, 20.

14. "New Deal Farm Plan Assailed at People's Lobby Luncheon," *WP*, November 18, 1934, M3; Gray, "Government Responsibility," *PLB* 5:8 (December 1935), 1–3; AP, "Capitalism Is Doomed, Economist Declares," *CSM*, December 14, 1935, 5.

15. *PLB*: Warne, "Taxation or Inflation," 4:13 (June 1935), 3; "Taxation and Socialization," 6:1 (May 1936), 1–4; "Why the People's Lobby Favors Socializing Ground Rent," 6:4 (August 1936), 1. Also "What's on the Air?," *New Republic*, May 6, 1936, 371.

16. *PLB*: Jackson, "The Dispossessed in Agriculture," 5:12 (April 1936), 1–2; "Sharecroppers and Tenants Strike," 6:3 (July 1936), 1–3. Also "3-Fold Fete Planned Here for May Day," *WP*, May 1, 1936, 17.

17. The PL operated on such a shoestring that before Marsh could organize the dinner, he had to ask Mrs. Clyde if she would be willing to pay the tab. She did.

18. "Speaking Trip of President, Vice President, and Secretary," *PLB* 5:11 (March 1936), 8.

19. Irving Brant, *Government Monopolies Are Constitutional*, February 1936 (Washington, DC: PL).

20. *CR*, February 7, 1936, 1647–1648. Even though the PL published Brant's essay as a booklet, it also reproduced the *CR* version and distributed copies to its mailing list (File: Dewey, John, No. 61-HQ-6611, FBI).

21. *CR*, May 17, 1935, 7759.

22. *CR*, August 22, 1935, 14081.

23. AP, "Eagle Has Its Day as Its Friends Come to Fore," *WP*, April 10, 1935, 2.

24. AP, "House Group Votes to Limit Tax Bill," *BS*, July 10, 1935, 2.

25. AP, April 14, 1936: "House Group Hits Relief under WPA," *HC*, 1, 5; "Foes Propose End of W.P.A.," *BG*, 15.

26. Robert C. Albright, "Disaster Lurks in New Tax Bill, Hearing Is Told," *WP*, May 6, 1936, 2.

27. The PL's domestic policy goal of public ownership of utilities and monopolies was largely absent from its lobbying efforts in 1935–36 compared with earlier periods. As there was no change in its support for the concept, there likely is another

explanation. During this period, a group called the Public Ownership League of America led the fight for this cause. As a result, the PL could let that organization take the lead on this subject. Indicating the PL's continuing support for that policy goal, Marsh spoke at one of the League's conferences ("1,000 Are Due at Prosperity Parley in D.C.," *WP*, February 17, 1935, 7).

28. While the press service coverage focused on his quotable criticism (controversy!), the *Times*' coverage was more substantively oriented, summarizing the contents of his proposed amendments (April 26, 1936: AP, "$876,000,000 Housing Plan Held Practical," *WP*, M10; "Loopholes Picked in Housing Plan," *NYT*, 29).

29. "People's Lobby Protests Housing Halt Proposal," *WP*, February 2, 1936, 7.

30. March 15, 1936: "Hits Land Buying against Inflation," *BS*, 6; AP, "Wallace Lashes Land Gambling as Disastrous," *LAT*, 2.

31. "Repeal Is Demanded," *CT*, July 4, 1935, 21.

32. Folders: Marsh, Benjamin (Reel 14) and People's Lobby (Reel 16), Part A, Series VII, Sidney Hillman Correspondence, *Records, of the Amalgamated Clothing Workers of America* (1989).

33. The Lobby was also marginally involved in the fight over a bonus to WWI veterans. When FDR vetoed the bill, Marsh ripped the veto as "hollow hypocrisy and sheer stupidity" ("Praise and Blame Greet Bonus Veto," *NYT*, May 23, 1935, 4). The Senate sustained that veto. In 1936, Congress overrode the president's veto of another bonus bill.

34. "The Powder Keg in Europe," *PLB* 4:8 (December 1934), 8.

35. AP, "Italy Sending 24 Airplanes and 80 Fliers to Abyssinia," *WP*, July 17, 1935, 1, 4.

36. Marsh, "Africa Brings League of Nations to Cross Roads," *PLB* 5:5 (September 1935), 1–3.

37. "U.S. Takes Steps to Lower World Tariff Barriers," *CSM*, September 28, 1935, 11.

38. Henry A. Atkinson letter to Dewey, October 30, 1936, No. 07809.

39. "The Executions in Russia," *PLB* 4:9 (January 1935), 7.

40. "Two Years Maximum Peace?," *PLB* 5:8 (December 1935), 4–5.

41. "Industrial Mobilization Plan," *PLB* 5:6 (October 1935), 1–3.

42. Folder: People's Lobby (Reel 16), Part A, Series VII, Sidney Hillman Correspondence, *Records, of the Amalgamated Clothing Workers of America* (1989).

43. Seventh Meeting of the Executive Committee, January 18, 1935. File: Minutes, Executive Committee 1932–1936, Box 2.

44. "New Deal Pictured at War with World," *BG*, July 17, 1936, 8; "Editor Pictures New Dealer as Conservatives in 1940," *CSM*, July 10, 1936, 4.

45. "Thomas Ridicules New Lemke Party," *NYT*, June 21, 1936, 25.

46. Given the sensitivities involved in playing *any* overt role in presidential politics, the Executive Committee explicitly approved Marsh attending both conventions to present the Lobby's policy suggestions (Eleventh Meeting of the Executive Committee, May 2, 1936. File: Minutes, Executive Committee, 1932–1936, Box 2).

47. Marsh, "Platitudinous and Perilous Platforms," *PLB* 6:4 (August 1936), 5–6; "Bankhead Scoffs at Hoover Speech," *NYT*, June 12, 1936, 17.

48. "Jackson Says Farley Made Deal with McNutt for Cabinet Post," *WP*, September 30, 1936, X10.

49. Sixth Meeting of the Executive Committee, January 7, 1935. File: Minutes, Executive Committee 1932–1936, Box 2.

50. "Tri-City Forum Hears Marsh Indict New Deal," *WP*, July 12, 1936, M10.

Chapter 7

1. n.d. (probably early 1933 or late 1932). File: Printed Matter 1916–1918 and 1930–1935, Box 4.

2. Sixth Meeting of the Executive Committee, January 7, 1935. File: Minutes, Executive Committee 1932–1936, Box 2.

3. "Lobby's Radio Broadcasts," *PLB* 4:9 (January 1935), 5.

4. "Lobby's February Radio Broadcasts," *PLB* 4:10 (February 1935), 5.

5. "Appreciation of Co-Operation of Broadcasting Systems," *PLB* 4:13 [typo, should be 5:1] (May 1935), 7.

6. For example, "Radio Programs and Features for the Week on the Metropolitan Stations," *New York Herald Tribune*, December 8, 1935, F7.

7. "Lobby's March Broadcasting Program" and "Radio Audience Approves Lobby's Program," *PLB* 4:11 (March 1935), 5, 8.

8. For example, see *PLB* 4:4 (August 1934), 1, emphasis in original.

9. *PLB*: "A Report in Headlines," 4:5 (September 1934), 4; "Secretary's Speaking Trip," 6:5 (September 1936), 8. As an indication of how systematically Marsh worked to promote his appearances in advance, see "People's Lobby Official to Give S.L. [Salt Lake] Address," *Salt Lake [UT] Tribune*, September 17, 1936, 6.

10. In October 1935, the title of his talk in LA was "America and the Mediterranean" ("Lobby Officer to Speak," *LAT*, October 17, 1935, A2). In 1934, he covered both international and domestic matters by titling his talk "New Deals in America and Europe" ("Marsh to Tell Forum of World New Deals," *WP*, October 11, 1934, 9).

11. "Secretary's October Trip," *PLB* 3:5 (September 1933), 8.

12. "Roosevelt Program Doomed, Speaker Says," *Salt Lake [UT] Tribune*, September 12, 1933, 11. His fifteen-year-old son and ten-year-old daughter accompanied him on a separate trip to LA in August (Gilbert Brown, "More Than NRA Needed, Says People's Lobby Man," *Los Angeles Record*, August 26, 1933. File: Printed Matter 1916–1918 and 1930–1935, Box 4).

13. "Relief Taxes Will Be Urged: People's Lobby to Demand Congress Assess Large Incomes," *WP*, October 29, 1933, R12.

14. "Secretary's Speaking Trip," *PLB* 3:7 (November 1933), 6.

15. "Secretary's Speaking Dates," *PLB* 5:10 (February 1936), 5. In Chicago, he addressed an African-American rally ("Aims of Negro Parley Told at Mass Meeting," *WP*, February 6, 1936, 13).

16. Jewish Telegraphic Agency, "Lawrence Dennis Speech Canceled Because 'He Is an Anti-Semite,'" May 1, 1934, retrieved February 6, 2014: http://archive.jta.org/article/1934/05/11/2812937/lawrence-dennis-speech-canceled-because-he-is-an-antisemite; "Marsh to Speak before Liberals on Thursday," *Harvard Crimson*, November 6, 1934; "Benjamin C. Marsh Calls Socialization Inevitable," *BG*, January 27, 1935, A23; "Marsh Will Speak Tonight," *HC*, June 1, 1935, 11.

17. Second Annual Meeting, January 1, 1934. File: Minutes, Stockholders and Directors 1931–1950, Box 3.

18. "Dewey Resigns as People's Lobby President," *PLB* 5:9 (January 1936), 5.

19. To fulfill corporate governance requirements, waivers of the thirty-day advance notice of meetings were to be physically signed by the corporate officers approving the waiver. Their signatures certified that the waiver complied with all provisions of the by-laws and other governing documents. Dewey's signature is on several of those waivers, including for the January 2 and November 16, 1933, meetings (File: Minutes, Board of Directors 1931–1950, Box 2). For the form letter soliciting members' proxies for the 1935 annual meeting, see Dewey letter to PL members, December 15, 1934, No. 18628.

20. This tradition was largely institutionalized by the precedent set by George Washington as the presiding officer of the Constitutional Convention in 1787. Based on that norm, nowadays when the Speaker of the House of Representatives wishes to participate in floor debates, he or she surrenders the gavel to another member of the majority party and then descends into the well of the House to speak as any other member would.

21. Seventh Meeting of the Executive Committee, January 18, 1935. File: Minutes, Executive Committee 1932–1936, Box 2.

22. Minutes: Board of Directors 1931–1950 and Executive Committee 1932–1936, Box 2; Stockholders and Directors 1931–1950, Box 3.

23. Grant F. Chase, public accountant, Annual Financial Report, February 24, 1936. File: Minutes, Stockholders and Directors 1931–1950, Box 3.

24. Sixth Meeting of the Executive Committee, January 7, 1935. File: Minutes, Executive Committee 1932–1936, Box 2.

25. Board of Directors, January 2, 1933. File: Minutes, Board of Directors 1931–1950, Box 2.

26. Second Annual Meeting, January 1, 1934. File: Minutes, Stockholders and Directors 1931–1950, Box 3.

27. Eighth Meeting of the Executive Committee, May 20, 1935. File: Minutes, Executive Committee 1932–1936, Box 2.

28. "Resources Socialization in U.S. Held Necessary," *HC*, November 14, 1934, 13.

29. Ninth Meeting of the Executive Committee, November 11, 1935. File: Minutes, Executive Committee 1932–1936, Box 2.

30. Fourth Annual Meeting, January 6, 1936. File: Minutes, Stockholders and Directors 1931–1950, Box 3.

31. Ibid.

32. "People's Lobby Hits Work Plan as New Farce: Prof. Dewey Asks Congress to Stop Experiments in Human Misery," *WP*, March 2, 1934, 2.

33. Luke I. Wilson letter to Dewey, March 2, 1934, No. 05165; Dewey reply to Wilson, No. 05167.

34. Dewey letter to Marsh, March 3, 1934, No. 05166. Dewey exhibited an astute reading of the political situation, showing his ability to analyze reality even when his conclusions went against his own preferences and ideology.

35. Dewey letter to Frank Tannenbaum, April 24, 1935, No. 07769.

36. Dewey letter to Marsh, April 24, 1935, No. 07770, emphasis added. For the exchange in the *New Republic*'s letters to editor, see Marsh, "Dangers in the Bankhead Bill," April 10, 1935, 246; Frank Tannenbaum, "More about the Bankhead Bill," June 5, 1935, 104.

37. For example, Dewey letters to Marsh, December 5[?] and 8, 1934, Nos. 05152–53.

38. For example, see columns by Charles F. Stewart: "Washington at a Glance" (syndicated column): *[Fayette, PA] Morning Herald*, September 27, 1933, 6 and *Kingsport [TN] Times*, January 1, 1936, 4. Also Albert L. Warner, "White House Parley Studies Money Issue," *New York Herald Tribune*, September 25, 1933, 2.

39. Arthur Sears Henning, "Organized Business Launches Fight against Roosevelt's 'Share-the-Wealth' Program," *CT*, July 10, 1935, 8.

40. *CT*: Arthur Sears Henning, "World Watches Roosevelt Use Special Power," April 10, 1933, 8; "Congress Finds Roosevelt Aids [*sic*] beyond Its Ken," April 13, 1933, 4.

41. "Homestead Plan Likened to Nazi Camp by Lobby," *CT*, January 20, 1935, 6.

42. " 'Little Fellows' Hit by New Deal Marsh Charges," *CT*, May 9, 1935, 4. The rest of the description of the PL accurately summarized its 1935 slogan, but without any commentary or condemnation: "working for legislation to balance consumption and production by eliminating profit."

43. UP, "Legion Commission Classes Jane Addams, Darrow as Communists," *Ames [IA] Daily Tribune-Times*, January 24, 1933, 2.

44. *CR*, January 30, 1934, 1613–1614. Other organizations included the Carnegie Foundation, the Foreign Policy Association, and the American Academy of Political and Social Science.

45. *CR*, June 27, 1935, 10332; Elizabeth Dilling, *The Red Network: A 'Who's Who' and Handbook of Radicalism for Patriots* (Kenilworth, Il: self-published, 1934), 214. Dilling was so extreme she considered the National Council of Churches and Quakers to be "toadies for Moscow." Ten years after she published her book, her comments against the administration and the conduct of the war were so far to the

right that she was one of the thirty people tried en masse in 1944 for sedition. It ended in a mistrial (Weintraub 2012, 180–181).

46. "Guffey Enters New Bill Based on Price Fixing," *CSM*, May 20, 1936, 2.

47. "Public Gets Warning of Danger in Social Panaceas of Minority," *CSM*, August 23, 1934, 2.

48. *CR*, June 16, 1934, 11949.

49. *CR*, April 22, 1935, 6175.

50. Private property and contractual rights had been a long-running theme of court decisions favoring management and capital in labor-management decisions long before the showdown over the constitutionality of the New Deal (Shesol 2010, 30).

51. Elliot Thurston, "Five Senators Deny Liberty League Link," *WP*, August 24, 1934, 2.

52. Smith was later famous, as head of the House Rules Committee, for trying to bottle up civil rights and liberal legislation. A major fight by President Kennedy and Speaker Rayburn was to expand the committee to break the conservative majority controlling it. They barely won. Smith was also famous for introducing in 1964 the one-word amendment "sex" to the list of protected classes in the pending civil rights bill. He insisted he proposed the amendment in good faith, as demonstrated by his record of co-sponsoring the Equal Rights Amendment to the Constitution (covering only women, not African-Americans). Nonetheless, it is more likely that he hoped either to kill the bill by expanding it too far or to weaken enforcement of equal rights for African-Americans by expanding the scope of the bill to cover such a large portion of the population. Smith's amendment passed and went on to become part of the 1964 Civil Rights Act as signed into law.

53. "Washington Lobbies for Next Congress," *PLB* 5:8 (December 1935), 8, emphasis added.

54. Charles F. Stewart, "Stewart Says Few Economists Have Courage to Face Facts: Radical Marsh Speaks His Mind" (syndicated column), *Hammond [IN] Times*, March 6, 1934, 1.

55. "The Knowmeter" and "Knowmeter Answers," *BG*, October 17, 1933, 16, 28, emphasis in original.

56. Frederic J. Haskin, "Questions of Readers Answered" (daily feature), *HC*, December 1, 1935, C8.

57. Tenth Meeting of the Executive Committee, January 6, 1936. File: Minutes, Executive Committee 1932–1936, Box 2; Fourth Annual Meeting, January 6, 1936. File: Minutes, Stockholders and Directors, Box 3.

58. "Dewey Resigns as People's Lobby President," *PLB* 5:9 (January 1936), 5.

59. *WP*, January 7, 1936, 21. In late January, a story in an Indiana newspaper still identified Dewey as president of the Lobby ("Doris Duke's Husband for Inflationists," *Hammond [IN] News*, January 27, 1936, 7).

60. Item No. 5619, Miscellaneous Documents, Folder 15, Box 219, Records of the Amalgamated Clothing Workers, Cornell Labor Archives; Warne, "Why the People's Lobby Favors Socializing Ground Rent," *PLB* 6:4 (August 1936), 1.

Chapter 8

1. Knox, a supporter of Theodore Roosevelt, had been a Bull-Mooser in the 1912 election, thus aligning himself with political progressives, some of whom later supported Dewey and the PL. Knox's political evolution made him a critic of FDR from the right, not the left. Later, in 1940, FDR shrewdly named Knox as secretary of the Navy, helping blunt accusations that the rearmament and national defense effort was a political tactic to help FDR run for an unprecedented third term. Knox served in that office through most of WWII, until his death in 1944.

2. William C. Lee, "The People's Lobby" (letter to editor), *WP*, February 2, 1939, 10. (No relation to the author of this book.)

3. "Federal Aid for Rural Schools Asked," *PLB* 8:3 (July 1938), 7–8.

4. "Lobby Dinner Speakers Urge Basic Economic Changes," *PLB* 7:2 (June 1937), 3.

5. Dewey, "Superficial Treatment Must Fail" (reprint), *PLB* 8:3 (July 1938), 1–3.

6. "What Is a World War Worth to Morgan?," *PLB* 9:6 (October 1939), 1–4.

7. John Chamberlain, "Books of the *Times*" (review of *Our Lords and Masters*), *NYT*, October 10, 1935, 23.

8. Dewey letter to Marsh, October 2, 1939, No. 05169.

9. The Dewey papers project was unable to locate Marsh's letter.

10. Dewey letter to Marsh, October 20, 1939, No. 05170.

11. Dewey letter to Marsh, November 29, 1939, No. 05171.

12. Marsh generally believed Catholics had an inordinate influence over FDR, as demonstrated by his policies during the Spanish Civil War. Catholics supported the rebellion against the Republic because of its anti-Catholic policies and because of the support for the Republicans by the SU.

13. Marsh's reply was not located. It may have been a phone conversation.

14. Dewey letter to Marsh, November 29, 1939 [typo, as Dewey's initial letter was on that day], No. 05172.

15. Board of Directors, October 17, 1936. File: Minutes, Board of Directors 1931–1950, Box 2.

16. Marsh, "The People's Lobby Program" (letter to editor), *New Republic*, December 2, 1936, 145; "Lobby's Legislative Program for Seventy-Fifth Congress," *PLB* 6:7 (November 1936), 4.

17. "To New Deal or Not to New Deal," *PLB* 6:9 (January 1937), 6–7.

18. Marsh, Report to the Fifth Annual Meeting, January 4, 1937. File: Minutes, Stockholders and Directors 1931–1950, Box 3.

19. "Wide Reform Plans Weighed at Session," *NYT*, April 18, 1937, 32.

20. "Bishop McConnell's Open Letter to President," *PLB* 7:4 (August 1937), 1–3.

21. "Cleric, Gorman Attack Present Economic Plan: McConnell Tells People's Lobby Capitalism Exists by Consent of People," *WP*, March 21, 1937, 10.

22. "Charges Campaign to Curb Labor Act," *NYT*, June 20, 1937, 5; Russell Smith, "Lewis Supports Reprisals for Court Bill Foes," *WP*, September 6, 1937, 2; "Nation's Prosperity Is Called Insecure: Leader of People's Lobby Blames New Deal," *BG*, December 12, 1937, A17.

23. Seventh Annual Meeting, January 2, 1939. File: Minutes, Stockholders and Directors 1931–1950, Box 3.

24. "Essential Changes in the Revenue Act," *PLB* 7:2 (June 1937), 5.

25. *PLB* 6:12 (April 1937), 1.

26. "No Recession Seen on Social Welfare," *NYT*, June 11, 1937, 7; AP, "Larger Federal Expenses in Social Security Hinted," *LAT*, June 11, 1937, 8; "Delegation Urges Revenue Revision at this Session of Congress," *PLB* 7:3 (July 1937), 1.

27. "U.S. Heads List of World High Income Nations," *CSM*, December 19, 1936, 1–2.

28. "2% of Families Have Seventh of U.S. Income," *WP*, February 27, 1939, 2.

29. "Decent Living for 45,000,000 in U.S. Urged," *WP*, February 14, 1937, 7; "Lundeen Urges Rail Purchases by Government," *WP*, May 29, 1938, 8; *CR*: April 10, 1939, A1371–1373; April 27, 1939, A1730–1731.

30. "House Committee to Take Up Revenue Revision," *PLB* 8:13 [typo, should be 9:1] (May 1939), 8.

31. *PLB*: "Consumers Win Place in Council for Industrial Progress," 6:9 (January 1937), 7–8; "President Asked to Appoint Consumers' Counsel on Freight Rates," 7:8 (December 1937), 1–3; "Subsidies against Consumers," 8:9 (January 1939), 2–4. In response to a typically tart Marsh letter urging consumer representation, an Interior Department official replied with an even tarter response, saying Marsh was being so brassy that "we will have to be ordering a limousine with sufficient head room for a top hat" for Marsh to be able to sit in. He ended on a slightly conciliatory note, but still a dig: "Some day when you have an excess of cash, give me a ring and I will let you take me to lunch" (John Carson, Consumers' Counsel, National Bituminous Coal Commission, Interior Department, reply to Marsh, May 29, 1937. File: Correspondence 1936–1939, Box 1).

32. AP, "Short-Line Rails Suggest Remedies," *BS*, March 23, 1939, 20.

33. AP, "Hearings on Rail Rate Rise before ICC Now Closed," *CSM*, February 10, 1938, 13.

34. Eliot Janeway, "Increasing Rates a Menace to Railroads," *PLB* 7:11 (March 1938), 1–3. Janeway's bylined article in the Sunday *Times* a month later appears to be based in part on the research paper he wrote for the PL ("Railroads a Key to Revival," *NYT*, April 10, 1938, E7).

35. Board of Directors, February 24, 1937. File: Minutes, Board of Directors 1931–1950, Box 2.

36. When introducing himself, he identified his position as "executive officer" of the Lobby, a conflation he made in no other congressional testimonies.

37. Dewey L. Fleming, "Democratic Leader Attacks Court Plan as Hearings End," *BS*, April 24, 1937, 1; "Court Forum Ends; Bill's Fate Unsure," *NYT*, April 24, 1937, 4. I found no letters to the editor from Marsh clarifying that the testimony reflected only his personal views. Marsh was permitting the misimpression to remain uncorrected.

38. Marsh, "Courts and Political and Economic Democracy," *PLB* 7:1 (May 1937), 2–3.

39. While cutting it very close, Marsh was ostensibly complying with the Board's decision that the PL would not have a position on court packing. As a result, there was no blowback or criticism from the Board regarding what he did and how he did it.

40. J. Fred Essary, "Jobs Are Held Chief Block to Reorganizing," *BS*, January 14, 1937, 12.

41. "Reorganization of Federal Government," *PLB* 6:10 (February 1937), 5. This Brownlow Committee recommendation eventually led to the creation of the Office of Government Reports (Lee 2005, chap. 3).

42. Public Administration generally has a hagiographic view of the Brownlow Committee. Like the budget law of 1921, the reorganization law definitely strengthened the president's hand vis-à-vis Congress in terms of controlling and directing executive branch agencies—precisely what congressional opponents feared.

43. "Reorganization of the National Government," *PLB* 8:13 [typo, should be 9:1] (May 1939), 6.

44. Marsh, "Government Aid to Private Schools," *PLB* 8:2 (June 1938), 2–3.

45. "Federal Education Aid Doomed Now," *PLB* 9:3 (July 1939), 5.

46. "Delegation Asks WPA to Provide Rural School Aid," *WP*, June 9, 1938, X30.

47. "Federal Aid for Rural Schools Asked," *PLB* 8:3 (July 1938), 7–8.

48. "Urge Funds for Rural Schools," *PLB* 8:4 (August 1938), 5.

49. However, in a 1941 letter, Marsh more accurately, but only privately, characterized the PL as "not primarily a peace organization" (Marsh letter to Eleanor Roosevelt, February 20, 1941, Correspondence of Eleanor Roosevelt, FDR Library).

50. Marsh gradually constructed an elaborate conspiracy theory that American Catholics, supporting the Fascist side, had successfully pressured FDR to impose a seemingly neutral arms embargo on both sides. Marsh and the left viewed this as implicitly helping the Fascist side, as it was being supplied by Germany and Italy. (Unmentioned was the SU's support for the Republican side.) From there, Marsh extrapolated that FDR (and Catholics) were secretly pro-Germany and pro-Hitler.

51. Board of Directors, February 24, 1937. File: Minutes, Board of Directors 1931–1950, Box 2.

52. "Europe and Neutrality," *PLB* 6:11 (March 1937), 7.

53. *PLB* 7:4 (August 1937), 8.

54. "Lifting the Embargo on Spain Blocked," *PLB* 8:2 (June 1938), 5–6.

55. "Referendum Favors Lifting Embargo on Spain," *PLB* 8:9 (January 1939), 8.

56. Seventh Annual Meeting, January 3, 1939. File: Minutes, Stockholders and Directors 1931–1950, Box 3.

57. AP, "Long Proposes Cash Neutrality to Avoid War," *WP*, April 20, 1939, 2.

58. Before Marsh and a few of his ilk could even testify, the committee members spent an hour and forty minutes arguing about whether to permit them to testify at all (Leland C. Speers, "Navy Build-Up Cost Set above a Billion," *NYT*, February 18, 1938, 2).

59. "Mexico's Example," *Times [of London]*, August 29, 1938, 14; "Hull Asked to Recall Note," *NYT*, August 28, 1938, 29. See also "Shall Mexico Be Another Spain?," *PLB* 8:5 (September 1938), 3–4.

60. "Committee of 100 Formed to Fight Mexico Seizures," *WP*, September 12, 1938, X2.

61. "Franco and Latin America," *PLB* 8:8 (December 1938), 3.

62. Marsh, "Will Britain Stop Operating Hitler?," *PLB* 8:5 (September 1938), 1–2.

63. "Heil American Property Rights!," *PLB* 7:12 (April 1938), 1–3. In slight exculpation, one needs to remember that at that point in history, Hitler was not yet *Hitler*. Plus, Marsh thrived on being provocative. That was one of the ingredients of his success at publicity.

64. John H. Gray, "Palestine the Danger Point of the World," *PLB* 8:7 (November 1938), 1. This comment reflects the anti-Semitism that was acceptable in polite WASP society (and American universities) before the Holocaust.

65. "La Follette War Referendum," *PLB* 7:8 (December 1937), 7–8.

66. "Collective Sense Essential to Collective Security; Why War Referendum was Killed," *PLB* 7:10 (February 1938), 3–5.

67. Gerald P. Nye, "Alien Imperialism—And America," *Vital Speeches of the Day* 5:18 (July 1, 1939), 574–575. One of the other speakers at the June event was second-term Congressman Jerry Voorhis (D-CA) ("Lobby's June Broadcast," *PLB* 8:14 [typo, should be 9:2] [June 1939], 8). Because of his views on issues, he became one of the PL's favorite congressmen. As a result, Voorhis was invited to speak at many PL events. From those appearances, it is clear that he was quite progressive, liberal, and a social democrat. But he was no Communist. Running for reelection in 1946, political newcomer and Republican Richard Nixon, in a red-baiting campaign that became his early political signature, successfully smeared Voorhis as, at least, a Communist sympathizer. That election launched Nixon's political career.

68. Marsh, "Neither War nor Peace in Europe Can Long Save Profit System," *PLB* 9:4 (August 1939), 3.

69. Even after Hitler's invasion of Poland, Marsh was still promoting the idea of a national war referendum (Marsh, "For Referendum" [letter to editor], *WP*, November 20, 1939, 8).

Chapter 9

1. Board of Directors, February 24, 1937. File: Minutes, Board of Directors 1931–1950, Box 2.

2. "Requests for Broadcasts," *PLB* 9:11 (March 1940), 7.

3. "Congressional Record Reprints Being Sent," *PLB* 8:4 (August 1938), 8. Also Seventh Annual Meeting, January 2, 1939. File: Minutes, Stockholders and Directors 1931–1950, Box 3.

4. Eighth and Ninth Annual Meetings, January 8, 1940 and January 13, 1941, ibid.

5. n.t., text: "A few of scores of headlines on Secretary's talks on speaking trip to Coast, Fall of 1938." File: Printed Material 1945–1946, Box 4.

6. "Sunday Sermon Announcements," *LAT*, October 11, 1941, A3.

7. Marsh, "Impressions on Reliefers, Reactionaries and Reform," *PLB* 7:7 (November 1937), 7.

8. "Secretary's Speaking Trip," *PLB* 9:7 (November 1939), 8.

9. "Secretary's Trip," *PLB* 10:7 (November 1940), 7.

10. "Nation's Prosperity Is Called Insecure: Leader of People's Lobby Blames New Deal," *BG*, December 12, 1937, A17; "Secretary's Trip in Massachusetts," *PLB* 7:8 (December 1937), 8; "News and Notes," *American Political Science* Review, 33:2 (April 1939), 297.

11. Letter from Marsh to PL members, December 20, 1939. File: Printed Matter 1936–1944, Box 4; "Annual Meeting," *PLB* 10:8 (December 1940), 8.

12. "Annual Meeting of the People's Lobby," *PLB* 7:9 (January 1938), 8.

13. In addition to examples cited earlier, also: "Radio Broadcast," *PLB* 6:11 (March 1937), 4; "Conference," *PLB* 9:8 (December 1939), 8; Membership recruitment letter from McConnell (and the other two officers), "Can We Maintain Eight Million Idle?," February 1940. File: People's Lobby, 9E3/313/3, Box 662, HUAC.

14. In 1940, Marsh testified on behalf of the Committee for Cultural Freedom, of which Dewey also was the honorary head (US Senate 1940b, 52–53). The group was opposed to a House-passed bill making it easier to deport aliens.

15. Ninth Annual Meeting, January 13, 1941. File: Minutes, Stockholders and Directors 1931–1950, Box 3.

16. "Dr. Israel Resigns," *PLB* 9:8 (December 1939), 8.

17. File: People's Lobby, 9E3/313/3, Box 662, HUAC.

18. Marsh letters to Joseph Schlossberg, Amalgamated Clothing Workers of America, June 30 and July 5, 1938. Document No. 5619, Folder 54, Box 142, Records of the Amalgamated Clothing Workers.

19. "Why the People's Lobby in Washington—And Its Program" (flier), April 20, 1937. File: New-York Historical Society.

20. "Some Members of the People's Lobby, Inc. in 1940." File: Dewey, John, No. 61-HQ-6611, FBI.

21. "Annual Meeting of the People's Lobby," *PLB* 7:9 (January 1938), 8.

22. "Bigger Social Welfare Budget, Robinson Forecasts for U.S.," *CSM*, June 10, 1937, 8.

23. Drew Pearson and Robert Allen, "Washington Merry-Go-Round" (syndicated column), *Joplin [MO] Globe*, September 30, 1939, 4.

24. AP, "Dollar-a-Year Officials Face Capitol Probes," *WP*, November 9, 1941, 11.

25. Willard Edwards, "Fight Gag on Dictator Bill Witnesses," *CT*, January 25, 1941, 2.

26. Turner Catledge, "Marshall Sways Congress Group on Army's Danger," *NYT*, July 24, 1941, 9.

27. "Mahoney Charges Communists Used Blanshard Office," *NYT*, October 25, 1937, 2.

28. *CR*, March 26, 1938, A1261.

29. *CR*, July 28, 1939, 10381.

30. Excerpt from "Termites in the Temple," 1940. File: People's Lobby, 9E3/313/3, Box 662, HUAC.

31. Marsh letter to Dies, December 1, 1939, ibid.; "Dies Committee Asked to Accept Own Verdict," *PLB* 9:11 (March 1940), 8.

32. Letter from Guy Hottel, special agent in charge [of Washington, DC, field office] to director, FBI, February 14, 1941; FBI Case File No. 100-704 on Marsh, February 14, 1941. File: Dewey, John, No. 61-HQ-6611, FBI.

33. Marsh, "Trip Shows Progress," *PLB* 11:7 (November 1941), 8.

34. Dewey reply to Professor (NFN) Heller, December 12, 1939, No. 05173.

35. Eighth Annual Meeting, January 8, 1940. File: Minutes, Stockholders and Directors 1931–1950, Box 3.

36. The last *Bulletin* listing him as honorary president was the June 1940 issue, and the last correspondence with his name on the letterhead was June 11, 1940 (Marsh letter to members of Congress, "Why Not Change This Record—Before Adjourning?." File: People's Lobby, 9E3/313/3, Box 662, HUAC).

37. Dewey, "Here at Home," *PLB* 10:12 (April 1941), 8.

38. Marsh letter to Eleanor Roosevelt, February 20, 1941. File: March–May 1941, Box 745, Series 100: Personal Letters, Eleanor Roosevelt Papers, FDR Library.

39. Mrs. Roosevelt's handwritten draft, ibid. Her formal reply to Marsh, March 4, 1941. File: Correspondence 1941–1943, Box 1, Marsh Papers.

Chapter 10

1. Marsh, "Japan Casts the Die," *PLB* 11:8 (December 1941), 1.
2. "Implications of Declaration of War," *PLB* 11:8 (December 1941), 4.
3. Ibid., 3.
4. "Program for 1942." File: Printed Matter 1936–1944, Box 4.

5. Marsh, "From People's Lobby" (letter to editor), *PM*, December 16, 1943, ibid.

6. Similarly, in November 1945, when Marsh testified against a postwar continuation of the draft, he emphasized that the PL's opposition to the draft occurred either before Pearl Harbor or after VJ Day, not *during* the war (US House, 1945, 201).

7. [H. R.] Baukhage, "Washington Digest" (syndicated column), *Brookshire [TX] Times*, April 9, 1943, 2. Reflecting an earlier style in American journalism, he only used his last name as his byline.

8. After the war, Marsh claimed at a hearing: "please do not misunderstand me; although I think [the bill] is inadequate, I certainly hope . . . you eventually will enact this legislation, because I don't believe in the theory of letting things get so bad that you are going to have a big ruction in this country" (US Senate, 1948, 378). Not true. He almost always depicted the good as the enemy of the perfect. For him, a half-full bottle was half empty.

9. "Week's Leading Events," *NYT*, January 25, 1942, X10.

10. "Listeners' Choice," *CT*, May 22, 1943, 14.

11. "*Half* Year Report," *PLB* 15:4 (August 1945), 8, emphasis in original headline.

12. "Farm Shortages Threatened; Says People's Lobby," *WP*, March 8, 1942, 13; Christine Sadler, "Stores Allowed to Cut Points and Hold Sales of Perishables," *WP*, March 21, 1943, 9; "Britain's Aid Asked in War on Cartels," *NYT*, February 13, 1944, 7; AP, "International Cartels Attacked by Berge," *AC*, February 13, 1944, 11B.

13. "War Taxes and War Economics," FBI Dewey file; "Maximum Food for Rationing," "The People's Stake in War Production," pamphlet collection, Wisconsin Historical Society; "Shall It Be [the] Century of the Common Man or Century of Cartel Control?." File: Printed Matter 1936–1944, Box 4.

14. "Service Men's Families' Addresses," *PLB* 14:9 (January 1945), 8.

15. Form letter from Marsh to wardens of federal penitentiaries, July 25, 1945. File: Correspondence 1945, Box 1.

16. March 29, 1945: Dewey L. Fleming, "Labor-Peace Code Offered," *BS*, 7; "Labor-Management Charter to Promote Postwar Prosperity," *WP*, 5.

17. "This Month's Letter," *PLB* 13:1 (January 1943), 8.

18. Letter from E. A. Ross to Marsh, May 18, 1942. File: Correspondence 1941–1943, Box 1.

19. Letter from Willard M. Kiplinger, *The Kiplinger Report*, to Marsh, April 7, 1942; Marsh reply, April 8, 1942. File: Correspondence 1941–1943, Box 1.

20. Letter from Broadus Mitchell to Marsh, April 4, 1945. File: Correspondence 1945, Box 1.

21. Frank L. Weller, AP, "No. 1 Hell Raiser: Ben Marsh, the Spokesman for the People's Lobby Here, Becomes Louder with Age," *WP*, February 13, 1944, B2. Newspapers publishing the column included the *Salt Lake [UT] Tribune*, *Milwaukee [WI] Journal*, *Galveston [TX] News*, and *Lima [OH] News*. Congressman

John Coffee (D-WA), a PL ally, inserted it in the *Congressional Record* (February 21, 1944, A863–A864).

22. AP, "Tips from Washington" (feature column), *AC*, April 8, 1945, 8A.

23. Michael Darrock, "What Happened to Price Control? The OPA vs. the Inflationary Tide," *Harper's* 187:1118 (July 1943), 128. The upper case ("People's Lobby") indicates that the author was not suggesting a generic lobby for the people, but the need for a specific organization called the People's Lobby.

24. Letter from Alfred Baker Lewis to Marsh, May 24, 1943; Marsh's reply, May 26, 1943. File: Correspondence 1941–1943, Box 1.

25. Letter from J. Walter Schirmer to Board of Directors, May 1, 1945. File: Correspondence 1945, Box 1.

26. Letter from Kirtley F. Mather to Marsh, March 23, 1945; Marsh's reply, March 27, 1945. File: Correspondence 1945, Box 1. Mather's unhappiness was not a bolt out of the blue. Two years earlier, he had seconded Alfred Baker Lewis's complaint to Marsh (Mather letter to Lewis with cc to Marsh, May 26, 1943. File: Correspondence 1941–1943, Box 1).

27. Letter from Frederick A. Dewey to Marsh, August 17, 1943; Marsh's reply, August 24, 1943. File: Correspondence 1941–1943, Box 1. Dewey *fils* concluded his letter with this relatively odd reference to his father: "Dad is summering in New Jersey. I have not seen him for some-time but understand he is well." This hints that there may have been a strained relationship between the two at that time.

28. "Responsibility of America for Palestine as a National Home for Jewish People," *PLB* 13:2 (June 1943), 7.

29. Letter from W. F. Stinespring to Marsh, June 30, 1943. File: Correspondence 1941–1943, Box 1.

30. Letter from Charles L. Carhart to Marsh, June 28, 1943, ibid.

31. "If Member—Disregard Appeal," *PLB* 13:10 (February 1944), 8.

32. Marsh, "*You* Need the People's Lobby" (mass mailing), November 1943, emphasis in original, FBI Dewey file.

33. Letter from Stone to Marsh, April 20, 1943; Letters from White to Marsh, February 9 and March 3, 1943. File: Correspondence 1941–1943, Box 1. At the time, Stone was the Washington editor for the *Nation*. In 1953, because of accusations that he was a Communist, he left the magazine and began self-publishing *I. F. Stone's Weekly* until 1971.

34. Annual meetings: Eleventh (January 11, 1943), Twelfth (January 10, 1944), Thirteenth (January 8, 1945). File: Minutes, Stockholders and Directors 1931–1950, Box 3.

35. Eleventh annual meeting, January 11, 1943, ibid.

36. Marsh annual letter to members with proxy for annual meeting, December 22, 1942. File: Printed Matter 1936–1944, Box 4.

37. Marsh letter to members with results of annual meeting, January 23, 1943. File: Correspondence 1941–1943, Box 1. The allusion is to the text in the Hebrew Testament of Pharaoh's punishment of his obstreperous slaves.

38. Board of Directors, January 8, 1945. File: Minutes, Board of Directors 1931–1950, Box 2.

39. "The People's Lobby, Inc., 1944 and 1945" (annual reports of treasurer and executive secretary for 1944; 1945 program and budget). File: Printed Matter 1936–1944, Box 4. Also: "Directors Ask Labor [and] Farm Leaders Position on Lobby Program," *PLB* 14:11 (March 1945), 1–2.

40. "Post-Election Prospects and Problems," *PLB* 14:7 (November 1944), 1.

41. The letter writer's name was redacted by the FBI before it was released in response to my Freedom of Information Act request. She lived at the Algonquin Hotel, and the letter was dated December 10, 1943. FBI Dewey File.

42. Internal FBI Memo from K. R. McIntire to Mr. Mumford, October 13, 1942; FBI Case File No. 100-25838 on Dewey, April 29, 1943, approved by E. E. Conroy, special agent in charge, New York Field Office, 7–8, ibid.

43. Letter from H. B. Fletcher, special agent in charge, Seattle Field Office, to Hoover, October 21, 1942; Hoover's reply, November 30, 1942, ibid.

44. Letter from P. E. Foxworth, assistant director, New York Field Office, to Hoover, May 11, 1942, ibid.

45. FBI Case File No. 100-25838 on Dewey, April 29, 1943, ibid.

46. "People's Lobby" (summary of available information), n.d. (probably late 1942 based on location in chronological file). File: People's Lobby, 9E3/313/3, Box 662, HUAC.

47. "Dies Reports" (summary of contents of HUAC files, known as the Dies Committee for its chairman, Congressman Martin Dies Jr.), FBI Case File No. 100-25838 on Dewey, April 29, 1943, 7–8.

48. Ibid.

49. "Lobby Secretary Says if People Accept Truman Program Shooting War Almost Certain" (press release), May 16, 1950. File: Printed Matter 1950, Box 5.

50. "Program for 1946." File: Printed Matter 1947, Box 5.

51. "People's Lobby Asks Office in White House," *NYT*, November 18, 1945, 36; John F. Gerrity, "Sad Tenants Prepare to Vacate Office Building of Low Rents," *WP*, November 29, 1945, 9; L. H. R. (Leonard H. Robbins), "About—" (column), *NYT Sunday Magazine*, December 2, 1945, 2.

52. December 27, 1948: "Joint Probe on Profits Is Protested," *WP*, B6; UP, "Committee Held Biased," *NYT*, 27.

53. "Capital's No. 1 Lobbyist Speaks Up on Labor Bill," *Washington Daily News*, June 18, 1947, 18. File: Printed Matter 1947, Box 5.

54. "The Dear People" (editorial), *Amarillo [TX] Daily News*, May 24, 1947, 4.

55. Some of the postwar conferences were "America Needs an Over-All Plan" (February 9, 1946), "Responsibility for Employment" (June 10, 1947), "World Planning or World Chaos" (May 29, 1948), and "What Responsibility to Consumers Have Government, Industry, Farmers, Labor, [and] Cooperatives?" (June 18, 1949). The PL published booklets with transcripts of the talks presented at the conference and distributed them as widely as possible. Coverage examples: AP, "C. of C.

Economist Sees No Depression in Next Few Months," *CSM*, June 12, 1947, 15; AP, "People's Lobby Chief Talks of Consumers," *LAT*, June 19, 1949, 21.

56. "Radio Today," *NYT*, May 11, 1946, 29; "Employment Parley Scheduled Tomorrow," *WP*, June 9, 1947, 14; "People's Lobby Holds Symposium Today at YWCA," *WP*, May 29, 1948, 7; "Inflation Conference Slated Today at YWCA," *WP*, November 20, 1948, B1.

57. Marquis Childs, "Washington Calling" (syndicated column), *WP*, July 18, 1947, 18. Marsh protested in a letter to the editor (July 27, 1947, B4).

58. Tris Coffin, "Washington Daybook" (syndicated column), *Charleston [WV] Daily Mail*, February 7, 1949, 4. Marsh and the PL had so faded from public attention that the reporter thought he was dead, referring to him as "the late" Ben Marsh.

59. "Influence Unlimited" (editorial), *Billings [MT] Gazette*, August 18, 1949, 4.

60. 1948: March 1 and 23, June 22, September 28, November 8. 1949: January 23, December 28.

61. *NYT*: September 20, 1946. *BS*: July 27, 1948; May 28, 1949.

62. "Lobby Calls Americans for Democratic Action Unwitting Allies of Fascism" (press release), July 21, 1949. That attack came two days after an earlier one: "Lobby Warns ADA Neither New Nor Old Deal Can Prevent Depression" (press release), July 19, 1949. File: Correspondence 1949, Box 2.

63. "Lobby Tells Civil Righters They Are Bamboozling Those without Economic Rights" (press release), January 18, 1950. File: Printed Matter 1950, Box 5.

64. "Holds State of the Union Speech Sounds Like Hitler's National Socialism" (press release), January 6, 1949. File: Printed Matter 1949, Box 5.

65. August 22, 1946: C. P. Trussell, "Lobbyists Report, as New Law Asks," *NYT*, 23; AP, "300 Lobbyists Get Form to Register," *BS*, 2. August 23, 1946; Philip Dodd, "Agent of W.C.T.U. 1st to Register as a Lobbyist," *CT*, 8; AP, "WCTU Lobbyist Registers," *NYT*, 38.

66. Lowell Mellett, "On the Other Hand" (syndicated column), *New York Post*, August 22, 1946, 26. File: Printed Matter 1945–1946, Box 4.

67. "People of the Week: What Registrars Tell Lobbyists," *United States News*, 21:10 (September 6, 1946), 72; William H. Stringer, "Filing Law 'Wilts' Lobbyists," *CSM*, September 14, 1946, 3.

68. "Lobbyist on Job for 30 Years," *WP*, March 1, 1948, 14; Jay Richter, "Washington's Number One Lobbyist Labors for, Not against, the People," King Features Syndicate, December 27, 1947; Harmon W. Nichols, UP, "Lobbyist No. 1 Works for People," *Bakersfield Californian*, September 25, 1948, 17; James C. Austin, UP, " 'People's Lobby' Leader Plugs Idea of Mixed Economy," *Niagara Falls [NY] Gazette*, April 4, 1950, 11.

69. "On the Lighter Side of the Capital: The No. 1 Lobbyist," *Nation's Business* 36:5 (May 1948), 94.

70. "Lobbyists May Get Closer Scrutiny," *BS*, November 16, 1947, 2; Robert Burkhardt, "Lobbyists' Turn to Listen," *CSM Magazine Section*, March 26, 1949, 2.

71. *CR*: January 3, 1947, 58, 67; January 29, 1948, 737; December 31, 1948, 10302; January 31, 1950, 1234.

72. "People's Lobby," *Tide: The Newsmagazine of Advertising, Marketing and Public Relations* 21:24 (June 13, 1947), 68.

73. "The People's Lobby, Inc., 1946 and 1947: Report of the Executive Secretary." File: Printed Matter 1947, Box 5.

74. Marsh letter to members, December 15, 1945. File: Printed Matter 1945–1946, Box 4.

75. Marsh letter to members, "Any Group Can Generate a Decisive Strength," December 1, 1949. File: Printed Matter 1949, Box 5.

76. Marsh letter to Irving H. Flamm, Chicago, October 2, 1946. File: Correspondence 1946, Box 1.

77. Board of Directors, January 9, 1947. File: Minutes, Board of Directors 1931–1950, Box 2. Bolstering that interpretation, months later McConnell wrote a very friendly and supportive letter to Marsh (October 22, 1947. File: Correspondence 1947, Box 1).

78. McGill letter to Marsh, December 12, 1947. File: Correspondence 1947, Box 1.

79. James H. McGill, "Lobby's New President Warns Makeshift Measures Are Futile," *PLB* 16:10 (February 1947), 1.

80. Eng Zimmerman Sr., "Death Takes James H. McGill: Founder of Local Plant Dies Monday," *[Valparaiso, IN] Vidette-Messenger*, April 27, 1948, 1, 6.

81. "Mitchell Elected President at Lobby's Annual Meeting," *PLB* 18:2 (June 1948), 7.

82. Edgar M. Shaw, minister, Grace Congregational Church, Cleveland, letter to Marsh, October 11, 1945. File: Correspondence 1945, Box 1.

83. Robert F. Skilling, Portland, Maine, letter to Marsh, March 24, 1948. File: Correspondence 1948, Box 2.

84. Capper letter to Marsh, August 30, 1946. File: Correspondence 1946, Box 1.

85. C. H. Coyle, Berwyn, Illinois, letter to McConnell, October 10, 1945. File: Correspondence 1945, Box 1.

86. Irving H. Flamm, Chicago, letter to Marsh, September 24, 1945, ibid.

87. Nathaniel M. Minkoff, secretary-treasurer, Joint Board of the Dress and Waistmakers' Union of Greater New York, letter to Marsh, November 21, 1945. File: Correspondence 1945, Box 1.

88. Marsh letter to Joseph Gaer, publications director, CIO Political Action Committee, New York, November 24, 1945, ibid.

89. The League for Industrial Democracy should not be confused with Dewey's political vehicle, the League for Independent Political Action, which folded in the late 1930s.

90. Laidler letter to Marsh, February 5, 1948. File: Correspondence 1948, Box 2.

91. Laidler letter to Marsh, May 19, 1950. File: Correspondence 1950, Box 2.

92. "Will Atomic Bomb Make Farce of 'Victory'?," *PLB* 15:5 (September 1945), 1.

93. "Hollywood Cartels and Un-American Activities Committee," *PLB* 17:7 (November 1947), 6.

94. Marsh, "The Vatican's Role in the War," *PLB* 15:6 (October 1945), 4–6.

95. Marsh response to letter from John F. MacCana, Boston, November 9, 1945. File: Correspondence 1945, Box 1.

96. Marsh, "Will We Back Cartel Controlled European Catholic Bloc?," *PLB* 20:2 (June 1950), 3–5; "Lobby Warns French-German Steel Coal Merger, Forecasts Western Europe Catholic Bloc" (press release), May 14, 1950. File: Printed Matter 1950, Box 5. That original steel and coal treaty was embryonic. It gradually morphed into the European Common Market and then into what is now (2014) the European Union.

97. Board of Directors, May 19, 1950. File: Minutes, Board of Directors 1931–1950, Box 2.

98. *PLB* 20:2 (June 1950), 2.

99. For example, there was a pro-FDR People's Lobby in Ohio in 1934 (*CR*, January 25, 1934, 1342); a very leftist People's Lobby in Minnesota in the late 1930s and early 1940s (AP, " 'People's Lobby' Ends Sit-Down in Minnesota Senate," *CSM*, April 6, 1937, 6); an isolationist woman's group in Chicago before Pearl Harbor ("Anti-War Mothers Hold Meeting: Plan a Lobby," *CT*, July 17, 1941, 8), which was sometimes called the People's Lobby for Action Now ("O'Brien Unable to Talk before Anti-War Rally," *CT*, August 2, 1941, 4); and a pro-FDR group of leftist lawyers associated with the National Lawyers' Guild (AP, " 'People's Lobby' Formed to Support President," *HC*, September 28, 1942, 12). The FBI was unable to differentiate between the Minnesota group and Dewey's, with information about both in the same file.

100. "Lobby Speaker Set," *LAT*, September 28, 1948, 12. It is unclear if this was the same group that existed in the 1930s ("More Evidence Refused Jury: People's Lobby Officials Decline to Testify," *LAT*, August 3, 1933, A8).

101. "FEPC Council Plans Lobby," *Chicago Defender*, March 15, 1947, 9.

102. INS, " 'Lobby' to Protest Filibuster," *Chester [PA] Times*, August 4, 1948, 3; "Picket Parade outside the White House: ALP [American Labor Party] Marches 3000 Here as 'Lobbyists,' " *WP*, June 9, 1949, 18. HUAC differentiated between this group and the PL by calling the former the National People's Lobby for Price Control and Housing Legislation.

103. Mary Hornaday, "Norman Thomas Sees Need for Strong People's Lobby," *CSM*, September 20, 1948, 11. One of the reasons Thomas called for creating the group was that he predicted Thomas Dewey's election to the presidency in 1948 was a "near certainty." Truman, of course, won in an upset.

104. Board of Directors, September 12, 1945. File: Minutes, Board of Directors 1931–1950, Box 2. The statement was not fully accurate. When the PL was first

created, Dewey and Marsh hoped to create local chapters in major cities to help with grassroots lobbying, though limiting them to lobbying on federal issues (Chap. 4).

105. "People's Lobby Is Incorporated," *PLB* 16:12 (April 1947), 8.

106. Marsh letter to editor, *Richmond [VA] Times Dispatch*, August 24, 1948. File: Correspondence 1948, Box 2.

107. The subject unfolded in a convoluted way. After stepping down as Truman's commerce secretary (and giving a speech opposing Truman's truculence toward the SU), Wallace became the editor of the *New Republic*. On his first day on the job, Wallace gave a speech in New York to local publishers and editors. Wallace said that the new bipartisan foreign policy (namely, that politics ends at the water's edge), as led by former isolationist Senator Arthur Vandenberg (R-MI), had been largely inspired by Reston's off-the-record conversations with Vandenberg ("Depression Seen Republicans' Doom," *NYT*, November 13, 1946, 2). The next day, the *Times* published Reston's denial, including an anecdote about a conversation Reston had with Wallace on the need for a "lobby for the people" (Reston, "Reply to Mr. Wallace" [letter to editor], November 14, 1946, 28). Marsh reacted by protesting the assertions Reston had made in his letter in a follow-up letter to the editor (Marsh, "'People's Lobby' in Existence," November 27, 1946, 24).

108. Marsh, "Other Lobby" (letter to editor), *New Republic*, September 6, 1948, 31. Giving a sense of the marginalization of the PL to liberals, the PL had not been mentioned or covered in the *New Republic* since 1939, a year before Dewey stepped down as honorary president.

109. John G. Harris, "Furcolo's Innovation Interests Congress," *BG*, January 16, 1949, C25.

110. Norman L. Smith, "Earlier People's Lobby" (letter to editor), *BG*, February 17, 1949, 18.

111. "Hollywood Cartels and Un-American Activities Committee," *PLB* 17:7 (November 1947), 5–6.

112. Letter from Harold U. Falkner to Marsh, June 18, 1947, emphasis added. File: Correspondence 1947, Box 1.

113. *CR*, January 31, 1946, 631.

114. *CR*, April 23, 1947, 3892.

115. See also "Per./Soviet Russia Today," July 1946. File: People's Lobby, 9E3/313/3, Box 662, HUAC.

116. Letter from Robert E. Stripling, chief investigator, HUAC, to Congressman James C. Davis, April 4, 1947, ibid.

117. Letter from Stripling to James Harvey Johnson, July 14, 1947, ibid.

118. Letter from Alfred H. Buschhorn, council member, Borough of Highland Park, New Jersey, to Thomas, May 29, 1947; Thomas reply, June 5, 1947, ibid.

119. Memo to Chiperfield, subject: Benjamin C. Marsh, June 19, 1947, ibid. This HUAC document has two markings on it: "Screened" and "Old material stored." I was unable to locate that additional material.

120. Cover letter and memo from Louis J. Russell, senior investigator, HUAC, to Senator Virgil Chapman, July 1, 1949, ibid.

121. Letter from Marsh to Rankin, September 11, 1946, and attachment: "People's Lobby Loans Economic Library to National Press Club" (press release), ibid.

122. "Lobby Warns Spy Scares Soar as Stocks Slump" (press release), June 14, 1949. File: Printed Matter 1949, Box 5; "Spy Scares Go Up as Stocks Go Down, People's Lobby Finds," *[NY] Daily Compass*, June 15, 1949, 7, HUAC files. The *Daily Compass* was a brief-lived newspaper and something of a successor to the leftist *PM*.

123. " 'Subversive' Should Be Defined," *PLB* 16:12 (May 1947), 7.

124. *WP*: "The FBI Checkup" (editorial), November 18, 1947, 10; Marsh, letter to editor, November 22, 1947, 8.

125. "McCarthyism, Korea and Cold War Preventative of Slump," *PLB* 20:3 (July 1950), 2.

126. Letter from Marsh to Congressman John Wood, chairman, HUAC, June 29, 1950. File: Correspondence 1950, Box 2.

127. "Communist Hunts Are Blind for Looting of American People" (press release), June __ (n.d.), 1948. File: People's Lobby, 9E3/313/3, Box 662, HUAC.

Chapter 11

1. "Secretary's Speaking Trip," *PLB* 15:7 (November 1945), 7.

2. "Clarke to Fill Marsh Date," *CSM*, November 9, 1945, 5.

3. McConnell letter to Marsh, November 26, 1945. File: Correspondence 1945, Box 1.

4. Board of Directors, March 25, 1946. File: Minutes, Board of Directors 1931–1950, Box 2.

5. Board of Directors, January 9, 1947, ibid.

6. Board of Directors, October 23, 1947, ibid.

7. Board of Directors, May 19, 1950, ibid.

8. Nineteenth Annual Meeting, May 19, 1950. File: Minutes, Stockholders and Directors 1931–1950, Box 3.

9. Marsh letter to Board of Directors, May 22, 1950. File: Correspondence 1950, Box 2.

10. "The Board of Directors and Council of the People's Lobby, Inc.," May__ (n. d.), 1950. File: Correspondence 1950, Box 2.

11. Marsh letters to Congressman Frank Buchanan, chairman, Committee on Lobbying Activities, June 26, 1950, and to Senator Walter George, chairman, Committee on Finance, September 20, 1950, ibid.

12. *CR*, July 14, 1950, 10321.

13. Press releases: "Lobby Secretary Calls Public Affairs Institute World Religious Conference Proposal Childishly Naïve," May 29, 1950; "Lobby Writes Congress 'The Tax Bill Kills Our Pleas of Democracy Abroad,' " September 7, 1950. File: Printed Matter 1950, Box 5.

14. Letter from Mrs. Clyde's lawyer, Olds Field, Huntington, New York, September 28, 1950. File: Minutes, Stockholders and Directors, 1931–1950, Box 3.

15. Marsh letter to J. B. Stein (landlord), September 30, 1950. File Correspondence 1950, Box 2; Reply from postmaster to Marsh, October 2, 1950. File: Correspondence October 1950, Box 2; Treasurer's Report, November 1, 1950. File: Minutes, Stockholders and Directors 1931–1950, Box 3.

16. For example: Letters of resignation to Marsh from Harry Laidlow, October 16; William Vickrey, professor of political science, Columbia University, October 20. File: Correspondence October 1950, Box 2.

17. Board of Directors letter to members and subscribers, September 30, 1950. File: Correspondence 1950, Box 2.

18. Dear Friend form letter, October 23, 1950. File: Correspondence October 1950, Box 2.

19. File: Correspondence October 1950, Box 2.

20. "People's Lobby Inc. Ends October 31—Secretary Warns Drastic Control Impend [sic]" (press release), October 12, 1950, ibid.

21. Arthur L. Edson, AP, "Ben Marsh, Dean of Lobbyists, to Retire after 32 Years on the Job: Now 74, He'll Quit on Doctor's Orders; Group to Disband," *Washington Star*, October 12, 1950, ibid.

22. "B.C. Marsh, People's Lobbyist, Will Retire and Close Office," *WP*, October 13, 1950, 12.

23. "Co-op Economy Near, People's Lobby Retires: 'We've Helped . . . People to Think,'" *Washington Daily News*, October 13, 1950. File: Correspondence October 1950, Box 2.

24. "A Veteran Lobbyist Retires" (editorial), *Portland Oregonian*, October 18, 1950, ibid.

25. Marsh, "People's Lobby Inc. Closes," *PLB* 20:6 (October 1950), 7.

26. "Dr. John Dewey Dead at 92; Philosopher a Noted Liberal," *NYT*, June 2, 1952, 21.

27. January 1, 1953: AP, "B. C. Marsh Dead; Welfare Leader," *NYT*, 23; ""B. C. Marsh Dies; Headed People's Lobby," *WP*, 16.

28. UP, "Capital Mourns Death of Famous Lobbyist," *Statesville [NC] Daily Record*, January 1, 1953, P–6.

29. *CR*, January 7, 1953, A59.

30. Ben W. Gilbert, "Fascinating Story about Lost Causes" (book review), *WP*, October 11, 1953, B6.

31. "Tribune of the People" (editorial), *Elyria [OH] Chronicle-Telegram*, November 20, 1953, 32; *Galveston [TX] Daily News*, November 21, 1953, 4.

32. There was a summary of the contents of the book from a Catholic academic perspective, but the reviewer expressed no personal opinion about the book (Goerdt 1954).

33. Letter from Virgil L. Flinn, superintendent, Kanawha County Schools, Charleston (WV), December 12, 1952; Hoover reply, December 17, 1952, FBI Dewey file.

34. Peter Kihss, "Aide at Monmouth Suspended Again," *NYT*, March 23, 1954, 11. Note that Republican President Eisenhower was by now in office and was trying to demonstrate that his administration was tougher on Communism than Truman and the Democrats had been. The president, at this point, had not yet openly broken with McCarthy. That happened as a result of the Army-McCarthy hearings, which started in April 1954.

35. "Marsh Denies People's Lobby Was Red Front," *WP*, March 25, 1954, 19. The term "hawkshaw" came from a comic strip titled and featuring Hawkshaw the Detective. Though now archaic, the name became a colloquialism for detective, similar to gumshoe or dick. Marsh *fils* followed in his father's ideological footsteps, for example, being a conscientious objector in WWII. For a short biography, see "Editor, Author Michael Marsh Dies at 75" (obituary), *WP*, April 9, 1993, B7.

36. Anthony Lewis, "Court Voids 6 'Risk' Dismissals; Says Army Must Tell Findings," *NYT*, June 20, 1958, 1, 12; "6 Monmouth 'Risks' Reinstated by Court," *NYT*, October 18, 1958, 1, 8.

37. Memo to Congressman B. Carroll Reece, n.a., June 22, 1954, emphasis added. File: Dewey, John, 9E3/2/14/1, Box 65, HUAC.

38. Letter from Congressman Martin Dies to Mrs. Juliette Joray, clerk, HUAC, May 19, 1956; reply by Richard Arens, director, HUAC, May 21, 1956, ibid.

39. "The New Postage Stamp for the U.S.A. to Commemorate— '? Great Americans?' " *San Diego Patriotic Society*, Bulletin #1123, n.d. (probably mid-1965). Attachment to letter from Congressman Charles Longstreet Weltner to Congressman Edwin E. Willis, chairman, HUAC, August 17, 1965, ibid. The newsletter also smeared and opposed stamps for Albert Einstein, Frank Lloyd Wright, Eugene O'Neill, Fred [*sic*] Douglass, and General George Marshall.

40. Memo from HUAC Files and Reference [section] to Mary Valente, August 19, 1965, Re: Attached Request from Mr. Weltner, ibid.

41. HUAC reply to Congressman Weltner, September 13, 1965, ibid.

Conclusion

1. "About Common Cause: Our Vision." Retrieved February 5, 2014: http://www.commoncause.org/site/pp.asp?c=dkLNK1MQIwG&b=4860183#VIS.

2. Retrieved February 6, 2014: http://www.peopleslobby.hypermart.net/.

3. Retrieved February 1, 2014: http://hernandogreens.4t.com/custom4.html.

4. Retrieved February 6, 2014: http://teapartysolutions.com/whoweare.html.

5. Retrieved February 2, 2014: http://images.nictusa.com/cgi-bin/fecimg/?C00459339.

6. Retrieved December 20, 2012: http://www.peopleslobby.co.uk/.

7. Also known as iGovUs. Retrieved February 6, 2014: http://www.prweb.com/releases/igovus/1/prweb10136932.htm.

8. Fraser Edwards, "Not All Lobbyists Get Jittery in Probes" (syndicated feature), *El Paso [TX] Herald-Post*, May 15, 1954, 22.

9. "It Doesn't Quite Fit" (editorial), *Billings [MT] Gazette*, September 9, 1952, 4.

10. Catherine Rampell, "An Estimate with a Life of Its Own," *NYT*, January 26, 2014, BU7.

11. Dewey letter to Oswald Garrison Villard, January 16, 1929, No. 04991; "Peace Agencies in the United States," *Advocate of Peace Through Justice*, 91:2 (February 1929), 101–104.

Bibliography

Archival Sources

A. Philip Randolph, Papers of. *Black Freedom Struggle in the 20th Century*, ProQuest History Vault (digital archives).

Amalgamated Clothing Workers of America, Records (microfilm). Frederick, MD: University Publications of America, 1989.

Brotherhood of Sleeping Car Porters, Records of. *Black Freedom Struggle in the 20th Century*, ProQuest History Vault (digital archives).

Dewey, John. *The Correspondence of John Dewey*. Past Masters, InteLex (database).

Federal Bureau of Investigation, Washington, DC.

House Un-American Activities Committee (HUAC), US Congress. Center for Legislative Archives, National Archives I, Washington, DC.

Kheel Center for Labor-Management Documentation and Archives, Cornell University, Ithaca, NY.

Marsh, Benjamin C., Papers of. Manuscript Division, Library of Congress, Washington, DC.

Naison, Mark, ed. 1989. *Department of Justice Investigative Files; Part II: The Communist Party* (microfilm). Bethesda, MD: University Publications of America/CIS.

Pamphlet Collection, Wisconsin Historical Society, Madison, WI.

Roosevelt, Eleanor, Papers of. Roosevelt Presidential Library, Hyde Park, NY.

Government Publications

US Congress (1937). House Committee on Labor and Senate Committee on Education and Labor. *Fair Labor Standards Act of 1937*, Part 2, joint public hearings. 75th Cong., 1st sess.

———. 1940. House Committee on Ways and Means and Senate Committee on Finance. *Excess Profits Taxation, 1940*, joint public hearings. 76th Cong., 3rd sess.

———. 1945. Joint Committee on the Organization of Congress. *Organization of Congress*, Part 4, public hearings. 79th Cong., 1st sess.

US House of Representatives (1929). Committee on Ways and Means. *Tax Relief for 1929*, public hearing. 71st Cong., 2nd sess.

———. 1930a. Special Committee to Investigate Communist Activities in the United States. *Investigation of Communist Propaganda*, Part 4, Vol. 3, public hearing. 71st Cong., 2nd sess.

———. 1930b. Special Committee to Investigate Communist Activities in the United States. *Investigation of Communist Propaganda*, Part 1, Vol. 4, public hearings. 71st Cong., 2nd sess.

———. 1931. *War Policies Commission*, H. Doc. 163. 72nd Cong., 1st sess.

———. 1932. Committee on Labor. *Unemployment in the United States*, public hearings. 72nd Cong., 1st sess.

———. 1933a. Committee on Interstate and Foreign Commerce. *Emergency Railroad Transportation Act, 1933*, public hearings. 73rd Cong., 1st sess.

———. 1933b. Committee on Labor. *Thirty-Hour Week Bill*, public hearings. 73rd Cong., 1st sess.

———. 1933c. Committee on Ways and Means. *National Industrial Recovery*, public hearings. 73rd Cong., 1st sess.

———. 1933–34. Committee on Ways and Means. *Revenue Revision, 1934*, public hearings. 73rd Cong., 2nd sess.

———. 1934a. Committee on Agriculture. *To Provide for the Purchase and Sale of Farm Products*, public hearing. 73rd Cong., 2nd sess.

———. 1934b. Committee on Ways and Means. *Reciprocal Trade Agreements*, public hearings. 73rd Cong., 2nd sess.

———. 1934c. Committee on Banking and Currency. *To Guarantee Bonds of the Home Owners' Loan Corporation*, public hearings. 73rd Cong., 2nd sess.

———. 1935a. Committee on Ways and Means. *Economic Security Act*, public hearings. 74th Cong., 1st sess.

———. 1935b. Committee on Labor. *Unemployment, Old Age, and Social Insurance*, public hearings. 74th Cong., 1st sess.

———. 1935c. Committee on Ways and Means. *Proposed Taxation of Individual and Corporate Incomes, Inheritances and Gifts*, public hearings. 74th Cong., 1st sess.

———. 1935d. Committee on Agriculture. *Amendments to Agricultural Adjustment Act*, public hearings. 74th Cong., 1st sess.

———. 1936a. Committee on Ways and Means. *Revenue Act, 1936*, public hearings. 74th Congress, 2nd sess.

———. 1936b. Committee on Appropriations. *First Deficiency Appropriation Bill for 1936*, Part II, public hearings. 74th Congress, 2nd sess.

———. 1936c. Committee on the Judiciary. *n.t. [Reporting of Contributions to and Expenditures by Political Organizations]*, public hearing. Unpublished, ProQuest Congressional ID: HRG-1936-HJH-0036. 74th Congress, 2nd sess.

———. 1937a. Committee on Agriculture. *Farm Tenancy*, public hearings. 75th Cong., 1st sess.

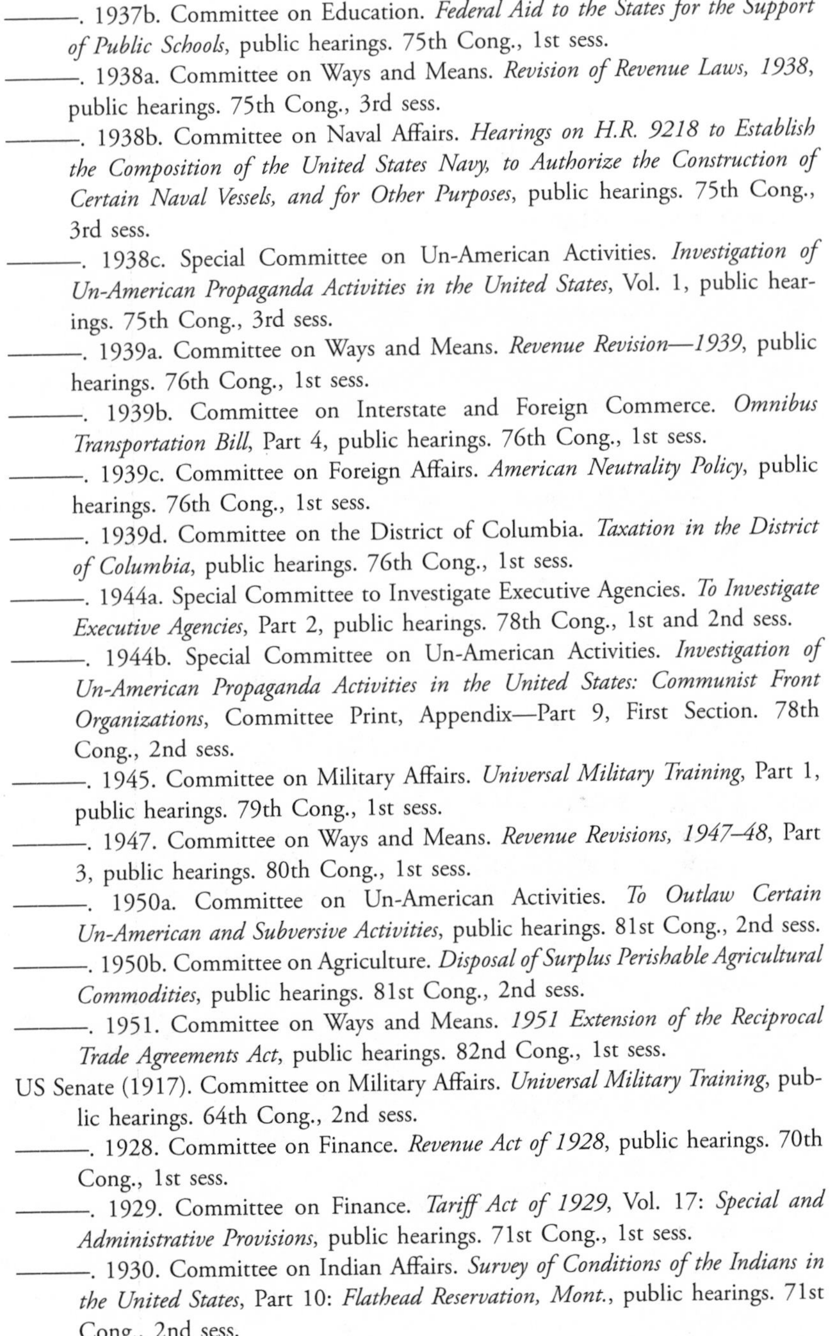

———. 1937b. Committee on Education. *Federal Aid to the States for the Support of Public Schools*, public hearings. 75th Cong., 1st sess.

———. 1938a. Committee on Ways and Means. *Revision of Revenue Laws, 1938*, public hearings. 75th Cong., 3rd sess.

———. 1938b. Committee on Naval Affairs. *Hearings on H.R. 9218 to Establish the Composition of the United States Navy, to Authorize the Construction of Certain Naval Vessels, and for Other Purposes*, public hearings. 75th Cong., 3rd sess.

———. 1938c. Special Committee on Un-American Activities. *Investigation of Un-American Propaganda Activities in the United States*, Vol. 1, public hearings. 75th Cong., 3rd sess.

———. 1939a. Committee on Ways and Means. *Revenue Revision—1939*, public hearings. 76th Cong., 1st sess.

———. 1939b. Committee on Interstate and Foreign Commerce. *Omnibus Transportation Bill*, Part 4, public hearings. 76th Cong., 1st sess.

———. 1939c. Committee on Foreign Affairs. *American Neutrality Policy*, public hearings. 76th Cong., 1st sess.

———. 1939d. Committee on the District of Columbia. *Taxation in the District of Columbia*, public hearings. 76th Cong., 1st sess.

———. 1944a. Special Committee to Investigate Executive Agencies. *To Investigate Executive Agencies*, Part 2, public hearings. 78th Cong., 1st and 2nd sess.

———. 1944b. Special Committee on Un-American Activities. *Investigation of Un-American Propaganda Activities in the United States: Communist Front Organizations*, Committee Print, Appendix—Part 9, First Section. 78th Cong., 2nd sess.

———. 1945. Committee on Military Affairs. *Universal Military Training*, Part 1, public hearings. 79th Cong., 1st sess.

———. 1947. Committee on Ways and Means. *Revenue Revisions, 1947–48*, Part 3, public hearings. 80th Cong., 1st sess.

———. 1950a. Committee on Un-American Activities. *To Outlaw Certain Un-American and Subversive Activities*, public hearings. 81st Cong., 2nd sess.

———. 1950b. Committee on Agriculture. *Disposal of Surplus Perishable Agricultural Commodities*, public hearings. 81st Cong., 2nd sess.

———. 1951. Committee on Ways and Means. *1951 Extension of the Reciprocal Trade Agreements Act*, public hearings. 82nd Cong., 1st sess.

US Senate (1917). Committee on Military Affairs. *Universal Military Training*, public hearings. 64th Cong., 2nd sess.

———. 1928. Committee on Finance. *Revenue Act of 1928*, public hearings. 70th Cong., 1st sess.

———. 1929. Committee on Finance. *Tariff Act of 1929*, Vol. 17: *Special and Administrative Provisions*, public hearings. 71st Cong., 1st sess.

———. 1930. Committee on Indian Affairs. *Survey of Conditions of the Indians in the United States*, Part 10: *Flathead Reservation, Mont.*, public hearings. 71st Cong., 2nd sess.

———. 1931. Select Committee on Unemployment Insurance. *Unemployment Insurance*, public hearings. 72nd Cong., 1st sess.

———. 1932a. Committee on Finance. *Revenue Act of 1932*, public hearings. 72nd Cong., 1st sess.

———. 1932b. Committee on Banking and Currency. *Unemployment Relief*, public hearings. 72nd Cong., 1st sess.

———. 1932c. Committee on Immigration. *Naturalization of Alien Conscientious Objectors*, public hearings. 72nd Cong., 1st sess.

———. 1933a. Committee on Manufactures. *Federal Aid for Unemployment Relief*, Part I, public hearings. 72nd Cong., 2nd sess.

———. 1933b. Committee on the Judiciary. *Thirty-Hour Work Week*, public hearings. 72nd Cong., 2nd sess.

———. 1933c. Committee on Agriculture and Forestry. *Agricultural Adjustment Relief Plan*, public hearings. 72nd Cong., 2nd sess.

———. 1933d. Committee on Finance. *Investigation of Economic Problems*, public hearings. 72nd Cong., 2nd sess.

———. 1933e. Committee on Interstate Commerce. *Emergency Railroad Transportation Act, 1933*, public hearings. 73rd Cong., 1st sess.

———. 1933f. Committee on Finance. *National Industrial Recovery*, public hearings. 73rd Cong., 1st sess.

———. 1934a. Committee on Agriculture and Forestry. *Confirmation of Rexford G. Tugwell*, public hearing. 73rd Cong., 2nd sess.

———. 1934b. Committee on Agriculture and Forestry. *To Provide for the Purchase and Sale of Farm Products*, public hearing. 73rd Cong., 2nd sess.

———. 1934c. Committee on Banking and Currency. *Stock Exchange Practices*, Part 15, public hearings. 73rd Cong., 1st sess.

———. 1934d. Committee on Finance. *Revenue Act of 1934*, public hearings. 73rd Cong., 2nd sess.

———. 1934e. Committee on Banking and Currency. *National Housing Act*, public hearings. 73rd Cong., 2nd sess.

———. 1934f. Committee on Education and Labor. *Additional Public Works Appropriations*, public hearings. 73rd Cong., 2nd sess.

———. 1934g. Committee on Commerce. *Foods, Drugs, and Cosmetics*, public hearings. 73rd Cong., 2nd sess.

———. 1935a. Committee on Finance. *Investigation of the National Recovery Administration*, public hearings. 74th Cong., 1st sess.

———. 1935b. Committee on Finance. *Economic Security Act*, public hearings. 74th Cong., 1st sess.

———. 1935c. Committee on Banking and Currency. *Banking Act of 1935*, Part 2, public hearings. 74th Cong., 1st sess.

———. 1935d. Committee on Education and Labor. *Slum and Low-Rent Public Housing*, public hearings. 74th Cong., 1st sess.

———. 1935e. Committee on Agriculture and Forestry. *To Amend the Agricultural Adjustment Act*, public hearings. 74th Cong., 1st sess.

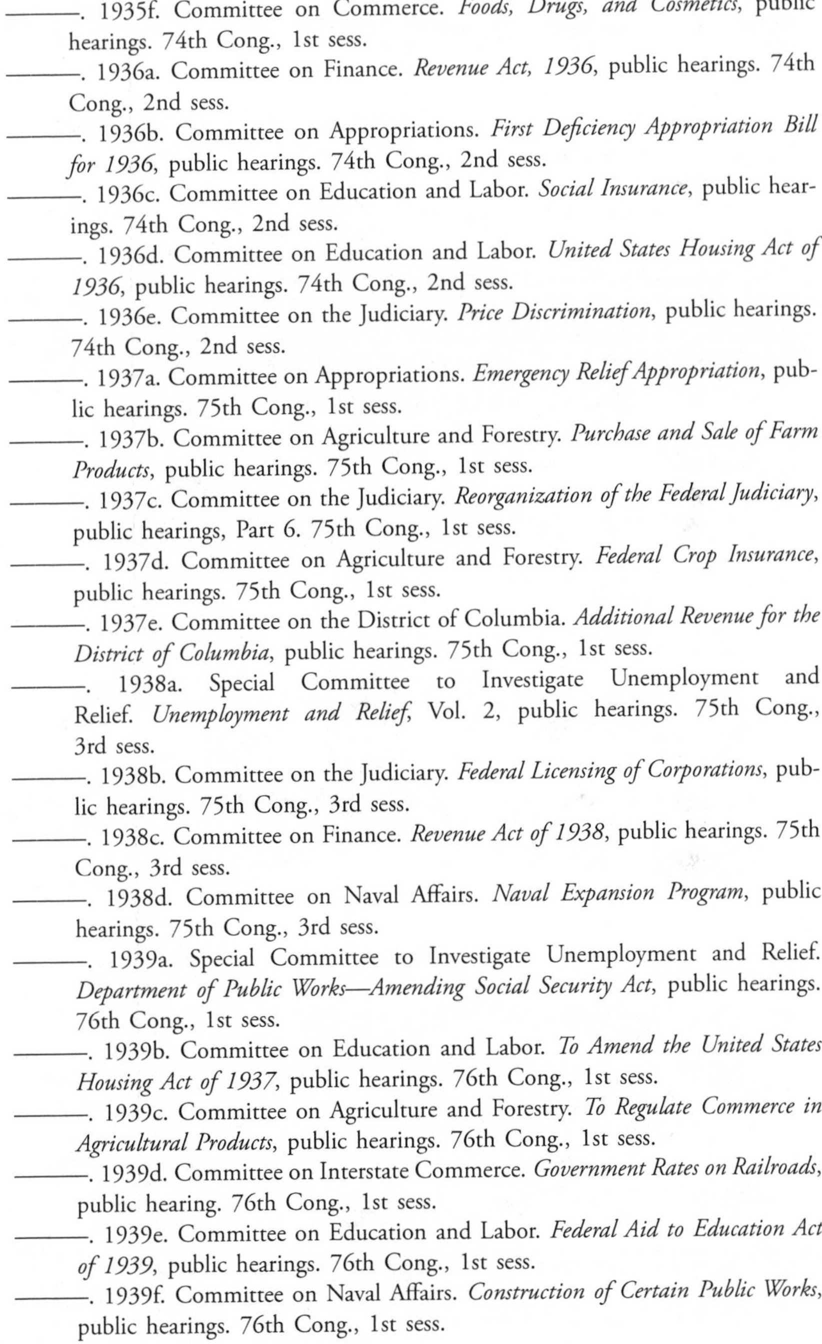

———. 1935f. Committee on Commerce. *Foods, Drugs, and Cosmetics*, public hearings. 74th Cong., 1st sess.

———. 1936a. Committee on Finance. *Revenue Act, 1936*, public hearings. 74th Cong., 2nd sess.

———. 1936b. Committee on Appropriations. *First Deficiency Appropriation Bill for 1936*, public hearings. 74th Cong., 2nd sess.

———. 1936c. Committee on Education and Labor. *Social Insurance*, public hearings. 74th Cong., 2nd sess.

———. 1936d. Committee on Education and Labor. *United States Housing Act of 1936*, public hearings. 74th Cong., 2nd sess.

———. 1936e. Committee on the Judiciary. *Price Discrimination*, public hearings. 74th Cong., 2nd sess.

———. 1937a. Committee on Appropriations. *Emergency Relief Appropriation*, public hearings. 75th Cong., 1st sess.

———. 1937b. Committee on Agriculture and Forestry. *Purchase and Sale of Farm Products*, public hearings. 75th Cong., 1st sess.

———. 1937c. Committee on the Judiciary. *Reorganization of the Federal Judiciary*, public hearings, Part 6. 75th Cong., 1st sess.

———. 1937d. Committee on Agriculture and Forestry. *Federal Crop Insurance*, public hearings. 75th Cong., 1st sess.

———. 1937e. Committee on the District of Columbia. *Additional Revenue for the District of Columbia*, public hearings. 75th Cong., 1st sess.

———. 1938a. Special Committee to Investigate Unemployment and Relief. *Unemployment and Relief*, Vol. 2, public hearings. 75th Cong., 3rd sess.

———. 1938b. Committee on the Judiciary. *Federal Licensing of Corporations*, public hearings. 75th Cong., 3rd sess.

———. 1938c. Committee on Finance. *Revenue Act of 1938*, public hearings. 75th Cong., 3rd sess.

———. 1938d. Committee on Naval Affairs. *Naval Expansion Program*, public hearings. 75th Cong., 3rd sess.

———. 1939a. Special Committee to Investigate Unemployment and Relief. *Department of Public Works—Amending Social Security Act*, public hearings. 76th Cong., 1st sess.

———. 1939b. Committee on Education and Labor. *To Amend the United States Housing Act of 1937*, public hearings. 76th Cong., 1st sess.

———. 1939c. Committee on Agriculture and Forestry. *To Regulate Commerce in Agricultural Products*, public hearings. 76th Cong., 1st sess.

———. 1939d. Committee on Interstate Commerce. *Government Rates on Railroads*, public hearing. 76th Cong., 1st sess.

———. 1939e. Committee on Education and Labor. *Federal Aid to Education Act of 1939*, public hearings. 76th Cong., 1st sess.

———. 1939f. Committee on Naval Affairs. *Construction of Certain Public Works*, public hearings. 76th Cong., 1st sess.

———. 1939g. Committee on the Judiciary. *War Referendum*, public hearings. 76th Cong., 1st sess.

———. 1939h. Committee on Interstate Commerce. *Nomination of Thomas R. Amlie*, public hearings. 76th Cong., 1st sess.

———. 1940a. Committee on Finance. *Second Revenue Act of 1940*, public hearings. 76th Cong., 3rd sess.

———. 1940b. Committee on Immigration. *Deportation of Aliens*, public hearings. 76th Cong., 2nd and 3rd sess.

———. 1947. Committee on Agriculture and Forestry. *Emergency Food Situation*, Vol. 1, public hearing. Unpublished, ProQuest Congressional ID: HRG-1947-AFS-0015. 80th Cong., 1st sess.

———. 1948. Committee on Banking and Currency. *Extension of Rent Control*, Part 1, public hearings. 80th Cong., 2nd sess.

———. 1950. Committee on Finance. *Revenue Revisions of 1950*, public hearings. 81st Cong., 2nd sess.

Books and Articles

Alter, Jonathan. 2006. *The Defining Moment: FDR's Hundred Days and the Triumph of Hope*. New York: Simon & Schuster.

Arnold, Peri E. 2009. *Remaking the Presidency: Roosevelt, Taft, and Wilson, 1901–1916*. Lawrence: University Press of Kansas.

Auerbach, Jerold S. 1966. *Labor and Liberty: The La Follette Committee and the New Deal*. Indianapolis, IN: Bobbs-Merrill.

Avner, Marcia. 2010. "Advocacy, Lobbying, and Social Change." In David O. Renz, ed., *Jossey-Bass Handbook of Nonprofit Leadership and Management*, 3rd ed., 347–374. San Francisco: Jossey-Bass/Wiley.

Beard, Charles A. 1911. "Reviews." *Political Science Quarterly* 26 (4): 714–715.

Bent, Silas. 1937. "International Broadcasting." *Public Opinion Quarterly* 1 (3): 117–121.

Berry, Jeffrey M. 1977. *Lobbying for the People: The Political Behavior of Public Interest Groups*. Princeton, NJ: Princeton University Press.

———, and Clyde Wilcox. 2009. *The Interest Group Society*, 5th ed. New York: Pearson-Longman.

———, and Sarah Sobieraj. 2014. *The Outrage Industry: Political Opinion Media and the New Incivility*. New York: Oxford University Press.

"Bibliography: USA, Social History." 1955. Review of *Lobbyist for the People* by Benjamin Marsh. In *Bulletin of the International Institute of Social History* 10 (2): 164.

Blacker, David J. 2007. *Democratic Education Stretched Thin: How Complexity Challenges a Liberal Ideal*. Albany: State University of New York Press.

Boorstin, Daniel J. 2012. *The Image: A Guide to Pseudo-Events in America*. New York: Vintage/Random House. Originally published in 1962.

Bordeau, Edward J. 1971. "John Dewey's Ideas about the Great Depression." *Journal of the History of Ideas* 32 (1): 67–84.

Boris, Elizabeth T., and Matthew Maronick. 2012. "Civic Participation and Advocacy." In Lester M. Salamon, ed., *The State of Nonprofit America*, 2nd ed., 394–422. Washington, DC: Brookings Institution.

Brands, H. W. 2008. *Traitor to His Class: The Privileged Life and Radical Presidency of Franklin Delano Roosevelt.* New York: Doubleday.

Breuning, Marijke. 2003. "The Role of Analogies and Abstract Reasoning in Decision-Making: Evidence from the Debate over Truman's Proposal for Development Assistance." *International Studies Quarterly* 47 (2): 229–245.

Bromley, Ray. 2005. "Marsh, Benjamin Clark." In Roger W. Caves, ed., *Encyclopedia of the City*, 305. London: Routledge.

Bullert, Gary. 1983. *The Politics of John Dewey*. Buffalo, NY: Prometheus.

Byrd, James D., and Amy Landry. 2012. "Distinguishing Community Benefits: Tax Exemption Versus Organizational Legitimacy." *Journal of Healthcare Management* 57 (1): 66–76.

Campbell, James. 1984. "Dewey's Method of Social Reconstruction." *Transactions of the Charles S. Peirce Society* 20 (4): 363–393.

Cannadine, David. 2006. *Mellon: An American Life*. New York: Alfred A. Knopf.

Carnovsky, Leon. 1936. "The Worst Periodical Usually Found in Library Reading Rooms with Reasons—from the Point of View of Its Influence on American Civilization." *Bulletin of the American Library Association* 30 (8): 737–740.

Carter, John Franklin. 1935. *Our Lords and Masters: Known and Unknown Rulers of the World*. New York: Simon and Schuster.

Clemens, Elisabeth S. 1997. *The People's Lobby: Organizational Innovation and the Rise of Interest Group Politics in the United States, 1890–1925*. Chicago: University of Chicago Press.

Curtis, Michael. 1991. "Introduction to the Transaction Edition." In Walter Lippmann, *Public Opinion*, xi–xxxvii. New Brunswick, NJ: Transaction.

Daymon, Christine, and Immy Holloway. 2011. *Qualitative Research Methods in Public Relations and Marketing Communications*, 2nd ed. London: Routledge.

Deen, Phillip. 2013. "John Atkinson Hobson and the Roots of John Dewey's Economic Thought." *European Journal of the History of Economic Thought* 20 (4): 646–665.

Delbanco, Andrew. 2008. "Lincoln's Sacramental Language." In Eric Foner, ed., *Our Lincoln: New Perspectives on Lincoln and His World*, 199–222. New York: W.W. Norton.

Dewey, John. 1970. *Characters and Events: Popular Essays in Social and Political Philosophy*. New York: Octagon. Originally published in 1929.

———. 1982. *The Middle Works, 1899–1924; Vol. 11: 1918–1919*. Carbondale: Southern Illinois University Press.

———. 1983. *The Middle Works, 1899–1924; Vol. 13: 1921–1922*. Carbondale: Southern Illinois University Press.

———. 1984a. *The Later Works, 1925–1953; Vol. 2: 1925–1927*. Carbondale: Southern Illinois University Press.

———. 1984b. *The Later Works, 1925–1953; Vol. 5: 1929–1930*. Carbondale: Southern Illinois University Press.

———. 1985. *The Later Works, 1925–1953; Vol. 6: 1931–1932*. Carbondale: Southern Illinois University Press.

———. 1986. *The Later Works, 1925–1953; Vol. 7: 1933–1934*. Carbondale: Southern Illinois University Press.

———. 2012. *The Public and Its Problems: An Essay in Political Inquiry*. University Park: Pennsylvania State University Press. Originally published in 1927.

———, and Tufts, James H. 1929. *Ethics*. New York: Henry Holt. Originally published in 1908.

———. 1961. *Ethics*, rev. ed. New York: Holt, Rinehart and Winston. Originally published in 1932.

Donohue, Kathleen G. 2010. "Choosing Conservatism in the 1930s: The Political Odyssey of F. J. Schlink." *Journal of the Historical Society* 10 (4): 437–473.

Eldridge, Michael. 1996. "Dewey's Faith in Democracy as Shared Experience." *Transactions of the Charles S. Peirce Society* 32 (1): 11–30.

Fehrenbacher, Don E. 2001. *The Dred Scott Case: Its Significance in American Law and Politics*. Oxford, UK: Oxford University Press. Originally published in 1978.

Foner, Eric. 1983. *Nothing But Freedom: Emancipation and Its Legacy*. Baton Rouge: Louisiana State University Press.

———. 2002. *Reconstruction: America's Unfinished Revolution, 1963–1877*. New York: HarperCollins. Originally published in 1988.

———. 2010. *The Fiery Trial: Abraham Lincoln and American Slavery*. New York: W.W. Norton.

Frumkin, Howard, Arthur M. Wendel, Robin Fran Abrams, and Emil Malizia. 2011. "An Introduction to Healthy Places." In Andrew L. Dannenberg, Howard Frumkin, and Richard J. Jackson, eds., *Making Healthy Places: Designing and Building for Health, Well-being, and Sustainability*, 3–30. Washington, DC: Island.

Gary, Brett. 1993. "Modernity's Challenge to Democracy: The Lippmann-Dewey Debate." *European Contributions to American Studies* 25: 35–46.

Goerdt, Arthur L. 1954. Review of *Lobbyist for the People* by Benjamin Marsh. In *American Catholic Sociological Review* 15 (1): 63–64.

Greenberg, David. 2011. "Theodore Roosevelt and the Image of Presidential Activism." *Social Research* 78 (4): 1057–1088.

Guth, James L. 1982. "Farmer Monopolies, Cooperatives, and the Intent of Congress: Origins of the Capper-Volstead Act." *Agricultural History* 56 (1): 67–82.

Hall, Peter Dobkin. 2006. "A Historical Overview of Philanthropy, Voluntary Associations, and Nonprofit Organizations in the United States, 1600–2000." In Walter W. Powell and Richard Steinberg, eds., *The Nonprofit Sector: A Research Handbook*, 2nd ed., 32–65. New Haven, CT: Yale University Press.

———. 2010. "Historical Perspectives on Nonprofit Organizations in the United States." In David O. Renz, ed., *Jossey-Bass Handbook of Nonprofit Leadership and Management*, 3rd ed., 3–41. San Francisco: Jossey-Bass/Wiley.

Hammack, David C. (2002). "Nonprofit Organizations in American History: Research Opportunities and Sources." *American Behavioral Scientist* 45 (11): 1638–1674.

Hammack, David C., ed. 1998. *Making the Nonprofit Sector in the United States: A Reader*. Bloomington: Indiana University Press.

Hansen, John Mark. 1987. "Choosing Sides: The Creation of an Agricultural Policy Network in Congress, 1919–1932." *Studies in American Political Development* 2: 183–229.

Hart, James. 1943. "National Administration." *American Political Science Review* 37 (1): 25–34.

Herring, Pendleton. 1967. *Group Representation before Congress*. New York: Russell & Russell. Originally published in 1929.

Hessenius, Barry. 2007. *Hardball Lobbying for Nonprofits: Real Advocacy for Nonprofits in the New Century*. New York: Palgrave.

Hoefer, Richard. 2012. *Advocacy Practice for Social Justice*, 2nd ed. Chicago: Lyceum.

Janeway, Michael. 2004. *The Fall of the House of Roosevelt: Brokers of Ideas and Power from FDR to LBJ*. New York: Columbia University Press.

Jeansonne, Glen. 2012. *The Life of Herbert Hoover*, Vol. 5: *Fighting Quaker, 1928–1933*. New York: Palgrave Macmillan.

Jenkins, J. Craig. 2006. "Nonprofit Organizations and Political Advocacy." In Walter W. Powell and Richard Steinberg, eds., *The Nonprofit Sector: A Research Handbook*, 2nd ed., 307–332. New Haven, CT: Yale University Press.

Jordan, David M. 2011. *FDR, Dewey, and the Election of 1944*. Bloomington: Indiana University Press.

Kantor, Harvey A. 1974. "Benjamin C. Marsh and the Fight over Population Congestion." *AIP [American Institute of Planners] Journal* 40 (6): 422–429.

Kennedy, Joseph V., and Vernon W. Ruttan. 1986. "A Reexamination of Professional and Popular Thought on Assistance for Economic Development: 1949–1952." *Journal of Developing Areas* 20 (3): 297–236.

Kochtitzky, Chris S. 2011. "Vulnerable Populations and the Built Environment." In Andrew L. Dannenberg, Howard Frumkin, and Richard J. Jackson, eds., *Making Healthy Places: Designing and Building for Health, Well-being, and Sustainability*, 129–145. Washington, DC: Island.

Laidler, Harry W., and Norman Thomas, eds. 1927. *Prosperity? Symposium* (conference proceedings). New York: Vanguard Press and League for Industrial Democracy.

———. (eds.). 1929. *The Socialism of Our Times; A Symposium* (conference proceedings). New York: Vanguard Press and League for Industrial Democracy.

Lande, Robert H. 1982. "Wealth Transfers as the Original and Primary Concern of Anti-Trust: The Efficiency Interpretation Challenged." *Hastings Law Journal* 34: 65–151.

Lane, Robert E. 1949. "Notes on the Theory of the Lobby." *Western Political Quarterly* 2 (1): 154–162.

Lee, Mordecai (2005). *The First Presidential Communications Agency: FDR's Office of Government Reports*. Albany: State University of New York Press.

———. 2007. "Revisiting the *Dartmouth* Court Decision: Why the US has Private Nonprofit Agencies Instead of Public Non-Governmental Organizations (NGOs)." *Public Organization Review* 7 (2): 113–142.

———. 2008. *Bureaus of Efficiency: Reforming Local Government in the Progressive Era*. Milwaukee, WI: Marquette University Press, 2008.

———. 2009. "Origins of the Epithet 'Government by Public Relations': Revisiting Bruce Catton's *War Lords of Washington*, 1948." *Public Relations Review* 35 (4): 388–394.

———. 2011a. "Historical Milestones in the Emergence of Nonprofit Public Relations in the US, 1900–1956." *Nonprofit and Voluntary Sector Quarterly* 40 (2): 318–335.

———. 2011b. "History of US Public Administration in the Progressive Era: Efficient Government by and for Whom?" *Journal of Management History* 17 (1): 88–101.

———. 2012. *Promoting the War Effort: Robert Horton and Federal Propaganda, 1938–1946*. Baton Rouge: Louisiana State University Press.

Leff, Mark H. 1984. *The Limits of Symbolic Reform: The New Deal and Taxation, 1933–1939*. Cambridge, UK: Cambridge University Press.

LeGates, Richard, and Frederic Stout. 1998. "Editors' Introduction." In *Selected Essays [Early Urban Planning]*, Vol. I, v–xiii. London: Routledge/Thoemmes.

Lippmann, Walter. 1927. *The Phantom Public: A Sequel to "Public Opinion."* New York: Macmillan.

———. 1993. *The Phantom Public*. New Brunswick, NJ: Transaction. Originally published in 1925.

———. 1997. *Public Opinion*. New York: Free Press/Simon & Schuster. Originally published in 1922.

Logan, Edward B. 1929. "Lobbying." *Annals of the American Academy of Political and Social Science* 144 [Supplement]: 1–91.

Marsh, Benjamin C. 1904. "Causes of Vagrancy and Methods of Eradication." *Annals of the American Academy of Political and Social Science* 23: 37–48.

———. 1910. "The Unused Assets of Our Public Recreation Facilities." *Annals of the American Academy of Political and Social Science* 35 (2): 166–169.

———. 1911. *Taxation of Land Values in American Cities: The Next Step in Exterminating Poverty*. New York: self-published.

———. 1912. *What Women Might Do with the Ballot; Needed: Women's Votes to Thwart Landlords Greed*. New York: National American Woman Suffrage Association.

———. 1914. "Can Land Be Overloaded? How Little Land Do People Need to Live On?" *Annals of the American Academy of Political and Social Science* 51: 54–58.

———. 1938. "Experiences of a Lobbyist." *Social Frontier* 5 (40): 81–82.

———. 1953. *Lobbyist for the People: A Record of Fifty Years*. Washington, DC: Public Affairs.

———. 1974. *An Introduction to City Planning: Democracy's Challenge to the American City*. New York: Arno. Originally published in 1909.

———, ed. 1916. *Real Preparedness*. New York: self-published.

McCarthy, Kathleen D. 2003. *American Creed: Philanthropy and the Rise of Civil Society, 1700–1865*. Chicago: University of Chicago Press.

McClay, Wilfred M. 1993. "Introduction to the Transaction Edition." In Walter Lippmann, *The Phantom Public*, xi–xiviii. New Brunswick, NJ: Transaction.

McFarland, Andrew S. 1984. *Common Cause: Lobbying in the Public Interest*. Chatham, NJ: Chatham House.

McGlashan, Zena Beth. 1976. "John Dewey and News." *Journal of Communication Inquiry* 2 (1): 3–14.

McNabb, David E. 2010. *Research Methods for Political Science: Quantitative and Qualitative Approaches*, 2nd ed. Armonk, NY: M.E. Sharpe.

———. 2013. *Research Methods in Public Administration and Nonprofit Management: Quantitative and Qualitative Approaches*, 3rd ed. Armonk, NY: M.E. Sharpe.

Menand, Louis. 2001. *The Metaphysical Club*. New York: Farrar, Straus and Giroux.

Mitchell, William A. 1949. "Religion and Federal Aid to Education." *Law and Contemporary Problems* 14 (1): 113–143.

Murphy, Cullen. 2012. *God's Jury: The Inquisition and the Making of the Modern World*. Boston: Houghton Mifflin Harcourt.

Myers, William Starr. 1954. Review of *Lobbyist for the People* by Benjamin Marsh. In *Annals of the American Academy of Political and Social Science* 293: 171.

Okrent, Daniel. 2010. *Last Call: The Rise and Fall of Prohibition*. New York: Scribner.

Olssen, Erik. 1978. "The Making of a Political Machine: The Railroad Unions Enter Politics." *Labor History* 19 (3): 373–396.

Outland, George E. 1954. Review of *Lobbyist for the People* by Benjamin Marsh. In *Western Political Quarterly* 7 (2): 312–313.

Papachristou, Judith. 1974. "An Exercise in Anti-Imperialism: The Thirties." *American Studies* 15 (1): 61–77.

Peirce, Neal R. 1972. "Foreword." In Judith G. Smith, ed., *Power Brokers: Money, Organization, Power and People*, ix–xi. New York: Liveright.

"Personal Notes." 1902. *Annals of the American Academy of Political and Social Science* 20: 97–105.

Peterson, Jon A. 2003. *The Birth of City Planning in the United States, 1840–1917*. Baltimore: Johns Hopkins University Press.

Piotrowski, Suzanne J. 2008. "Obtaining Archival and Other Existing Records." In Kaifeng Yang and Gerald J. Miller, eds., *Handbook of Research Methods in Public Administration*, 2nd ed., 279–290. Boca Raton, FL: CRC Press/Taylor & Francis.

Prakash, Aseem, and Mary Kay Gugerty, eds. 2010. *Advocacy Organizations and Collective Action*. New York: Cambridge University Press.

Ratner, Sidney. 1985. "Introduction." In John Dewey, *The Later Works, 1925–195; Vol. 6: 1931–1932*, xi–xxiii. Carbondale: Southern Illinois University Press.

Ravitch, Diane. 2000. *Left Back: A Century of Failed School Reforms*. New York: Simon & Schuster.

Reds in America. 1924. n.a. New York: Beckwith.

Reid, Elizabeth J. 2006. "Advocacy and the Challenges It Presents for Nonprofits." In Elizabeth T. Boris and C. Eugene Steuerle, eds., *Nonprofits & Government: Collaboration & Conflict*, 2nd ed., 343–371. Washington, DC: Urban Institute.

Riccucci, Norma M. 2010. *Public Administration: Traditions of Inquiry and Philosophies of Knowledge*. Washington, DC: Georgetown University Press.

Richan, Willard C. 2006. *Lobbying for Social Change*, 3rd ed. New York: Haworth.

Ritchie, Donald A. 2007. *Electing FDR: The New Deal Campaign of 1932*. Lawrence: University Press of Kansas.

Rockefeller, Steven C. 1991. *John Dewey: Religious Faith and Democratic Humanism*. New York: Columbia University Press.

Rogers, Melvin L. 2012. "Introduction: Revisiting *The Public and Its Problems*." In John Dewey, *The Public and Its Problems: An Essay in Political Inquiry*, 1–29. University Park: Pennsylvania State University Press.

St. John, Burton, III. 2010. *Press Professionalization and Propaganda: The Rise of Journalistic Double-Mindedness, 1917–1941*. Amherst, NY: Cambria.

Saloutos, Theodore. 1946. "The Expansion and Decline of the Nonpartisan League in the Western Middle West, 1917–1921." *Agricultural History* 20 (4): 235–252.

Sanders, Elizabeth. 1999. *Roots of Reform: Farmers, Workers, and the American State, 1877–1917*. Chicago: University of Chicago Press.

Sargent, Noel. 1930. *Public Unemployment Insurance and National Economics* (mimeograph, conference paper). New York: Industrial Relations Department, National Association of Manufacturers.

Sautter, Udo. 1991. *Three Cheers for the Unemployed: Government and Unemployment before the New Deal*. Cambridge, UK: Cambridge University Press.

Schmid, Hillel, and Michal Almog-Bar, eds. 2014. Symposium on Nonprofit Advocacy in Public Policy Making. *Nonprofit and Voluntary Sector Quarterly* 43 (1): 7–120.

Sheingate, Adam D. 2007. "'Publicity' and the Progressive-Era Origins of Modern Politics." *Critical Review* 19 (2–3): 461–480.

Shesol, Jeff. 2010. *Supreme Power: Franklin Roosevelt vs. the Supreme Court*. New York: W.W. Norton.

Shlaes, Amity. 2007. *The Forgotten Man: A New History of the Great Depression*. New York: HarperCollins.

Sillars, Malcolm O. 1952. "Henry A. Wallace's Editorials on Agricultural Discontent, 1921–1928." *Agricultural History* 26 (4): 132–140.

Steinkraus, Warren E. 1957. "Two Philosopher-Bishops." *Journal of Bible and Religion* 25 (1): 24–29.

Stoker, Kevin, and Brad L. Rawlins. 2005. "The 'Light' of Publicity in the Progressive Era: From Searchlight to Flashlight." *Journalism History* 30 (4): 177–188.

Strong, Donald S. 1954. Review of *Lobbyist for the People* by Benjamin Marsh. In *Journal of Politics* 16 (2): 400–402.

Thorndike, Joseph J. 2013. *Fair Share: Taxing the Rich in the Age of FDR.* Washington, DC: Urban Institute Press.

Tichenor, Daniel J., and Richard A. Harris. 2002–03. "Organized Interests and American Political Development." *Political Science Quarterly* 117 (4): 587–612.

———. 2005. "The Development of Interest Group Politics in America: Beyond the Conceits of Modern Times." *Annual Review of Political Science* 8: 251–270.

Tobin, Eugene M. 1974. "The Progressive as Single Taxer: Mark Fagan and the Jersey City Experience, 1900–1917." *American Journal of Economics and Sociology* 33 (3): 287–297.

———. 1986. *Organize or Perish: America's Independent Progressives, 1913–1933.* New York: Greenwood.

Truman, David B. 1997. *The Governmental Process: Political Interests and Public Opinion*, 2nd ed. Berkeley: Institute for Governmental Studies, University of California-Berkeley. Originally published in 1971.

Wapshott, Nicholas. 2011. *Keynes Hayek: The Clash That Defined Modern Economics.* New York: W.W. Norton.

Weintraub, Stanley. 2012. *Final Victory: FDR's Extraordinary World War II Presidential Campaign.* Boston: Da Capo/Perseus.

Weller, Charles Frederick, ed. 1935. *World Fellowship: Addresses and Messages by Leading Spokesmen of all Faiths, Races and Countries.* New York: Liveright.

Westbrook, Robert B. 1991. *John Dewey and American Democracy.* Ithaca, NY: Cornell University Press.

Westwood, Howard C. 1970. "The Influence of Washington Lawyering." *George Washington Law Review* 38 (4): 607–618.

Williams, Mason B. 2013. *City of Ambition: FDR, La Guardia, and the Making of Modern New York.* New York: W. W. Norton.

Williams, R. Hal. 2010. *Realigning America: McKinley, Bryan, and the Remarkable Election of 1896.* Lawrence: University Press of Kansas.

Wilson, Edmund. 1996. *The American Earthquake.* New York: Da Capo. Originally published in 1958.

Young, Dennis R. 2006. "Complementary, Supplementary, or Adversarial? Nonprofit–Government Relations." In Elizabeth T. Boris and C. Eugene Steuerle, eds., *Nonprofits & Government: Collaboration & Conflict*, 2nd ed., 37–79. Washington, DC: Urban Institute.

Zelizer, Julian E. 2012. *Governing America: The Revival of Political History.* Princeton, NJ: Princeton University Press.

Zeller, Belle. 1948. "The Federal Regulation of Lobbying Act." *American Political Science Review* 42 (2): 239–271.

Ziobrowski, Alan J., Ping Cheng, James W. Boyd, and Brigitte J. Ziobrowski. 2004. "Abnormal Returns from the Common Stock Investments of the U.S. Senate." *Journal of Financial and Quantitative Analysis* 39 (4): 661–676.

Index